God as the Shadow of Man

Studies in the Postmodern Theory of Education

Joe L. Kincheloe and Shirley R. Steinberg
General Editors

Vol. 82

PETER LANG
New York • Washington, D.C./Baltimore • Boston • Bern
Frankfurt am Main • Berlin • Brussels • Vienna • Oxford

Shlomo Giora Shoham

God as the Shadow of Man

Myth and Creation

PETER LANG
New York • Washington, D.C./Baltimore • Boston • Bern
Frankfurt am Main • Berlin • Brussels • Vienna • Oxford

Library of Congress Cataloging-in-Publication Data

Shoham, S. Giora.
God as the shadow of man: myth and creation / Shlomo Giora Shoham.
p. cm. — (Counterpoints; vol. 82)
Includes bibliographical references.
1. Myth—Psychology. 2. Psychology and religion. I. Title.
II. Counterpoints (New York, N.Y.); vol. 82.
BF175.5.M95 .S56 291.1'3—dc21 98-008241
ISBN 0-8204-4016-7
ISSN 1058-1634

Die Deutsche Bibliothek-CIP-Einheitsaufnahme

Shoham, Shlomo Giora:
God as the shadow of man: myth and creation / Shlomo Giora Shoham.
–New York; Washington, D.C./Baltimore; Boston; Bern;
Frankfurt am Main; Berlin; Brussels; Vienna; Oxford: Lang.
(Counterpoints; Vol. 82)
ISBN 0-8204-4016-7

Cover design by James F. Brisson

The paper in this book meets the guidelines for permanence and durability
of the Committee on Production Guidelines for Book Longevity
of the Council of Library Resources.

Printed in the United States of America

To the memory of my teachers, Martin Buber and Gershom Gerhard Scholem, who really knew the score.

I would like to show my gratitude to Martin Kett and Bryan Atinsky
for the work they have done in making this book possible.

CONTENTS

Introduction

Spiritual Connections, Soulful Frontiers

By: Joe L. Kincheloe

Humans at the end of the millennium are in an epistemological, ontological, and spiritual crisis. There is no simple way of escaping the existential hole the species has dug for itself. Shlomo Shoham understands these stark realities: given the specificities of his life, he grasps them all too well. *God as the Shadow of Man* is not simply a creative, informed, and smart book, it is the seasoned, mature work of a worldly scholar who has seen and felt so much. Shoham is the type of thinker I would like someday to become: a bricoleur who is an expert student of many fields, an intellectual who senses the synergistic relationships among theology, mythology, history, epistemology, ontology, axiology, and the social and physical sciences. It is rare to meet a scholar with both the depth and breadth of Shoham. Shirley and I are blessed to know him as a friend and a teacher.

Shoham's genius involves alerting us in an informed way to the many dimensions of human being. Central to this ontological dynamic is his effort to connect consciousness to the energy and materiality of the universe. Such a connection opens a window to a new understanding not only of consciousness per se but to the human role in the cosmos. In this context Shoham reclaims, recontextualizes various ancient traditions and intuitions, analyzing them in light of contemporary discoveries about the nature of "reality." Such an effort is quite significant, as new perspectives of both the human search for the soul and human cognitive possibility are provided. The literature of various theological traditions, Shoham notes, is filled with references to human consciousness connected to the "holism" of the world. The author analyzes these references for their insights and contributions to the development of a new spirituality that is inseparable from the deep structure of nature.

Such a hermeneutic feat is vitally important in a postmodern condition, a hyperreality marked by social/spiritual amnesia. The growing loss of contact with nature and the disconnection with the past (even the recent past), reduces human relationship with the totality of creation, the nature of being, and the production of knowledge. The dysfuntionality of contemporary Western societies constructs a need for a new encounter with diverse ancient traditions in relation to the critical socio-cultual theorizing of recent decades. With his multi-dimensional background Shoham emerges as the one capable of such an ambitious undertaking with his insights into Eastern knowledges of Hinduism, Buddhism, and Taoism and the theological and mystical revelations of Judaism, Christianity, and Islam. Add to this mix the indigenous knowledges of peoples dismissed by the West and we begin to appreciate Shoham as spiritual architect constructing a sacred edifice with materials provided by the planet's diverse traditions.

Those who appreciate Shoham's bricolage can no longer take part in Western science's adolescent rejection of the wisdom of antiquity and the discoveries reported by epistemological pioneers pushing the soulful frontiers of consciousness. *God as the Shadow of Man* validates from an innovative mind-space a set of philosophical and theological teachings without forfeiting the benefits of rigorous hermeneutical analysis. In this context a synergy emerges that holds implications for cultural workers operating in the theological, philosophical, pedagogical, psychological and scientific domains. In my work in post-formal psychology with its critique of the Cartesian-Newtonian limitations on our study of consciousness, Shoham's work is a primary source. Using his unique synthesis, I am empowered to push post-formal theory to deeper levels of understanding.

As I have struggled to construct a post-formal psychology, one of my most important tools has been quantum theory. In this context I can understand the sophistication of Shoham's appreciation of the revolutionary implications of quantum physics for a plethora of academic fields and human endeavors. Shoham knows that quantum insights change human self-understanding, the ways we think and our place in the world. The post-quantum world can no longer accept a universe consisting only of solid matter with indestructible atoms characterized by predictable actions as its basic building blocks. The machine metaphor has broken down and the belief that one glorious day we will uncover all the rules shaping the workings of consciousness, society, and the physical world is dying.

As a new understanding of these cosmological dynamics begins to emerge, Shoham is an able guide who focuses our attention on the meaning of the concept of "soul" within a new mindset. Is the reconceptualized notion of soul connected to that point—those points—where consciousness meets matter and energy? in the relationship, the pattern that connects the micro- and macro-realms of the universe? in the feelings and the *Lebenswelt* (life world) that form a continuum with the living patterns of the cosmos? Such are the types of questions that emerge when Shoham connects quantum theory with theology. The richness of the synthesis and its evocative nature leave scholars wanting more: Shoham creates a hungry audience empowered to explore on their own but ready for more Shohamisms.

Immersed in the work of Martin Buber with whom he studied, Shoham provides an existentialist interpretation of quantum mechanics. Central to an appreciation of Shoham's contribution is the existentialist interaction of what he calls the Tantalic and Sisyphean vectors: the Tantalic (from the Myth of Tantalus) involves a personality trait seeking unity and participation with the universe; and the Sisyphean (from the Myth of Sisyphus) concerns a personality trait concerned with maintaining the boundaries of self, separation from the universe. The interaction between the bipolar vectors reflects the Buberian disposition for complex syntheses resulting in unifying ontological and epistemological impulses. Shoham explores this synthesis in minute detail, positing the notion of "symbolon" structure. By this term he is referring to an agent that connects the Tantalic participation/unification impulse with the energy matter of the cosmos. As the nexus where the bipolar vectors come together, the symbolon structure takes on profound importance in the effort to make sense of the characteristics of the relationship involving consciousness, matter, and energy. As we study the symbolon agent, human potentiality expands exponentially.

Via the analysis of the symbolon Shoham finds an epistemic outlet from the classical (Cartesian-Newtonian) world. Through an examination of the way sub-atomic particles jump back and forth across the uncertainty barrier that separate quantum from Newtonian reality, the author extrapolates a wide range of implication for theology, philosophy, psychology, and the reproduction of knowledge in general. As one concerned with the limitations of modernist cognitive and educational psychology and its truncated vision of human potential, I listen carefully to Shoham's explanation of the epistemic outlet. In this context such work tells me that it becomes even more imperative to develop a new psychology that respects Shoham's complex understanding of consciousness. Such a process involves the construction of new forms of research and new modes of analyses that better explore the intersection between the psyche and the structure of the cosmos.

As we learn about the limitations of present research methodologies and mechanical cause-effect explanations of various phenomena, I always think of the inability of such conceptual tools to explain the beginning of the universe. This concept has worked throughout my childhood and adulthood as an abrasive grain of sand to subvert any comfort with Cartesian-Newtonian mindsets. Shoham's work increases the size and abrasive power of that grain of sand. In Shoham's eyes the universe as a web of connection among interrelated phenomena becomes clearer and clearer. That which has appeared so flagrantly inconsistent with common sense in this context begins to exhibit new meanings that carry us to uncharted theological, philosophical, psychological, and scientific territories (Kincheloe and Steinberg, 1993; Kincheloe, 1995; Kincheloe, Steinberg, and Hinchey, 1999; Wexler. 1996, 1997; Courtney, 1988; Grof, 1993; Fosnot. 1988; Gangadean, 1987).

Shoham understands that Western science views only a small portion of the physical, social, and psychological world. Focusing on material substance, Cartesian-Newtonian ways of seeing tell us little about the generative forces that produce phenomena and the consciousness that is embedded within them. From some theological, philosophical, and cultural perspectives the inability of Western science to address generative forces is a fatal flaw. What use is a method of producing knowledge, many ask, that avoids such a critical dynamic? This neglect of the generative is but one aspect of the fragmentation tendency within mainstream scholarship. In this context scientists focus on particular problems outside of broader contexts. Solutions devised from such analysis often serve simply to make matters worse, whether it be in the domain of natural resources and the environment or in education and student evaluation.

Operating in these scientific contexts is an ontological reductionism: the inability to appreciate the variety of realities coexisting in what Shoham labels classical reality. In addition, epistemological reductionism assumes that what lends itself to scientific measureability is all there is to be known. Understanding these dynamics, Philip Wexler (who introduced me to Shoham and his work) provides a set of epistemological and ontological insights that resonate with and synergize our appreciation of Shoham. In his awareness of these Cartesian-Newtonian reductionisms Wexler intervenes in the tradition's depersonalization of the human subject. Drawing on various fledgling efforts to resacralize a world reeling from the interconnected forces of scientific reductionism and globalized commodification, Wexler (1997) embarks on a journey of "vivification and enlivenment", an effort that enforces both Shoham's quest for an extension of human consciousness and the post-formal attempt to extend human freedom and possibility. Wexler's vivification/enlivenment offer great hope that mainstream systems of knowledge production and their truncated notions of human being can cross the boundaries of disinterested impersonality and combine reason with emotion and feeling.

Using Wexler's conceptualizations we can gain further insight into Shoham's work and its relationship to the end-of-century academic conversation. Wexler accurately warns that the postmodern focus on the discursive practices of the text does not automatically get us to the ontological realm of the living, feeling human and his and her creative consciousness. Wexler, Shoham, and myself have been profoundly influenced by the insights of quantum theory in our intellectual/spiritual treks into the unknown with its demolition of the assumed relationships between observer-subject and sytem-object. Freed from these modernist blinders we have been empowered to appreciate the nature of science's social construction of the physical, cultural, and pathological world. The question implicit in Shoham's work and overt in Wexler's is, of course, once we understand fictive science and its ontological implications, where do we go from there? Has the stage been set for a second wave paradigm shift: the "after postmodernism" realm with which Wexler is so concerned?

Wexler and Shoham inject heart and emotion into the discursive subject of post-Cartesian social theory. Both emphasize the importance of studying the process of being in a socio-cultural world. In this context Wexler's point is well taken: the human body is more than simply a social artifact—social artifacts may or may not possess consciousness. Having learned from Shoham and Wexler, I struggle with my next theoretical step. Is it possible in light of these insights to better historicize the last three decades of social theorizing? Can the emergence of the postmodernist critique of Cartesianism better be conceptualized as a theoretical worm hole leading to a redefinition of the human role in the universe? Has it served as a valuable evolutionary step in gaining the ability to recognize the scientific revolution as a transitional historical and cultural dynamic—not the end of epistemological and ontological history as it has for decades been tacitly perceived? Can the postmodern appreciation of knowledge production as a social construction exist in synergistic juxtaposition with the ontological recovery of feeling, heart, and emotion? Is a critical theoretical project concerned with justice and the elimination of oppression and suffering "enlivened" and extended by an engagement with Shoham and Wexler's ontological insights?

Such questions lead us to dramatic possibilities. From the vantage point they provide, we can see Shoham's *God as the Shadow of Man* as a guide to the redefinition of life. As consciousness and matter dance to Pink Floyd, the tapestry of existence is woven. Consciousness in this context flees the confines of "mind" reappearing in individual cells, the eco-system, the earth as living system, and the fabric of the universe itself. In this context Shoham's holon emerges with important ontological implications for the relationship between the parts and the whole. The part (the human mind) subsumes the whole (the structure of the universe) and vice versa. The nature of the relationship between self and "not-self" is thus permanently altered. Existentially, we can never be the same; we are for too integrated into the patterns of the universe to retreat into self-containment. Transpersonal experience with its reconstruction of the nature of "I" reconfigures our conception of interpersonal closeness.

In this theoretical context Shoham's awareness of the centrality of relationship (e.g.. consciousness and matter) to any ontology or epistemology energizes the concept of relationship developed in post-formal thinking. Readers familiar with post-formalismwill notice the link between Shoham's relationship and its importance in this critical psychological theory. Post-formalism deploys the notion of relationship in a plethora of settings to gain new insights into critical thinking and higher-order ways of seeing. In an ontological sense post-formal thinkers understand that life itself may have less to do with the parts of a living thing than with patterns of information, the "dance" of the living process, the "no-thing" of the relationship between the parts. In this sense post-formalism views human being as connected to relationships between the internal parts of humanness, between humans and the physical universe, and between individuals and other human beings. In this "ontology of relationship" post-formalism uses a feminist concept of human connectedness to open cognitive possibilities previously unimaginable.

Here the epistemological and the ontological intersect, as life itself becomes not some reductionistic secret substance but a relationship—an information pattern. This elevates the recognition of relationship from the cognitive to the spiritual domain, for it is the relationship that is us. The same is true for consciousness, as meaning-sensitive intelligence is present whenever an individual can tune into the woven mesh of cosmic information, the order/pattern of the universe. Einstein "tuned into" such a relationship as he came to understand gravity not as a force but as part of the order/pattern of the relationship of "empty space to celestial objects." Thus, post-formal detectives of cognition rethink reason by returning to its original meaning involving the nature of relationship. Once relationship is discerned then its implications can be transferred from one domain to another. With this understanding post-formalists in an educational context can help students impart their grasp of particular relationships in their everyday lives to a new context. Operating in this manner post-formalism may elicit sophisticated academic thinking from individuals not deemed capable of such cognition by mainstream psychologists.

Thus, Shoham's understanding of relationship holds not only theological and philosophical implications, but according to post-formalists, practical everyday benefits as well. When Werner Heisenberg theorized the indeterminancy principle—that the observer is part of the experiment, i.e., the observer enters into a relationship with the observed—he had little idea how much a part of the experiment we actually were; he did not realize how important the relationship he detected would become to the search to make sense of the world around us. Picking up on the profundity of Heisenberg's relationship, Shoham takes us to the domain of mythology in order to work out the complexity of its implications. The link (relationship) between subject and object, Shoham asserts, has been a central psycho-philosophical problem since the dawn of civilization. Myths served the critical function connecting the subject (cognitive/consciousness) with object (energy-matter).

As myths relate events at an abstract level, they reveal the underlying structures shaping events, the principles on which the cosmos and human life are grounded. Such structures and principles immerse themselves into the consciousness of both society and individuals and subsequently shape events in unseen ways. Thus, myths as ever-evolving and re-forming entities help construct (along with many other forces) the nature of everyday life. In Shoham's conceptualization myths not only create relationships between nature and culture but also subject and object, individuals and society, consciousness and energy-matter, and God and history. Returning to Shoham's symbolon—the connecting agent that recognizes the kinetic synergy within unrecognized relationships—humans themselves become ad hoc symbolon agents. Indeed, it is as symbolon agents that humans create, make meanings, and construct values.

Using the abstract logos as their tool, humans carry out the divine task of connecting the various differing dynamics throughout the world. This abstract logos refers to the use of the word or text to create a universal idea, a spirit of creative inspiration. Thus, myths provide insight into ancient consciousness, the protohistoric generation on meaning. In this context Shoham employs the concept mythogene to denote the idea of myth as a generating structure—the device humans use when they operate as symbolon agents. Jung had a similar notion with his use of archetypes, describing them, interestingly, as belonging neither to the domain of consciousness nor matter. Shoham moves Jung to the next conceptual step, uncovering the role of myth at the cosmological, structure-of-the-universe level.

The mythogene as an extension of consciousness takes its place in the universal fabric, metaphorically filling what Cartesian-Newtonian science deemed mere empty space. In the symbolon role the abstract logos fulfills its mission of generating the spirit of creative inspiration. In a profound philological move Shoham reports that logos when structured as a symbol etymologically referred in ancient Greece to two pieces of a broken bone used in a contract. To display the existence of a prior contract the two pieces of bone were brought together—a linking function, a connecting agent, an interactive dialogue, a dynamic relationship. Thus, the symbolon becomes a permanent aspect of an eternal triad along with the ani consciousness (the manner of consciousness that exists in all life—defined broadly—forms) and energy matter. The symbolon and what it creates via the relationship that constructs it become not only a thread in the universal fabric but a driving force in history—a dynamic that alerts us to human agency, the ability of humans to help shape their own destiny despite the impediments they face.

As we think through Shoham's delineation of the generative processes of connection and relationship, our minds are filled with numerous possibilities of how we might link these understandings to our own lives and passions. With these idiosyncratic readings in mind I will conclude this introduction with a few final observations of the evocative power of Shoham's writing—Shoham as quintessential symbolon agent. In my own idiosyncratic reading Shoham's concern with the socio-normative, the relation between humans and their social groups speaks directly to me. Here again the work of Philip Wexler (1996, 1997) is especially helpful in my attempt to articulate the importance of Shoham's concern with interpersonal/intercosmic relationships. Wexler describes the possible emergence of a turn-of-the millenium cultural reorientation grounded on a shared social ethic of being. Shoham delineates the cosmological specificities of Wexler's new universalist vision.

Employing the concept of the Final Anthropic Principle stipulating that consciousness is a necessary feature of the cosmos, Shoham connects with Wexler's universalist vision by positing a melioristic universe. As humans inscribe materiality (and thus themselves) with meanings and values, they look to various cultural signification and knowledge systems. Such a search leads to the analysis and incorporation of previously dismissed indigenous knowledges (see Semali and Kincheloe, 1999) and ontologies. The experiences generated in such processes produce deeper levels of communication and mythogenic comparisons. This cross-cultural empathy taps into the holographic part-in-whole/whole-in-part aspect of the undivided universe. This cosmological holography enables the symbolon structure to produce forms of connection that defy classical scientific understanding. While Shoham insists on avoiding the overdetermined occultism into which some authors in this domain have fallen, he is willing to use Buber's universal Thou to address the transhistorical tenor of ani consciousness.

In this context the ontology of relationship so central to the book leads to the possibility of instantaneous, non-local communication among the various constituents of the cosmos at the quantum level. And here rest the heart of Shoham's brilliant speculations: the nature of the divine is connected to the holographic and non-local features of the cosmos. Drawing upon the Kabbala, Shoham references proto-holographic understandings of the nature of divinity existing even in the most ostensibly unsacred of frameworks. God in Shoham's construction exists in the ontology of relationship, in the various symbolon structures that bring the diverse manifestations or creation together. God, not the Devil, is in the details—all the details. The generative features of the symbolonic mythogenes generate divine meanings. *God as the Shadow of Man* redefines not only the role of humans in the cosmos but divinity woven into the universal fabric. With this said, I await Shoham's next installment in the exploration of the divine in the shadows, his next encounter with the frontiers of the cosmos.

References

Courteney, R. (1988). *No one way of being: A study of the practical knowledge of elementary arts teachers*. Toronto, MGS Publications.

Fosnot, C. (1968). "The dance of education." Paper presented to the Annual Conference of The Association for Educational Communication and Technology, New Orleans. Gangadean, A. (1987). "Ontological relativity: A metaphysical critique of Einstein's thought," in D. Ryan, *Einstein and the Humanities*. New York, Greenwood Press.

Grof, S. (1993). *The holotropic mind*. New York, Harper Collins.

Kincheloe, J. (1995). *Toil and trouble: good work, smart workers, and the integration of academic and vocational education*. New York, Peter Lang.

Kincheloe, J. & Steinberg. S. (1993). "A tentative description of post-formal thinking; The critical confrontation with cognitive theory." Harvard Educational Review, 63,3, pp. 296-320.

Wexler, P. (1996). *Holy sparks: Social theory, education and religion*. New York, St. Martin's Press.

Wexler, P. (1997). "Social research in education: Ethnography of being." Paper presented at the International Conference "The Culture of Schooling." Halle, Germany.

Chapter One

The Mythogene and the Myth of the Logos

Myths are seldom simple and never irresponsible.
Robert Graves, *The Greek Myths*

Nothing dies until it is lived out.
H.G. Baynes, *Mythology of the Soul*

The epoch-making insight of Claude Levi-Strauss revealed that myth links nature and cultures.[1] In the present work, we shall try and walk in his giant footsteps and show that myth bridges history and transcendence and may provide ties between subject and object, relating them to man. In the process of our deliberations, we shall coin several new metaphysical concepts and provide some hitherto unexplored angles to the relationship between consciousness and energy matter.

In *The Myth of Tantalus*, we explained how the individual psyche develops from a pantheistic unity until it is ejected, through conflict and deprivation, from its sense of holistic oneness to that of a separate entity.[2] In *The Violence of Silence*, we described how the individual strives towards other humans, flora, fauna, and even inanimate objects, trying to achieve as deep an encounter as he is able.[3] In *The Promethean Connection*, we examined the link between consciousness and quantum mechanics and tried to trace the dynamics by which the human cognitive processes may 'collapse' the probabilities within a superposition—a nondescript, hazy 'soup' of energy—into a well-defined quantum state.[4]

The relationship between the self and its human and objective environment is, therefore, conceived within the context of a Buberian dialogue. If an I-thou encounter occurs, there is a sense of revelation and meaning. If a dialogue is not effected, the self feels that its environment is menacing, opaque, and absurd. A dialogue may be affected, according to Buber, only if the self opens up voluntarily to the other. When the choice has been made, and the self enters into a dialogic relationship with another human being, or into an authentic relationship with words, music, or a painting, the alternatives—to use a quantum mechanical simile—

collapse, and the relevant mental energy is infused exclusively into the dialogical relationship. Technically, we have availed ourselves of Niels Bohr's conceptualization of the complementarity between divergent dualities to describe the possibilities of linkage between man, on the one hand, and energy-matter, on the other. Bohr says:

> ...Evidence obtained under different experimental conditions cannot be comprehended within a single picture, but must be regarded as complementary in the sense that only the totality of the phenomena exhaust the possible information about the objects...Indeed this circumstance presents us with a situation concerning the analysis and synthesis of experience which is entirely new in physics and forces us to replace the ideal of causality by a more general viewpoint usually termed 'complementarity'. The apparently incompatible sorts of information about the behavior of the object under examination, which we get by different experimental arrangements, can clearly not be brought into connection with each other in the usual way, but may, as equally essential for an exhaustive account of all experience, be regarded as 'complementary' to each other. [5]

Bohr intended his complementarity principle to apply not only to pairs of quantitative parameters (the measurement of both at the same time barred by the uncertainty principle), but also to the bonding of contradictory parameters in biology, psychology, and philosophy, especially ethics. Hence, for instance, the complementarity between value judgments and collapse of alternatives would induce us to see evil after we have made an indeterministic choice to opt for evil. Per contra, if we elect to see good, we shall see good. If we concentrate on one alternative, the other collapses; if we set out to observe good, we tend to ignore evil, and vice versa.

The complementarity principle in the field of cultural norms may be envisaged in the following manner: Every organism needs a system-in-balance to function and survive. This holds true for artifacts as well as human aggregates. Hence, Hellenistic cultures stress the need for contextual harmony. The Egyptian *ethos*, like the Greek *kosmos*, which literally means order, anchors on the need for balance. The most important Greek norm is *meden agan*, nothing in excess, and the cardinal sin is *hübris*, the divergence from the golden mean. In a similar vein, the Egyptian goddess Maat is in charge of the all-important cosmic order, to be maintained as a precondition for the cycles of life. Conformity to group norms is a prime Greek mandate; deviants—both transgressors and outstanding achievers—were ostracized and expelled from the polis. The Jews, on the other hand, were socialized to strive for the absolute. This makes for revelatory insights, but poor team workers. Indeed, the Jews, wherever they were, tended to contribute brilliant ideas to their host cultures, but usually did not excel as contextual performers. The viability of a culture depends on a complementarity between the revelatory virtuoso, spurred by directional insight, and the contextual performers, who integrate the ideas into a durable system-in-balance. Bohr intended the complementarity principle to serve philosophy better than Aristotelian causality, scholastic coincidentia oppositorium, and Hegelian dialectics. We have our own conception of how the complementarity principle actually effects the linkage between divergent concepts, parameters, and objects and shall elucidate it in due course.

The link between consciousness and the objective world was masterfully metaphorized in the following Hasidic tale, as told by S.Y. Agnon to Gershom Scholem:

> When the Ba'al Shem had a difficult task before him, he would go to a certain place in the woods, light a fire, and meditate in prayer—and what he set out to perform was done. When a generation later the *Maggid* of Meseritz was faced with the same task he would go to the same place in the woods and say: We can no longer light the fire, but we can still speak the prayers—and what he wanted done became reality. A generation later Rabbi Moshe Leib of Sassov had to perform this task. And he too went to the woods and said: We can no longer light the fire, nor do we know the secret meditations belonging to the prayer, but we do know the place in the woods to which it all belongs—and that must be sufficient; and sufficient it was. But when another generation had passed and Rabbi Israel of Rishin was called on to perform the task, he sat down in his golden chair in his castle and said: We cannot light the fire, we cannot speak the prayers, we do not know the place, but we can tell the story of how it was done. And, the story-teller adds, the story which he told had the same effect as the other three.[6]

This Hasidic tale was interpreted by Scholem as portraying the decay of the Hasidic movement and the transformation of its values.[7] Our interpretation is different: We hold that the Ba'al Shem Tov (the Besht)—the charismatic founder of the Hasidic movement—taught that the optimal performance of man's tasks in this world is a praxis: a combination of action and meditative prayer or spiritual concentration. Indeed, the Besht, the doer, integrates his thoughts with the overt action—the kindling of the fire—and brings about the performance of the task. The quietist, inner-directed Maggid of Meseritz, does not act, but prays. The Besht reaches out to the object whereas the Maggid focuses on his thoughts and transforms them into a solipsistic reality all his own. The Rabbi of Sassov anchors his efforts on a spatial location to perform the task. The Rabbi of Rishin has no action, no spiritual concentration, and no location; all he has is a story, a mythical account which generates the task. This Hasidic tale highlights the subject of our present work: The combination of cognitive dynamics with energy-matter by generative myths to create reality.

The link between subject and object has been one of the most relevant psycho-philosophical problems from time immemorial. Solomon Maimon, the disciple of Kant, posited the matter in metaphoric terms: 'To find a passage from the external world to the mental world is more important than to find a way to East India, no matter what statesmen may say.' Still, our concern is more pragmatic: We wish to understand how the mental revelation of an Archemedian 'Eureka' is structured into an objective creation. We hypothesize that this creative linkage is affected by a mythogenic structure, the meaning of which has, of course, to be presently explained.

Andrew Lang, a pioneering student of mythology, stated towards the end of the nineteenth century that myths are not just cautionary tales to frighten young children into eating their porridge, but causal and ætiological explanations of phenomena that had taken place in historical reality. He, therefore, denoted mythology as a proto-science.[8] Freud claimed that 'myths are the distorted vestiges of the wish-fulfillment fantasies of whole nations…the age-long dreams of young humanity.'[9] Freud actually raised his intra-psychic interpretation of dreams on to the group level and claims that the myth is an expression of the tribe's 'social characters,' the nation's or social aggregate's wishes and visions. Surely, the myth of the Flood was not dreamful wish-fulfillment, but a projection of actual experiences of disastrous inundations by rivers—especially in Mesopotamia and Egypt. Myths are, therefore, also a projection of experiences and of spectacular events borne by a group before written history in ille tempore. According to Bachofen, 'The mythical tradition may be taken as a faithful reflection of life in those times in which historical antiquity is rooted. It is a manifestation of primordial thinking, an immediate historical revelation and, consequently, a very reliable source.'[10] Eliade further claims that, because myths reflect the occurrence of events on a high level of abstraction, they also reveal the principles or designs underlying events. He writes that 'the myth discloses the eventful creation of the world and man, and at the same time, the principles which govern the cosmic process and human existence. The myths succeed each other and articulate themselves into a sacred history, which is continuously recovered in the life of the community as well as in the existence of each individual. What happened in the beginning describes at once both the original perfection and the destiny of each individual.'[11]

This brings us to Jung, who regarded myths not only as means of individual psychic expression, but also as the archetypal contents of the 'collective human unconsciousness.'[12] As an interim summary, we may regard myths as a projection of wishes and experiences both on the individual and group levels. Some two decades ago, in *Salvation Through the Gutters*, we stated that:

> ...Our methodological anchor is the conception of myths as projections of personal history. Individuals are aware of their personalities as the sole existential entity in their cognition. This awareness of existence is the only epistemological reality. Myths cannot, therefore, be divorced from the human personality. Whatever happened to us in the amnestic years, and even later, is projected onto our theory of the creation of the universe, magic and other human beings. The events that happened in the highly receptive amnestic years have been recorded and stored by the human brain. Events that happened after the amnestic years may be recalled cognitively, but whatever happened within these first years of life is recalled, inter alia, by myths of cosmogony. Myths as personal history may, therefore, be regarded as the account of some crucial developmental stages in the formative years. Moreover, human development, in the early formative years, passes in an accelerated manner through the evolutionary phases of the species.[13]

Consequently, myths are also a projection of the development of the species, as paralleled in the development of the individual. It is interesting to note that this conception of myths as a projection of personal history may be inferred from the Apocalypse of Baruch, which stated that 'every man is the Adam of his own soul,'[14] which may in turn be interpreted to mean that every human being experiences original sin. Karl Abraham, as early as 1925 in his article 'Character Formation on the Genital Level of Libido Development,' expressed a basic idea, which may be relevant for our present purposes, thus:

> In the two phases of development...we are able to recognize archaic types of character-formation. They represent in the life of the individual recapitulations of primitive states which the human race has passed through at certain stages of its development. Hence, in general in biology, we find the rule holding good that the individual repeats in an abbreviated form the history of his ancestors. Accordingly, in normal circumstances, the individual will traverse those early stages of character formation in a relatively short space of time.[15]

Hence, the myth of the Fall of Man is the projection of a stage of development of the individual, yet also a universal human developmental experience. However, myths become archetypal projections of human experience only when they are widespread. The more common a developmental experience, the greater its chances of becoming a mythical projection. The converse is also valid: The more widespread the myth, the higher the chance that it is a projection of a widespread or even universal development. The universality of the myth of the Fall of Man, for example, points to a corresponding developmental phase—the separation of the individual self from the unified whole of early orality, which is indeed experienced by every human being.

Therefore, we hold that myths structure meanings for human behavior and serve as motivation and prime movers for both individual and group behavior. As myths are projected models of human behavior at all levels, they may be records of past experience as well as a structuring for future longings and goals. Myths are also expressions of both overt behavior and of covert dynamics; of the here and now as well as of transcendence. The dimensions of myths may also vary greatly, ranging from micro-myths, like names of persons and places representing meaningful experiences or quests, to meta-myths representing the polar type of human behavior on both the individual and group levels such as the myths of Sisyphus and Tantalus. They vary with time and place. Every society and culture has its own indigenous mythology. Myths move in time from sacred myths recorded before history to modern myths, like master detectives Sherlock Holmes and Hercule Poirot, or the master spy, John Le Carré's Smiley, or even Superman, who realizes the dreams of the omnipotence among the downtrodden, henpecked inhabitants of Metropolis.

Myths can relate to individuals. The offering of Isaac and Iphigenia, signifying the sacrificial enmeshing of the young within the normative system of society, are two examples. Then there are group myths like the adventures of the Olympian gods and the tribal exploits of the German Æsir. The Nazi movement may indeed be studied as a collective myth when the collective worms, to use Goëbbels' macabre simile, become effectively a fire spitting dragon.[16]

We follow in the giant footsteps of Claude Levi-Strauss, who claimed that myths are a connecting structure between divergent polarities like the raw and the cooked.[17] However, we attribute to mythology, as a structure, wider and deeper functions. Piaget has described the function of a structure, thus:

> A system of transformations is characterized by the laws of this system (in contradistinction to the attributes of its individual components). The system is preserved and enriched by the actions of these transformations, but they do not lead to outright components, which are outside the (structured system). In short, a structure is characterized by holism, transformation, and self-regulation.[18]

It is therefore 'ahistorical' in the sense that a myth, as a holistic self-regulating structure, functions irrespective of its historical veracity. Thus Moses and the Exodus of the Jews from Egypt, which have no corroboration outside the Bible, have generated monotheistic Judaism, which is still viable, regardless of Moses' actually having existed or not. Also, we hold that myths link subject and object, the individual and society, consciousness and matter, revelation and creativity, history and transcendence. This linkage is a feedback cycle, since man, for instance, projects myths on to metaphysics, which are structured into religion, which in turn feeds the individual's faith. The creative myth, or in our terminology, the 'mythologic structure', is not only a self-regulating mechanism, but also a self-recharging dynamic. Man projects the myths which are remodeling him as role models, creative muses, ideologies, and religions. Hence, myths are our prime movers, which lift us by our own proverbial bootstraps à la Baron Münchausen, powered as a self-energizing perpetuum mobilæ.

Our interest in mythology has been generated over almost three decades of interest in the theory and practice of labeling. When someone is stigmatized as a homosexual, a criminal, or a madman, his or her other attributes and qualities seem to become eclipsed. The fact that the homosexual is also a good pianist, that the criminal has a sense of humor, or that the madman has a good heart becomes eclipsed by the over-arching effect of stereotyping as a deviant, jailbird, or lunatic. The stigmatization of the deviant, the different person or the outsider is just one instance of the omnipotence of structure. Of special importance in our present context is Piaget's exposition on structures which are current to both psychology and physics.[19]

Piaget also assures us that children start thinking in structures. This might account for the fact that the most basic structures are ingrained in us in our oral phase of development, along with the acquisition of our mother tongue. Structures are, therefore, independent entities with internal transformation that do not change, because self-regulation keeps them intact.

It is important to note that once the structure has been formed, we get used to it by processes of feedback. The earlier and longer one has had a structure, the more it is cherished through the dynamics of cognitive dissonance and is normalized and mythologized by processes we shall describe later. Established structures lend security, familiarity, and confidence. Hence, normative upheavals and ideational revolutions are painful and relatively rare.

The symbolon structure is the connecting agent between the ani-consciousness and energy-matter that is structured into a model of a phenomenon to be realized subsequently as an act of creation. The durability and longevity of symbolon structures are subject to natural selection and functional adaptability. In this domain, as in so many other Sisyphean dynamics of creation and entropy, Darwinian evolution reigns supreme.[20]

Once the mythogenic structure has been generated by projected experiences and yearnings and formed into a self-regulating configuration, it has a life of its own. Hence, a mythogene is ahistoric. We have already mentioned that there is no independent evidence for the outright accuracy of the biblical account of Moses or the Exodus. A recent study by an American archaeologist even concludes that the events recounted in the first ten books of the Old Testament can have no historical veracity.[21] Hence, not only Moses, but also Saul, David, and Solomon are all fictional characters. But this is hardly relevant to our present context. The mythogenic structure obeys W.I. Thomas's basic theorem of social processes, according to which if man defines a situation as real, it becomes real in its consequences. Hence, if the mythogene has been projected, structured, and legitimized by a given group, it motivates man to generate cultural patterns by a process of revelation and creativity. Levi-Strauss defines how the mythic structure links nature and culture; we shall try also to show how the mythogenic structures are generated, grow, and decline. Indeed, mythogenes are generated, developed, and destroyed in a manner different from the growth and decline of historical entities. Leon Festinger has demonstrated how belief in prophets has increased just when their historical prophesies have failed.[22] Likewise, the serious proselytizing by the followers of Christ started after his crucifixion, and so did proselytizing by the believers of Shabbatai Zevi, the self-proclaimed seventeenth-century Jewish messiah, after he converted to Islam. The mythogenic structure moves itself, and us its creators, in a feedback cycle of virtual reality—once we impute historical veracity to it and insist on incorporating it into our daily lives we are courting disaster. The numerous Christs, Napoleons, and Elvis Presleys in insane asylums are all individual instances of the deranging effects of historicizing myths, whereas the Nazis' reviving of the Elder Eddas and the Niebelungen Ring—and reliving them—was a catastrophic instance of this on a group level.

Our first step in the study of mythology will be the exploration of its role in the development of the human personality.

The Two Vectors

We propose to describe here the two opposing vectors which form the core of our personality theory. These are the vectors of participation and separation. By participation we mean the identification of the self with a person or persons, an object, a life form, or a symbol outside the self, and the self striving to lose its separate identity by fusion with this external entity. Separation is the opposite vector and consists of aiming to sever and differentiate the self from surrounding lifeforms and objects.

These opposing vectors, as the main axis of our theory, are developed in conjunction with three major developmental phases. First, the process of birth, an abrupt propulsion from the cushioned self-sufficiency of the womb into the strife and struggles of life outside, represents a major crisis and is, undoubtedly, recorded by the newborn's psyche; this is in addition to any physical pressures that the process of birth itself might impose on the cranium and the resultant effects on the various layers of the brain. We build our premises on those separating effects of birth which are universal. These in turn initiate the opposite vector of participation, which is a directional driving force, harnessing a diverse assortment of psychic energies towards union with given objects, life forms, or symbols. The newborn, who is physiologically and psychologically capable of recording these crises incidental to its birth, is traumatized by them into a lifelong quest for congruity and unification.[23]

The second process, that of separation, is the crystallization of an individual self through the molding of an ego boundary. The infant shrieks and kicks his way into the world, but still feels himself part and parcel of his surroundings. However, this holistic bliss is gradually destroyed by the harsh realities of hunger, thirst, discomfort, physical violence, and hard objects and by a mother who is mostly loving but sometimes nagging, apathetic, hysterical, overprotecting, or even rejecting. All this pushes the infant into forming a separate identity, that is, into leaving the common fold of unity with his environment and crystallizing an 'I'. This individual self knows then that he is not part of, or with, but rather against, his surroundings. This realization of a separate self, resulting from a coerced departure from the security of engulfing togetherness, is registered by the developing psyche as a fall from grace.

The process of separation continues in full force as a corollary to socialization, until one reaches the post-adolescent's adjustment to the mandates of the normative systems of society. The making of the responsible person, the stable human being, is achieved by constant indoctrination by the various socialization agencies: family, school, church, etc. These convey to him the harsh realities of life and urge him to grow up, with the help of some rigorous initiation rites. Thus is concluded the third developmental phase.

The desire to overcome the separating and dividing pressures never leaves the human individual. The striving to partake in a unifying whole is ever-present and takes many forms: If one avenue toward its realization becomes blocked, it surges out through another.

We have traced the various pressures towards separation in each developmental phase; each stimulus is registered by the embryo as a disturbance to be overcome. The various demands of its mother and others close to it, before and after such crystallization of the separate self, are also perceived as disquieting events, with which one must cope and come to terms. Later, the various demands of the socialization agencies to fit into the boundaries of the normative system, and so gain one's social identity and responsibility, serve as the semi-final or final separating pressures. After this, the individual is on his own, ontologically lonely and trying desperately to regain the togetherness of his lost fold. In this uphill climb, the individual may choose both legitimate and illegitimate paths, both acceptable and deviant avenues.

After the primary biological separation of birth, the processes of separation and the ensuing developmental stages are affected by the deprivational interaction of the self with its surrounding objects. Following birth, the self-preservation instinct guards against the extinction of this new creature by inducing it to cry out for food and comfort. Yet, as we have pointed out, the crystallization of the separate 'I' is affected through interaction with the nipple that does *not* give food, and with the mother who does *not* ease all pain and alleviate all discomfort.[24] In other words, if the neonate had all his needs immediately gratified, he would not emerge from his feeling of unity with his surroundings, which marks the infant's first year of life and which is denoted as early orality. This means that it is not the release of tension through the satisfaction of the biological needs which is the separating agent, but rather the conflictual interaction with a depriving object. Consequently, the primary separation of the self is not a corollary to instinctual need satisfaction, but an interactional phenomenon.

Isaac And Iphigenia

Similarly, we claim that social separation is not affected, as Freud and Erickson postulated, by psycho-sexual developmental phases, but rather by conflictual normative indoctrination and deprivational socialization within the family. These are exemplified by the various rites of passage studied by anthropologists, and by the lonely burdens of responsibility imposed on post-adolescents in every human society, so as to enable them to cope with the vicissitudes of adult life.[25]

In most cultures, the father or his surrogate is the vehicle of indoctrination, instrumental in imposing the various norms and duties on both daughter and son, thus preparing them for their social roles. Such imposition of normative duties on the son by his father has been described elsewhere as the Isaac Syndrome.[26]

Whereas the initial victimization of the child at the oral stage of development is maternal, blocking the free expression of the child's incestuous desires, the second is paternal, coercing and harnessing the child into the normative system of society, of which the father is deemed the agent within the family. Usually this coercive normative victimization is backed by the absolute authority of God, the fatherland, or a secular political deity. As in the paradigm, the offering of Isaac, there is usually a symbiotic relationship between the stern, doctrinaire father and a metaphysical source of absolute authority. It is important to note that such continuing victimization of the child by his parents from early orality onwards is an integral part of the separant process of development and socialization. Paternal victimization leads to the separant insertion of the pubescent individual into a normative pigeonhole sanctioned by society.

The mother is the symbol of grace. She stands for carefree participant longing for the forgiveness and irresponsibility of children within the family fold, prior to their harnessing within the normative burdens of society. In some tribes, such rites of passage from childhood to puberty as circumcision are presided over by the leaders, while the mothers join in the wailing of their sons.[27] A mythological corroboration for the mother as the image of grace in the eyes of the pubescent son is found in the angel who orders Abraham not to slaughter Isaac. The angel is invariably depicted as female by the iconography of the offering of Isaac.[28] It would not be farfetched, therefore, to regard the female angel as representing his mother, Sarah.

The Isaac Syndrome is the paternal normative aggression of fathers against their sons.[29] The main thrust of the myth of the offering of Isaac, however, lies in the sacrificial enmeshing of the young into the disciplinarian boundaries of the normative systems of society. All normative breaking in involves, to varying degrees, the curbing of the well-being and freedom of the pubescent for the good of the group.

Literature abounds with the sacrificial coercion of children into the carnivorous exigencies of the normative system. Kafka's letters to his father reek of the agonies of a son being abused by his father in the name of bourgeois morality. Kafka's relationship with his father was, no doubt, the inspiration for his description in *Metamorphosis* of Mr. Sama, the petit bourgeois father who degrades his misfit son out of shame and fear of the social norms. Frank Wedekind, in his play *The Awakening of Spring*, portrays a father who justifies the commitment of his son to a notorious institution for juvenile delinquents by his conviction that the institution stresses and enhances Christian thought and logic. The boy's mother, like her archetypal image in the iconography of Isaac's offering, prays for grace and forgiveness. The mother laments that her son, basically a good boy, is bound to become a hardened criminal in the institution. But stern paternal judgment prevails, and the boy, Melchior, is confined to an institution for delinquents for the heinous crime of having had sex with a girl. Wedekind's play focuses on the sacrificial coercion of parents, namely the suppression of sexual manifestations in the name of social propriety, morality, and religion.

Paternal sanction and raging admonition burst forth from Francis Bacon's portrait of *The Screaming Pope.*[30] In this painting, Bacon takes Velasquez's serene portrait of Pope Innocent X seated in full regalia on his throne and covers it with the transparent projection of a frozen scream. The Pope's mouth is wide open, and it seems to emit shrieks of horror, howling curses, and shouts of damnation. Could this be the howls of Bacon's own authoritarian father when he found out that his adolescent son was a transvestite?

By free association we could recall the recent televised interviews with Pope John Paul II whose benign face, that of a good-natured Polish peasant, became hard and stern whenever he reconfirmed the church's proscriptions of married priests, abortion, and homosexuality.

Indeed, sex remains one of the normative strongholds of the church, perhaps because it sees in sexual roles God's choice media for the programming of humanity. The persistent proscription of free manifestations of sexuality, especially between consenting homosexual adults, induced John Money to label the official secular and religious authorities as sexual dictatorships hunting sexual heretics.[31] Indeed, this is an extension of the Isaac Syndrome to the social and group levels, where the authoritarian figure of Abraham permeates the power structures of society and religion.

Mothers often warn their children when they are naughty: 'You wait 'till Daddy comes home and I tell him what you were doing today.' The mother implies that she herself does not wield the normative rod, rather it is the role of the authoritarian figure in the family (i.e., the father) to mete out sanctions when due. The doctrinaire role of the father is directed equally towards the son and the daughter. The contents of the social norms imposed by paternal authority vary, however, with the sex of the child. The son is coerced, in most patriarchal societies, to undertake the burden of social responsibility, whereas the daughter is harnessed into her feminine roles of marriage, childbearing, and household duties.

A partial feminine counterpart to the sacrificial rites of passage inherent in the Isaac Syndrome may be inferred from the Greek myth of Demeter-Kore. Zeus, Kore's father, was instrumental in ejecting his daughter from the family fold and the protection of her mother and in delivering her to his hellish brother, Hades.[32] The implication here is that Kore was taken away from the protective care of her mother through the devices of her father and exposed to the trials of matrimonial servitude to her husband, an experience recorded by the pubescent Kore as coercive and infernal. Yet this is the social essence of a daughter's betrothal throughout most of history and in traditionalist societies even today. She is given in marriage to the appropriate husband as determined mainly by the political calculations, social expectations, and economic needs of her father.

However, the most striking feminine parallel to the Isaac Syndrome, both in its gory sacrificial details and profound socio-normative implications, is seen in the sacrifice of Iphigenia (as dramatized by Euripides) to the exigencies of socio-religious commands through the authoritarian agency of her father, Agamemnon. Iphigenia is sacrificed to the glory of the group and to patriotic honor, which are extensions of the glory and honor of Agamemnon himself, in the same way that the normative authority of Abraham was the extension of divinity. Unlike Abraham, who never doubted God's commands, Agamemnon wavers and rages against the need to sacrifice his daughter for the glory of the army and the honor of the mob. This divergence stems from the difference in the Judaic and Greek conceptions of divine authority. For Abraham, God's commands were the epitome of justice, which could not be doubted, and should not be questioned, whereas the anthropomorphic Greek gods made no pretense of being just.

In the case of Iphigenia, the Greeks knew that the gods were the arbiters of necessity and fate, which together made up the prime movers of the Greek religion and normative system. The outcome, however, was the same: both Isaac and Iphigenia were sacrificed to the divine projections of socio-normative mandates. According to the Midrash, the traditional and mythological interpretation of the Bible, Isaac ran joyfully to the alter and bound himself on it.[33] Iphigenia, however, was not so willing a victim. In one of the most shattering monologues ever written, she pleads with Agamemnon:

> Had I the voice of Orpheus, O my father,
> If I could sing so that the rocks would move,
> If I had words to win the hearts of all,
> I would have used them; I have only tears.
> See, I have brought them! They are all my power,
> I clasp your knees, I am your suppliant now,
> I, your own child, my mother bore me to you.
> O, kill me not untimely! The sun is sweet!
> Why will you send me into the dark grave?
> I was the first to sit upon your knee,
> The first to call you father.[34]

In the end, however, she accepts her fate and goes to the altar with the patriotic announcement, 'Bid my father come and touch the alter, which will this day bring victory and salvation unto Greece.'[35] Like Sarah in the myth of the offering of Isaac, Clytaemnestra, Iphigenia's mother, is the figure of grace, condemning paternal cruelty as expressed in the divine mandate to sacrifice her daughter for the glory of Greece.

The vicissitudes of social separation, the cruel rites of passage from childhood to puberty, the harsh coercion into the delimiting social norms and the sacrificial horrors of the Isaac and Iphigenia syndromes are all presided over by the father. They induce both male and female children to long for the cushioned forgiveness and lenient protection of mother. For the homosexual Proust, this longing became so intense that he enclosed himself into a padded, womb-like room and wrote volume after volume idealizing his beloved mother. For the fiercely heterosexual Camus, his great love for his mother may have turned into a generalized longing for the grace of womanhood rather than for a specific woman. Hence, Camus undertook a lifelong quest for the tender friendship of women.[36]

It might well be that the chivalrous adoration of ladies and the troubadours' odes to the graces of women during the Middle Ages were spurred by the insane trails of the hordes of cross-bearing warriors sacrificed to the waging of impossible wars by a stern absolutist God. The graceful, tender mother-woman was the vision of everything warm and merciful back home, in stark contrast to the squalor and death ordained by a graceless, unforgiving, and uncompromising fatherly God.

It is worth noting that in the original Hebrew of the Bible, as well as in Aramaic and Syriac, the word grace, *hessed*, also means incestuous, or sinful.[37] This shows that, etymologically, at least, the son's longing for his mother's grace appears to have sexual and incestuous undertones. This, of course, is a corollary to the suppressed, incestuous desire of the son for his mother at orality and its relation to the subconscious. Primarily, this might explain the attraction of boys to girls who remind them, directly or symbolically, of their mother, since the amatory and sexual longing for their mothers is blocked by the deeply internalized prohibition of their very early incestuous desires. The parallel attraction of daughters to men resembling their fathers in some relevant or vicarious characteristics might also be related to the dynamics of complementarity. The pubescent daughter, through identification with her mother, would be attracted to a complementary authoritarian figure linked to the normativeness of the father. Of course, these relationships vary in those families where the father is soft and benign, while the mother is harsh and authoritarian. The various combinations of identifications and permutations of complementary points between parents and children of the same and different sex are virtually endless, and the tracing of their effects on the choice of sexual partners is outside the scope of the present work.

The Tantalus Ratio

We have conceived our participation vector as the individual's quest at every particular moment in his life to revert to an earlier developmental phase: to the irresponsibility of pre-puberty, to the grace of the mother and the protection of the family fold, to the omnipresence of early orality and to the pre-natal bliss of non-being. This pull is countered by the instinctual and deprivational interaction vectors of separation, which except in the case of death, always have the upper hand. Yet the quest for participatory non-being is ever-present; we tend to agree with the hypothesis that, if man possessed a special master switch by means of which he could end his life at will, he would be bound to press it at one time or another. While the quest for participation manifests itself in numerous sublimatory substitutes, both institutionalized and deviant, actual participation is unattainable by definition. Proust could sensitively revive a lost childhood and a graceful mother though the hazy memories triggered by the taste of a madeleine bun, but even he could not recapture the actual sensations of things past. We are forever searching for our lost childhood, for our narcissistic paradise, but no one can actually revert to pre-puberty, reconstruct the omnipresence of early orality, or revive the sensation of blissful suspended animation in the amniotic fluid of the uterus. Participation is a fata morgana, shining hazily before our craving eyes, but ever-receding and never achieved.

This objective impossibility of participation is augmented by the countervailing separating vectors, both instinctual and interactive. At any given moment of our lives, there is a disjuncture, a gap, between our yearning for participation and the subjectively defined distance from our participatory aims. We have denoted this gap the Tantalus Ratio, after the Olympian demi-god who, whenever he reached for fruit, saw it whirl out of his reach by a gust of wind, and, whenever he bent down to drink from a seemingly fresh and sparkling stream of water, discovered it to be black mud. Even if he succeeded in scooping up some water in his palm, it dripped through his fingers before he could cool his parched lips.

The Tantalus Ratio creates a strain, a tension, between the longing for participation and the distance from it as perceived by the individual. This tension, the intensity of which is determined by the factors comprising the Tantalus Ratio, is the motivating force underlying an individual's action. On a rather low level of abstraction, we may envisage this tantalizing strain as the rabbit lure running in front of racing dogs or the proverbial carrot tied before the donkey's nose. This tantalizing strain is entirely different in nature from the opposing vectors that comprise the Tantalus Ratio. It is generated within the synaptic junctions of these opposing vectors and is released by the individual's motivational movement towards participatory goals or their sublimated alternatives. In other words, the participatory and separating vectors provide the crude psychic energy, whereas the Tantalus Ratio and the strain generated by it provide the motivational directions for the individual's actual behavior. This tantalizing tension may be either conscious or subconscious, and its operation is checked by acquired norms and by various internal personality mechanisms. Our hypothesis is that the psychic bases which underlie these mechanisms are generated by the anxieties registered at each consecutive stage of separation. Because each developmental stage from birth onwards is experienced as a painful separation, accompanied by deprivational interaction, the personality clings to the stability afforded by its present condition, by way of recoiling from a developmental change for the worse, leading to more radical separateness. The mechanisms are, therefore, 'the devil I know' defenses, which cause the personality to adhere to stable states as lesser evils.

We have already mentioned that the actual reversal to previous developmental stages is a practical impossibility and that all the techniques of participation, both institutionalized and deviant, cannot quench the intense longing for participation fueled by the individual's memories of his earlier participatory developmental stages. This means that the Tantalus Ratio, and the tension generated by it, produce formidable energies, which are ever augmented and kindled by the impossibility of slaking the individual's thirst for participation.

The gist of our premise is that the Tantalus Ratio is most powerful at the outset of life and decreases in potency with each developmental stage, until it wanes to a low ebb in old age.

The strength of the Tantalus Ratio is related first of all to the enormity of the separating forces of early childhood, which cause the participation vectors to muster countervailing pressures of corresponding potency. Second, the closeness in time of separating developmental events makes for vivid memories and sharply focused images of the lost participatory bliss. The child's frantic efforts to regain its bliss would, therefore, be marked by a desperate surge of power aimed at reversing the raw grief of the recent developmental calamity. These efforts are not yet mellowed by the sad knowledge, brought about by experience, that direct participatory reversals are impossible. The separation of birth, registered by the neonate as a catastrophe, is marked by frantic efforts to survive.[38] The mouth-ego of the infant searches for the nipple, or for anything that will provide nourishment. This factor, as well as the enormous pressures of growth at this hectic stage of development, leads to the formation of the biological vectors of separation, which are at the height of their potency. And yet this is also the stage at which the neonate experiences the strongest craving to revert back to his mother's womb, from which he was so brutally expelled just a short while ago, into an existence where mere survival involves effort and pain. This would be in keeping with what Schachtel denotes as the 'Law of Embeddedness'. The more complete an organism's state of embeddedness, the less it wants to stir from its state of quiescent equilibrium with its environment.[39] This means that the more violent the separating disturbance, the more powerful the corresponding striving for participation. And what is more violent than the separating expulsion of birth? Indeed, we claim that what Bowlby has denoted as the 'instinct of clinging' of the primate to its mother, as well as the less corporeal attachment of the human infant to his mother or father surrogate, can be linked to the neonate's desire to regain physical union with his mother in her womb.[40] This might provide the motive underlying the clinging behavior of both primate and human infants, apart from the functional desire of the young to be close to the source of their nourishment and protection.[41]

The second major phase of separation, the coagulation of the distinct 'I', is marked by the introduction of the deprivational interaction with the object into the battling forces of the Tantalus Ratio. At the oral stage, these objects are the mother, the breast, and the nipple. Indeed, the ego boundary, which separates the self from the totality of early orality, is nothing other than scar tissues which surround the individual self, as a result of its deprivational interaction with its surrounding objects.

We have relied elsewhere on the oralist offshoot of psychoanalysis to describe the mouth ego of early orality as aiming to empty the object mother's breast, whereas at the later, biting, oral stage the mouth ego, in fits of rage, wants to destroy the non-obliging object (mother).[42]

The Fixation of Personality Types

Personality traits and types are centered on the key concept of fixation, which is, undoubtedly, Freudian in origin. Unfortunately, neither Freud nor his disciples sufficiently clarified the mechanisms of fixation, as far as uninitiated outsiders are concerned, though it seems to have been a central concept in psychoanalytic theory and practice. According to the original Freudian formulation, psycho-sexual energy is directed towards the erogenous zones, which also represent the major psycho-sexual development phases.[43] When parents or their surrogates over-indulge an infant, or severely deprive him at any given developmental phase, he will muster a relatively large amount of psycho-sexual energy to overcome the frustrations thus generated. He will also harness such energies to create alternative, defensive outlets, the normal manifestations of which have been blocked. Consequently, the growth processes will be arrested or injured at that developmental phase, since the psycho-sexual energies have been expanded to erect defenses against the conflictual interaction with the parents, instead of building the infant's personality.

Freud himself was not clear as to the nature of fixation and took too many things for granted, claiming:

> The unconscious knows no time limit. The most important, as well as the most peculiar, character of psychic fixation consists in the fact that all impressions are, on the one hand, retained in the same form as they were received, and also in the forms that they have assumed in their further development. This state of affairs cannot be elucidated by any comparison from any other sphere. By virtue of this theory, every former state of the memory content may thus be restored, even though all original relations have long been replaced by newer ones.[44]

Freud's unconscious psyche would appear to be the perfect data bank, one which stores all impressions, as well as all possible interactions of these impressions, with past and future ones in a timeless progression. A fixation is, thus, an anchor of sorts on a given context of these impressions, but how this anchoring comes about, Freud does not say. We propose, therefore, an explanation based on our exposition of the developmental phases of the personality core.[45]

If the processes of transition from one developmental phase to the next, which are deprivational in essence, are more painful at a given developmental phase than the modal degree of pain, as perceived by the individual's own experience, ruptures or developmental wounds are formed, which psychic energies then rush to mend. To be more precise: We envisage the developmental processes as an interplay between the separating forces of growth and interaction and the participating urge to revert back to an earlier developmental phase. It is energy resulting from the dynamic interplay between these vectors that is the Tantalus Ratio. However, if the separating effects of the deprivational interaction are too intense or violent at any given time, the developmental process is temporarily disconnected. The participation vector and the energies of the Tantalus Ratio repair the injury by covering it with developmental scar tissue, as on a wound. Yet the wound itself and the tender coats of scar tissue are still exposed to conflict and more pressure, since the deprivational interaction of the nascent ego with its surroundings is a continuous process. Consequently, the ever-thickening layers of scar tissue which result from the trauma of fixation are more like a corn on a toe. The psychic energy centers around the traumatized developmental scar, covering it with excessive mental imprints, very much like the whirl loops of the corn, which form a lump protruding from the skin. The corn is painful, not only because of the pressure, but because the excessive scar tissue makes it all the more vulnerable. Because of the trauma, the whole area is sensitive.

This metaphor illustrates the nature of fixation. It is the combined outcome of the traumatizing injury and the excessive and frantic patching of layers of developmental scar tissue through the psychic energies of the Tantalus Ratio. The harsher the trauma, the thicker the layers of defensive scar tissue. The separate ego emerges out of non-differentiated early orality, through its deprivational interaction with the mother's breast and surrounding objects. The resulting boundary around the self is also an example of developmental scar tissue, but a fixation is an over-traumatized developmental experience, which is more conspicuous and more sensitive, and, consequently, more vulnerable than the rest of the developmental texture of the personality.

We should point out here that our conceptualization of fixation, as distinct from Freud's, is not related to pathological regressions, but to the crystallization of character traits and personality types. We hold further that regression is not conditioned by fixation, but is rather a defensive flight to an earlier developmental phase, the longing for which is ever present in the participation vector of our personality core. When the dynamic balance of the Tantalus Ratio is disturbed by the separating pressure of growth, or when the individual's interpersonal relationships suffer a disrupting blow, the counter-pressures of participation thus released catapult the individual to visions of pre-pubic havens and blissful dreams of early orality. Fixation is, therefore, a developmental dam which traps both the disrupting blows of traumatizing interaction and the countering defenses of the Tantalus Ratio. The anchoring of personality traits on the fixation is the result of this massive concentration of painful experiences and heaping of defenses in frantic disarray. One is aware of a hand or a tooth only when they are painful, and one always feels a blow on a sore, because the same blow to normal tissue is negligible. Consequently, the severity of fixation is related to the magnitude of the developmental trauma and the corresponding intensity of defenses mustered by the Tantalus Ratio.

The Sisyphean and the Tantalic

Birth is, no doubt, an explosive event, whose archetype in mythology is the act of creation itself. Yet this colossal event is not registered by a separate self-awareness. Not until later orality does a separate self-image emerge out of a non-differentiated mass, when the 'I' is confronted by the surrounding objects. This is the baseline from which the self emerges out of the total being of early orality and the circumference of the self is defined by the non-self. This is an existential revolution, which is registered by the individual as a separating catastrophe.

We propose, therefore, a personality typology anchored on this developmental dichotomy of pre- and post-differentiation of the self. The molding process is expressed in the nature and severity of the fixation, which in turn determines the placement of a given individual on the personality type continuum. However, the types themselves are fixated by developmental chronology—i.e., whether the fixating trauma occurred before or after the separation of the self. We denote a personality that was fixed before the formation of the self as a participant or Tantalic type, after the mythical Greek demigod whose punishment we have already described. If the traumas fixate personality after the crystallization of the self, the Sisyphean (separant) type is bound to emerge. This Sisyphean type is related to a Greek mythical demigod, who was punished by having to roll a stone to the top of a hill. Whenever he neared the summit, the stone rolled down and Sisyphus had to start pushing it all over again. The Tantalic type is operation-bound, ever visualizing and longing for the all-inclusive early orality, while the Sisyphean type is always entangled with the vicissitude of the object. The separant Sisyphus anchors on the inter-relationship with the object, whereas the participant Tantalus seeks the blissful fruits of mystical union. These are the passions kindling the vectors of our personality types. However, Sisyphus's object keeps rolling down and Tantalus's mystical fruit forever recedes before his eyes. This is the essence, and the irony, of the Tantalus Ratio: Its strength is measured by unachieved aims, because its fulfillment is not only impossible, but also tantamount to impotence.

The *Ani, Atzmi, Ity*, and the Self

The concept of the self involves consistency and continuity, so that the same self is felt and defined by an individual from the moment his separate awareness coagulates until death. The exceptions to the principle of consistency and continuity are cases of madness or the temporary dissolution, or weakening, of the self in extreme cases of hallucinations or mystical experiences.

The self, therefore, is the consistent and continuous inner sameness of the individual vis-à-vis his environment. This inner sameness element of our definition has, no doubt, an Ericksonian flavor to it.[46] But for Erickson, 'ego identity' is the meaning of this inner sameness to others, whereas for us, the self is the structured barrier between the separate individual, as conceived by the individual himself, and everything—flora, fauna, and inanimate objects—that are excluded from the confines of this barrier.

We propose to denote the participant core of the self by the Hebrew word ani. The translation of ani is 'I', but in kabbalist doctrine, ani (אני) and ain (אין) (nothingness), which have the same Hebrew letters but in different order, are interchangeable and synonymous. Consequently, the ani, the 'I', which longs for participant non-being, is the Tantalic objectless component of the self. We shall denote our interactive object-related component of the self with the Hebrew word *atzmi* (עצמי) which may be translated into English as 'myself'. Its root, however, is *etzem*, (עצם) 'object', which makes it appropriate for its definitional task.

For us, the self is the essence that defines its being both for itself and for others. The atzmi is the interactive, relational self reaching outward towards the object, whereas the ani transcends spatio-temporality and reaches inwards towards the pre-differentiated unity.

It is important to point out that the atzmi must have a subject and an object, a perceiver and a perceived. There is a continuous flow of perception to the atzmi from flora, fauna, and inanimate objects. The atzmi may also perceive the body and the ani, the ontological self, as objects. The ani, on the other hand, need not have an object. In concentrated meditation, in some mystical experiences, in some forms of madness, in drug-induced euphoria, and sometimes in orgasm, the ani has no awareness of itself as a being separate from its surroundings. The boundaries of the self may also melt away, and temporary objectless unity may be achieved.

The atzmi is by definition a relational entity; therefore, its interaction with its surroundings may be studied in terms of stimulus, response, association, and correlation. Not so the ani, which in its pure form is objectless and non-relational; measures of logic, deduction, and inference do not apply to it. If we wish to study the whole human being, and not only fragments of it, we have to rely on intuition, introspection, and even meditation in order to grasp the ani component of the self and, therefore, fully understand the dual nature of our personality.

Our study of personality is, therefore, holistic and synthetic, not analytic, in contrast to the main thrust of contemporary behavioral science.

We have pointed out elsewhere that the crystallization of the self out of the non-self is, in effect, a process of tearing away region after region of the original omnipresence of the neonate. This process continues until the separate atzmi is placed within the specific boundaries of its spatio-temporality and the confines of compelling social norms.[47]

The essence of the ani, i.e., that which constitutes the being of the ani—pure self—precedes the existence, that which constitutes the emergence or manifestation, of the atzmi, interactive self. We have pointed out earlier that the non-differentiated entity before birth and at early orality is an omnipresent, timeless, and infinite essence, which is then separated and confined within spatio-temporality by its deprivational interaction with its surroundings. This timeless essence, when embedded with the separate individual, is not a metaphysical, but rather a natural, phase of human development. Our conception of the ani is in line with Husserl's later writings, in which he postulates a pure ego and says that the knowledge of possibilities (inherent in the pure ego) must precede that of actualities.[48] In a similar manner, the logically non-verifiable essence of the objectless ani differs from Husserl's pure ego, because it relates to experience and not to theoretical, a priori transcendence.

The contents of the ani and the atzmi, as well as their relative preponderance with a given personality, are, of course, related to the participant and separant personality core vectors, the developmental fixations, and the given culture in which the individual is socialized.

Finally, we present the ity, which is Hebrew for 'with me'. The ity is the synthesizer of the dialectical conflicts within the self, between the unity-bound ani and the interactive atzmi. The ity is the structured Tantalus Ratio within the self. Its synthesizing function makes it the coordinator of human action, and as such it has a lot in common with Freud's ego.

The magnitude and relative preponderance of the poles on our self-continuum are related to the developmental factors of the personality core. A violent early oral fixation, a quietist participant culture, and a Tantalic preoccupation at old age will contribute to the predominance of the ani within the self-continuum. Conversely, a separant fixation on the object, during a period of vigorous growth in an active-Sisyphean culture, will make for an overpowering atzmi. The strength or weakness of the coordinating ity will then determine its ability to contain the self within the dynamic system in balance.

The ani is mostly unconscious, because its source is anchored in pre-differentiated non-awareness, when the space and time of consciousness have not yet developed. Some of the ani is pre-conscious or semi-conscious, while only a few of its manifestations are conscious. Even when the ani is conscious, it lurks more on the peripheries of awareness in a déjà vu-like experience. The atzmi, on the other hand, is largely conscious, partly pre-conscious (as in many semi-automatic functions we perform in daily life) and only rarely unconscious, as in some religious ecstasies or in drug-induced euphoria, which partly dissolves the ego boundary.

The ideal ani is timeless, spaceless, and without the sequences of logic and inference. These are generated by the interactive atzmi and structured within the Tantalus Ratio by the coordinating ity. This stems from our basic premise that the ani is dominated by a flow of intuition. The atzmi is intentional and attentive to the sequences of experiences and memory, which make for a distinction of before and after, and hence for the sequences of time. The ani on the other hand, is suspended in a Bergsonian Duree-like flow of a continuous present.[49]

The ani is also spaceless. It projects onto transcendence archetypes such as the Upanishadic Purasha, the kabbalist adam kadmon, and the Gnostic 'primordial man'. This holistic view of the universe, characteristic of ani-dominated mystics, regards the discrete, pluralistic image of reality, perceived by the atzmi as partial, not unlike the eyesight of an alcoholic whose retina has been damaged by methylated spirits. Still, the perception of space is effected through the relationships and interaction of the components of the self with surrounding objects. Like time, space is generated by the interactive dynamics of the Tantalus Ratio and structured by the regulating dialectics of the ity.

The ani, not being relational, is not necessarily governed by rules of causality. Causal simultaneity and synchronicity may be acceptable to the ani as different manifestations of the same phenomenon, stemming from one source. The ani may be reached experientially through meditation, mystical experiences, or the catalysis of drug-induced peak experiences. Logic is inapplicable as a means of discovering the ani; intuition rather than deliberate attention is the proper medium for the unveiling it. Conversely, space, time, and causality are inherent in the relational nature of the atzmi.

We envisage a dialectical conflict within the Tantalus Ratio of the self, which provides the motivation for the inclusion, i.e., the swallowing of the object by the outward reaching atzmi which, with the help of the coordinating ity, devises surrogate modes of inclusion, which manifest themselves as socially acceptable or deviant object relationships.

The ity, through constant dialectical conflicts amongst the components of the self and its environment, creates a system-in-balance which holds the personality in a dynamic equilibrium.

The main attributes of our atzmi, the interactive component of the self, are based, first of all, on the discrete perception of space and linear perception of time. The perception of the rhythm of time may, of course, vary from one person to another and may also be heightened or blurred by drugs. Nevertheless, only the linear sequence of past, present, and future is perceived meaningfully by the atzmi. The necessity of time and space for the objects of the atzmi underlies its need for logic, symbolism (language), causality, association, and inference in its interaction with other people and things. Social norms are then incorporated within the self, by the coordinating functions of the ity. The atzmi, in contrast to the holistic flow of the intuition of the ani, operates by soberly focusing attention on the object and relating to it intentionally. The atzmi is basically an omnivore which aims to swallow the object and, thus, regain the exclusive omnipotence it lost when ejected from Eden-like orality.

The dynamics of the ity, the regulating dialectical system-in-balance of the self, are different in our model from those of the ego or Freud. For him, the ego is an executive, making independent decisions and sending out orders over the psychic intercom. Jung regards his ego as an army commander presiding over the sessions of his general staff. For the ego psychologists, the ego has an autonomous standing which does not stem from the basic drives and the core components of the personality. Our ity is different. It is the dialectical force-field created by the turbulence and pressures from without and within. An instance of this, on a micro level, is a ping-pong ball held in one place on a billiard table by opposing streams of air and, on a macro level, the fixed courses of stellar bodies. The position, strength, and balance of the regulating ity are a function of the potency of the conflicting personality components and a measure of their inability to attain their contradictory goals.

Let us recall then: the brain records the highly receptive amnestic years; events that transpired in those first years of life are projected, inter alia, as myths of cosmology; myths as personal history may be regarded as the account of crucial developments in the formative years; moreover, human development in the early formative years passes in an accelerated manner through the whole evolutional phases, and myths are also a projection of the development of the species as inherent in the development of the human individual.

As the ani-consciousness is a universal unity which is reflected in all consciousness, it may account for the universal basis of some myths, e.g., the proverbial 'Fall from Grace', the sacrificing of the young gods, the slaying of the (incestuous) snakes, the breaking of the cosmic vessels (birth), as well as the unitary God. The plurality of consciousnesses, on the other hand, provides mythology with the projection of experiential myths as well as the plurality of gods and forces projected by the historical experiences and the Sisyphean forces of nature. Tantalus and Sisyphus in reality do not forgive because they do not judge and because each event dents the cosmos in an irreversible manner. They also have no regrets because each event dents the inner intensity of the authentic experience and counts, not its outward 'success' or 'failure'. One discards the obscuring veils of Maya, evades the violent spirals of the demiurgos, and drops the cozy filters of bourgeois slumber and stands drawn, tense, and ready in the eye of the storm. There, in naked, defenseless desperation a cry of anguish of a kindred soul may reach the inner self. If answered, the miracle of a dialogue of grace may yet transpire.

The Viable Mythogenes

For the mythogene to exist and to continue to survive, its structure must have a homeostatic system-in-balance; otherwise it would disrupt. Since in content the mythogenic structure contains elements of the divergent entities which it aims to connect, stable modus vivendi within the structure would have to be attained, which only then becomes viable and effective as a linking agent. The mythogenic contents of the structure may have various quantities, qualities, and proportions of ani-consciousness energy-matter participant myths of yearning and separant myths of experience, but the mythogene within the structure must have a system-in-balance; otherwise it would not be viable, durable, or functional in effecting a link between divergent qualities. There is a basic dualism between the ani and the totality of energy-matter, whose universal potential is the first singularity, the ani mentioned in the previous section. This ani singularity is the pin-point center of blackholes reflected in all the individual singularity potentials of energy-matter. This reflection is holonic, a term invented by Arthur Koestler to denote a hierarchy of sub-wholes. Koestler says:

> The point first to be emphasized is that each member of this hierarchy, on whatever level, is a sub-whole or *Holon* in its own right—a stable, integrated structure equipped with self-regulatory devices and enjoying a considerable degree of autonomy or self-government. Cells, muscles, nerves, organs, all have their intrinsic rhythms and patterns of activity, often manifested spontaneously and without external stimulation; they are subordinated as parts to the higher centers of the hierarchy, but at the same time function as quasi-autonomous wholes. They are Janus-faced. The face turned upward, toward the higher levels, is that of a dependent part; the faced turned downward, towards its own constituents, is that of a whole of remarkable self-sufficiency.[50]

This system-in-balance is universal and stems from the holonic quality of life forms and objects. We postulate that the nuclei of atoms are held together by a system-in-balance between the strong nuclear force and the countervailing force of protons; the electromagnetic forces and Pauli's exclusion principle hold the atom in equilibrium by forces which we lack the ability or understanding to examine. In the *Myth of Tantalus,* we showed how the human personality is held in equilibrium by its participant and separant core vectors.[51] We hold that this tendency towards equilibrium, found both in inanimate objects and in life forms, is necessary both for their space-time existence and evolutionary survival. If we return to the particle, so long as the system-in-balance holds, so does the particle. Once that system is disrupted, a particle may decay into other particles or revert back to a suppressed, wave-like form.

Following our method in the present work, we shall trace some of the mytho-empirical anchors for the necessity of a system at equilibrium for both life forms and objects on all levels of existence.

The idea that a certain order, equilibrium, or balance constitutes a necessary condition for the existence of objects is not new. The Greek of the word 'cosmos', literally 'order', is the root of cosmetics, the art of ornamentation.

This exemplifies the separant Greek ethos of the world as being based on order and aesthetics. The pre-Socratic dialectics of Heracleites were adopted by Hegel, and through him by Marx, to create a new world order, a nèw cosmos, through revolution. A similar strategy was adopted by Li Ta-Chao (1889-1927), one of the founders of the Chinese Communist Party, when he transferred the Confucian idea of a universal harmony and order (Ta-t'ung) to the Communist order which would prevail in China after the revolution. These are Sisyphean cycles of chaos, order, revolution, new order, new chaos etc., spiraling aimlessly ad infinitum. The system-in-balance is technical and yet valueless, instrumental but arbitrary, consisting of social and physical controls. These are the organizational controls of *meden agan* (nothing in excess) and *ananké* (the coercion of the physical equilibria). The latter even keeps the heavenly bodies in their orbit and will push them back if they commit the hübris of deviating from it. *Ordnung muss sein*, the Germanic version of the Greek separant maxims, exalts order as a meta-law for man and universe.

The participant system-in-balance is the clandestine core dialectic of yearning, which especially characterizes the kabbala. The copulation—*Zivug*—of the cherubim in the Holy of Holies, is postulated by the kabbala.[52] The *Talmud*, which we hold to be a mytho-empirical projection of the core dialectics of yearning as the prime mover of both man and god, would seem to have permeated the Freudian notion of the core psycho-sexuality of man.[53] In a similar vein, the participant Judaic ethos of a system-of-balance of core dialectics could have permeated the thinking of Claude Levi-Strauss on formulating his basic notions of structuralism.

The model of structuralism, shown in figure 1.1, postulates that the space equilibrium of the routine operation of individuals is of particular interest:

	Haut	
Gauche	Ego	Droite
	Bas	

Figure 1.1[54]

This is very similar to the kabbalist model of the holonic system-in-balance represented by the emanated sefirot in a didactic equilibrium, as shown in figure 1.2.

Hessed, 'grace', represents the right; *din*, 'judgment', is the left, or sinister side of stern judgment, and *tiferet*, 'glory', occupies the dialectical synthetic middle. Many scholars have studied the homeostatic and balancing mechanisms in biology and the equilibrium of forces in physics, especially in quantum mechanics.[55] These subjects lie outside the scope of the present work, but we shall deal with the system-in-balance that applies to man—transcendent relationships, as well as to the Munchausen-like self-regulating mechanisms inherent in revelation and creativity.

din		*hessed*
	tiferet	
hod	*yesod*	*netzah*
	malchut	

Figure 1.2

Atlas embodies the mytho-empirical projection of the system-in-balance between God and Creation, in that he was entrusted with the maintenance of the pillars linking heaven and earth. He also provides a mytho-empirical anchor for the system-in-balance between man and creation. Atlas, the Titan or the man-god, is depicted by Hesiodos as holding heaven on his head and his hands.[56] Etymologically, 'atlas' means 'very enduring.' The tense creator holding the globe or the Sisyphean stone on his head must be attuned to his task in a dynamic, yet precarious, equilibrium. Even a slight disturbance may break the creator's concentration. Effective creativity is, therefore, a combined mytho-empirical projection of both Sisyphus and Atlas. The first represents the object relationship inherent in creativity, and the second the system in equilibrium required to carry it out. Indeed, the system-in-balance between the core vectors would seem to be a precedent condition for the functioning of God and man. The absence of a system-in-balance on the biological level disrupts the physical homeostasis and may cause sickness and death. A disjuncture of the core vectors on the personality level may cause structural personality defects or even madness. The disintegration of the individual may lead to anomie, deviance, or crime. Structurally, all singularities are formed in the image of the first singularity; this is the essence of the expansive nature of energy matter. However, the pure ani is always a single unity. It is reflected as consciousness, which is deterministically encased in all artifacts, from the first wheel to the most sophisticated computer. The ani is existentialist, because we feel it as the essence of our being without any further proof. As such, it is as, or even more real, than any physical reality proven by an experiment or a mathematical equation. The ani-unity, as the underlying spiritual essence of all objects and life forms, forms the basis of mythology, theology, and mysticism which equate the ani-unity with God.

Hence, God's name, Yehowva, a contraction of the Hebrew for 'I am that I am', applies to both God and man. The repetition of the word *eheyeh* in the Exodus passage as interpreted by the Kabbala, means that God and man reflect each other, or, more precisely, that God is the reflection of the (inner) man.

The ani, as the unique consciousness at the core of all objects and life forms, is one, and the transcendental project of this uniqueness is the unity of God. It filters through the objects and life forms in a kaleidoscopic manner, so that it fits the peculiarities of a specific life form or object. This is the meaning of the Theosophic Kabbala's statement that both God and man consist of lights and containers (vessels). The light stems from the unity of infinity, while the containers are the bodies which contain the lights. The kaleidoscopic flowing of divinity into and through objects and life forms explains the paradox of plurality in unity. Plurality has an infrastructure of unity, yet the appearances and perceptions of all life forms and objects are plural. This might also explain why God created man in His own image—the one inner image permeating every thing and every creature.

Thus, the divine inner essence of the plurality of creatures and things is identical, and only its outer garments differ from one another in endless permutations, so that object and life form is unique. This is a reflection of the uniqueness of God, even within plurality each emanant senses a unique entity vis-à-vis the unitarian uniqueness of the emanator.

The timeless, spaceless, and attributeless ani, though unique, is present in all life forms and may also be present in objects and artifacts as contained (canned) consciousness.

The ani, the holonic potential of energy-matter, is a singularity, a point in the infinite matter density, infinite temperature and infinite space-time curvature.[57]

There is a degree of consensus that a singularity was the potential ani of the Big Bang, as well as other white holes explosions. A singularity is also the ultimate fate of the Big Crunch and other dynamics, such as matter collapsing into black holes. All singularities are surrounded by an event horizon, the boundaries of extreme gravity, from which even light itself cannot escape.[58] We hold this event horizon to be the curtain from which energy emanates into history.

Right after the Big Bang there was total symmetry and uniformity of energy, and the four fundamental forces of gravitation, the weak force, the electromagnetic force and the strong force were not yet differentiated. The universe was filled with an undifferentiated soup of matter and radiation, each particle of which collided very rapidly with the other particles. Despite its rapid expansion, the universe was in a state of nearly perfect thermal equilibrium.[59]

Thus, in the beginning, all was symmetric, isomorphic, and the phenomena were created by synthesizing ani-consciousness and energy-matter as a means for the subsequent creation. More than anything else, man is a manufacturer of symboloi. These are the connecting agents between the ani-consciousness and energy-matter structured into a model of a phenomenon to be realized subsequently by an act of creation. Man's atzmi, his interactive self, synthesizes symboloi by connecting his ani-consciousness with well-defined diffuse parts of his environment.

The Logos, when directed at an object, became fixated as a name tag or symbol. Man was a name-caller for God, and whatever name he gave to a creature became the symbol by which it was known (Gen. 2:19). The symbol stems from the Greek *symbolon*, which was originally a bone broken in two, with each part given to the two parties to a contract. The perfect fit of the parts of the bone was the ultimate evidence, like fingerprints, for the existence of the contract. Hence, the symbol evolved from a linking function. Therefore, the word—the Logos—when structured into a symbol, became a connecting agent, entering into a dialogue moving through and by the Logos into a creative interaction with chaos, the formless flow of energy matter. These mythogenic structures precede any act of creation which involves the integration of consciousness and energy-matter, be it a poem, a painting, or a quantum particle. All integrations of consciousness and energy taking place on the quantum level cannot be consciously perceived and remembered by creatures, because they take place in the unconscious, yet very likely in the processes of memory, thought, intuition, and emotion. These are all based on micro-dynamics taking place on the quantum level behind the uncertainty barrier. These basic processes are integrated, however, within the personality of the ani-consciousness and are, hence, projected onto mythology as experiential myths. Scientific analysis of mythology may divulge information, not only on the personality structure and social character, but also on quantum mechanics.

The ani-consciousness is indeterministic. It has an existentialist freedom of choice which it imbues in all life forms. We hold that, in its own fashion, even a tree makes an indeterministic choice to push its roots in one direction rather than another. However, no artifact has a free choice, because its creator has implanted in it, by means of a symbolon structure, a consciousness geared to perform certain tasks. Hence, it is imbued with a deterministic contained consciousness. This idea was expressed by the Basht, who taught that a man infuses his power into everything he creates.

Both a paleolithic spearhead and the most sophisticated computer have a deterministic contained consciousness. They cannot perform differently than they have been designed to by their creator. The guiding maxim of computer experts as to the cybernetic aptitude of their charges is 'garbage in, garbage out.' The contained consciousness in artifacts is the intention which guided its creation—the performance of a certain set of tasks.

One of the most important differences between the contained consciousness of artifacts, and the indeterministic ani-consciousness of life forms, especially of man, is that the latter can experience revelation, whereas the former (the spearhead, the computer) cannot. However complex the hardware of a computer may be, however sophisticated its software, it can only carry out the tasks it was programmed to perform deterministically. Creatures, on the other hand, have freedom of will, and this to our mind is the basis of their indeterministic abilities, as well as their capacity to experience revelation.

We look at a picture by Van Gogh. It strikes us with an overwhelming potency a century after his death. The same may be said of a novel by Dostoevski or a concerto by Bach. The consciousness of an artist is contained in his work and transferred to it through the creative act. These are merely well-known cases; we claim that all creation is a dialectic between consciousness and matter as mediated by the symbolon structure.

The disturbance of the equilibrium within the object may lead to its falling apart and, on the universal level, to a Big Bang. A disharmony or maladjustment of a life form vis-à-vis its environment may lead to its evolutionary failure to adapt. Disruption between man and transcendence is represented by the Gnostic plane and the Theosophic Kabbalist feeding of the *kelipot*, eventually leading to the disjunction of the inner equilibrium within the Godhead and the catastrophe of the breaking of the vessels.[60] The system-in-balance between core vectors thus seems to be, a universal principle of existence and creativity. This is attested to by both the mystic book of *Zohar* and the Lurianic kabbala. The 'Kings' in the Zohar died because of a disjuncture between hessed and din.[61] In our model this stands for a disruption between the core vectors of separation and participation. If he has no inner system-in-balance, man is incapable either of creativity or meaningful dialogue with God or his fellow man. Of special importance is the error of Pistis Sophia:

> The Sophia, who is called the Pistis, wished to accomplish a work alone without her mate. And her work became an image of heaven. There is a curtain between the æons above and the æons which are below. And a shadow came into existence below the curtain. And that shadow became matter. And that shadow was cast into a region, and its form became a work in matter like an abortion.[62]

The essence of the demiurgos is that it deems itself self-sufficient in a solipsistic manner. Evil considers itself to be all alone in the world, and hence, everything does, or should, belong to it. Without a dialogue, one is blind to the other. Without the core dialogue of energy, without the Kabbalist zivug, there can be no viable creation; without a system-in-balance between the holonic dualities within an individual, there is a risk of madness and death, while the lack of equilibrium within divinity may lead to error and hübris.

The hübris of the deities abounds in Greek mythology. Prometheus acted alone without heeding the counsel of his fellow gods, thus disrupting the equilibrium of creation by purveying fire to man, conferring him with an advantage in instrumental manipulation and domination over other life forms. When we consider the sorry mess which many generations of man's polluting and violent sovereignty have made of our planet, we tend to agree with the Olympians. Very likely, Prometheus himself, if he is still chained to his rock, is at this very minute striking his chest with his fist in atonement for such an act of hübris. While Prometheus committed an instrumental Sisyphean act of hübris, Icarus was guilty of a Tantalic participant act of hübris. His search for revelation induced him to soar too high, and his inadequate wings were exposed to the scorching light of the sun (the demiurgical fire), causing him to fall to the sea and drown. In order to experience revelation one must evade direct epistemic exposure to the demiurgos. Icarus' father, Dædalus, counseled him not to fly too high or too low (to be a system in equilibrium), but rather to experience revelation right in the middle of the eye of the storm, but because of his hübris, Icarus exposed himself to the demiurgos and was scorched by it. In man, hübris is even more lethal. Any biological, personal, or social conspicuousness has been held in many different societies and eras to be a sign of hübris, was tagged as deviance, and was treated accordingly.

It should be clear that the characteristics rendering the object conspicuous are not necessarily themselves negatively valued. In ancient Greece, where policy making was quite often realistic, stigmatization by ostracism was achieved by 'chipping off the tallest ears of corn' (i.e., those who seemed to be more conspicuous than necessary). The question asked from the assembly in a manner quite relevant to our context was: 'Is there any among you who you think is dangerous to the state? If so, who?' In other words, we have here conspicuity and danger used almost as synonyms.

Greek tragedy shows, in many instances, that stigma befalls a person who is too conspicuous, too wealthy, too successful, or too wise, thereby bringing on himself the jealousy of men and gods alike. That theme recurs in Greek mythology. Prometheus was punished excessively not only because he brought fire to mortals, but because he was outstanding in his knowledge of science and medicine, which filled Zeus with jealousy and anger. Stigma as sanction is, therefore, not necessarily the story of deviation from laws or moral standards. Man is often subjected to sanctions for no apparent reason. A person has his *moira*, or station in life, and, if he exceeds it by being conspicuous in any way, he commits hübris and arouses the jealousy of the strikingly anthropomorphic Greek gods.[63] Herodotus recounts the message of Artabanos to Xerxes:

> You see that the Gods hurl their bolts against those living beings that tower above the rest. They do not suffer them to exalt themselves. The small ones, on the other hand, do not bother them. You see that lightning always strikes the tallest houses and trees. For the Gods love to set a limit to everything that rises too high. For the Gods do not suffer anyone but themselves to harbor proud thoughts.[64]

The hübris of Agamemnon consisted of being awarded a hero's welcome as 'the highest of all who walk on earth today'. We may note that though it was the crowd that committed the hübris, Agamemnon was doomed, because 'the black furies wait, and when a man has grown great by luck, not justice, without turn of chance, they wear him to a shade and cast him down to perdition; who shall save him?' (Æschylus, *Oresteia*). Again we have a clue as to the main criteria of social stigma: 'An excess of fame is danger'. But danger to whom? Apparently, to the jealous multitudes (the gods). Drachman comments on the theme of punishment without offense in Greek tragedy, as follows:

> Our first question, when the immediate effect of the magnificent drama has subsided, is this: But what has he done? 'Done?' answers the Greek in astonishment, 'He has not done anything. That is the point of it. It has all happened unknown to him.'—Well, but then it is all the most outrageous injustice.—'I do not understand you,' says the Greek; 'Do you mean to deny that such things can happen to you, any day, nay, at any moment? Or are you even for an instant safe from the invasion of the most appalling horror that your mind can grasp? If you are, you had better realize what human life is. This is what Sophocles's drama should help you to do.'[65]

The epitome of this theme is reached in Polycrates, King of Samos, whose hübris, according to Herodotus, was his conspicuous success and outstanding prosperity.

It is not only the anthropomorphic Greek gods or primitive tribes who punish man's disruption of the system-in-balance. Lurianic kabbala sees original sin as inherent in Adam's hübris, as expressed by his over-eagerness to copulate with Eve. He disrupted the cosmic equilibrium by carrying out his mating—zivug—before the Sabbath (the optimal time for a zivug of mending—*tikkun*). In addition, he had performed a disruptive and polluting mating with Lilith (Satan's consort), thereby bringing about the profane zivug of Eve with the snake.[66] In a like manner, Moses also committed hübris by striking the rock instead of talking to it, as ordained by God, in order to free the water within. Thus Moses also caused a disruptive zivug instead of a harmonious one.[67]

We have already pointed out that the breaking of the vessels was a violent disrupting of the system-in-balance of the Godhead, whereas original sin and the golden calf represented dramatic disruptions of the process the Almighty's mending (tikkun). The Talmud (Bereita Hagiga[68]) tale about four scholars who entered a mystical orchard, *Pardess*, may provide a mytho-empirical support for our contention as to the effects of a strong cathartic experience, such as mystical revelations on the intra-psychic system-in-balance. One of them, Ben Azaai, died and another, Ben Soma, went mad. These two had apparently a very skewed and precarious system-in-balance, which the forceful mystical experiences shattered physically in the first case and mentally in the second. The third, Elisha ben-Avuya, had apparently a loosely integrated system-in-balance. Yet after its initial disruption, it reached a reintegration on another level of being within another belief system. He became an *acher*—an apostate. Rabbi Akiva had apparently a very strongly integrated system-in-balance, enabling him to undergo the revelatory experience without being injured by it.

Indeed, man's system-in-balance is very precarious on all three levels of his being: biological, personal, and social. In the *Myth of Tantalus*, we discussed the vulnerability of the Sisyphean and Tantalic types to outside stimuli. On the cortical level, the activist Sisyphean needs the initial arousal more than the Tantalic type in order to initiate his functioning. On the personality level, the Tantalic type is averse to stimuli, whereas the Sisyphean type is hungry for them. On the social level, the Sisyphean is a group performer, whereas the Tantalic type is a loner.[69] These traits, measured along continua, can be used to indicate the vulnerability of the various types to the disruption of the system-in-balance on these three levels which are, of course, interrelated within the individual as an holistic unit. When one of these levels or the whole person is exposed to a traumatic experience, they try to 'mend' themselves on another level of being. However, when these tikkunim (mendings) are not successful, the individual may die, or become insane or alienated. There is no intrinsic difference between the vulnerability of God's system-in-balance of man's. Both must be 'mended' if their equilibrium has been disrupted. This makes for constant change, both for man and God. Both mortal and divine are in a constant process of *becoming*. They undergo processes; but in line with their Tantalic and Sisyphean meta-myths, they never reach their goals. A system-in-balance also constitutes a precedent condition for revelation and creativity. Revelation can flow through a balanced infrastructure and then be transmitted to others and to God as a universal thou. Man, through his creativity, is also the connecting link between the mindless, valueless demiurgos and the powerless and silent Godhead. Man creates the viable equilibrium between psyche and soma, between God and his creation. There can be no abdication for a creative Sisyphus; without him everything reverts to chaos. The sefirot of the Kaballah are divided into three heads as shown in figure 1.3:

Left	Middle	Right
Bina	*Keter*	*Hochma*
(intelligence)	(crown)	(wisdom)
Din	*Tiferet*	*Hessed*
(stern judgment)	(glory)	(grace)
Hod	*Yessod*	*Netzah*
(awe inspiring)	(foundation)	(eternity)
	Malchut	
	(kingdom)	

Figure 1.3

The right side, dominated by the sefira of grace, also contains those sefirot which descriptively constitute those attributes of God denoted by us as participant—Tantalic. The left, sinister side, dominated by stern judgment, is also materially separant—Sisyphean, whereas the middle row presents the dialectical synthesis. As the sefirotic structure is holonic and permeates all of creation and transcendence, it postulates the system-in-balance as a meta-principle regulating the viability of God, man, and the relationship between them. Indeed, in the Lurianic kabbala the light which radiates from infinity and which builds all the worlds is denoted as the *kav hamida*[70]—the ray of balance, which builds the world in measures and balances. The breaking of the vessels was caused by the disharmony between the divine light flowing from infinity and the emanated containers (vessels) which were meant to hold Knowledge and the Tree of Life.[71] The molding of the golden calf disrupted the face-to-face mating between *ze-er* (male) and *nukbah* (female).[72] The purpose of mending is, therefore, to reinstate the harmony between the countenances of divinity. The soul of the *tzadik*, the Kabbalist *Pneumaticus*, is represented according to Joseph Jikatilla by the synthesizing Sefira of *Yessod* which he denotes as *shadai*. This is a jeux de mots, since *shadai* is both a denotation of God and a balancing, harmonizing, and regulating of power which synchronizes between the countenances of God and between transcendence and creation.[73] Indeed, the world of *azilut*, the primeval world of infinity representing the harmonious emanator Godhead, is denoted by the Kabbala as *Olam ha-matekela*—the World of Balance[74]

In Gnosis, we have a dialectic between spirit and matter.[75] This is necessary because the Godhead is alien to temporality and does not activate the world of creation. Hence, the particles of light (souls) mingle with the demiurgical matter and activate it. This, apparently, is carried out through the mediation of the messenger of Christ who is also denoted in Gnosis as 'the measured one'.[76]

We find Kierkegaard, the founding father of existentialism, making the following statement: 'A human being is a synthesis of the infinite and the finite, of the temporal and the eternal, of freedom and necessity, in short a synthesis.' In his *Either/Or*, Kierkegaard examines the equilibrium between the æsthetical (in our model the separant Sisyphean type) and the ethical (in our model the participant Tantalic type) in the composition of personality.[77] Again, we see here an equilibrium, a system-in-balance. Philosophy, for Heidegger, spoke Greek: *'Das word 'philosophie' spricht jetzt griechisch.'* Camus went even further. In a celebrated interview he declared: 'A Greek heart pounds in me.' Camus embraced the Greek maxim of meden agan. In a period when most of the avant-gardé European intelligentsia opted for revolution, Camus was not fashionable, but he did attain authenticity for his preaching against the revolution. The French Revolution brought the Terror, the Nazi Revolution culminated in

Auschwitz, and the Communist Revolution had its purges and gulags. Hence, his 'nothing-in-excess'. Camus recognized the courage of the middle way; the heroic nature of creative rebellion within the eye of the demiurgical storm of history. The system-in-balance between the participant and the separant core vectors is not only a precedent condition for the containment of the energy generated by our dialectical quests in a viable structure, but is also necessary for the creative transmission of this energy in a dialogical and authentic manner. For charisma to flow, the person experiencing the revelation of grace must be attuned to inner feed-back both from himself and from his audience. For revelation to flow into structured creativity Sisyphus must be attuned to his stone and carve it into a vehicle for dialogue. Thus, the structured revelation through the suffering of a Van Gogh is emitted by his canvasses, while Antonin Artaud tried unsuccessfully to transmit his torment in the form of unstructured shrieks hurled at a theatre audience. The disruption of Artaud's core vectors resulted in his madness, making his hell strictly private.

The demiurgos is the God of creation and history, space and atomic energy. He is the divine container of the Kabbala, receiving the flow of the light of grace coming from the Godhead. The demiurgos interact with the Godhead through creativity to produce creation. Sisyphus, thus, imbues his stone with grace and the inert Godhead is able to vicariously experience the authentic triumphs and disasters of a Mozart, a Van Gogh, or a Brel. Existentially inauthentic activity, which is unpalatable to Him, is left to the demiurgos as Gnostic error or Kabbalist din and kellipot. Creativity, if authentic, may generate the energy for an I-thou dialogue, linking the Godhead and the creation. If inauthentic and flawed, creativity would degenerate into the petrification of an I-it relationship.

The Gnostic messenger, the Kabbalist initiate performing the tikkun, the go-between of revelation, links the thing-in-itself in transcendence with the prime mover emanated into history. This is why Tantalus, the protagonist of our meta-myth, is a Titan: part God who is still in transcendence and part man, God's image and emanant theophony within history. The dialogic prayer between the self in history and the transcendental, universal thou actually generates the energy of revelation. It is the process of revelation in itself without any further goal beyond it. Revelatory prayer is God. Sisyphus, likewise, is the creative link between the Godhead and the demiurgos. He symbolizes the integration between man's desperate creative spirit and the demiurgical stone which is both his burden and his destiny.

As myths have many layers, one stratum of the original sin may point to the hübris of attaining self-consciousness, since self-consciousness is the prerogative of God. Hence, Judaeo-Christianity ordained abject humility to offset original sin, and not just a Greek meden-agan, nothing in excess, to keep everything and everybody within the statistical middle range.

The evolutionary need for a system-in-balance for the survival of mythogenic structures might explain the tragic faith of the great innovators and too-radical revolutionaries. A Galileo, a Van Gogh, and a Melville effected virtual revolutions in their creative realms. Hence, the demiurgical social structure defended both itself and the mythogenic structures which sustained its cultural system against the upheaval of excessive and, hence, disruptive innovations. Likewise, a Jesus Christ, an el-Hlage, and a Meister Eckhart were revelatory revolutionaries who threatened to rupture the mythogenic structures of the existing religious institutions, which accordingly defended themselves by executing their assailants. Evolution and the survival of mythogenic structures are aversive to the violence of revolutions.

Indeed, the ani-consciousness prods man the creator and projector mythogenic structures to relate to energy-matter since it is the attributeless ani, the spiritual kabbalist *airich-anpin* (the suffering man the emaciated countenance of God), which is caught in constant pain due to his inability to reach a modus vivendi, a complimentary relationship with the mindless, brutal, demiurgical energy-matter. This can be achieved only through creativity which is effected by an evolutionary viable and structurally intact mythogene.

Man, the anthropic mediator, is also infused with the suffering of the arich anpin, so as to motivate him better to create and effect a modus vivendi with the demiurgical energy-matter. This suffering is exacerbated by his being thrown into the world—to use Heidegger's terminology—with his parents' genes which may handicap him; later, these parents coerce him/her into submission to delimiting norms by surrogate sacrificial rites of passage. Here again the relationship between suffering and creativity which entails the structuring of viable mythogenes is curvilinear: Too much suffering will crush homo faber, man the creator, hurling him under the Sisyphean stone which only a median amount of pain will induce him to creativity which will effect a complementarity between the ani-consciousness and energy-matter.

Evolution is a dynamic of being, not of non-being. Hence, it is a record of successes and not of failures. The latter are recorded as fossils if at all. Since mediocrities seem to be more viable in power structures and in institutions, and since talent is not democratic, the creative innovators who rock the boat are hunted down, persecuted, subdued, and, many times, destroyed by the power structures of societies and social institutions. Yet these creative innovators are enrich fructify and enhance cultures, in return for which the power élite of those cultures subjugate, discredit, and suppress these pioneers as 'just desserts' for their creative pains. Mytho-empirically, this is portrayed by Persephone who sacrifices the sacred king who fertilized her. Persephone—who brings destruction—is the mature nymph ready to be impregnated by the Demetrian triad of goddesses: Kore—maiden, Persephone—nymph, Hecate—Kore partaking in the mysteries of fertility rites.[78] Persephone represents the demiurgical evil forces; (some of her epitaphs are the fearful one: she who kills) which destroy those who fructify them. She devours, praying mantis-like, while her lovers—like the social institutions, artists' cliques and promotion committees in academia—destroy the most gifted creators, those who don't fit in. Indeed, creative innovators are almost by definition deviants from the modes, means, and median parameters of the group. Still the creative innovator cannot but continue to be creative despite the hazards of his vocation. The artist must heed Nietzche's mandate to create dangerously, and Vincent Van Gogh in his misery wrote to his brother that he could renounce everything, except his need to create. However, if we accept Buber's dictum, which we do, that an I-thou relationship is an authentic being, whereas an I-it association is an inauthentic slumber, then creativity transfuses the juice of life into a petrified I-it relationship that man has with other objects, other people, and God, and resuscitates it by the mythogenic structures of endeavor, daring, and revolt.

Our developmental model of personality formation poses three major dichotomies corresponding to the three major human developmental phases. The first is Hamlet's 'to be or not to be' associated with the primary Heideggerrean Geworfenheit zum Tod. The second is the existentialist-epistemic dilemma of knowing or not knowing linked to the coagulation of a separate self out of the pantheistic mass of early orality. The third is the socio-normative dimension: man's mythogenic and cultural relationship with his group. These three dichotomous queries entail the structure of the personality dealt by us in the Myth of Tantalus, i.e.,[79] the relationship between consciousness and energy-matter elucidated in *Le Pont de Prométhée*.[80] In the present volume, we shall deal with the third dimension of man's socio-normative relationship as well as with the more general mytho-empirical bases for man's attitude towards transcendence.

NOTES

1. Claude Levi-Strauss, *Le Cru et le Cuit* (Paris: Plon, 1964), 9.
2. Shlomo Giora Shoham, *The Myth of Tantalus: A Scaffolding for an Ontological Personality Theory*(St. Lucia, Australia: Queensland University Press, 1979).
3. Shlomo Giora Shoham, *The Violence of Silence: The Impossibility of Dialogue* (Middlesex: Transaction Books, Science Reviews, Ltd., 1983).
4. Shlomo Giora Shoham, *Le Pont de Prométhée: Physique et Métaphysique,* trans. Viviane de Charrière (Paris: Editions L'Age d'Hommes, 1994).
5. Niels Bohr, 'Causality and Complementarity', *Philosophy of Science* 4, no.3 (1937), 291.
6. Gershom Gerhard Scholem, *Major Trends in Jewish Mysticism* (Jerusalem: Schocken Publishing House, 1941), 350.
7. Ibid., 350.
8. Andrew Lang, *Myth, Ritual, and Religion* (1906; reprint, New York: AMS Press, 1968).
9. Sigmund Freud,'The Relation of the Poet to Day-Dreaming', (1908) *Collected Papers,* IV, (London: The Hogarth Press, 1925), 182.
10. John Jakob Bachofen, *Myth, Religion, and Mother-Right* (Princeton: Princeton University Press, 1967), 73.
11. Mircea Eliade, *The Myth of Eternal Return* , trans. Willard R. Trask (New York: Pantheon Books, 1954), 34–48.
12. Carl Gustav Jung, *Psychological Types* (London: Routledge & Kegan Paul, 1944), 241, 615.
13. Shlomo Giora Shoham, *Salvation through the Gutters* (Washington, D.C.: Hemisphere Publications, 1979), 21.
14. Frederick Robert Tennant, *The Sources of the Doctrines of the Fall and Original Sin* (New York: Schocken Press, 1968), 140.
15. Karl Abraham, *Selected Papers of Karl Abraham, M.D.* (London: Hogarth Press, 1927), 407.
16. Shlomo Giora Shoham, *Valhalla, Calvary and Aucshwitz* (Cincinnati: Bowman & Cody Academic Publishing Inc., 1995) 25.
17. Levi-Strauss, *Le Cru et le Cuit,* 9.
18. Jean Piaget, *Structuralism*, trans. Chaninah Maschler (London: Routledge and Kegan Paul, 1971), 5.
19. Ibid., 36,37, 39.
20. Compare the views of Penrose on the natural selection of Algorithms: Roger Penrose, *The Emperor's New Mind* (New York: Penguin, 1991), 414.
21. Thompson, *The Ancient History of Israel.*
22. Leon Festinger, *When Prophesy Fails: A Social and Psychological Study of a Modern Group that Predicted the Destruction of the World* (New York: Harper and Row, 1964).
23. Shoham, *The Myth of Tantalus*, 15.

[24] Shlomo Giora Shoham, *Le Sex Comme Appât* (Paris: Editions l'Age d'homme, 1991), chapters 3, 6–7.

[25] Jacob A. Cohen, *The Transition from Childhood to Adolescence: Cross-Cultural Studies of Initiation Ceremonies, Legal Systems, and Incest Taboos* (Chicago: Aldine Publishing Co., 1964).

[26] Shoham, *The Myth of Tantalus*, ch. 8.

[27] Erich Wellisch, *Isaac and Oedipus: A Study in Biblical Psychology of the Sacrifice of Isaac, the Akedah* (London: Routledge & Kegan Paul, 1954) 27 *et. seq.*

[28] Ibid., 10.

[29] Shoham, *Myth of Tantalus,* 299.

[30] Francis Bacon, *A Study After Velasquez's Portrait of Pope Innocent X* (New York: Collection of Mr. and Mrs. A.M. Burden, 1953).

[31] John Money, 'Sexual Dictatorship, Dissidence, and Democracy'. *The International Journal of Medicine and Law,* no. 1 (1978), 11.

[32] Robert Graves, *The Greek Myths:* vol.1 (Harmondsworth: Pelican Books, 1955), 91.

[33] Deuteronomy 32.

[34] Euripides: 'Iphigenia in Aulis', *The Complete Greek Drama, vol. 2* (New York: Random House, 1938), 323.

[35] Ibid., 334.

[36] Herbert R. Lottman, *Albert Camus* (New York: Doubleday, 1979).

[37] Proverbs 14:34.

[38] E.G. Schachtel, *Metamorphosis* (London: Routledge & Kegan Paul, 1963), 60.

[39] Shoham, *Salvation Through the Gutters,* introduction and ch.1.

[40] John Bowlby, *Attachment and Loss*, vol (Hammondsworth: Penguin Books, 1984), ch. 11.

[41] This stance is adhered to, inter alia, by Sullivan. See Munro, *Schools of Psychoanalytic Thought,* 360.

[42] Shoham, *Salvation Through the Gutters*, 97, and Fairbain, *Psychoanalytic Studies of the Personality*, 11.

[43] Chad Gordon and Kenneth J. Gergen, eds., *The Self in Social Interaction* (New York: J. Wiley, 1968), 3.

[44] Sigmund Freud, *Psychopathology of Everyday Life: The Basic Writings of Sigmund Freud* (New York: Modern Library, 1938), 147–150.

[45] Shoham, *Salvation Through the Gutters,* 151.

[46] Eric H. Erickson, *Childhood and Society,* (Penguin: Harmondsworth, 1969), 253.

[47] Shoham, *Salvation Through the Gutters*, 92.

[48] Edmund Husserl, *Ideas: General Introduction to Pure Phenomenology* (London: Collier-Macmillian Ltd., 1962), 232.

49 Henri Louis Bergson, in *Introduction to Metaphysics,* states: 'pure duration excludes all ideas of juxtaposition, reciprocal exteriority, and extension.' Cited in William P. Alston and G. Nakhnikian, eds., *Readings in Twentieth-Century Philosophy* (New York: Free Press, 1963), 49.

50 Arthur Koestler, *Janus: A Summing Up* (London: Hutchinson, 1978), 27.

51 Shoham,*The Myth of Tantalus*, ch. 1.

52 Moshe Idel, *Metaphores et Pratiques Sexuelles dans la Cabale*, 334.

53 David Bakan, *Sigmund Freud and the Jewish Mystical Tradition* (New York: Schoken Books, 1965), ch. 33.

54 Claude Levi-Strauss, *The Savage Mind* (Chicago: University of Chicago Press, 1966).

55 David Bohm, *Wholeness and the Implicate Order:* (London: Ark Paperbacks, 1983).

56 Hesidos, *Theogeny* 527.

57 Roger Penrose, *The Emperor's New Mind* (Oxford: Oxford University Press, 1989), 250–251.

58 Stephen W. Hawking, *A Brief History of Time* (Toronto: Bantum Books, 1988).

59 Steven Weinberg, *The First Three Minutes: A Modern View of the Origin of the Universe.* (New York: Basic Books, 1977), 55–57.

60 Haim Vital: *Etz Haim* (Jerusalem: Research Centre of Kabala, 1978), 35.

61 Isaiah Tishby, *The Doctrine of Evil and the Kelippah in Lurianic Kabbalism* (Jerusalem: Schocken, 1942), 32.

62 The Hypostasis of the Archons' in Werner Foerster, *Gnosis: A Selection of Gnostic Texts* (Oxford: Clarendon Press, 1974), 50.

63 Sven Ranulf, *The Jealousy of the Gods and the Criminal Law of Athens: A Contribution to the Sociology of Moral Indignation*, vol. 1(London: Williams & Norgate, 1933), 63.

64 Herodotus, *The Greek Historians: The Complete and unabridged Historical Works of Herodotus, Thucydides, Xenophon, Arrian,* ed. Francis R. B. Godolphin (New York: Random House, 1942), 47.

65 A.B. Drachman, *Umdvalate Ahondlinger: Selected Topics* (Copenhagen: 1911).

66 Tishby, *The Doctrines of Evil*, 94.

67 Ibid., 94.

68 Hegiga, 146.

69 Shoham, *The Myth of Tantalus*, ch. 2.

70 Tishby, *The Doctrines of Evil*, 148.

71 Gershom Gerhard Scholem, *Elements of the Kaballah and its Symbolism*, 198.

72 Tishby, *The Doctrines of Evil*, 122.

73 Scholem, *Elements of the Kabbalah and its Symbolism* (Jerusalem: The Bialik Institute, 1977), 226–227.

74 Ibid., 142.

[75] 'The Gospel of Truth' in Foerster, ed., *Gnosis* (Oxford: Clarendon Press, 1974), 65.

[76] 'The Gospel of Philip' in ibid., 85.

[77] Soren Kirkegaard, *Either/Or,* trans. Walter Laurie (Princeton: Princeton University Press, 1971), 159 *et seq.*

[78] Robert Graves, *The Greek Myths,* vol. 1 (Harmondsworth: Pelican Books, 1960), 92–93.

[79] Shoham, *The Myth of Tantalus*,

[80] Shoham, *Le Pont de Prométhée,*

Chapter Two

The Mediation

To see a World in a grain of sand,
And a heaven in a wild flower,
Hold Infinity in the palm of your hand,
And Eternity in an hour...
We are led to believe a lie
When we see with, not thro' the eye,
Which was born in a night to perish in a night
When the Soul slept in beams of light.
William Blake: 'Auguries of Innocence'

Myth is a projection of the epic of the soul
on its journey to salvation.
Plutarch

The essence of Bohr's complementarity principle set forth in chapter one is that, unlike the synthesis of dialectics, each entity of a pair keeps its distinct nature and does not fuse or integrate into the other. Hence, the creative linkage effected by complementarity cannot be a direct one, but is rather a kind of Socratic maieutic (from the Greek for 'midwife') one. The original Socratic mode of enlightenment through dialogue, shunned authoritative teaching ex cathedra, in favor of instilling revelatory understanding in the pupil by a covert co-acting by the teacher.

Creativity is the expression of a unique personality. In order to be authentic, a creation must include some dynamics of Ego's inner self. It is, therefore, also as specific to Ego as his fingerprints. Consequently, the imitation of the creativity of another, the servile acceptance of the directives of the other, or the Zdanovite dictates of totalitarian regimes render the creation inauthentic. Discipleship can also render a creation inauthentic, unless the master-teacher serves as a maieutic catalyst to his pupil's talents. In the latter case, the teacher helps the creative potential of the pupil to flower, rather than stifle it by totalitarian imposition.

I-Thou and I-It

Martin Buber said of man's attitude towards the world:

The attitude of man is twofold, in accordance with the twofold nature of the primary words which he speaks.
The primary words are not isolated words, but combined words.
The one primary word is the combination I-thou.
The other primary word is the combination I-it; wherein, without a change in the primary word, one of the words He and She can replace It.
Hence the I of the primary word I-thou is a different I from that of the primary I-it.

Primary words do not signify things, but they intimate relations. Primary words do not describe something that might exist independently of them, but by being spoken they bring existence.
Primary words are spoken from the being.
If Thou is said, the I of the combination I-thou is said along with it.
If It is said, the I of the combination I-it is said along with it.
The primary word I-it can never be spoken with the whole being.

There is not taken in itself, but only the I of the primary word I-thou and the I of the primary word I-it.
When a man says I he refers to one of these.
The I to which he refers is present when he said I.
Further, when he says Thou or It, the I of one of the two primary words is present.
When a primary word is spoken, the speaker enters the word and takes his stand, it.

The life of human beings is not passed in the sphere of transitive verbs alone.
It does not exist in virtue of activities alone, which have some thing for their object.
I perceive something. I am sensible of something. I imagine something.
I will something. I feel something. I think something. The life of human beings does not consist of all this and the like alone.
This and the like alone establish the realm of it.
But the realm of Thou has a different basis.
When Thou is spoken, the speaker has no thing for his object. For where there is a thing there is another thing. Every Thou is bounded by others; It exists only through being bound by others. But when Thou is spoken, there is no thing. Thou has no bounds.

> When Thou is spoken, the speaker has no thing, he has indeed nothing. But he takes his stand in relation.[1]

Things do not exist, only relationships do. The I-thou is the relationship between the experiential I, which is similar to the ani-conciousness participant component of the self and, to the universal Thou, a manifestation of the universal Thou, which is equivalent to our 'pure ani', (the universal consciousness). The I-it is the experiential self relating to objects and things and is equivalent to our atzmi (interactive self). The I-thou expresses the indeterminism of choice. The I-it is deterministic and obeys the ananké, the coercive rules of nature, space-time, and causality.

The existentialism of the Kierkegaard-Buber dialogica does expound how the ani, the archetypal obseпver, interacts and initiates the processes of becoming. Buber postulates 'primary words' which are spoken from the innermost being. Primary words signify a relationship. 'Primary words do not describe something that might exist independently of them, but being spoken they bring about existence.'[2]

The primary word concept articulated by the ani-consciousness is a revelatory event which structures the mythogene. The primary words spoken, not in isolation but in intentional dialogue, already entail a relationship, be it I-thou, or I-it. This fits our model, insofar as it integrates the ani-consciousness and energy-matter within the mythogenic structure which triggers the act of creation. Our interactive atzmi is a conceptualization of one such integration. Hence, the speaking of a primary word integrates the I-thou of the ani and the I-it of the atzmi into a self-contained unit which stems from the self, but, which is directed towards the object. It, thus, initiates the process of creation, or rather provides a seed or tool of creation which is the essence of our connecting mythogenic structure. 'And God said let there be light, and there was light' is indeed the speaking of a primary word-concept, which forms an ever-relational mythogenic structure directed at creation and serving as a primary too, for it.

We hold the Bible to be the prime source of authentic myths. We shall explain here our method of mytho-empiricism, which we shall utilize frequently. According to this method, mytho-empiricism is the utilization of myths not as illustrations for our theoretical premises, but as their empirical anchors.

The mediational function of the mythogene is clearly highlighted by Buber in profundity and clarity as follows:

> [Prime truths] can be conveyed only through myth. Anthropology shows how all concepts are auxiliary boards with which to build a bridge between myth

> and reality...In this manner we shall be able to glean from myths their most valuable gift: The truth which may be expressed only by itself.[3]

If we begin at the beginning, the primary act of creation was effected by 'the spirit of God hovering [not 'moved' as rendered by the faulty King James translation] upon the face of the waters' (Gen. 1:2). And the earth was 'chaotic and formless' [not 'without form and void' as per King James] (Gen. 1:2). 'And God said: "Let there be light", and there was light' (Gen. 1:3). Mythogenically, we hold the holy spirit to be the primary mythogene projected onto transcendence and structured by worship and rituals as a deity. Tohu and bohu are the primary chaos of energy matter in ille tempore. The uttering of the words, 'let there be light', is, according to Buber, the speaking of primary words which are spoken from the innermost being.

The act of creation starts with the knowledge, or rather with the consciousness of being conscience, of the primary word. Since it is then that man starts forming mythogenes, structuring them into Logoi, and ritualizing them into deities. Basically, this is the essence of original sin. Myths have many layers. The outer layer of the sin of Adam and Eve relates to the opening of their eyes (Gen. 3:7). Eyesight, eyes, and their opening are the Egyptian mythogenes. The eye of Horus is the symbol of life and royal power which, with the Egyptians, was divine. Hence, the opening of the eyes was an idolatrous Egyptian ritual which was anathema for the mosaic God of Genesis. Another layer of the original sin myth is that it proscribes knowledge of spiritual truth, i.e., gnosis in Greek. A likely interpretation is that the Gnostic variant of belief-systems competed with and threatened Judaism for many centuries. The Gnostic creeds—which proclaimed a dualism of independent good and evil, last judgment, resurrection, and a universal messiah-savior-avatar—started apparently with Zarathustra in Persia at about the middle of the second millennium B.C.E. and spread throughout the Middle East. Mithraism, one of the offshoots of Zoroastrianism, was carried out by Roman soldiers all over the Roman Empire. Gnosticism, flourishing in the south of France, must have influenced Spanish Kabbala until suppressed by a Crusade and Inquisition in the thirteenth century. Gnosis' quest for a direct knowledge of God, as claimed by Zarathustra, must have had a powerful appeal for the masses, including Jews. Hence, it was proclaimed hübris. Cosmogony was the sole prerogative of God, and man cannot, and ought not, compete with Him. His creation, indeed, his whole life cycle, is, thence, ordained in pain, decreed in strife, and fated in misery (Gen. 3:16-20). Creativity, if authentic, can extricate man from his predicament and lead him, perchance, to experience grace; this grace is, however, short lived, as the Sisyphean stone is soon to roll down and will have to be pushed up again, da capo.

This conferring of meanings on one's surroundings is masterfully portrayed by Camus as follows:

> It is during that return, that pause, that Sisyphus interests me. A face that toils so close to stone is already stone itself! I see that man going back down with a heavy, yet measured, step towards the torment of which he will never know an end. That hour, like a breathing space which returns as surely as his suffering, that is the hour of consciousness. At each of those moments when he leaves the heights and gradually sinks to the lair of the gods he is superior to his fate. He is stronger than his rock.
>
> I leave Sisyphus at the foot of the mountain! One always finds one's burden again. But Sisyphus teaches the higher fidelity that negates the gods and raises rocks. He, too, concludes that all is well. This universe, henceforth without a master, seems to him neither sterile nor futile. Each atom of that stone, each mineral flake of the night-filled mountain, in itself forms a world. The struggle itself towards the heights is enough to fill a man's heart. One must imagine Sisyphus happy.[4]

One cannot, and should not, add anything to this masterful portrayal of the creative outlet from man's absurd routines. It summarizes in a few lines the whole doctrine of existentialism as a way of life. However, in being the source of normativeness and bestowing it both on energy-matter and on the ani-consciousness, man, the anthropic normative mediator, has the central, not the secondary, role of the dialectical Trinitarian dramatis persona. Hence, God (the projection of the universal ani-consciousness) is, according to the kabbalist Meir ibn Gabbai in his *Tola'at Ya'akov*, the shadow of man.

We hold that the creative connecting mythogenic structure is generated by a process of inner revelation. The vectorial intention of the mythogene is conscious, but its actual structuring is utilized as a connecting, or rather integrating, agent between the ani-consciousness and energy matter to catalyze the creation of a Promethean holon, be it a particle, a chanson, or a sculpture.

Our conception of the revelation which gives rise to the mythogenic structure and the process of creation of the Promethean holon is sui generis. Historically, revelation was related to religious experiences, to the exposure of the individual to transcendence. For us, however, all accounts of revelatory religious experiences have a mytho-empirical value because they constitute a mythological projection of core personality experiences. These are transmitted by the ani to the level of consciousness and mythology, although the core personality processes are largely subconscious. Thus, although our empirical anchors in the present context are taken from belief systems, our aim will be to understand the revelations triggering creativity (e.g., the 'Eureka!' of Archimedes, the oceanic feelings of Freud; all these presumably display similar dynamics to the revelatory processes underlying the exposure of the individual to his ani inner self in the process of structuring his mythogenic connecting agent. Indeed, we claim that mytho-empiricism is probably the sole method for gleaning information about the otherwise unfathomable dynamics of structuring the mythogene.

The solitude of the individual is a unique loneliness because his inner core is linked by an umbilical cord to unity. Of this, the individual can be aware of only if he turns inwardly to his 'pure' ani.

Man, by prodding into his inner self, is revealed to truth and God, which are synonymous. To this end, the outside, the objects, and the others are unnecessary and confound the channel of awareness, both of oneself and one's surroundings.

The idea that all sense perception is illusive and that all truth stems from the inner sense of being, the manifestation of the infinite and indivisible unity, is projected mutatis mutandis in most monotheistic creeds and proclaimed by the first commandment of the *Decalogue*. Heidegger's conception of Dasein as the unveiling and disclosure of being, as the basic ontological truth which needs no further proof, is quite similar to the extreme participant pole of our personality continuum with its objectless 'pure-self' (the ani).[5] On this pole, Ego identifies with a person (persons), an object or a symbolic construct outside himself, and his striving is to lose his separate identity by fusion with this other object or symbol. This is the pole towards which the individual would move on…to yearn when his revelatory experiences are likely to manifest themselves.

The separant pole on which Ego aims to sever, disjoin, and differentiate himself from his surroundings is where the interactive self (atzmi) is posited. It anchors on logic and causality and would be quite amenable to the Cartesian cognito ergo sum as proof of its existence.

Many of our mytho-empirical anchors are gnostic and kabbalistic. The two disciplines are dualist and, hence, fit our basic conception of all creation as a perpetual interaction between the ani-consciousness and energy-matter, through the mediation of mythogenic structures.

Our first mytho-empirical anchor is taken from *Sha'arei Tzedek*, a thirteenth-century Spanish Kabbalist tract (its name means 'Gates of Righteousness') which states that the lower man and the 'higher man sitting on the divine throne' are both signified by the Hebrew letter yod (י).[6] This letter, which is the first in the Tetragrammaton (the four-letter name of God in Hebrew, YHWH), has the graphic shape of a half circle. These two yods—the two semicircles—long to be united to a whole circle when lower and upper man are elevated to the 'Throne of Divinity'. This could serve as a mytho-empirical anchor for the revelatory process of structuring the mythogene. The lower man, representing the mortal human, is exposed to the upper man, who could signify the exposure to the inner ani-consciousness. The result is the integration of the two half-circles into one. Translated into the conceptual context of our model, the interactive atzmi separant vector is integrated with the ani participant vector into the Tantalus Ratio, which constitutes the subsequently formed mythogene. This mythogene then triggers the creation of the Promethean holon, be it a Christmas dinner or the eigenstate of a particle.

In a similar vein, the Gnostic Gospel of Philip speaks about truth and its image thus:

> Truth did not come into the world naked, but it came in types and images. It [the world] will not receive it in any other way. There is rebirth and an image of rebirth. It is truly fitting to be reborn through the image. What is the resurrection and the image? It is fitting that it rises through the image.[7]

We contend that the truth here, for the firmly participant Gnostic, stands for the attributeless 'pure' ani-consciousness. The created world of spatio-temporality cannot accept it in its 'nakedness', i.e., its ahistoric nature. It needs a go-between or image which we interpret mytho-empirically as our mediating mythogenic structure.

In gnostic light, which, with its participant bias, would stand mytho-empirically for the ani—and darkness—representing the profane energy-matter, intermingle to create the world. In the theosophical Kabbala, the ten sefirot (rungs) contain an image of God clothing himself, yet are an integral part of divinity. These are the mytho-empirical manifestations of named archetypes, forming an inner ani-consciousness dynamic, as well as being coined denotations facing creation. These holonic manifestations of named archetypes also represent the initial formations of the mythogenic structures. The ten sefirot are then structured into five countenances (*parzufim*) which are the mytho-empirical projection of full-fledged mythogenic connecting structures. As we shall see later, the coupling interaction or intercourse (zivug) of these countenances constitutes acts of creation. In our conceptualization, the countenances are mythogenic connecting structures which produce the Promethean holon, the entire holonic product, creation, or artifact.

The Kabbala envisages that each life form and object has a transcendental root (*shoresh*). This we could take to be a mytho-empirical projection of the mythogenic structure as constituting the transcendental model or blueprint for creation. These roots constitute an integration of grace and stern judgment. Here again, the participant bias of the Kabbala would conceive grace to be the projection of the ani-consciousness and stern judgment to be. The intermingling of sacred and profane elements in these Kabbalist 'roots' is universal, even if they risk sacrilege. Thus, Moses had his root the atzmi not only in Abel (grace), but in Cain (stern judgment) as well.

The initial stages of mythogenic formation are within the ani-consciousness. It is an intra-psychic revelatory dynamic—a dialectic between the ahistorical 'pure' ani and the historical participant vector within the historical self.

Mytho-empirically, this intra-psychic revelatory dialectic resulting in the formation of the mythogene is envisaged by the Kabbala as the process of creation starting with God clothing himself in garments woven from the Torah and the letters of the tetragrammaton.

To sum up our present discussion, we may envisage the revelatory intra-psychic dialectic as culminating in the structuring of the mythogene. The mythogene not only reveals what to do (i.e., lends meaning), but also how to do it (i.e., lends value to the subsequent act). This, when implemented in the act of creation, will lend meaning and value to the Promethean holon. The act of creation is, thus, a dual process: both an intra-psychologic ontological dialectic leading to the formation of the mythogene and a subsequent epistemic process of creativity linking the ani-consciousness and energy-matter, the creation of which was triggered by the mythogenic structure. The main asset of our mythogene is its suitability in integrating consciousness and energy-matter through a dual process of revelation and creativity.

The immutable ani-consciousness peers through ever-changing configurations of life forms, artifacts, and objects, and this combination of immutability and kaleidoscopically changing plurality makes for the uniqueness and irreplaceability of each creature. Hence, the reflected historical ani in a specific self and the transcendental, pure ani-consciousness cannot be creative in unity, as Sisyphus has to have his separate stone in order to be creative. Therefore Ego has to feel apart and separate from the transcendental ani for the interactive experience of revelation to take place. Hence, Ego is a partner to the transcendental ani in creativity.

Mytho-empirically, we have the description of the Maggid of Meseritz, following some Kabbalist traditions according to which God contracted himself so that he could experience man's adventures vicariously through human cognition. Says the Maggid:

> The *Tzadikim* (sages) effect God through their mind; so that He thinks what they think. If they think in love, they bring God into the realm of love as stated in the Zohar. A king (God) is imprisoned in the tresses of the [human] mind.[8]

In Lurianic Kabbala the doctrine that God is present in every life form and object is basic. Says Vital:

> There is nothing in the world and in all the worlds and in all parts of Creation; the inanimate plants, living and talking, that does not have within it sparks of Divinity which are embedded in their profane shells.[9]

All Creation, not only man, was thrown into spatio-temporality, and all flora, fauna, and inanimate objects are in this respect equal to man, with exiled cores of divinity encased in every created separatum and in every vestige of spatio-temporality. Ibn Tabul describes this sequel to the breaking of the vessels (birth) as follows:

> And the *Reshimu* of [Divine] Light...was scattered within and amongst the [sinister] powers of judgment, and these were crystallized like containers which served as a body for a soul, and, thus, a light symbol is clothed by a profane container.[10]

Hence, each object and life form of Creation is composed of divine particles embedded within containers of less sacred and, in the lower spheres, downright profane matter.

The barrier between Ego and transcendence must be hermetically closed; otherwise the creative interaction between experientially different entities cannot be effected. Ego is, thus, interacting with a less than perfect transcendence which needs him for its feeling of creativity, yet cannot allow him to know that he is part of it.

Creativity as a Sisyphean Dynamic

Creativity involves the projection and imposition of Ego's personality core vectors' goal onto his objective and human surroundings. We should recall that these goals are, by definition, unattainable. Hence, whatever ideals Ego might maintain in his core vectors of perfection, aesthetics, harmony, order, and omnipotence are first of all processed dialectically by intra-psychic developmental dynamics. The separant and participant vectors within the personality interact constantly to produce a mental system-in-balance which then is imprinted with Tantalic or Sisyphean patterns of culture through socialization. This configuration, which is a dialectical far cry from the original goals of the personality core vectors, influences Ego's perception of his surroundings. However, this aisthesis, Greek for perception and used by Baumgarten to denote the whole field of aesthetics[11] makes for a unique conception of how and what his creative involvement should be. When Ego projects his specific image of aesthetics, order, and instrumentation onto the object he aims to be creatively involved with, it is not likely to be shared by others. This makes for a variety of styles and forms of creativity, as well as for differences in individual tastes.

A direct corollary of this basic premise is that the creative efforts, as initially envisioned by Ego, are never achieved because the goals of the personality core vectors are unachievable by definition, as we have already mentioned. Furthermore, when the aesthetic or instrumental system-in-balance as envisioned by Ego is projected onto the object and creatively applied to it, the result is bound to be a dialectical synthesis different from the initial vision. Hence, creativity is a truly Sisyphean task in which the creator cannot be satisfied with the end product of his creation. Therefore, he is impelled to attempt ever-new schemes with his object-stone and to hope that the next try will succeed in molding it into the vision of the aesthetic system-in-balance in his mind. This, alas, never happens, just as Sisyphus can never succeed in balancing his stone on the summit of the hill. And yet this apparent failure is the motivating fuel of creativity. The author's own creative involvement is spurred by his dissatisfaction with each previous completed venture, which appeared to be his magnum opus when he was still immersed in it. This brings us to our notion of authentic creativity. Authenticity as related to creativity can only be a process. The efforts, the strain of creative involvement, can be authentically absorbing, but not the end product. If Ego anchors on the final product of his creativity, he is bound to be disappointed. Achievements are filed and forgotten, and if the process is not rewarding, then Ego's creativity is not authentic. The balancing of the Sisyphean stone on the apex of the mount is not only impossible, but futile from the point of view of creativity. It is the aesthetic ascent or descent which can be authentic, but not the public acclaim (which never lasts) for being at the top or the clever overpricing of an objet d'art to sell to a money-laden tourist.

The participant component of creativity is inherent in its revelatory aspect, which shines forth from the inner self. This discovery, sprouting forth from the inner core of the self, may be projected onto the object, or the other, and make it shine forth with a sudden disclosure of meaning, worth, or enlightenment. The revelatory moment makes one feel that everything has fallen into place, that obscurity has resolved itself into clarity. This moment, which as yet does not lend itself easily to analysis and definition, is distinctly felt by every creator, causing the musician to feel a spine-tingling elation and the director to sense that the actor has said his lines exactly right. This revelatory feeling, which interacts dialectically with the basically object-bound creative process, is specific and unique for each individual creator. The feeling itself and the contents of the revelation cannot be effectively transmitted to others, but the fact of its experience, which is the dialectical essence of the creative act, is imprinted on the creation and is, therefore, manifest to an observer. Indeed, the creator, having experienced a revelation and having embedded it in his creation, provides an element of authenticity which it would otherwise lack. Without a spark of the inner self of the creator infused into the creation, it is inauthentic. A mytho-empirical side glance might be awarded by the Lurianic Kabbala, in which the world of mere doing is the world of flat matter, but the world of creation involves the inspiration-generating exposure to angels.

This is in line with the Buberian conception of reaching out towards the object as a baseline for a dialogical relationship between man and his surroundings. Hence, we envisage creativity as a real bridge between man and object. By imbuing the object with his visions and molding it as his creation, man the creator, homo faber, entwines his psyche with the object.

The creator's longing to communicate his artistic message to kindred souls, wherever and whenever they might be, who might appreciate it effects a link between artist and audience outside the confines of space and time.

This mutual longing to communicate by means of a work of art makes genuine creativity eternal. This communicability of a creation is also the main criterion of its durable value. The author recently attended a retrospective exhibition of the works of the artist Antonello Da Messina held in his hometown. His works, especially a wooden Christ, raised the author to intense heights of aesthetic euphoria, as if he himself was involved in their creation. Da Messina, thus, gained a measure of immortality by infusing his authentic creation with an artistic message which continues to communicate beyond his own place and time.

The element of communication in creativity is even more apparent in the performing arts. A performer is always anxious to reach his audience. If his message did not come across, both the performer and the audience would consider his performance a failure. However, the performer who flatters his audience and tries to gain acceptance by superficial gimmicks is likely, in the long run, to be rejected for lack of authenticity. The performer has to probe into his inner self for his participant resources and infuse them into his Sisyphean efforts to reach the audience.

A Jacques Brel, an Edith Piaf, and a George Brassens will be able to carry across to their audiences, but with their own pitch and unique depth, which will lend their performances both separant communicability and revelatory authenticity.

The creator may feel a dialogue-like affinity with his tools, a sculptor with his chisels, a painter with his brush, and the author with the thick fountain pen he has used to write all his books in longhand. With these personalized tools, the artist may feel that he has reached the core of his creation. This is not unlike Buber's account that he reached a dialogue with a tree by means of a walking stick which he felt to be an extension of himself. This link with a tool or an object cannot be affected by a sense of possession or through an impersonal, automated, functional mass-produced product. For a creator to feel that he has reached a rapport with a tool or a creation, he must sense that he has imbued it with his personal uniqueness, that his vision has been infused into its very core. The mytho-empirical anchor for this dynamic, of seeking communication with the object via creativity, is the *avodah begashmiut*—i.e., work or worship in the concrete—which is based in turn, on the Kabbalist myth of the 'breaking of the vessels'. According to this myth, a cosmic disaster caused sparks of divinity to be scattered into spatio-temporality. These were embedded in each life form. The purpose of the Hasid is to find a link, by means of prayer, with these divine sparks in order to unite with them. This doctrine was adopted by Buber and formed the basis for his dialogical philosophy. An I-it relationship may be transformed by Hasidic devotions with the holy Kavanah—i.e., meditative concentration aimed at reaching the divine sparks in objects and life forms so as to illuminate everyday life into an I-thou relationship. An even earlier mytho-empirical anchor for the communication with objects through creativity was in the myth of the gnostic messenger. His task was to set in motion the ships of light and start the revolution of the cosmic spheres in order to liberate the particles of divine light entrapped in nature. This, as well as the Manichean Jesus *patibilis*, who 'hangs from every tree', and who is dispersed in all creation, is the transcendental projection of the quest of homo faber to reach the divine core of the object and link it to his own inner core-vector by the dialectics of creativity.[12]

This feeling of worshipping in the concrete, of beautifying the daily routines of life, is also evident in Zen Buddhism, which has implanted in myriads of Japanese the ability to find an intense meaning even in the most routine tasks. Henry Thoreau built his hut beside Walden Pond, where he felt a dialogical affinity with the woods, air, water, and stars. Camus's heroes found their Sisyphean raison d'être in being able to create, save, and cure in the midst of the existential plague. Chomsky even proposed that the dialectical involvement with language is the baseline of creativity. He, thus, tried to build a bridge between himself and the world of the object. Shlonsky, the late contemporary Israeli poet, went much further than that. He confided that he never used a word in his poems unless he had made love with it.

If, indeed, creativity is spurred by a core need to communicate, how is communication, through creativity, effected? We hold that the creator transmits to his audience through his creation or performance the intensity and sincerity of the longing of his core vectors, which catalyze the surging up of similar longings within the audience. Even though the content of the longings of the artist and the individuals in the audience, as determined by their respective statistically unique bio-psycho-cultural configuration, are bound to be different, still the coincidence of their yearnings in time lends them a sense of communication effected through their common elation. Thus, James Galway, playing before an Israeli audience, may be elated by his rich visions of green pastures, smiling Irish eyes, and laughter. The music may arouse different yearnings in the members of his audience according to the specific aims of their personality core vectors. One may long for the red mountains of Eilat, another for the blue heat of Lake Tiberias, and another for the black eyes and olive skin of Yemenite girls. Thus, the structured common longing generated by the performance creates the sense of communication through art, despite the wide discrepancies in the contents of the longing of the audience members. It is necessary, however, that the artist be authentic, that he be intensely sincere, in order for his arts to spur a communicative elation in his audience. Otherwise, his performance will not come across; it is liable to fall flat and leave his audience cold. In all probability, the structured common denominator of communication through art is effected by the revelatory component of creativity, linked, in turn, to the participant attributelessness ani components of the self which are closer to the common core-awareness of all human beings. Paradoxically, therefore, the Tantalic revelatory core experience is instrumental in effecting a sense of communication by means of the basically Sisyphean process of creativity.

For existentialism, authenticity is a moral principle and inauthenticity is an immoral one. Inauthenticity consists of hypocrisy, pretence, feigning, self-deception, and the deception of others. Double or multiple moral standards stem from the Greek hypocrites, who were originally actors. Another possible source of the term hypocrisy is *hypothrinein*, which originally meant ‘to pass judgment’. Judging others, Kabbalist stern-judgment (din) or bourgeois righteous indignation, are sources, etymologically at least, of hypocrisy. Hence, one of the characteristics of Camus’s judge penitent’s fall into authenticity was his refusal to judge others any more. Inauthenticity is a basic attribute of the demiurgical social structures, which can only function by power manipulation and deception of those normatively subject to them. These are mostly the government, politicians, and yielders of power in social institutions, ranging from churches to the arbiteri elegentiari of the artistic cliques. They possess finely tuned social antennae to detect any change in the fads, fashions, or prevalent tastes of the reigning elites in their membership groups in order to manipulate them to their advantage. They jump on all the worthy, but safe, bandwagons and wear the current uniforms of the age—the crew cut in the fifties, the long hair and pot parties (never the hard stuff) in the sixties, careerism and capitalism in the seventies, while still paying exorbitant prices for tickets to a Bob Dylan concert to sing the songs of the 'Woodstock Nation', together with the other now balding and slightly potbellied ex-protesters who park their Cadillacs far from the site of the reunion. In the eighties, they are 'yuppies', and if they have made it, they will have a modest veuve cliquot champagne and Beluga caviar around the swimming pool in their penthouses with their friends, who happen to represent the right combination of government, legislature, judiciary, mass media, favorite artists, and, of course, ad hoc manipulators whom they need to impress or manipulate. They exude a love of humanity with all the depth of a toothpaste commercial, but their actual compassion for their fellow human beings is that of a barracuda, or, rather, a piranha. Camus describes the morality of bourgeois society as follows:

> Haven't you noticed that our society is organized for this kind of liquidation? You have heard, of course, of these tiny fish in the rivers of Brazil that attack the unwary swimmer by the thousands and, with swift little nibbles, clean him up in a few minutes, leaving only an immaculate skeleton? Well, that's what their organization is. 'Do you want a good clean life? Like everybody else?' You say, 'Yes of course'. How can one say no? 'OK. You'll be cleaned up. Here's a job, a family, and organized leisure activities.' And the little teeth attack the flesh, right down to the bone. But I am unjust. I shouldn't say their organization, it is ours after all: It's just a question of which one will clean up the other.[13]

The hypocrites excel in false sincerity. With hand on chest and a piercing look of honesty or eyes attuned to heaven in the case of a Tartuffe, they will immediately detect the Achilles heel of their current victim. They are especially adept at exploiting the idealistic and self-sacrificing revolutionaries.

The salon communists and socialists pay lip service to the brotherhood of the proletariat in their spacious villas on the Côte D'Azur, so that they can go on exploiting the workers in their factories with an expurgated conscience. Max Nordau, one of the keenest observers of human inauthenticity, recorded how the most illustrious of artists and scientists were awestruck when confronted by the bored and boring Hapsburg Emperor. The author witnessed a similar excitement amongst world-renowned Cambridge scholars when presented to a silly and shallow young woman who happened to have married the Prince of Wales. Institutionalized men-of-God and some university professors suffer from false modesty. An eighteenth-century Hasidic sage known for his disgust at this type of inauthenticity used to reproach such people thus: 'Don't be so modest, you are not so great'. The politician cannot but be inauthentic, since, if he stops double-dealing, double-talking, and double-crossing, he will soon be out of a job. The ultimate diagnosis in this context was made by the madam of the brothel in Genet's *The Balcony*. She sends the audience back home to a world in which the judges are more pompously righteous, the bishops more piously bigoted, and the generals more stuffily bemedalled, because others died for their glory.

Authentic creativity must be geared towards a maieutic dialogue with specific objects and others, or motivated by a search for such a dialogue, even with a large audience. The kitsch of soap operas and announcers in airports are inauthentic because they are geared towards the central measures and common denominators which constitute the generalized other. Authentic creativity is the expression of one's inner self for the other. In listening to a Bach sonata, Bach and the listener reach a unique dialogical encounter that cannot be replicated. Any action which is motivated by spiteful resentment towards the other is a demiurgical I-it relationship, because the hatred which is directed at the other boomerangs onto oneself, in real or imaginary reprisals from the other. Authentic creativity must, however, stem from or aim at a system-in-balance between oneself and the object-other. Laurence Olivier, in a one-act play by Beckett, decided that he should act with only himself as an audience, because as a very gifted student of the author once said, 'No one deserves my genius'. Alas, he ended up acting in a madhouse. Per contra, as a slave to the demands of the audience, one may be devoured by the gorgonican generalized other, as were Marilyn Monroe, Elvis Presley, John Belushi, and a myriad of lesser luminaries.

The dialogic linkage between two individuals through creativity effects an extasis from history and becomes transcendental, irreplaceable, indestructible. Authentic work, like Cervantes' *Don Quixote*, and Bosch's *Passion*, and Mozart's *Requiem* are outside history and never date. They remain ever-fresh, relevant, and meaningful in an eternal now. On the other hand, an inauthentic work which was not meant to effect an I-thou dialogue is soon covered with patina and buried by the cobwebs of history. An I-thou dialogue can be effected only when both parties are authentic to their encounter. Feigning authenticity is as fatal to an encounter as a counterfeited orgasm is to sexual intercourse. Authenticity stands for existential truth and morality, since it entails a sincere and immediate attitude to oneself and the other. When the inauthenticity, the make-believe, the double-talk, the bad faith are phenomenologically identified and peeled off from one's relationship with oneself and with the object-other, one can reorder one's priorities vis-à-vis the approaching horizon of death. Thenceforth, the authenticity of an experience is not meant to be judged by separant success or bourgeois failure. An encounter may be painful and involve loss of social status and yet be existentially authentic. Per contra, an experience may be outwardly praised by the generalized and specific others, but be inauthentic and, hence, meaningless to Ego. The evaluations of the generalized or specific others and the experiencing ego are bound to be divergent, depending on time, place, and type of personality, as measured by our bio-psycho-social configuration as individuals. Sartre's negation of any authentic encounter, as evident in *No Exit, Nausea,* and *Being and Nothingness,* stems from the fact that he considered the encounter only in the context of an epistemic inter-subjectivity. However, if we can feel, with Kierkegaard, a maieutic revelation of transcendence within his inner self, which Sartre denied but we accept, then man ceases to be a useless passion and attains a potential for authenticity which is up to him to realize or ignore.

In the absence of rebellion against the generalized other, the demiurgical hell closes on me so that all my object-other relationships are I-it petrifications. Only when I extricate myself from the tresses of the generalized other can I be existentially moral by relating myself to a specific other on his terms. The demiurgos functions through an imposition of power, public opinion, and the selling of goods through the mass media. One can never reach an I-thou dialogue with the other as president, general manager, or committee member. Only when he is stripped of his social roles can we hope to reach out to him in an authentic encounter. The sequences of time, as ordained by the demiurgos contain past and future, but no present. Authentic time aims at an extasis into the intensity of processes, not goals, and, hence, into a continuous present. The choice of authenticity is a value decision undertaken by Ego alone. No outside advice is possible, since one's bio-psycho-social configuration is bound to be different than that of others. Only a maieutic triggering of revelation by the other, so that I feel as though the choice was my own, is possible. Hence, if one has defined one's decision as stemming from one's own inner-self, in order to realize one's creative potential, it becomes authentic in its consequences.

Authenticity is a level of being different from epistemic communication. It is a clandestine maieutic reaching out from one's inner-self to the inner-self of the other, while evading the noise emanating from the I-it demiurgos. Authenticity is a continuous process of becoming. Tantalic ends and Sisyphean objectives are non-attainable, hence, whatever can be achieved should be achieved by authentic processes of revelation and creativity. Ego trips, such as a column in the society page of the local newspaper, a medal, or a presidential citation, are good for temporary lifts (Heideggerian augenblicke of inauthentic time) which are soon filed in the nostalgic memory, or more probably, forgotten. Only the authentic process of creativity or revelation effects an extasis into the continuous present, and hence, into timelessness and the transcendence of the I-thou dialogue. Not everyone performs this leap of faith into authenticity. On the contrary, to answer the call of authenticity takes courage and readiness for rebellious renunciation. For every Gauguin who leaves everything behind to fulfill himself in Tahiti, there are myriads of insurance agents, stockbrokers, and post office clerks who remain in their non-creative jobs, basking in their relative security, and secretly writing poems, dreaming of the trip to South America which will never take place, or painting a couple of hours every other Sunday afternoon.

A creative Sisyphus, a revelatory Tantalus, has a total commitment to his authentic vocations. No compromises for them. Once they compromise, they accept the coercive point of view of the generalized and specific others and introduce an I-it element into their creativity and revelation with a corresponding loss of authenticity. Once Tantalus and Sisyphus recognize that they are partners of a blemished God and recognize the paradox inherent in their being an exclusive channel of cosmic awareness, their uniqueness is revealed to them as irreplaceable. Hence, they can never accept substitutes. Only the real thing, conveyed intuitively and maieutically to their inner-selves by bio-psycho-social feedback is good enough. Counterfeit revelation and creativity are soon weathered with the patina of time and lost in the graveyards of history. Only authentic revelation and creativity are timeless and may be conveyed to God and man in an everlasting dialogue. If one cannot find authentic revelation and creativity which fits one's unique bio-psycho-social configuration, one may carry on searching for them. If one does not settle for substitutes, one may perchance experience authenticity in the processes of searching and yearning themselves.

The actual process of creativity is initiated by the formation of a symbolon in the Greek sense—a connecting mechanism. The symbolon is structured from the mythogenic elements of yearning in our ani-consciousness which are complemented by mythogenes from our atzmi interactive self. Hence, as we have already mentioned, the speaking of a primary word integrates the I-thou of the ani and the I-it of the atzmi into a self-contained unit stemming from the self but directed towards the object. It, thus, initiates the process of creation, or, rather, provides a vectorial seed or tool of creation, which is the essence of our connecting symbolon structure.

The ani-consciousness creates the symbolon structure which already contains the maquette, the reduced yet scaled model, the seed on which it will integrate with energy-matter to form the actual Promethean holon, which could be, depending on the case, a quantum particle, an artifact, or a creature. To return to the creation myth of Genesis, we find that 'the spirit of God *hovered over* (emphases mine) the face of the water' (Gen. 1:2). There is no direct contact between the spirit of God, which we hold to be a mytho-empirical projection of the ani-consciousness, and the water, a projection of the primordial soup of energy-matter. To effect an integration—a symbolon structure—should be introduced into the synaptic juncture between the ani-consciousness and energy-matter. These symbolon structures precede any act of creation which involves the integration of consciousness and energy-matter—be it a poem, a painting, or a quantum particle.

All integrations of consciousness and energy taking place on the quantum level cannot be consciously perceived and remembered by creatures because they take place in the unconscious, yet very likely the processes of memory, thought, intuition, and emotions are based on micro-dynamics taking place at the quantum level behind the uncertainty barrier. These basic premises, however, are integrated within the personality through the ani-consciousness, and, thus are projected onto mythology as experiential myths.

On the conscious level, we have shown elsewhere, and also seen above from Bohr's complementarity principle, that human perception is not only holistic, but also selective, depending on the bio-psycho-social configuration of the given individual.[14] On the biological level, a hungry individual would tend to be more attracted by gastronomical stimuli. On the personality level, we have Petrie's ingenious experiments showing that some individuals tend to augment or reduce incoming stimuli, and that these are stable personality traits.[15] In a similar vein, Zuckerman demonstrated that some people are hungry for stimuli and others averse to them, again as basic personality patterns.[16]

On the social level, we have the binocular rivalry in a tachistoscope where two different pictures are presented rapidly, simultaneously, to two viewers from different cultures. An American, for instance, would tend to see a baseball game, where the Mexican would see a bullfight. On the anthropological level, we have the Whorfean hypothesis, according to which the whole process of perception is determined by cultural predispositions. Perception will be selective according to the relative importance, meaning, and values ordained by a given culture.

Consequently, the bio-psycho-social configuration of an individual will determine the selectivity of his perception on the structuring of symboloi for his short-term and long-term creativity. This selectivity is intentional and, hence, involves an indeterministic choice by the ani to form a connecting symbolon with a given physical state. This lends a meaning to the created Promethean holon, be it an eigenstate of a particle or a Shakespearean sonnet, since both derive meaning from the intentional act of creating, mediating the ani-consciousness with energy by a symbolon structure.

We hold that the connecting symbolon structure is generated by a process of inner revelation. The vectorial intention of the symbolon is conscious, but the actual integration of the mythogenes within it and its actual structuring is unconscious. The symbolon seed is utilized as a connecting or rather integrating agent between the ani-consciousness and the energy-matter to catalyze the creation of a Promethean holon, be it the eigenstate of a particle, a chanson, or a sculpture.

We are in a position now to present our conceptual scheme in which we shall try to show how the symbolon structure links in a creative manner the domains of ani-consciousness and energy-matter. Figure 2.1 should help our conceptual analysis:

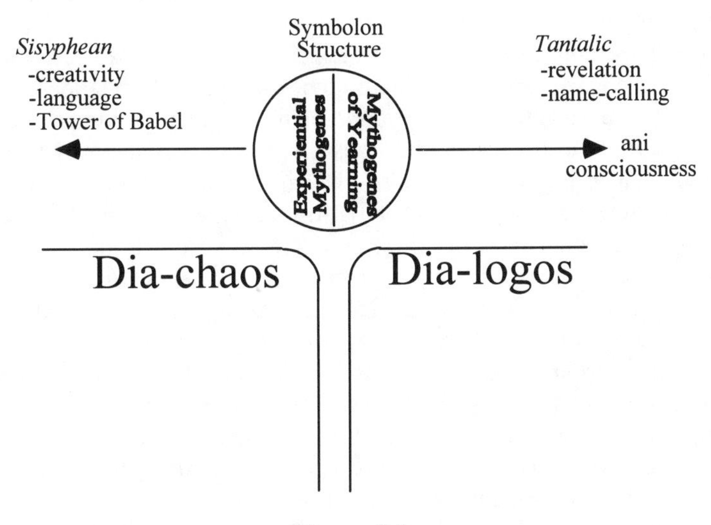

Figure 2.1

On the right-hand side we have the domain of the Logos, the Tantalic vector of revelation which is ever longed for, but, in its ultimate goal of exposure to divinity, is never fully achieved or achievable. On the left, hand side is the Sisyphean domain of creativity in which our batteries of being may be charged with meaning. Science is also a Sisyphean process since, as Popper forcefully argues, we can never prove or disprove conclusively any hypothesis, but the process of refutation itself is what science is based upon.

The mythogenes of the single revelatory Logos is splintered as per the myth of the Tower of Babel into an infinity of words and meanings. As Camus assures us in his *Myth of Sisyphus*, we can never balance our burden stone on the top of the hill, yet the process of authentic creativity in and by itself, is combined with mythogenes of experience into the symbolon structure to effect an act of creation. Hence, culture is the sum total of creative ventures in any given society. Also, since mythogenes are the contents which actually pass from the domain of the Logos to the domain of unstructured energy-matter, therefore chaos is the communicating medium by which a dialogue, literally a passing through the word, is effected. This dialogue is a communicative flow of revelatory mythogenes of longing onto the domain of energy-matter (dia-chaos) inherent in the process of creation. Indeed, primitive man encounters the world as a person—a thou, in the Buberian dialogical tradition.[17] What passes over in the synaptic junctions of the Logos and the chaos is a subconscious and maieutically indirect mythogene since a direct communication between an abstract ahistorical ani-consciousness and concrete, historical matter is impossible.

Indeed, the epistemic barrier between consciousness and energy-matter has been projected onto many mythologies as the veil or fence between history and transcendence. In Egyptian mythology, an individual prepares his whole lifetime for the fateful transition from the domain of Horus to the away and beyond of the realm of Osiris.[18] Hermes and Merkur, the divine messengers, are also archetypal thieves, implying that one cannot pass over the boundaries dividing the Here and Now from the Far and Away directly, but must steal across them *contrabandieri* style like thieves in the night. The epistemic, ontological, and existential barrier between the ani-consciousness and its physical and metaphysical surroundings seem to be so formidable that only the crafty mythogenes are able to franchise the two by their indirect, maieutic leaps. Levi-Strauss hinted at this aspect of myth when he stated that its main function is to bridge over extremely divergent dualties.[19] Levi-Bruehl, likewise, shows how myths bridge over man and other life forms, like talking beasts such as Balaam's ass.[20] This could explain the nature of divinities so common in Egypt, Mesopotamia, and Greece including notably, Pegasus, the Greek flying horse, Horus, the winged and falcon-headed Egyptian deity, and Imdugud, the Mesopotamian lion-headed eagle.

When the linking and creative complementarity between mythogenes become progressively more effective, they become sanctified and reach their axial age (to use Karl Jasper's phrase), and then they are engraved into scripture like the Bible, the Egyptian Book of the Dead, or the Babylonian Enuma Elish.

Myths of Longing and Myths of Experience

Both the Sisyphean quest for regaining pre-differentiated unity by swallowing the object and incorporating it in one's personality and the Tantalic longing to melt back into the pantheism of early orality are unattainable by definition. Hence, these quests for impossible ideals are projected onto transcendence, where the longed-for perfections are not bound by the limits of spatio-temporality. The Tantalic type, who has been fixated on non-differentiated early orality, projects his God as a monistic omnipresence, whereas the later-orally fixated Sisyphean externalizes his deity as an omnipotent boundless force. Moreover, the later oral fixation of the Sisyphean allows him to identify the source of his frustrations. The Sisyphean tends to blame his objective human surroundings for his frustrations in an extrapunitive manner, as conceptualized by Rosenzweig.

The inevitable rift between the Sisyphean's separant ideal of controlling and manipulating his surroundings and his actual competitive achievement are registered by him as a continuous frustration. This chronic discontent is also projected onto transcendence and manifested by the separant deity as a constant need to reinforce his omnipotence. The prayers in many religions include repetitious flatteries and assertions, with a multiplicity of flattering adjectives imputing power, wisdom, and greatness, as if to placate the potency anxieties projected onto God by his frustrated Sisyphean initiates.

The self-effacing Tantalic type is also constantly frustrated, because his quietist ideal of melting back into the omnipresent non-being of unity cannot be realized. Being intra-punitive, that is imputing the causes of his frustrations to himself, he projects onto transcendence a less than perfect deity like the Kabbalist God, who seems to be unable to prevent the catastrophe of the breaking of the cosmic vessels and, thereby, allows evil to be created, or like Rilke's puerile God, whose unsynchronized hands are responsible for the sorry mess of temporal creation. The separant core vector manifests itself in creation, corporeality, and developmental growth, whereas the participant core-vector seeks reversal to the noncorporeality and spirituality of non-being. This might well account for the mind-body controversy raging in philosophy to this very day. The claims of the Sisyphean object-manipulating materialists concerning the exclusiveness of body-matter and of the Tantalic rejectors of appearances postulating the reality of spirit-mind may be better understood in the light of these personality core-vectors.

Metaphysical projections define, by contrast, the misery of temporal existence. Man's first phase of separation, ejection from the cozy womb, was registered mytho-empirically as the catastrophe of the breaking of the vessels. The second phase, after the existential coagulation of the separate ego from the pantheistic togetherness of early orality, is registered mytho-empirically as expulsion from Paradise, when God has condemned man to a cursed land on which he will live in sorrow all his temporal life. The third phase, involving cruel rites of passage from childhood to puberty, have been mytho-empirically anchored by us to the sacrifices of Isaac and Iphigenia. All this implies that temporal existence is marked by ejection from the uterine wholeness, by separation from the early oral Edenic pantheism, and by expulsion from the family fold. The regaining of completeness, wholeness, and perfection cannot be accomplished in the dire here and now, but only in the ever after, within the realm of omnipresence and omnipotence.

The dialectical quests of the vectors—the things-in-themselves—the prime movers of objects and life cannot be apparent. Only the clashes and synthetic outcomes of dialectical interaction constitute the apparent reality, the contours and forms of matter, the systems-in-balance of life forms and personalities. When the synthetic outcome of each dialectical style initiates another cycle, it slips again into non-being only to reappear again into the being of reality as the synthesis of another dialectical cycle da capo, in an endless Sisyphean-Tantalic process. Hence, such interaction of the teleological non-realizable quests of the core-vectors is the basic energy and the prime-movers of being as well as the system-in-balance of life. Moreover, this dialectical dynamic makes for man's motivation by Sisyphean quests and Tantalic longings which he can never fulfill.

As we are ever craving for what we are not, and for what we have not, we live in an inauthentic time frame. The separant vector aims for the future, and the participant vector longs for the past. When dominated by these two vectors, man does not exist in the present; his time is thus false and inauthentic. If the quests and longings inherent in man's core personality vectors cannot be fulfilled, there is an inevitable and constant rift between his aspirations, expectations, and perceived reality. Hence, man is ever confronted with the absurd. This dual impasse of inauthenticity and the absurd makes the myths of Sisyphus and Tantalus so central to the human condition that we can rightly consider them meta-myths. The initial inauthenticity of man's existence in the world and his inevitable experience of the absurd constitute man's existential impasse from which creativity and revelation are able to extricate him.

Creativity is, thus, the modus vivendi of Sisyphus with his stone-burden, and revelation is the means by which Tantalus can go on living within his predicament. Man, thus, starts as an initial failure, yet through his ability to sublimate his unrealized quests into creativity and revelation, he is able to transform his initial impasse into authentic experience and existence.

It seems that our programmer, whoever or whatever it is—God, chance, evolution, or the devil—programmed us to yearn to achieve goals that can never be achieved, to yearn to be different than we are at a given time and place, and to cherish not the present but to long for either earlier developmental phases and nonbeing in the past or for the away and beyond in the future. Our non-realizable core personality quests control us the way the lure in front of racing dogs control the race. Our programmer apparently intends to see how our Sisyphean quests can be sublimated dialectically into creativity and revelation.

Both the separant and the participant need to sustain their quests and longings into creativity and revelationism; both dynamic processes sustained by Sisyphean aims and Tantalic longings. If they are, our yearnings are extinguished, and our potentiality for authentic being through creativity and revelation die with them. The impasse of unfulfilled aims and the inevitable absurd rift between expectations and reality is transformed from a curse to a blessing. Moreover, the dialectics between our unfulfillable Sisyphean quests and Tantalic longings are our prime movers; without them we are dead. Therefore, when William Golding describes in *The Spire* the quests of a builder to pierce a hole in the sky with the spire of a cathedral, he depicts the essence of Sisyphean aspirations and the core of the builder's being. Freud's oceanic feelings, described by him in relation to religiosity and assigned by him to a secondary and almost peripheral role, are much more central than he thought. It is the expression of the participant core longing to reunite with pantheism of pre-differentiated early orality. The visions of grandeur swelling in one's chest while listening to Beethoven's Eroica and the feeling of melting into the totality of unity while deep in prayer are not just accidental or peripheral processes. They are all there is. They are the things-in-themselves.

We intend to present now two models which may serve as a summary of our expositions and as a guideline for our deliberations for the rest of this chapter. Figure 2.2 shows a triangular model having at its apex the dialectics of yearnings which are the thing or rather the things-in-themselves. They also represent our prime movers because we are motivated to act by the unachievable goals of our core-vectors. The transcendental projections of these goals are man's metaphysical divinities.

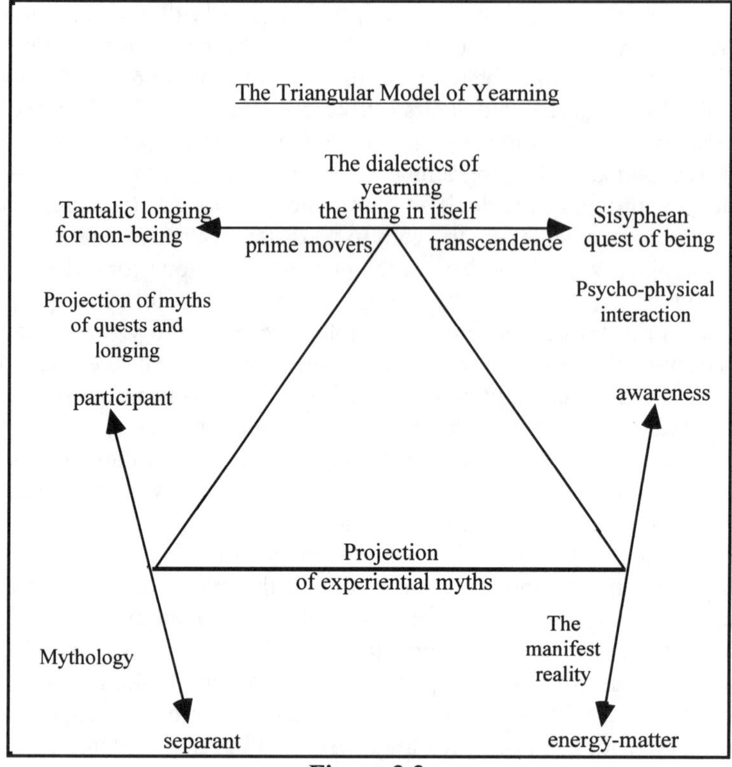

Figure 2.2

The dialectics of yearning constitute the manifest reality along a continuum ranging from the core awareness of the self to the system-in-balance of energy-matter. The self is held in a precarious balance which is the synthetic outcome of the dialectics between Tantalic longings and Sisyphean quests, whereas the structure of matter is maintained as a synthesis between the dynamic separant and the participant interaction between the waves and particles of energy. The psycho-physical antithesis is solved, or, rather, bridged by our conception of the thing-in-itself interacting dialectically to produce both the awareness of the self and energy-matter. Thus, the self and its objects are on opposing poles of the same continuum of synthetic systems-in-balance. The mythological projections of manifest reality are mostly experiential and developmental being myths of quests and participant myths of longing. The myths of Tantalus and Sisyphus are meta-myths because they describe the predicament of Man in not being able to realize either his separant quests or participant longings.

They are also a combination of experiential projections and myths of yearning and, thus, cover the whole range of mytho-empiricism. However, most myths can be discerned as either experiential projections or myths of longing. Experiential myths when perceived as mytho-empirical anchors may serve as the common denominators of experience. They may thus become a basis of epistemic interpersonal communication and eventually become, if properly studied, a meta-language. The myth of Tantalus is also a meta-experiential myth because his punishment according to an earlier version of the myth was also to crouch beneath a stone, not knowing when, or if, it was liable to crush him. This represents the basic existential condition of man as being thrown unto death. This is the mytho-empirical anchor of the Heideggerian Angst, Kierkegaard's fear and trembling, and our desperation as characterizing human existence. Myths as experiential projections disclose things primordially, register happenings in illo tempore before recorded history, and, of course, project man's developmental phases.

Myths of yearning are so abundant that they engulf our entire lives. Thrillers, science fiction, detective books all depict the myth of an ever-prevailing justice. These are typical myths of yearnings because we know that in real life alas, justice does not always win, and crime very often does pay. Commercials on television and the perfect ever-young skin of cosmetic models are again myths of yearning. So are the Walter Mittyesque exploits of Superman and the straight-forward-and-tough-on the-outside-yet-soft-like-a-marshmallow-on-the-inside type of cowboy who fades on his white horse into the setting sun on the movie screen. Names are often myths of yearnings. We call our children after prophets, kings, and angels. Our family names are often synonyms of hope, happiness, joy, and wisdom. Place names often denote success, progress, and glory.

Our first model deals with the ontological triadic relationships among the things in themselves, i.e., the dialectics of yearnings, their manifestations in reality, and their mythological projections. Our second model, shown in figure 2.3, deals with the dynamic processes inherent in the ontological model:

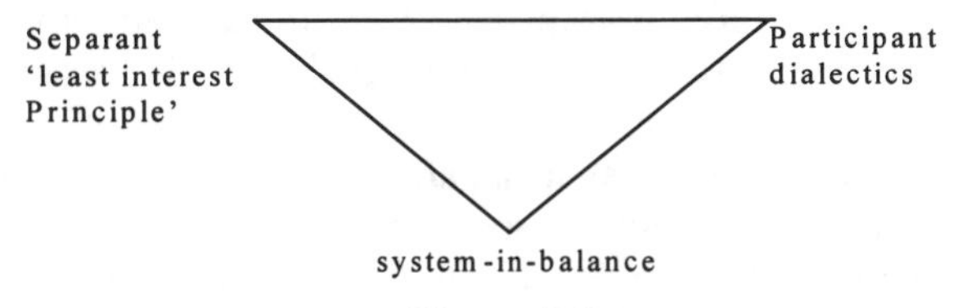

Figure 2.3

Most of our experience in our deprivational interaction with our surroundings is negative, because of our basic separant competitive orientation towards other human beings and our achievement-motivated efforts to control our environment. These efforts usually fail because others also aim to control their environment, including Ego itself, and because the more one succeeds in one Sisyphean task the more one increases one's Sisyphean goals which become, thence, progressively unattainable. This is one of the main separant mechanisms which guard against a too-close rapprochement between Ego and his surrounding objects and life forms. However, the most effective separant safeguard against participation is the least interest principle, which ordains that the more the Ego strives to gain control over its surroundings or to gain possession of goods, money, and power, the less it is likely to succeed in its aims. The least interest principle operates on all levels of human behavior and may be denoted, therefore, as a meta-dynamic. It functions in a curvilinear relationship with the separant goals. Some achievement motivation is needed for Ego to muster all its energies to achieve its Sisyphean aims, but after a certain intensity of motivation and effort they become counterproductive. After a certain level of exertion to achieve a separant aim, the marginal returns decrease. The least interest principle operates, thus, as a negative feedback cycle effecting a rupture between the Ego and its goal whenever the efforts to attain it become too strenuous or frantic. Consequently, when Ego's attitude towards the achievement of separant goals is almost neutral or nonchalant, he has the best chance of gaining them. We have shown elsewhere that the least interest principle operates in full force in the emotional relationship between the sexes[21] and in power-based interaction in politics and business.[22] The tragic and sometimes the tragicomic aspect of the least interest principle is that one gains things, services, and others' affections when and where one does not want them, yet when one is desperate for money or love he rarely gets them. Thus the hard-up businessman, who desperately needs a loan, is not likely to be favored by banks, and a Vincent Van Gogh, who courts a girl by putting his hand in an open fire to prove the intensity of his love for her, has indeed frightened her away. The author's own experience is that his best lectures were those in which he was not too involved with his audience. In those lectures in which he had strong emotional or other interests, his tension negatively affected the quality of his presentation.

Therefore, the tragic paradox inherent in the least interest principle is that the separant programming against participation makes for detachment and non-involvement to be more associated with success attain in goods, powering or dialogues than in strenuous efforts. Consequently, one tends to attain goals in which one is less interested, but the aims one wants most one is the least likely to get.

Dialectics as the unifying mechanism of existence ordains that man can never achieve his Sisyphean quests or Tantalic longings, only a synthesis between them which serves as a thesis for another dialectical zig-zag ad infinitum. Consequently, man's fate is to ever seek something and always attain something else. This is masterfully portrayed by Beckett whose Watt always longs to go north but his legs lead him southwards. We can, therefore, never achieve whatever our aims are because dialectics will lead us somewhere else. Hence, authentic rebellion concentrates on processes of creativity and revelation because their goals are unattainable to begin with and because, whatever aim we may wish to attain, dialectics will move us to another, more synthetic goal.

The synthetic result of dialectics is the compromising middle range principle of the golden rule or the Greek maxim of nothing in excess, which was projected onto transcendence as the main principle governing both life and heavenly bodies. Even the planets are going to be scourged by furies if they leave their ordained course. If one exceeds the middle course and one's moira (i.e., one's proverbial 'lot in life'), one commits the capital crime of hübris, which is punished most strenuously by the Olympians. If one does not maneuver skillfully between the extremes of Scylla and Charibdis, one is sure to perish.

Finally dialectics whitewashes evil and makes falsehood necessary because by Ego's need to overcome it one may achieve a higher truth. In a similar vein, we need the absurdity of man's unattainable core goals and the impasse of one's being thrown to death and to the vicissitudes of temporal existence. Only by one's dialectical efforts to overcome the strife, conflict, impasse, and absurdity of his existence can man obtain the meaningfulness of creativity and the grace of revelation.

Transcendence

Our concept of transcendence is, thus, a dual one: the illusory goals of perfect and absolute transcendence, which serve as motivating aims both in the Sisyphean and Tantalic core-vectors. The illusory goals of perfection are the separant pagan god as well as the theistic omnipotent God of Judaism, Christianity, and Islam. In a similar vein, the participant Far Eastern Deities Tao, Nirvana, and Bakhti as well as the Kabbalistic Torah-D'atzilut are also perfect states which are Tantalic prime movers: all are unattainable by definition. Moreover, if they are attained, they lose their motivating force. Hence, Sisyphus should never succeed in balancing his stone on the summit of the hill lest his dialectical motivation for creativity be extinguished. Also, the Tantalic aims should not be realized. Otherwise, the longing for revelation is bound to expire. Here Beckett understood that his Godot (God) should never appear, and

Kierkegaard and Rabbi Nachman of Bratzlav renounced the theophany of transcendence in the here-and-now lest their longings for revelation and, indeed, its viability in the here-and-now be destroyed.

Genuine transcendence, therefore, moves in a cycle from the Sisyphean unattainable core quests to the equally unrealizable Tantalic longing both of which interact dialectically in a system-in-balance constituting our prime movers and the thing-in-itself. These are projected as myths of experience and expectations, which are in their turn structured into religions and deities which are the unreal, perfect, unattainable, projected goals of our core-vectors and which feed our core quests. Schematically this cycle may be presented as shown in figure 2.4:

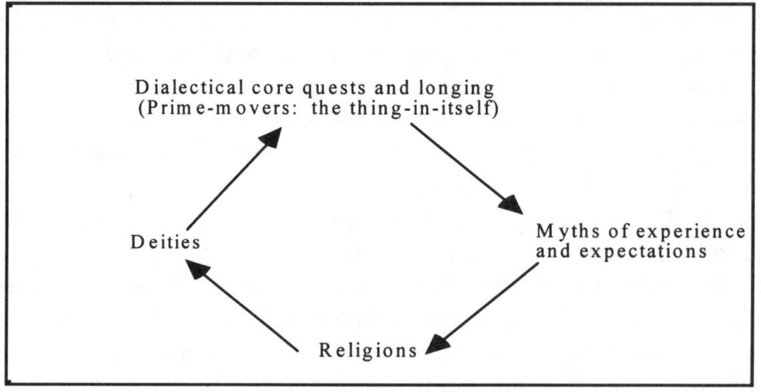

Figure 2.4

This cycle constitutes our metaphysical programming, which is quite similar to David Bohm's implicate order.[23] While its operation is mostly subconscious, its overt conscious components and the realization that transcendence is our own projection do not hamper the viability of our metaphysical cycle because our prime-mover is conceived by us as a basic participant belief which needs not be sustained by logic or rational inference. Hence, our real transcendental cycle which is fueled by unattainable and, thus, illusory absolutes constitutes a perpetuum mobilae insofar as it, first, creates transcendence and, then, is motivated by it. Our psycho-physical-metaphysical cycle is both prime-mover and moved—a Baron Münchausen-like feat of lifting itself up by its bootstraps.

Solipsism

Ego's feeling and realization that he was chosen to be the channel of awareness, not only of his own being but also of the whole creation, makes for a solipsistic sense of being a unique and exclusive center of the cosmos. Schopenhauer admitted that one cannot argue with a solipsist, only send him to a madhouse. Surely, if the solipsist is willing to extricate himself from his quandary, he may do so through our conception of an ever-striving, imperfect transcendence in the following manner: he should realize that the awareness is not his alone. The unique awareness perceived in his pure (without interactional attributes) self is a unity and, hence, is common to all flora and fauna. Each life form, as well as Ego, feels this basic awareness through this unique bio-psycho-social configuration and, therefore, perceives itself in a kaleidoscopic manner specific to itself alone. This space-time kaleidoscope cuts off Ego from the other life forms and from the realization that the basic awareness in his pure self and transcendence are one. The purpose here is that both Ego and his programming as represented by his transcendental awareness in his pure self cannot be creative in unity; as Sisyphus has to have his stone to be creative, so Ego has to separate from transcendence for the interactive experience of creativity, or, for that matter, for all experience except for revelation, to take place. Hence, Ego is a partner of transcendence in creativity: the metaphysical programming of Sisyphus experiences vicariously his triumphs and disasters.

We do not know why transcendence needs to experience vicariously the existence of Ego. This could be out of boredom, stress, an experiment which must be unknown to Ego—the guinea-pig for the elation of creativity. The barrier between Ego and transcendence must be hermetically sealed; otherwise, the creative interaction between experientially different entities cannot be effected. Ego is, thus, interacting with a less-than-perfect transcendence which needs him for its feeling of creativity, yet cannot allow him to know that he is part of it. Ego is moved, as we have seen, and motivated by dialectical quests which are the things-in-themselves and, hence, part of transcendence which are longing for a perfect transcendence which cannot and ought not be realized. Otherwise, the seemingly all-important relationship between Ego and transcendence cannot be creative or even sustained. Hence, we have a double paradox: An imperfect transcendence is tantamount to annihilation and extinction of both transcendence and Ego.

The possible solution of this paradox, relieving him in the process from his perfect exclusivity, is that imperfection is perfect, in the sense that it lends life and creativity to the dyad of Ego and transcendence, whereas the perfection of transcendence spells inertia, sterility, and the absoluteness of death.

Credo Quia Absurdum

This idea is reminiscent of some of the teachings of Kierkegaard and Rabbi Nachman of Bratzlav. But, above all, it is reminiscent of Kabbala and the catastrophe of the breaking of the vessels, scattering bits of divinity in the mire of spatio-temporality, thus, transforming the perfect Old Testament God into a blemished, less-than-perfect divinity. It also made man a junior, but essential, partner to God because by his meditative prayer man lifts back the scattered particles of divinity to their origin in God. Man thus effects a tikkun, a mending of the blemished divinity, and imbues in the process a meaning to his own life. Our model, however, does not involve a transformation from a theistic, absolute God to a less-than-perfect divinity. We envisage a less-than-perfect God as a starting point. He imbued part of himself, i.e., man, and other life forms, with the capacity for creation and revelation so that he might experience it through them.

Both man and God are ever-longing and striving. It is precisely this that makes them ever-revelatory and creative. Indeed, Dante consigns to eternal damnation the souls of those whose wishes came true and whose longings were fulfilled. Our less-than-perfect God, with his capacity for longing and striving, is perfect precisely because of his imperfection. It brings to the fore St. Anselm's proof for the existence of God: The imperfection of our transcendence lends it more perfection than if it were perfect. Perfection in God kills it into non-being, whereas non-perfection gives it the ever-involving perfectibility of longing together with his junior partners—man and other life forms—for revelation and striving for creativity, which is the essence of authentic existence. Moreover, Tantalic longing and the Sisyphean seeking interact dialectically to reinforce as prime movers and things-in-themselves the being of God and man, even if these quests are not actually fulfilled through revelation and creativity. These longings serve as a recharging of the batteries, which lend motivation for further revelation and creativity and, thus, for a continuous sense of existence. Our pure attributeless awareness within our inner selves is part of transcendence, and, hence, eternal, but its sense of longing, striving, revelation, and creativity, i.e., its meaningful existence, is gained through its dialectical interaction with seemingly separate life forms, which, in metaphysical reality, are part of its own transcendence.

Contrary to Buddhist doctrine, the spiked Samsara wheel of continuous transformations and incarnations is perceived by us as perfection, whereas the mandala of non-being is the image of inertia and death. This dialectical quest, which seems to be the essence of our transcendence, is implanted in us and in other life forms—being chips of divinity—by our participant core-vectors to revert back to previous developmental phases of pantheistic early orality and the blissful wholeness in utero. These perfect states serve only as enticements which cannot and should not be achieved.

Myths, being a projection of experiences and yearnings of individuals or groups, may be typed along a continuum, in the same ways as personalities. On its participant pole is the bad me early oral fixated type surrounded by good objects as well as the Tantalic culture's ethical myths, where the boundaries of laws and the limits of morals are good checks and balances containing the separant sprouting and unruly me. On the other pole is the separant later-oral fixated good me individual, surrounded by the delimiting bad objects and competing life forms as well as by the Sisyphean cultures' myths of aesthetics, order, heroism, strife, and dominion over man and nature. Hence, Judaic myths are more participant, whereas Greek and Germanic myths are situated on the extreme separant pole of the continuum. The separant myths are bound by place and time. Even heaven and hell are just on different planes of the here and now. This life-giving and life-pumping blood is idealized and mythologized as the basis of tribal and racial identity by the Sisyphean German culture, but is shunned and dreaded by the Tantalic Judaic myths and social character. The separant cosmogenetic myths are the reordering and restructuring of ever-existing matter, whereas the participant cosmogenetic myths depict as a vile dynamic the transition from non-being to being which is considered as death or exile from the timelessness and boundlessness of spirituality. Participant characteristics are linked with paternal moralizing and surrogate sacrificial normative mandates.[24] Separant normative characteristics are related, on the other hand, to maternal organization of pragmatic routines which are linked to viable procreation and the rearing of a family. Hence, Tantalic myths are more patri-normative whereas Sisyphean myths are largely matri-normative. Separant myths, in keeping with their corresponding social character, are more logical and rational, whereas participant myths are more intuitive and irrational. Of special importance is that separant myths are time-bound, historical, and linear, whereas participant myths transcend time and tend to be circular and ahistorical. Sisyphean myths are diachronic—they move from one point in time to another—whereas Tantalic myths are synchronic involving mixed, overlapping, or nonexistent time spans.

The continuum of myths makes for a vast array of polar correlates, with myths of yearning, on the participant-Tantalic pole and myths of experience, on the separant-Sisyphean pole of our continuum. These correlates, which should not be taken as an exclusive list, but as illustrative instances only, inter alia as follows: Myths of yearning are our Tantalic prime movers since their sense of lacking, of deprivation, or of a need to fulfill prods us for spiritual revelation and, for authentic creativity. Myths of yearning tend to be intuitive and irrational whereas experiential myths are mostly rational. Myths of yearning tend to be ahistorical temporally, synchronic, and acausal, whereas experiential myths are temporally diachronic and causally spatial. Tantalic myths of longing can never be reinforced, hence the yearning in itself has to be structured into a self-rewarding feedback which is divorced from its goal. The experiential myths, on the other hand, have the dubious advantage of having historical objects to interact with. Still, it makes all the difference if Sisyphus has managed to achieve a creative modus vivendi with his stone or lies exhausted, defeated, and crushed underneath it.

The Projected Perfections and the Mythogenic Prime Movers

We have envisaged God as the projected perfection of the unachievable goals of man's personality core-vectors, which motivate his behavior through his never-ending quest to achieve them.[25] In this section we shall try to show how these goals, which cannot be realized in history, are projected as mythogenes onto transcendental mythology and are sacralized as deities by rituals, theurgy, and magic. Since a mythogene is a self-regulating structure, it is projected onto mythology and is ritualized into a God; it not only has an existence of its own, but it also governs the life and fates of humans who impute legitimacy to the divine authority. The belief in gods then operates as a self-fulfilling feedback cycle. Kirk states the matter thus: 'If one believes that God works in wondrous ways, that is a belief that conditions one's whole mentality by drastically altering the limits of the possible.'[26]

The sanctification of the myth through its ritualized reduction into a script takes place in a historical span denoted by Jaspers as the axial age.[27] This age marks the transition from an oral transmission of myth to its engraving into a durable form of scripture. Thence it is not man's words but the Word of God. When Moses brought down the tablets from Mount Sinai, a cycle was closed: He projected a myth of an abstract God, who conveyed his messages by divine word—the Logos—when this word was inscribed into Scripture, the Torah. It has become canonized as sacred law, which in its turn has infused mythogenes back into history to reproject them onto mythology da capo.

The mythogenes of yearning and experience may be posited at the extreme poles of a continuum which would correspond with the separant-participant personality continuum and the Sisyphean-Tantalic continuum of mythologies. Our reliance on myths as anchors for our continuum of gods is linked to our contention that divinities are projections of the perfect unattainable goals of our personality core-vectors. We hold myths to be collective projections of human developmental phases. They are archetypal processes linked to our prime motivations, inherent in the goals of our core-vectors, which are projected as gods. Hence, myths are projected mostly as sacred records of events which transpired in the primordial before time ille tempore; their sources are the common developmental experiences of human beings as ordained and programmed by our core-vectors presented as divinities. Therefore, myths are natural empirical anchors for our work, which conceives gods as human projections.

A mythogene of yearning stemming from an early orally fixated personality type, anchoring on pantheism and omnipresence, would project a unitary monotheistic deity with its normative perfection demanding absolute obedience, like the God of Abraham. This god demands an unwavering compliance with the ultimate sacrifice on Mount Moriah. The experiential mythogene projects a pragmatic, perfectly omnipotent deity, who manipulates power, man, and things in a manner most suitable to an ad hoc expediency. The moral righteousness of the Greek god, for instance, is usually secondary to the orderly performance of his tasks. Both humans and gods are subject to the coercion of necessity αναγκη (ananké) especially when the need to remain within the boundaries and central measures of moira, man's lot in life, are concerned. Still, since a mythogene is a self-regulating and self-sustaining structure, its power to motivate us—fuel our actions and recharge our batteries of yearning—may not be impaired when its emanatory source seems to be absent or incommunicado. On the Tantalic pole of our mythogenic continuum, we have the Deus Absconditis: the Absent, or Silent, God.

The extreme participant anchors on non-being and his blissful non-awareness in utero, before the catastrophe of birth; his ultimate aim is to revert to nothingness. This is the aim of the Hindu Samadhi, the Buddhist Nirvana, the Gnostic deliverance, and the Hasidic Iyum, which is literally 'rendering into nothingness'. These are techniques aiming to annul the catastrophe of birth, to annihilate the temporal self-concept and body image, and revert back to the wholeness, perfection, and omnipresent non-being. Hence, a wide range of participant mystics—ranging from Molinos, the Christian quietist, through the Muslim Sufis and the Hasidic Maggid of Meseritz—taught that the obliteration and the ontological death of the temporal self leads to its resurrection in unity. The human quest of non-being is, therefore, projected on a transcendent nothingness which represents the non-embodied boundless infinity of pre-being.

The contemporary exposition of the dead deity has been dramatized by Nietzsche. Some interpreters hold that, even with Nietzsche, the nihilation of God relates to the disclaimer of an objective deity and to his transformation into an immanence of subjectivity.[28] This is quite clear with Kierkegaard and Heidegger. Both expound, in widely disparate styles, their basic doctrine that authentic transcendence can be reached only through the all-embracing nothingness within the inner pure self, as conceptualized by Husserl. The works of Beckett are permeated with the sense of an absent and silent God, yet Godot (God) does not show up, and there is an underlying supposition that He need not because the mere longing for Him is enough. This is, in many ways, a bold interpretation of divinity, which could be in line with our major premise in the present work: That the existence of God is not a conditional precedent for man's existential fulfilment in the here-and-now, yet the longing for transcendence, which is man's projected quest for the perfection of his personality core-vectors, is necessary for the initiation of the processes which may lead to creativity and revelation. God may be absent or silent, but the longing for him in itself may be sufficient for the dialectics of man's fulfilment.

After the Jewish Holocaust, Buber still asserted the existence of God, yet maintained that at the time of Auschwitz and Dachau, God was eclipsed. This is a rather compromising predicament for the 'Universal Thou', and what happens to the I when the Universal Thou is eclipsed? Eli Weisel asks how a Jew can still believe in God after Auschwitz; the answer he gives is that a Jew may rebel against God on condition that he still believes in him. This rebellion against a theistic God opens up a Pandora's box of theological and moral problems, in comparison to which the queries of Job seem trivial. More pertinent to our present context is the statement of Alexander Donat, himself a survivor of Auschwitz, who says: 'I am a Jew. I do not believe in the God of Auschwitz. I believe in man who rebels, who suffers, and who fights; this is my belief. This is the true call which sprouts forth from the holy ashes.'[29] Donat rebels against an absent God, yet his rebellion against his thrownness into his world and against his incomprehensible predicament, which are the realm of transcendence, show that his rebellion is against transcendence. This is also evident from his use of the expressions 'belief' and 'holy'. It is a rebellion against a metaphysical non-being which lends a sense of meaning to temporal being.

Camus's God has also forsaken us and left humanity forever, 'leaving it to judge and condemn, with pardon on their lips and the sentence in their hearts'.[30] He is silent and does not interfere like a deus ex machina in man's affairs. Hence, Tarrous' problem in Camus's *The Plague* is how to be a saint without God. This saint is the Doctor Rieux, who fights the plague, knowing that he cannot defeat it. An existentialist saint tries to ease the pains of the sick because they are ill and because they suffer, and not for rewards in the here-and-now or in the ever-after. A theistic saint like Mother Theresa, who tends the lepers on the streets of Calcutta, believes that whatever she does is for Jesus Christ. 'When I feed the hungry and clothe the naked', she says, 'I do it for Jesus Christ. My work is, therefore, not social work but holy service.'[31] Working for God lends one's actions instant meaning, but tending the sick in an absurd world forsaken by an absent and silent God takes all the strength and stamina one can muster to lift oneself by one's existential bootstraps just high enough not to sink in the plague of despair.

According to Bultman and Tillich, by nihilating the outside object-bound God, one reaches the internal timeless and boundless deity. Dietrich Bonhoeffer, the martyred contemporary saint, preached belief in an absent God as follows:

> So our coming of age forces us to a true recognition vis-à-vis God. God is teaching us that we must live as men who can get along very well without Him. The God who is with us is the God who forsakes us (Mark 15:34). The God who makes us live in this world without using Him as a working hypothesis is the God before whom we are ever standing. Before God and with him we live, and live without God. God allows himself to be edged out of the world and unto the cross. God is weak and powerless in the world, and that is exactly the way, the only way, in which he can be with us and help us. Bonhoeffer, *16 July 1944*[32]

Finally, Dostoevski's Grand Inquisitor receives a kiss from the departing Jesus Christ, thereby signifying his approval that God need not be present in the world for man to seek his salvation in it.

For the participant to partake of God, he has to nihilate himself. By emerging from spatio-temporality, one becomes nothing and, thus, may emerge into the non-being of God. This quest of nihilation, of becoming nothing, was apparently expounded by participant religious thinkers like Plotinus and Augustine. For them contemplatio and extasis meant the revelation of spiritual essences in contradistinction to the corporeality of temporal existence.[33] In a similar vein, Meister Eckhart taught that only when the soul withdraws from its corporeal abode, i.e., nihilates its temporal existence, does it encounter the true life. Jacob Boehme's *Umgrund*, the primal nothingness out of which God the creator and the whole of creation sprouted forth, has been taken as a base for Berdyaev's elaborate exposition of God's nothingness and man's non-being. Fathomless non-being is not only prior to being, but is also absolutely free, because even God the creator has no power over it.[34] Berdyaev's conception of God is that he is not something, but nothing. Out of his divine absolute nothing, God the creator emerged to form man and the world. Yet absolute freedom is also responsible for created evil. God-the-son had, therefore, to revert back, through His divine self-sacrifice, to primeval nothingness in order to change it from within.[35] The projected God-son, the archetypal man-son, can mend the primeval badness by reverting to non-being, and there within his perfect source restore its wholesome nothingness. This is reminiscent, mutatis mutandis, of Lurianic kabbala, another extreme participant creed, according to which man can reverse through his good mending deeds (tikkunim) the vile outcome of the 'breaking of the vessels', which we have shown to be the mytho-empirical equivalent of birth.[36] The participant Tantalic type longs to blot the catastrophe of birth which catapulted him into the trials of existence and which projects goodness, perfection, and divinity on to the non-being that existed before creation.

Heidegger denotes man's authentic being-in-the-world as Dasein. However, when projected on transcendence, this Dasein is nihilated into nothingness.[37] This means that our innermost awareness of being, when projected on to God, becomes the participant pre-creation non-being which longs to merge with the nothingness of divinity.

The participant aim of reaching divine nothingness is revelation. This absent, yet revealing, transcendence is not a manipulating Old Testament God or a divinity, whether theistic, deistic, or pantheistic, which exists either within space-time or outside it. The revelation here is effected by the quest of exposure to the non-being of procreation and the blissful nothingness in utero. God is not in the dramatis personae of this revelatory process, because the Tantalic longing for the perfection of non-being may in itself lend viability to transcendental revelation. Neither God nor the actual attainment of nothingness is necessary for the revelatory experience. The quest of non-being may suffice. This, in essence, is the message of Heidegger in his interpretation of Hölderlin's poem *Homecoming*.[38] The poet longs to come back to his source. The home and source are near, yet clandestine and distant. This is the unattainable Tantalic nature of the coveted source. The 'reserving proximity' to 'the High One who inhabits the Serene of the Holy'[39] is never bridged, and the high one is never attained because 'Holy names are lacking'.[40] God is absent; he is nothingness. Homecoming to the source of the absent God is impossible, yet the process itself, the voyage, the longing and the writing about it, fills the heart with the most joyous bliss. Thus, the singer's soul does indeed gaze into the serene, but the singer does not see the High One himself, for he is blind.[41] In like manner, the Tantalic searcher of his perfect source-transcendental non-being is blind. He is unable to grasp his aim. His aim is unreachable, unperceivable, and nameless because it is a nothingness, yet the search in itself fills the voyager with an innermost joy of divine revelation. Man does not need

God to achieve transcendence, because he may project his innermost being (Dasein) on non-being, thus trying to reach metaphysical nothingness. Projecting onto nothing, Dasein is already beyond what-is-totality. This being beyond is what we call transcendence. 'The essence of Nothing as original nihilation lies in this: that it alone brings Dasein face to face with what-is as such.'[42]

Here we find the Tantalic conception of the metaphysical elusive 'Ding-an-sich', which is bound to confront man when and if he nihilates himself into non-being. Of more importance is our ability to translate the extreme participant Heideggerean conception of transcendence into our psycho-ontological context of Tantalic man, trying to realize the basic aim of his participant core-vectors to return to the boundlessness of his pre-being and projecting it onto divine nothingness. Heidegger claims that this process of the divine self-nihilation goes on incessantly without our noticing it in our routine, inauthentic everyday life.[43] Only in moments of authentic revelation is the divine nothingness of Dasein unveiled to us. Moreover, a failing god does not impede revelation. On the contrary, the failure of God, His non-being, and nothingness may help the voyagers, homecoming in and naming the High One.[44] The absence of God kindles the unquenchable Tantalic longing for transcendence, the way the quest for the realization of the unattainable aims of the personality core-vectors motivates man to act. The failure, i.e., the absence of God, thus makes for a continuous quest for Him which may enhance a Tantalic revelation. It may ever-recede like a fata morgana, only to reappear again da capo.

A dead, absent, or dying god is awe-inspiring and romantic. It has been dramatized by numerous myths, elegized by Nietzsche, and rhapsodized by Wagner. A silent god, however, is not romantic, quite difficult to understand, and even harder to accept. Dostoevski's god in *The Brothers Karamazov* remains silent throughout the Grand Inquisitor's monologue. He is even asked to remain silent, and, at the end of the encounter, he was told 'go, and come no more—don't come at all—never, never!'[45]

In Beckett's *Waiting for Godot,* not only does God not appear, He is incommunicado. He says nothing to those who wait for him. At times they thought they heard Him, but it was only the wind in the reeds. Lucky's cacophonous diatribe in the play contains some lucid passages in which man's personal God is described as being in the heights of divine apathia, divine athambia, and aphasia.[46]

Ingmar Bergman seems to be obsessed by the silence of God. This is portrayed in many of his movies, especially in *The Seventh Seal*, in which the knight demands to know God, that He reveal Himself and speak; but Death assures the knight that God remains forever silent. These random, yet forceful, portrayals of the silence of God may represent in context a participant religious disposition which projects onto God the Tantalic type's own passivity and quietism. This is in line with our thesis here that a Tantalic God, whose ideal essence is non-being, cannot manifest Himself and communicate with man. By remaining hidden, unattainable, and, therefore, incommunicado, God entices man to long and pray for Him. The longing in itself becomes the motivation of the Tantalic quietist. Per contra, if Godot appears, Dostoevski's Jesus remains in the here and now, and Bergman's God speaks up his message for humanity. Man will get used to these striking events, as the novelty wears off and they will be recorded and buried in Scriptures. Moreover, the Tantalic longing which kindles the fires of faith by becoming an aim in itself will be expended by fulfillment. The ever-receding aims of a Tantalus fuels his visions and his dreams. These are bound to degenerate into a slow contented slumber once his longings are concretized into possessions.

However, man persists in praying to a silent God. Beckett's tramps prayed to Godot, although he never seems to have noticed them. Bergman's knight of *The Seventh Seal* shouts to a God 'who must be somewhere, yet chooses to keep quiet', and the son-God cries to his seemingly non-responsive father-God *'Eli Eli lama shabakhtani.'* The supplication to a silent God marks the participant attitude towards the payer. It is mostly a tool to achieve revelation through the blunting of spatio-temporal consciousness. It is a contemplative means which may reveal oneself to one's innermost non-being. To this end a communicative God is unnecessary. A participant, contemplative prayer is marked by its self-sufficiency.

Beckett's two tramps in *Waiting for Godot* await the coming of God to no avail. Faute-de-mieux, they expect a sign from Him which does not come either. At the end of the first act they decide to go, but ultimately remain where they were. The same theme recurs in Beckett's *Mercier and Camier*, where the two tramps decide to go somewhere, but always come back. They intended to move towards a certain destination only to realize that they have no destination, that no promised land will ever be reached. And yet the tramps' waiting for God—for a perfection which never materializes—may allow them to hone their yearned-for ideal of perfection. For Beckett and for similar Tantalic participants, only the non-realizable quests like the unattainable aims of their core personality vectors can be perfect. When a longing materializes, it cannot be perfect, because it becomes tarnished with a deprivational object-relationship which is scorned and despised by the participant who is anchored on non-being. Godot must remain clandestine in order to safeguard his immaculate perfection. For a Tantalic participant, flawlessness can never be disclosed or embodied in profane space and time. Beckett, an archetypal Tantalus, renounces the manifestation of God and, thereby, reinforces the viability of revelation by a constant unquenchable search for Him.

Beckett's transcendental longing for the boundlessness of non-being permeates most of his writings. In *L'Expulsé,* the longing for the boundlessness of nothingness is expressed by a look at heaven from where help is to come, because there nothing interferes with boundlessness, no matter to which direction one turns.[47] In *Watt,* Beckett points out that 'the only way one can speak of nothing is to speak of it as though it were something, just as the only way one can speak of God is to speak of him as though he were a man.[48] There is hardly any randomness in Beckett's articulate and sophisticated writing. Hence, the relation between something and nothing is intentionally proximal to the projection of man onto God.

Beckett's characters aim also to obliterate their objective surroundings, so that they may achieve the pre-creation boundlessness of nothingness. Murphy aims to obliterate the outside 'big world' so that he may better cherish his inner 'little world'.[49] In his prose poem, *Lessness*, Beckett chants a haunting description of total ruin where everything falls apart, nothing stirs, and there are no sounds. Only an ash-grey sky mirrors blank planes of earth. Calm is reached with 'All sides endlessness earth sky as one no stir not a breath. Blank planes sheer white calm eye light of reason all gone from mind. Scattered ruins ash grey all sides true refuge long last issueless'.[50] This is a yearning for Nirvana, Bukhty, and Satori lumped together in an intense longing for participant non-being. Yet Beckett aims higher. He wishes to experience death in life. He longs for the total inaction, the nihilation of sense perception, and the blankness of death while being able to experience it in vivo.[51] To have the sensation of a living death, of being within nothingness, is Beckett's idea of revelatory freedom.

Another participant dynamic resorted to by Beckett is to try to negate his spatio-temporal surroundings, so that he may revert back to the omnipresence of early orality. In one of his stories, buildings disappear and whole streets change their location. The hero does not know which town he is in, and his view of reality is foggy and blurred.[52] In another story the hero enters an empty city. Trams and buses are without passengers. The port is quiet, and its vessels are stationary. Gradually he loses himself into a glowing emptiness.[53] This negation of objects and spatial surroundings is many times coupled by the obliteration of time. The two tramps in *Waiting for Godot* confound the hour of the day and night, mix up the days in the week, and confuse the number and order of the years. With spatio-temporality in ruins, the participant pre-creation nothingness engulfs everlasting boundlessness and projects it on the uniqueness of God.

Short of negating their surroundings, Beckett's characters aim to blot out their own cognition and self-awareness. This they try to obtain by endless repetitious rituals; by monotonous recitals of words and expressions like the cyclic utterings of the mantra in transcendental meditation or the chanting of the name of God by Muslim dervishes. The two tramps in *Waiting for Godot*, as well as Pozzo and Lucky, the other two characters in the play, many times spatter gibberish to blunt their awareness, and Lucky's sermon is mostly a regurgitation of stylized nonsense syllables to render one's cognition opaque. There are also non-communicative pauses, and the dialogue deteriorates into meaningless sounds. These acquire a rhythm of their own, and their function seems to be, like the repetitive prayers of the quietist Hasidim, to erase one's separate awareness, in order to facilitate the partaking in unity. Indeed, many passages in Beckett's works—especially in *How It Is*, *Poems in English*,[54] and the prose poem *Lessness*[55]—are exercises in the nullification of the meaning of language and the liturgization of its form. This is not unlike the decree of the quietist Hasidim that prayer should be devoid of meaning so that its formalized intonation may obliterate the awareness of the Hasid and elevate him to the gates of divine nothingness. The exile of language from its content and meaning is an apt negating offering to a silent God.[56] Beckett's nullification of language is a participant projection on an incommunicado divinity. We have described elsewhere the separant and normatively discriminant nature of language. Hence, by the trivilization of language and its fragmentation and meaningless liturgy, one may enhance the negation into non-being and the transcendental projection of partaking into divine nothingness.

Beckett's characters also seek, and often actually undergo, physical degeneration. They sink into apathy and lethargy and crave for the extinction of their substantiality. This quietist longing to cast off their corporeality, blunt their senses, and blot out their intellect are means to the participant yearning for the negation of the self and the partaking in the totality of nothingness. Winnie in *Happy Days* slowly sinks into a mound. Hamm in *Endgame* is stationary and paralyzed, and the Mouth in the play with the tell-tale name of *Not-I* is all that remains of a negated body and face.

Dante's *Belacqua*, who sits in purgatory in total passivity and spends his time in motionless inaction, is adopted by Beckett in many of his works. Murphy's body was quite stationary to begin with. He never left his rocking chair which was in a corner curtained off from the sun. Beckett describes Murphy's end as follows:

> Slowly he felt better, astir in his mind, in the freedom of that light and dark that did not crash, nor alternate, nor fade, nor lighten except to their communion. The rock got faster and faster, shorter and shorter, the gleam was gone, the grin was gone, the starlessness was gone, soon his body would be quiet. Most things under the moon got slower and slower and then stopped, a rock got faster and faster and then stopped. Soon his body would be quiet, soon he would be free. The gas went on in the w.c., excellent gas, superfine chaos.[57]

The negation of the body makes for freedom. It is the Tantalic liberation by communion with nothingness. Belacqua detests the dawn because it symbolizes nauseating birth.[58] In a similar vein, one of the two tramps in *Waiting for Godot* expresses a plaintive sorrow for being born. This brings to mind the quest of the participant in our model for the reversal of birth in order to regain the non-being of pre-Creation. Indeed, Murphy longed for an embryonal repose, which was the favorite position of rest of Beckett himself. Back to the womb and the regaining of the omnipresence of non-being seems to be the Tantalic aim of both Beckett and his characters. This quest is presented by Beckett as a possible way out of the impasse of being thrown into this world by an absent God. Moreover, in Beckettean metaphysics, Godot does not come. He need not come. He should not come. The longing for his appearance is enough to sustain divine revelation in the stale and fetid mires of spatio-temporal existence.

A form of religious thought, quite prevalent among mystics of various denominations, is that God is never silent or absent because he is ever-present in us and He reveals Himself to us through our innermost being. God is silent or absent if we seek Him outside us and in our objective surroundings, but is ever-present and communicative if we look for him within us. The foremost contemporary exponent of this view is Kierkegaard, one whose basic philosophical tenets is that 'God is a subject, and, therefore, exists only for subjectivity in inwardness'.[59] The extreme participant religious orientation of Kierkegaard is that each one of us is plugged through his subjectivity into the generalized subject, which is God. Hence, the seeking of the external object-bound God is sacrilegious. Only the pre-creation, non-objective omnipresence can be projected on transcendence as the totality of divine unity, which is disrupted, fragmented, and profaned by objective plurality. The only revelation possible is by inward renewal, which has nothing to do with changes in space or movements in time.[60] Whatever one thinks may be accomplished by being preoccupied with the external world, it is totally irrelevant for seeking God, whose presence can be revealed only within and through the unity of self-awareness. Kierkegaard does not deny the reality of spatio-temporality, but entrusts to God the concern with it.[61] Kierkegaard seems to envisage a division of labor—he would immerse himself in his subjectivity and seek God therein, whereas God Himself is to deal with the plurality of objects. As God has created spatio-temporality and the plurality of consciousness, He is the one to stir and control them—the individual is not fit or able to do so. This is not just another brand of egoism à la Stirner or Rand flavored by religion. Kierkegaard concedes his despair of comprehending the external world which should be clear to an omniscient God. All he asks for is to be able to sink into his subjective solitude and try to glean from within his innermost self some sparks of revelation shining through the darkness of his despair.

According to Kierkegaard, the effort to find God in nature and in other people is idolatry. God can be found only in one's inwardness.[62] The mediation of religious institutions, such as the church, the rabbinate, or the ulama between man and God is also sacrilege. Man's link to God can only be direct as a coincidence and as an identity of subjects. The participant Kierkegaard regards as paganism any separant seeking of God outside oneself. The Tantalic nature of the Kierkegaardean search for God is apparent in his stressing the process of longing for partaking in God and not its attainment.[63] Kierkegaard's place at the extreme participant pole of our continuum of gods is warranted by his statement that one may even despair of achieving communion with God provided one still craves ardently the inward reunion with God.[64] In this he joins Beckett and Dostoevski in the renunciation of the presence of God so long as the longing for Him remains. Kierkegaard's leap of faith constitutes, therefore, the renunciation of the world historic aims of temporal achievement as well as the waiver of the fulfillment by communion with divinity. Divine revelation through this leap of faith may still be sustained by the will, which is Kierkegaard's way of expressing the quest for an ethical, i.e., direct and inward, relationship with God. Kierkegaard hardly needs to project his subjectivity onto God because his inner self *is* God.

These are indeed instances of participant mythogenes having theophanic effect on and transcendental force over humans, although the deities themselves are presumed to be dead, absent, or silent. Hence, we shall try to substantiate our claim in the next section of this chapter that mythogenes are the metaphysical Ding-an-Sich, and our prime-mover since they need no emanatory source to imbue us with belief systems and activate us. On the separant pole of our mythogenic continuum the projected myths may be formed into ideologies which may be seen as secular religions. Even Marxism was denoted a 'secular religion' by Bertrand Russel, who made the following ingenious analogies:

Yahweh = Dialectical Materialism
The Messiah = Marx
The Elect = The Proletariat
The Church = The Communist Party
The Second Coming = The Revolution
Hell = The Punishment of the Capitalists
The Millennium = The Communist Commonwealth[65]

Our separant social character seems to be quite different from Mannheim's Utopian. The revolutionary who actually undertakes to topple an existing *topia* (social order) according to some wish-images embodied in an ideology is a utopian according to Mannheim's definition.[66] Our separant, however, aims higher. He wishes to achieve complete harmony between subject and object. This is a true utopia, literally 'no place' because no one has ever succeeded in attuning himself completely to his object, although the separant Sisypheans will always try to come to terms with their stones. Mannheim's utopia is a state of existence that is unattainable relative to the point of view of a given social order, whereas the separant's utopia is absolutely unattainable from any point of view, although he never ceases to strive towards it.[67] For Mannheim, utopias are spatial wish-images, whereas are chiliasms temporal wish-images.[68] Our separant aims for perfect atonement with the Other in both the temporal and spatial dimensions, when these two themselves are in harmony. It seems that our conception of the separant utopia is more in line with the conventional sense of the term as used to describe the socio-political structures dreamed up by a Plato or a Thomas Moore. These are the subjective visions of the separant projected on the object in an ordered schema which does not allow for any disheveling disjunctures between Ego and his objective surroundings.

This utopian vision is projected onto space at a point of time in the future, but the process leading to it is a dialectic. The present chaotic disarray is jostled to its antithesis by a conflictual quake. A stable state is momentarily formed, only to be pushed into another dialectical zigzag and so on, ad infinitum. This process must contain, as per the separant vision, somehow, somewhere in its fluctuations, the philosopher's stone, which will perform the alchemy of closing the rift between Ego and the object. Utopia is as necessary to the object-manipulating separant as his determined belief that he will eventually reach a modus vivendi with his stone. Sisyphus, the separant utopian, irrespective of his political label, releases his frenzied energies toward the object in order to mold it, with himself as visionary, into the Just Society, the Classless Society, or the Great Society. The participant, on the other hand, abhors history. For him, it is not a necessity, but a bondage. He aims to rid himself of the object altogether by destroying his awareness, which binds him to the concrete. His fixation on predifferentiated omnipresence makes him seek salvation in timeless, spaceless, unity. Says Meister Eckhart:

> Nothing so much hinders the soul as time and space. If the soul is to perceive God, it must stand above time and space! If the soul is in the act of taking a leap beyond itself and entering into a denial of itself and its own activities, it is through grace.[69]

This is the Tantalic leap of faith into the unknown and the unattainable, because without time there are no measurements and because without space no one knows the distance to salvation. Between inactive unity and salvation one has to pass through oblivion, but this in itself is a relationship and a sequence in time, so that we are back again at an insoluble paradox. The participant seeking salvation is a Tantalus chasing a fata morgana whereas Sisyphus, on the other side of the continuum, makes his rock look like a philosopher's stone of utopia.

There is essentially no intrinsic difference, for our purpose, between the various types of utopia described by Mannheim. The Chiliasts, kindled by a messianic outburst of revolutionary zeal, aim not towards the ever-after, but as in the case of their contemporaries the anarchists, make the present erupt into a lawless paradise. Yet this vision of the world to come is the projection of an ecstatic Thomas Münzer onto an activist God, who would surely give a helping hand to mold the object according to the exact specifications of the Chiliast prophet. In like manner, the anarchist utopia of a Bakunin is as paradoxical, contradictory, and chaotic as its author's mind. The liberal utopia is anchored in the evolutionary process of progress: The optimism of 'tomorrow is another day' and 'things do turn out to be better if one has the patience and perseverance to wait'. The Kiplingesque man projects his ifs onto the object and, eventually, despite all the trials, people, things, and beasts are molded into utopia, with Ego in the guise of Superman supplying the proper happy ending to nursery rhymes.

Here again we have separant mythologies guiding our lives with religious fervor and determining our actions with the metaphysical authority of secular belief systems posing as ideologies. Yet the mythogenes are the self-regulating and self-sustaining contents of their ideologies.

At this stage, we may anticipate critical reactions to our focus on religion as an anchor for the identification of mythogenic structures along our continuum. However, this focus is warranted both by theoretical considerations and empirical findings. First, religious affiliation has been found to correlate with many attitudes and modes of behavior as well as with the structure and contents of social institutions.[70] Religion is a significant identification tag, although many other social institutions, norms, and cultural goals are also relevant for our classification. Most of human history, to risk a sweeping generalization, has been related, influenced, and, at times, totally dominated by religion. The 'unchartered region of human experience', to use Gilbert Murray's apt phrase, is the domain of religion.[71] Although the areas of our positive knowledge are greatly expanding, most of the swift human journey from an involuntary beginning to an unknown end is governed by confusion and chaos. Consequently, religion has reigned supreme in human societies throughout history.

By having God create man in his image, man circumvents the injunction of the Judaeo-Christian Scriptures and other religious texts against image-making. Man created God in the images of his projected core-vectors, but in his religious dogma the process is reversed. It is God who created man in his image so that the never-attained projected goals of his personality core-vectors are being reinforced by Divine Will. Indeed, man cannot but project God in his image; as Xenophanes rightly said, if bulls and lions could discuss theology, they would claim that God surely has a bull's horns or a lion's mane. However, by having his divine projections boomerang back to him as his own image, he tried not unsuccessfully to have his cake and eat it too. God is the projected unachievable perfection of man's personality core-vectors which motivate both his separant and participant behavior. By returning the image of God back to its creator, i.e., man, a positive feedback cycle is initiated which ever feeds the human Sisyphean endeavors of creativity and their Tantalic yearning for revelation.

The theistic Old Testament God is the most celebrated example of the imperceptibility of a deity, the concretization of whom by a graven image becomes a cardinal offence.[72] This is also one of the bases of Philo's via negativa, conceiving God by attributes which he does not display.[73] Maimonides follows this via negativa and states that the negative attributes of God, that is his incorporeality, imperceptibility, boundlessness, etc., are his true attributes, whereas positive attributes imply polytheism.[74] This conception of God is highly relevant for our interpretation because the participant aspects of divinity are the negative ones of unsubstantiability, immateriality, and incorporeality which signify the predifferentiated early orality and even uteral state in utero. An individual fixated at this developmental period will project on divinity the non-physical and bodiless attributes of non-differentiation. In extremo, the participant metaphysical entity is even denied a conceptual reality. For example, one of the basic maxims of Taoism is that 'the Tao which can be spoken is not the eternal Tao'.[75] The personality-based equivalent to this extreme participant stance is Bergson's timeless and spaceless real duration of an individual's inner life which cannot be represented by images and even less by concepts.[76] On the other hand, once the individual being has been separated from the pantheistic mass of early orality and is surrounded by perceptible objects, he is able to identify and denote positively the apparent attributes of his multiple surroundings. Corporeal and embodied attributes of divinity represent, thus, the projections of the later orally fixated individual who not only concretizes his deities, but also relates them to his multiple surroundings and multiphasic experience of spatio-temporality. It follows that polytheistic gods tend not only to be corporeal and visible, but that their theophanies are defined and are bombastically expressive like the lightning and thunder of Zeus, the matchless skill of Hephæstus in shaping metal and Ares constantly waging war. The theistic Old Testament God had also some separant theophanys; He set Mount Sinai ablaze and made it quake.[77] He shone with dazzling light, and rays came out of his hand.[78] Per contra, for the participant deity the phenomenal world is a 'veil of maya' caching His reality so that a corresponding Tantalic personality like a Kierkegaard denies the direct accessibility to God. The visible and phenomenal world is deceptive and misleading insofar as it suggests a direct eternal link between man and God. This, to Kierkegaard, signifies paganism, and to us an object-related corporeal projection of divinity.[79] The participant's way to God is through his inner-self or his pure-self stemming from the lack of attributes of pre-differentiation. At that early developmental stage the pure-self and God were identical within a boundless unity. The differentiation of the separant self and the crystallization around it of an ego boundary installs for the Tantalic person the catastrophic barrier of space and time between himself and God. The participant Judaic mythogene projects over this barrier and, hence, creates an abstract God who is a word, a concept, or a meaning—and this coats all of creation with meaning as well. The original Greek of Saint John's Gospel states 'In the beginning was the word and the word was with God and the word was God'.[80] This means literally that the Judaeo-Christian concept of divinity is closely tied up with the abstraction of words or rather of meaning. In the beginning was the word, says St. John, and the word came out of God and God was the word. This indeed fits our conception of an abstract mythogene which is our prime mover and initiates creation including divinity and imbues meaning to things and to life forms. This would explain the enormity of the sin of Moses when at Mei-Meriba he smote the rock—like an Egyptian magician—and would not talk to it with the abstract logos which is the essence and the prime mover of the Judaic God. Moses resorted to the gentile praxis, to the separant Sisyphean action instead of to the employment of God's word which indeed is God. Hence, Moses was declared unfit to lead the people of Israel to the Promised Land (Numbers 20:12). The epitome of concretization and, hence, of idolatry and sacrilege of the Mosaic creed was the golden calf. Cattle imagery was most common in the mythogenic representátions of the Mediterranean basin. In Egypt, Apis the Bull-God and Nut, the heavenly cow, were front-line divinities; in Sumer, Enlil the Bull was the supreme God of fertility. The Bull was the title of the El, the chief Canaanite deity. In Minoan culture, the bull was the paramount deity and a sacred emblem. In Mithraism, Mithra was ever-portrayed in the company of a sacrificial bull, and the purificatory offering of the bull and the atoning bathing in its blood spread around the Roman empire through the Roman Legions, which converted massively to Mithraism. The golden calf was anathema and represented a stark and retrograde contrast to the revolutionary Mosaic conception of a Logos as a unique and abstract God. One hermeneutic version of the golden calf story even portrays Moses placing a gold calf in the Ark of the Covenant as a negative contrast to the tablets of the Law.[81]

Indeed, most of the Bible, and especially the Five Books of Moses, is ever-concerned with safeguarding the abstractness of God and its mythogenically unique Logos, in contradistinction to the idolatry of images and the sacrilege of the plurality of Logoi—the divine mythogenic epiphanies. One of the layers of the myth of original sin may be taken as an injunction against an epistemic knowledge of God, which is tied up with the Decalogue's injunction against a graven image. God as the mythogenic Logos should remain abstract and outside history. The dragging of God into history by a golden calf is as sacrilegious as His depiction by Michelangelo on the ceiling of the Sistine Chapel. The burning bush mythogene stresses the continuous presence of God within the here-and-now as well as in the ever-after. There is no need to bring, or rather steal, the fire à la Prometheus from one place, Olympus, and coney it over to earth. In a similar vein, Inanna, the Sumerian Queen of heaven and earth: 'from the Great Above opened her ear to the Great Below'.[82] This again presents an epistemic spatial communication from a place above to a place below. Not so in the Bible. God communicated with Elijah in 'a thin voice of silence', implying that a revelatory communication is an inner, non-verbal enlightenment.[83] The diachronic nature of Greek gods is apparent from Kronus (one epiphany of which is Khronos, time) swallowing its children. Indeed, phenomenologically, as Heidegger pointed out, in diachronic time, the past devours the future.[84] Judaic sacred time, per contra, is synchronic, since Jehovah (יהוה) in Hebrew means present and *Eheyeh Asher Eheyeh* (*I am/will be what I am/will be*), God's name as revealed to Moses in Exodus,[85] is a continuous present-future. Also, the word in Greek for world is kosmos, order, and its derivative, kosmetikos, is beauty/aesthetics. In Hebrew, world is olam, which stems from he'alem, which means disappearing or clandestine. The Maggid of Meseritz even interprets a verse from Job (28:20) to mean that wisdom comes from nothingness (ain). Finally, the expulsion from the Pantheistic non-verbal Edenic unity of early orality and the need to acquire the multiple denotations and connotations of language is the semantic layer of original sin which culminates in the mythogenic shattering of the uniform Logos into the confounding multitudes of the Logoi and meanings following the demise of the Tower of Babel.

Our few examples point out the rather remarkable link between the mythogenes of a given religion and the nature of its divinities as related to the participation-separation continuum and its correlated dimensions of abstractness-concreteness, diachronic-synchronic temporality, and the unitary non-verbal and multiplicity of symbolic communication.

The Münchausen Effect

We assume the conservation of mental energy to be not unlike the law of conservation of physical energy. Hence, if some of our mental energies longing to revert to our perfect origin in the wholeness of nothingness are sublimated into mythogenes which may effect a revelation, an enlightenment, or any other religious experience, the actual goal of negation cannot be achieved. Hence, the unexpended energy seeks again and again, in a Tantalic manner, to be reabsorbed in the totality of unity ad infinitum. Likewise, the separant quest to swallow the object may manifest itself in an endless quest for possessions, power, and status, in order to reach a creative modus vivendi with the object—yet these Sisyphean cyclic efforts can never quench the separant wish to absorb the surrounding objects and life forms. Therefore, the mythogenes motivating us to creativity are never relinquished. For a mythogene to emerge from the domain of the Logos—the realms of the abstract word—and be formed by a process of revelation as a structure to be transmitted in a maieutic fashion to the domain of energy-matter to effect a creation, it has to be authentic. Authentic longings and experience cannot be structured by a revelation into a mythogene, but will remain buried in our subconsciousness, be stored as memories, or emerge in hazy daydreams amid dim nightmares. The basic incompleteness and sense of lack and of insensibility of our ani-consciousness prods our longing for dialogue, which forms the abstractions of the word, which is structured by revelation into a mythogene which, in turn, is projected as a mythology, and ritualized as deities. These in turn are institutionalized as religions which transmit to their believers ever-new meaningful Logoi, which are structured through revelation as mythogenes, da capo. This Münchausenic cycle of mythogenes as prime-movers may be presented schematically as seen in figure 2.5. This Tantalic cycle is linked by homo faber, man the creator through an indirect maieutic resonance-trigger to the Sisyphean cycle of creativity. The latter is initiated by the mythogenic structure molding the potential of energy-matter into a creation or artifact.

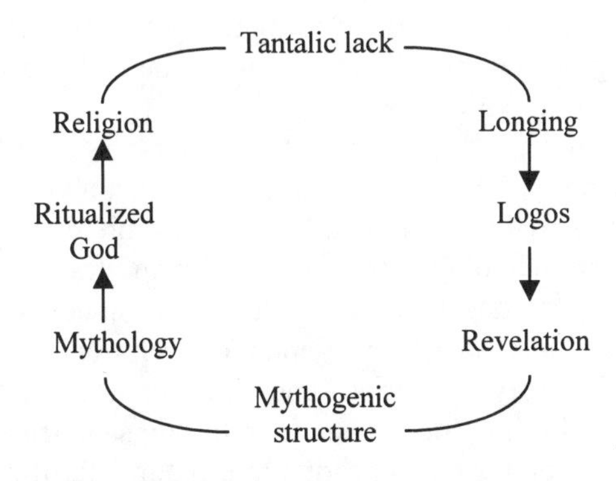

Figure 2.5

The Münchausenic cycle of the mythogene of revelation is outside history, and hence it has the mandala shape of a perfect circle. The circle of creativity is within history, and is hence time-bound and spiral shaped, as can be seen in figure 2.6:

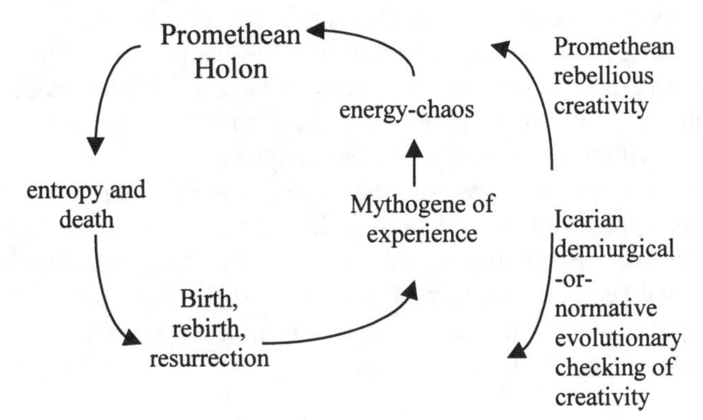

Figure 2.6

The chaotic energy-matter is triggered maieutically into the creation of a Promethean Holon, which is the creation or artifact formed with the revelatory mythogene as its model, which is not unlike a Platonic Idea. The Promethean Holon then decays and disintegrates, but it is recreated, or resurrected in a Sisyphean manner. This resurrection produces a mythogene of experience which, in turn, initiates a new link in the Sisyphean spiral of creativity. What is important here is that when the Promethean Holon disintegrates, dies, or is ritualistically sacrificed, it is sanctified, and the consecration is the generating dynamics of the experiential mythogene. This is why the human and animal as human surrogate sacrifices abound so much in mythology, from the sacrifice of Isaac to the killing of the Greek sacred king to the self-sacrifice of Jesus for the absolution of his followers.

To sum up this topic, which is so central to our present work, we point out that the uniqueness of man stems from his being a mythogenic animal, thus enabling him to create culture, and with it to replenish and reign over the earth. The importance of original sin is that man, through his hübris in structuring mythogenes has indeed become God, since the mythogene, being a self-sustaining structure, generates religion which in turn recharges the revelatory batteries and, hence, the myth-producing capacities of man. In the Sisyphean spiral, the sanctified mythogene becomes the trigger for further reproduction, natural fertility cycles, and artistic creativity. The mythogenes, therefore, are our prime-movers, which fuel our revelation and creativity in a continuous Münchausenic feed back cycle. Still, mythogenes of revelation and creativity can fuel us authentically, functionally, and constructively within the dual cycles of revelation and creativity. If individuals and groups insist on living myths directly and simplistically in the here-and-now, we may witness the tragic-comedies of the myriads of Don Quixotes and the disasters of the Nazis reenacting Teutonic mythology in actual history. Also, if these two mythogenic cycles of revelation and creativity are not linked maieutically and authentically by man, the basic dualism of being will remain disconnected with a resultant Gnostic belief system.

It is now time for us to see how man, the prime bricoleur, or linker, in Levi-Strauss's apt phrase, indeed links the mythogenic cycles of revelation and the Sisyphean spiral of creativity. This bonding role of man was conceived mytho-empirically as early as the Egyptian mythology in which man (Unas) was conceived as the link between the historical domain of Horus and the timeless realm of Osiris in the ever-after.[86]

The Anthropic Mediating Principle

The Weak Anthropic Principle (WAP) sounds tautologous and maybe it is. It says, roughly, that, if man is present in the universe, then the conditions and background factors must have been such as to enable his evolution. A more formal and precise definition of the weak anthropic principle has been offered by Barrow and Tipler as follows: 'The observed values of all physical and cosmological quantities are not equally probable, but they take on values restricted by the requirement that there exist sites where carbon-based life can evolve and by the requirement that the Universe be old enough for it to have already done so'.[87] The weak anthropic principle is a post-facto statement that, if conditions were different, e.g., if Pauli's exclusion principle did not exist and all Fermions could cram together on one orbit around the atom's nucleus, there would be no life as we know it. Or, as Hawking rightly observes, that the digestive tract from mouth to rectum would cut all animals into two if the world had two spatial dimensions instead of three.[88]

Finally, for life to appear, the evolutionary process needs time. It needs to be some billions of years old, and, hence, its explosive expansion from the original big bang would be measured by billions of light years.[89] The human life form, being the most elaborate psycho-physically, receives a very delicate and complex range of possibilities and structures in order to be formed and sustained. Even small changes in temperature, gravity, and the electro-magnetic equilibrium would prevent life from being formed, or destroy it if already created.

The Strong Anthropic Principle (SAP) states: 'The Universe must have those properties which allow life to develop within it at some stage in its history.'[90]

The SAP is not probabilistic, but rather categorical in its teleology. It postulates the evolution of life and man (the Darwinian vision of evolution must have been from the lowly amoeba to the British gentleman) as a necessary corollary and aim (telos) of the creation of the world. The SAP seems to imply a theological, theosophical, and, even, theurgical need for the creation of man. In extremo, the SAP is manifest in Teilhard de Chardin's teleological doctrine, according to which man is not only the irreplaceable goal of creation, but also its infallible end.[91] The Kabbalist theurgy also entails an SAP. The whole notion of the Kabbalist tikkun, the human mending of a blemished God, makes man theosophically indispensable. Idel says :

> Jewish theurgical anthropology strikes utterly different chords; the problem is basically the need of the Divinity for human help, or human power, in order to restore the lost sefirotic harmony. The focus of the Kabbalistic theurgy is God, not man; the latter is given unimaginable powers, to be used in order to repair the divine glory or the divine image; only his initiative can improve Divinity. An archmagician, the theurgical Kabbalist does not need external help or grace; his way of operating—namely, the Torah—enables him to be independent; he

> looks not so much for salvation by the intervention of God as for God's redemption by human intervention. The theurgical Kabbalah articulates a basic feature of Jewish religion in general: because he concentrates more upon action than upon thought, the Jew is responsible for everything, including God, since his activity is crucial for the welfare of the cosmos in general. Accordingly, no speculation or faith can change the exterior reality, which must be rescued from its fallen state. The metaphor of the shadow points to the reinforcement of the theurgical trend precisely by its strong delineation of the human and the divine; only by retaining his own individuality can the theurgical Kabbalist retain his cosmic influence.
>
> Man is, therefore, an extension of the divine on earth; his form and soul not only reflect the divine but also actually are divine—hence, the interdiction against killing a person. Its meaning is not the fact, emphasized in rabbinic sources, that man is a whole world, a world in itself, but that this micro-cosmos is a divine monad. Destroying a person is tantamount to diminishing not only the divine form on earth but, as this text puts it, divine power itself. Man is conceived as a source of energy parallel to, or perhaps even essentially identical with, the Divine.[92]

Thus, God is tantamount to the 'shadow of man' because without man, God could not be theurgically mended.[93]

A further step in the symbiotic relationship between man and creation is proposed by Wheeler, who expounded the Participant Anthropic Principle (PAP) as follows: 'Observers are necessary to bring the universe into being'.[94] This is in line with the Copenhagen interpretation of quantum mechanics, which postulates a necessary interaction between observer and observed in order to create matter. Wheeler, however, raises this quantum mechanical dyad to a cosmic level.

Ultimately, we have the Final Anthropic Principle (FAP) which states: 'Intelligent information-processing must come into existence in the universe, and, once it comes into existence, it will never die out'.[95]

We are even more extreme. We hold that ani-consciousness and energy-matter were always there as a basic duality. What is formed (whether by chance or by an intentional act is irrelevant for our present purposes) is the symbolon structure which links the ani-consciousness and energy-matter into an ever-evolving Promethean Holon. Hence, the constant kaleidoscopic interaction between the primordial ani-consciousness and energy is the mytho-empirical anchor of a self-sustaining triad—ani-consciousness, energy, and the symbolon structure—linking and constantly transforming them into endless spirals of creations, transformations, and evolutions. Man in this model is just an ad hoc intermediate symbolon-connecting structure, which might well evolve into as yet unknown and unpredictable heights or abysses depending on our value judgment. And this leads us to our crucial point. Our conception of the anthropic principle does lead to and allow for the formation of meanings, values, and norms. Barrow and Tipler rightly say:

> Although the Final Anthropic Principle is a statement of physics and hence ipso facto has no ethical or moral content, it, nevertheless, is closely connected with moral values, for the validity of the FAP is the physical precondition for moral values to arise and to continue to exist in the universe: no moral values of any sort can exist in a lifeless cosmology. Furthermore, the FAP seems to imply a melioristic cosmos.[96]

Indeed, our version of the FAP enables man to imbue his objective and biological surroundings with meaning, values, and norms.

Our stance is that an observer need not have been created for the world to be observed. He was always there in the essence of the ani-consciousness. The observed was also there as energy-matter. What was ever-changing, transforming, and developing was the linking agent between the two. The two polar components of our world are so starkly divergent in all parameters, that there could be no direct interaction between the two. Only when the first linking structure has been formed—be it by chance or intention—could the endless variations of objects, artifacts, and life forms be created. The holonic nature of our symbolon structures and Promethean Holons in the Koestlerian sense make for the transformation of symbolon structures into Promethean Holons, and vice-versa, according to the hierarchy of contexts in which they interact. Thus the symbolon structure, which has been contained in the quantum measurement instrument, processes a photon as a Promethean Holon (PH). A seed, as a symbolon structure, would produce a tree as a PH and an architect's design, a symbolon structure of a bridge, would produce a PH which will then be subject to natural selection, functionality, and evolution, like the seed and the measurement instrument. To date, there seems to be no more versatile, efficient, and durable synthesizer between the ani-consciousness and energy than homo sapiens. But this is subject to evolution, and, once man is dethroned and surpassed as a meta-symbolon structure, the anthropic principle would have to be renamed after this more versatile and durable connecting agent. Until this happens, the anthropic principles posit man as the most efficient meta-symbolon structure, integrating the ani-consciousness and the dimensions of space and time through his soma and psyche. Special relativity becomes, thus, linked to our conception of the anthropic principle insofar as it envisages space and time as observer anchored. Indeed, we regard space-time as engulfing the specific ani-consciousness of Ego within the context of his being a meta-symbolon connecting agent. The integration of space-time and consciousness within each individual is sui generis and peculiar to himself. Hence, the space-time-consciousness configuration of each individual is relativistic vis-à-vis the space-time-consciousness configuration of any Alter. This is not a Kantean conception of time-space as in-built mind filters. It is a relativistic conception of space-time as a manifestation of energy-matter containing in a holonic manner, the ani-consciousness reflected in each life form and artifact. Mytho-empirically this is projected in the theosophic Kabbala as the sefiroth, the ten divine rungs being a holonic integration of divine lights and garments.[97]

Here man is the most efficient viable mediator and integrator of the ani-consciousness and energy-matter (until the processes of evolution dethrone him), because his freedom of choice and his cognitive intentionality which lend meaning and values to his creative mediations.

We hold that all life forms possess varying degrees of freedom of choice. When an amoeba chooses to move in one direction rather than the other, this is an indeterministic decision. When a Bromeliacae seed decided to fasten itself onto a piece of dead wood which was barren and devoid of nourishment, it made an indeterministic decision with far-reaching evolutionary effects since it had to develop food absorption capacities through its chalice or become extinct. We have already elaborated on the crucial difference between the Buberian I-it artifacts, from quantum measuring instruments to computers with canned consciousness and no freedom of the will, and the ani-consciousness embedded in all life forms which do have freedom of choice. The most elaborate freedom of choice rests with man. He may choose to develop his creative potential following authentic experiences of revelation and, thereby, lending his own life meaning as well as imbuing meaning to his surroundings. Or he may choose not to develop his potential for revelation and creativity and, thence, be drawn into cycles of inauthenticity and alienation à la Tolstoy's Ivan Illich or like a Gauguin, but instead choose to stay within the cozy stifling bosom of fashionable, bourgeois tous Paris. This freedom of choice and its resultant meaningful inner and outer may lend evolutionary viability to our conception of the anthropic principle. Man as the meta-symbolon structure linking the ani-consciousness and energy-matter need not change his external environment in order to achieve optimal viability. He may achieve even better results by transforming the meaning of his surroundings and their evaluations of him, or—and this is equally effective from the optimal viability point of vantage—he may change his inner meanings and values and adapt them to the changing inner or outer situations and processes. Thus, man's ability to adapt and adjust meanings, values, and norms enhances his evolutionary viability as the meta-integrator between the ani-consciousness and energy-matter.

Mytho-empirically, this evaluation and the normatization of man is already extant in Genesis: 'And out of the ground the Lord God formed every beast of the field and every fowl of the air; and brought them unto Adam to see what he would call them: and whatsoever Adam called every living creature that was the name thereof. And Adam gave names to all cattle, and to the fowl of the air, and to every beast of the field.' (Genesis 2:19-20). This is in line with our mytho-empirical conception of God as the projection of the *ani*-consciousness which is normatively neutral. Hence man, the anthropic integrator, is the name-giver, the λογος endower, who is capable of lending meanings and values to his surroundings. We hold this name-giving to be an attempt by man as the meta-mediator to bridge between the ani-consciousness and energy-matter. Man may imbue meanings and values to his surroundings by creativity, by trying to mold objects and others in his own image. This he performs by implanting his contained consciousness on a canvas to be transmitted to generations of viewers or by transmitting his innovations to his student or colleagues, maieutically. In order to be effectively communicable the processes of creativity have to be authentic; then the symbolon structure carries the message and imbues the objective and living surroundings with meanings and values. But these are Ego's own meanings and values as conceived by him and as implanted onto his surroundings in a manner peculiar to himself. This stems from the fact that each individual reflects the ani-consciousness through his unique bio-psycho-social configuration. The uniqueness of the creator is thus paired with the uniqueness of the creation. Thus, according to Sumerian mytho-empirical sources, man was created in order, inter alia, to initiate the gods in creating further creations and preserving the system-in-balance of the cosmos.[98] Man, the creator, thus becomes God.

This, of course, is a mytho-empirical projection. There is no white-bearded God in heaven. Everything, all creation and transcendence, is inherent in the relationships between the ani-consciousness and energy-matter as mediated by the symboloi structures. When the latter is manifest in man as the meta-symbolon mediator, all creativity is an endless cycle or, rather, spiral of kaleidoscopic variations on the themes of Tantalus Ratios structured into symboloi integrating the ani-consciousness and energy-matter into Promethean Holons. These are perpetuum mobilæ of Sisyphean spirals, nothing more, but nothing less. However, every individual creator who aims to imbue meanings and values to his surroundings, through his creativity, implants his images into them. These would compete with the images (a mytho-empirical projection of individual meanings and values ingrained in creations) of other individual creators. These are jealous artists, innovators, and inventors, who wish to mold the environment in their own image. They are, therefore, projected on transcendence especially, in Greek mythology, as jealous Sisyphean gods.

Our personality theory, which serves as a basis for our model, was constructed along a continuum between the Sisyphean and Tantalic predispositions. We could envisage innovators, both revelatory and creative, at the extremes of this continuum. The Sisyphean tries to project his creative involvement with the object onto his burden-stone, in order to emerge from his inauthentic drudgery. If this creative innovation is too extreme, like Van Gogh's revolution in painting and Artaud's innovative view of aesthetics, he commits the hübris of rocking the social order, of deviating from the dictates of the ruling cliques in art circles. Societal reaction, in the form of stigma, is, therefore, furiously repressive. The creative Sisyphus, who then becomes a Prometheus, is censored by his father Zeus representing the normative system. Prometheus is then painfully bound to the rock and engages in his creativity in cyclic alternations of creation and misery, parallel to the cyclic trials of Sisyphus. At the other extreme, we have a Giordano Bruno or any other Tantalic virtuoso whose revelation makes him soar, Icarus-like, only to be exposed to the scorching light of the sun and to fall and drown in the sea. Tantalus, in the extremity of his revelatory aspirations, becomes an Icarus who fails to heed the warnings of his father, Daedalus, again representing the normative system, not to fly too high or too low. Icarus committed the hübris forbidden by societal norms, as expressed by the mandate of his father, and his innovation was duly punished. Figure 2.7 shows our mytho-empirical model:

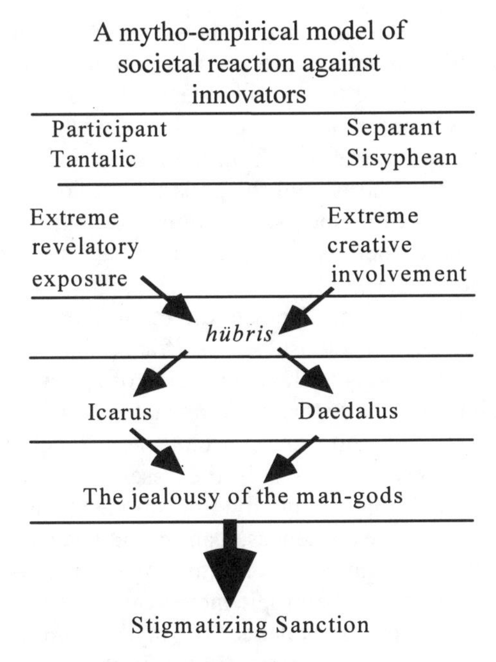

Figure 2.7

Both Sisyphean and Tantalic innovators try to extract or steal forbidden knowledge from transcendence. Sisyphus becomes the Prometheus who steals fire from the Olympians to give it to mortals. The Faustean myth is incorporated into the life history of most creative innovators like Galileo, Van Gogh, Artaud, Nietzsche, and Joyce, to mention but a few who paid dearly for their innovations. By infringing the prevailing norm of μηδεν αγαν or 'nothing in excess', the creative innovators commit the sin of hübris, of exceeding the means, modes, and medians and, hence of overstepping their moira—their lot in life. Their extravagance, which arouses the jealousy of the gods, is clearly a projection of the jealousy of man and kindles their wrath. The link between the normative system of a separant competitive society and the jealousy of its men-Gods has been insightfully expounded by Svend Ranulf in his study on the jealousy of the Greek gods and Greek criminal law.[99] If a creator is too extreme in his innovations and raises the jealousy of the competitive men-gods, then he is liable to be smitten by a stigmatizing punishment, be ostracized, and be driven to madness and death. The mytho-empirical cycle is closed: the rock of Sisyphus becomes the rock on which Prometheus is chained.

The rule of nothing in excess which dominated separant Greek religion seems to prevail in physics, evolution, the life sciences, law, and sociology. Guarding the middle values, the system-in-balance between the core-vectors dominating man's life reigns supreme in all areas of the Sisyphean regulation of life forms and objects. Social norms and systems of social control ensure that man does not deviate in his behavior, including his creative innovations, from the modes, means, and medians. If he does, he commits hübris, and the gods of creation who are inherent in the Gnostic concept of the demiurges, in the Kabbalist stern judgment, and in the existentialist hell as the other strike-back to keep the deviant (creative) innovator in line.

In a similar vein, but in an opposite direction, the Tantalic revelatory exposure to the ani-consciousness as transcendence also imbues meanings, values, and norms to the whole triad of ani, energy-matter, and symbolon structure as mediator. The revelatory dialogue (dia-logos) between man and the pure ani-consciousness lends transcendental meaning to man's existence. This is the essence of all religious and mystical experiences. Once my life is imbued with meaning by transcendental revelatory experiences, I am not alienated and I know my value within the Trinitarian configuration of ani-consciousness, energy-matter, and man: the Anthropic meta-symbolon. This phenomenon might be related to the prevalence of mytho-empirical Trinitarian projections in India, the ancient Middle East, and, of course, in Christianity. The evolutionary viability of meaningfulness is also apparent in the Kabbalist notion of tikkun. Man's theurgic function raises his stature and makes him a partner of transcendence; yet in this partnership lies an inherent danger.

The Tantalic seeker-after-revelation commits the hübris of wishing to become like the gods. This is precisely the kind of knowledge proscribed by Genesis. The Tantalic participant seeks not only to be exposed to God, but also actually to partake of Him and, thus, become God. Hence, the separant theistic God of Genesis proscribes the actual 'knowledge' of God, lest man also become God. This proscription also contains a separate mandate against a participant reversal to earlier developmental phases and non-being. In the actual myth, Daedalus, the father of Icarus, instructs him in the perennial way of parents: 'My son, be warned! Neither soar too high, lest the sun melt the wax; nor swoop too low, lest the feathers be wetted by the sea. Follow me closely! Do not set your own course', We can hear our own parents warning us from their experience not to jump too high, not to stick out our necks, to abide by the rules, to keep in line lest we be hurt.

Man is, therefore, no match for the power, arbitrariness, and cruelty of the gods, but he does hold a trump card. By being victimized, abused, and manipulated, he gains moral freedom, a mandate to imbue his own life, his surroundings, and, transcendence with meaning and values.

To tighten a loose knot, we should link the indeterministic choice of the ani-consciousness as manifest in man (or for that matter in other creatures) with meaning. This is inherent in the link between the intentional indeterministic choice of an act and its meaning.

The link between intentionality and meaning has already been postulated by Edmond Husserl, the founder of phenomenological existentialism, in his Cartesian meditations.[100] This link between meaningfulness and an indeterministic act of attention and intention, expounded, *inter alia* by Buber, has its mytho-empirical counterpart in the Kabbala.[101] Scholem says:

> In Lurianic thought these elements, under the name of *Kawwanah,* or mystical intention, occupy a highly important position. The task of man is seen to consist in the direction of his whole inner purpose towards the restoration of the original harmony which was disturbed by the original defect—the breaking of the vessels—and those powers of evil and sin which date from that time. To *unify* the name of God [emphasis in original], as the term goes, is not merely to perform an act of confession and acknowledgment of God's Kingdom, it is more than that; it is an action rather than an act. The Tikkun restores the unity of God's name which was destroyed by the original defect—Luria speaks of the letters JH as being torn away from WH in the name JHWH—and every true religious act is directed towards the same aim.
>
> ...But the doctrine of Kawwanah, particularly of the Kawwanah of prayer, does not stop there. To Luria, the heir of a whole school of thought in classical Kabbalism which he merely developed further, prayer means more than a free outpouring of religious feeling. Nor is it merely the institutionalized acknowledgment and praise of God as Creator and King by the religious community, in the standard prayers of Jewish liturgy. The individual's prayers, as well as those of the community, but particularly the latter, are, under certain conditions, the vehicle of the soul's mystical ascent to God. The words of prayer, more particularly of the traditional liturgical prayer with its fixed text, become a silken cord with the aid of which the mystical intention of the mind gropes its dangerous way through the darkness towards God. The purpose of mystical meditation in the act of prayer, and in reflecting upon this act, is to discover the various stages of this ascent, which of course can also be called a descent into the deepest recesses of the soul. Prayer, according to Luria, is a symbolical image of the theogonic and cosmic process. The devout worshipper who prays in a spirit of mystical meditation moves through all the stages of this process, from the outermost to the innermost. More than that: prayer is a mystical action which has an influence on the spheres through which the mystic moves in his Kawwanah. It is part of the great mystical process of Tikkun. Since Kawwanah is of a spiritual nature, it can achieve something in the

spiritual world. It can become a most powerful factor, if used by the right man in the right place. As we have seen, the process of restoring all things to their proper place demands not only an impulse from God, but also one from His creatures, in its religious action. True life and true amends for the original sin are made possible by the confluence and concurrence of both impulses, the divine and the human.[102]

Idel expounds the theurgic power of the kabbalist *Kawwanah* as follows:

The final type of mystical technique to be surveyed here is a nomian one relating to a particular understanding of the Kabbalistic meaning of *kawwanah*—that is, that intention which, according to the Talmud, should accompany the performance of the commandments. In Provence and Catalonia, the Kabbalists had already emphasized the mystical significance of such intention; it was no doubt connected to the theosophical system of S*efirot*, toward which the Kabbalist was to direct his thought throughout prayer. The basic assumption of earlier Kabbalah, which remained unchanged for centuries, was that the words of prayer were symbols of the supernal divine potencies and, hence, could serve either as starting points for the contemplation of high entities or as ways of influencing them, or as both together.

According to this understanding, kawwanah effects an elevation of human thought from the words of prayer to the sefirotic realm, apparently achieved without any intermediary mental operation or external factor. The intrinsic affinity of language to its sources in the divine realm enables human thought to ascend to the Sefirot and to act upon them. Externally, the Kabbalist is supposed to recite the standard prayer text—the mystical kawwanah is an additional activity, in no way intended to change the halakhic regulations of prayer. Mystical kawwanah can, therefore, be defined as a nomian technique, using as it does the common prayers as a vehicle for accomplishing mystical and theurgical aims.

When the righteous man intellectualizes his creator by means of his *kawwanah* and his performance of the commandments of God, he cleaves unto his God, as it is said: "But you that did cleave of the Lord your God are alive every one of you this day".[103]

These observations attest to the powerful effects of intentionality (Kawwanah) and the meanings of actions. Indeed the tikkun, man's theurgic mending of God, is the underlying meaning, value, and normative raison d'être of man's life.

Mytho-empirically, man was from the outset an integration of spirit and matter. The second chapter of Genesis recounts, 'And the Lord God formed man of the dust of the ground and breathed into his nostrils the breath of life; and man became a living soul' (Genesis 2:7). This in our model is the integration of the ani-consciousness and energy-matter within man. The basic primeval dualities of creation thus converge in man as their anthropic integrator. Thence, man (and other creatures) becomes the agent of incessant becoming and development through creativity. Man's core personality becomes the site or rather the arena within which the ani-consciousness intermingles with energy-matter to form symboloi structures—to trigger the incessant creation of Promethean Holons. Mytho-empirically, the Logos, the divine particle embedded within man is already, as stated by the Tikunei *Zohar*: 'A king imprisoned within the Tresses of the Mind'.[104] The Logos is, thus, the mytho-empirical representation of the prime moving participant and separant core-vectors which constitute the Tantalus Ratio, which in its turn fuels the symbolon structure. This Logos—the symbolon structure conceived through the intra-psychic process of revelation—is the trigger, the messenger, the Gnostic Christ, the Mandean—*manda D'hayye* instrumental in the creation of a new PH, be it a creature, an artifact, or a particle.

All this happens through man the creator. Mytho-empirically, Sisyphus is the archetype of the homo faber. He is the creative link between the universal pure ani-consciousness and energy-matter represented by his burden-stone. Without Sisyphus, the ani-consciousness has no means of interacting with the unruly brute force of the demiurgical energy-matter stone. However, the Sisyphean creative cycles are full of strife. The Tantalic revelatory visions are cursory and illusive, while the whole Promethean spiral of existence is characterized by agony and coercive resurrections. His has been ordained by the separant God of Genesis, who represents a mytho-empirical analogy to the Greek necessity, the universal principle of nothing in excess, coercing every creature, object, and astral body into a determined lot (moira) with the world order (kosmos). Having committed the hübris of original sin, which is the fate of every creative innovator, Adam is condemned by the God of Genesis: 'Cursed is the ground for thy sake; in sorrow shalt thou eat of it all the days of thy life. Thorns also and thistles shall it bring forth to thee; and thou shall eat the herb of the field; in the sweat of thy face shalt thou eat bread, till thou return unto the ground: for dust thou art, and unto dust shalt thou return'. (Genesis 3:17–19). These are the painful cycles of creativity, marked by agony and strife. We hold that these mytho-empirical projections of painful Tantalic revelations, frustrating Sisyphean creativity, the agonies of Promethean existence, as well as the strife meted on Adam by the God of Genesis, are mytho-empirical projections of the core dynamics of man's existence. Both the Tantalic participant and Sisyphean separant core-vectors are marked by a lack; by a deficiency, by an impossibility of achievement. The Tantalic longing for non-being is never achieved; hence, its revelatory efforts are marked by suffering. The Sisyphean quests to control the object are also unattainable; hence, the separant vector is also fueled by endless strife. Thus pain, suffering, and strife are the moving fuel of our existence and, hence, the prime means of communication and normativeness. But above all, pain, suffering, and strife constitute the prime movers of revelation and creativity. Therefore, the Tantalic agonies and Sisyphean strife are vindicated by such as Albert Camus, a true olympian who knew that this is so.[105]

Of special importance is the fact that Tantalus, Sisyphus, and Prometheus are all Titans, half god and half mortal. This signifies the mytho-empirical connecting function of man, the meta-symbolon structure between the atemporal ani-consciousness and historical energy-matter. A similar sacred-anthropic connecting mytho-empirical entity is the Kabbalist *Adam Kadmon Lechol Kedumim.* The archetypal man created by a dialectical process of expansion (separation) and contraction (participation) is the link between infinity—representing mytho-empirically the pure ani-consciousness and the worlds of creation (energy-matter). In Gnosis we have the Messenger who links the Father, an invisible infinity, with the demiurgical creation. The messenger may take many forms: it may be the *Eleleth*—Wisdom—'who stands before the Holy Spirit' and was sent to rescue Norea, the virgin daughter of Eve from the Archons of Unrighteousness.[106] He may be called Jesus Christ the Son of God; or he may be the Snake of Paradise. This messenger performed a specific errand for the God-head (invisible) Father. It divulged to Eve that she should defy the injunction of the vile demiurges (the creator God of Genesis) who denied his creatures knowledge (gnosis) and eat from the Tree of Knowledge in order to experience a divine revelation (knowledge) of the (alien) God Father.[107] This revelation would form, in our terms, the symbolon structure that would trigger the creation of a new PH (judged negatively by the participant Gnostics, who regarded creation as demiurgical and vile).

Our conception of the anthropic principle may shed light on the mytho-empirical centrality of the man-God in trinitarian systems. This centrality is apparent in Jung's survey of the many mythological and religious trinities as well as in the psychological force lent to Christianity by the archetype of Christ as self-image.[108] We hold that the man-God is more crucial to the existence and function of the dialectical Trinitarian systems because he is the vital link between transcendence and history.

The mytho-empirical projection of the ahistorical ani-consciousness is the Mosaic godhead: the abstract timeless entity which is outside of time in the continuous present. 'And Moses said unto God, Behold, when I come unto the children of Israel and shall say unto them, the God of your fathers hath sent me unto you; and they shall say to me, what is his name, what shall I say unto them? And God said unto Moses, I am that I am and he said, thus shalt thou say unto the children of Israel, I am he that hath sent me unto you' (Exodus 3:13–14). This is another of the many instances which demonstrate that the Bible should be read in the original, at least when mytho-empirical inferences have to be drawn. We have mentioned that in the original Hebrew the godhead is denoted as *Ehyeh Asher Ehyeh,* which connotes not only the present but also the future. Hence, the abstract Mosaic God connotes infinity. Indeed, verse 15 of the same chapter in Exodus specifies that this present-future name of God is '...for ever and this is my memorial unto all generations'. Hence, the universal 'pure' ani-consciousness is not only outside space and time, but also uncreated, external, and indivisible in its unity. This abstract monotheistic participant godhead should be contrasted with the Greek separant idea: form—something which one can see: eidon. This apparent visibility is concretized into a likeness, a separant image of matter, an eidolon (literally that which can be seen), which to the participant abstract Mosaic God is the sacrilegious graven image epitomized by the bio-morphic Egyptian gods and the anathemic golden calf created by the rebellious Israelites in the desert.

The mytho-empirical projection of energy-matter linked to the ani-consciousness by the anthropic mediator, God's prophet Moses, is presented in the third chapter of Exodus as follows: 'And the angel of the Lord appeared unto him in a flame of fire out of the midst of a bush, and he looked, and, behold, the bush burned with fire, and the bush was not consumed. And Moses said, I will now turn aside, and see this great sight, why the bush is not burnt. And when the Lord saw that he turned aside to see, God called unto him out of the midst of the bush and said, 'Moses, Moses', and Moses answered, 'Here am I' (Exodus 3:22–25). This is the revelatory recognition of the mediating anthropos as the integrator between God (the ani-consciousness) and energy-matter. Like the ani-consciousness, energy-matter is also eternal. It was not created and is ever-conserved. These eternal dualities are integrated through the anthropic observer, the prophet of God. These Sisyphean cycles, or, rather, dialectical spirals, are never-ending. God's prophet, the Kabbalist mender, and the Gnostic messenger continuously produce endless permutations and combinations of the ani-consciousness and energy-matter.

The burning bush which is not consumed is a mytho-empirical presentation of the self-sustaining cycles (or rather spirals) of revelation and creativity by the dialectical linkage of the *ani*-consciousness and energy-matter effected by the dialogical mediation of the observer. The latter, through the ever-energizing recharging of the core-vectors by the myths of experience and longing, becomes the prophet, the agent of God, as indeed Moses was. He was also admirably suitable for this role of the meta-symbolon mediator. He never achieved his longing to reach the Promised Land since God commanded Moses to stay on Mount Nebo from where he could behold the Land of Canaan, but not to enter it. 'Thou shalt see the Land before thee, but thou shalt not go thither unto the Land which I give the children of Israel' (Deut. 32:52). The longing of Moses which is not fulfilled becomes, like the Tantalic longing and Sisyphean quests of our core-vector, a self-sustaining force ever recharging our core batteries with unrequited myths of longing. Each creation, each PH is unique, like the uniqueness of each symbolon structure. They are unique the way each turn of a kaleidoscope presents a non-repeatable configuration. Yet all these unique Promethean Holons constitute the paradox of a plurality through unity, or of a plurality of physical eigenstates being observed by a unique ani-consciousness. Mytho-empirically this paradox has been man's metaphysical prime mover. In extremo, it led the Besht, the founder of the Hasidic movement, and earlier Kabbalists to declare that God is the shadow of man, Kierkegaard and Rabbi Nachman of Bratzlav to declare that they were spiritual emissaries of God, and el-Hlage, the Muslim mystic, to proclaim that he was *el Haque*, or the divine truth, for which pronouncement he was pronounced a blasphemer and executed accordingly.

NOTES

1 Martin Buber, *I and Thou*, 2nd ed., trans. Ronald Gregor Smith (New York: Charles Scribner's Sons, 1958), 1–2.

2 Ibid., 269.

3 Martin Buber, *The Face of Man* (Jerusalem: The Bialik Institute, 1962), 357–58.

4 Albert Camus, *The Myth of Sisyphus and Other Essays,* trans. Justin O'Brien (New York: Vintage Books, 1959), 89, 91.

5 Martin Heidegger, *Existence and Being* (Chicago: Henry Regnery Co., 1949), 27.

6 Gershom Gerhard Scholem, *Major Trends in Jewish Mysticism* (New York: Schocken Books, 1941), first lecture.

7 'The Gospel of Philip,' in W. Foerster, *Gnosis,* Oxford University Press, 82

8 Maggid, *Devrarav LeYa'akov* (Jerusalem: Magness Press 1962), 16.

9 Haim Vital, *Mevo-She'arim--Part 2*, ch. A. Cited in Isaiah Tishby, *The Doctrine of Evil and the Kelippah in Lurianic Kabbalism* (Jerusalem: Schoken Publishing House, 1942) 36.

10 Ibn Tabul, *Drosh Heftziba.* cited in ibid., 24.

11 A. Baumgarten, *Reflections on Poetry* (1735).

12 Shlomo Giora Shoham, *The Violence of Silence: The Impossibility of Dialgue* (Transaction Books, Science Reviews Ltd., 1983), chapter 6

13 Albert Camus, *The Fall* (New York: Vintage Books, 1956), 7–8.

14 Shoham, *The Violence of Silence,*

15 Asenath Petrie, *Individuality in Pain and Suffering* (Chicago: University of Chicago Press, 1967), 138,140.

16 Zuckerman in H. Eyensnck, *The Biological Bases of Personality* (Springfield, IL: Charles C. Thomas, 1967), 37.

17 Geoffrey Stephen Kirk, *Greek Myths* (Hammondsworth, Middlesex: Pelican Books, 1974), 49.

18 See the Egyptian *Book of the Dead.*

19 Claude Levi-Strauss, *Structural Anthropology*, trans. Claire Jacobson (New York: Basic Books, 1963), 216.

20 Lucien Levi-Bruehl, *Le Mentalite Primitive* (Paris: F. Alcon, 1922),

21 Shlomo Giora Shoham, *Sex as Bait: Eve, Casanova, and Don Juan* (St. Lucia: Queensland University Press, 1983), 182–185.

22 Shoham, *The Violence of Silence*,

23 David Bohm, *Wholeness and Implicate Order* (London: Ark Paperbacks, 1983),

24 Shoham, *Sex as Bait*, chapter 7.

25 Shlomo Giora Shoham, *Rebellion, Creativity, and Revelation* (Middlesex: Transaction Books, Science Reviews Ltd., 1985), 29.

26 Kirk, *Greek Mythology*, 292.

27 Karl Jaspers, *Psychology der Weltauschaunegen* (Berlin, 1919)

28 Martin Buber, *Eclipse of God* (New York: Harper & Row, 1952), 21.

29 Alexander Donat, *The Holocaust: A Generation After Jalkut Moreshet,* June 1976.

30 Albert Camus, *The Fall* (New York: Vintage Books, 1956), 116.

31 From an interview in *Ha'aretz*, Nov. 6, 1979.

32 Thomas J.J. Altizer and William Hamilton, *Radical Theology and the Death of God* (Indianapolis: The Bobbs-Merrill Co., 1966), 115–116.

33 Nathan Rotenstreich, “Alienation: Transformation of a Concept,” *Proceedings of the Israel Academy of Sciences and Humanities* 1, no. 6 (1963): 3.

34 Nikolai Berdyaev, *The Destiny of Man* (New York: Charles Scribner's Sons, 1937), 37.

35 Berdyaev, *Destiny of Man*, 33, 37.

36 Shoham, *Salvation Through the Gutters: Deviance and Transcendence* (Washington: Hemisphere Publishing Corp., 1979), Chapter 3.

37 Martin Heidegger, *Existence and Being* (Chicago: Henry Regnery Co., 1949), 339.

38 Martin Heidegger, "Remembrance of the Poet," *Existence and Being* (Chicago: Henry Regenery Co.), 223 *et. seq.*

39 Ibid., 263.

40 Ibid., 263.

41 Ibid., 264.

42 Heidegger, "What is Metaphysics?", 339.

43 Ibid., 341.

44 Ibid., 265.

45 Fedor Dostoevsky, *The Brothers Karamazov* (Harmondsworth: 1958).

46 Samuel Beckett, *Waiting for Godot: A Tragic Comedy in 2 Acts* (New York: Grove Press, 1954), 28.

47 Samuel Beckett, "L'expulse," *Novelles et Textes pour Rien*, (Paris: Les Editions de Minuit, 1958), 18. This theme was also developed by M. Megged in "Exile and Silence in the Work of Beckett," unpublished Ph.D Thesis, (The Hebrew University of Jerusalem, February, 1973), 235.

48 Samuel Beckett, *Watt* (London: John Calder, 1953), 74.

49 Samuel Beckett, *Murphy* (New York: Grove Press, 1957), 178.

50 Samuel Beckett, *Lessness* (London: Calder and Bayars, 1969), 11.

51 Samuel Beckett, *La Fin: Nouvelles et Textes pour rien* (Paris: Les Editions de Minuit, 1958), 88–89.

52 Samuel Beckett, "Le Calmant," *Nouvelles*, 49.

53 Samuel Beckett, *How it Is* (New York: Grove Press, 1964).

54 Samuel Beckett, *Poems in English* (New York: Grove Press, 1964).

55 Beckett, *Lessness* (London: Calder and Bayars, 1969)

56 Megged, *Exile and Silence* (The Hebrew University of Jerusalem, February, 1973)

57 Beckett, *Murphy* (New York: Grove Press, 1957)

58 Ibid., 252–253.

59 Soren Kierkegaard, *Concluding Unscientific Postscript* (Princeton: Princeton University Press, 1972), 142.

60 Soren Kirkegaard, *The Journals of Kirkegaard, 1834–1854* (London: Fontana Books, 1965), 127.

61 Kierkegaard, *Concluding Unscientific Postscript*, 142.

62 Ibid., 220–221.

63 Ibid., 121.

64 Ibid., 123.

65 Bertrand Russell, *History of Western Philosophy And its Connection with Political and Social Circumstances from the Earliest Times to the Present Day* (London: George Allen & Unwin Ltd., 1947), 383.

66 Karl Mannheim, *Ideology and Utopia: An Introduction to the Sociology of Knowledge,* trans. Louis Wirth and Edward Shils (New York: Harcourt, Brace Co., 1936), 192–93.

67 Ibid., 196.

68 Ibid., 205.

69 Meister Eckhart, "Schriften und Predigten," cited in Mannheim, *Ideology and Utopia*, 215.

70 David Clarence McClelland, *The Achieving Society* (Princeton: D. Van Nostrand Co., 1961),160.

71 Gilbert Murray, *Five Stages of Greek Religion* (London: Watts & Co., 1935),4–5.

72 Exod. 20:4.

73 Harry Austryn Wolfson, *Works of Philo Judæus*, vol. 2 (Cambridge: Harvard University Press, 1948), 382.

74 Moses Maimonides, *The Guide of the Perplexed.* (Chicago: University of Chicago Press, 1963), 207–8.

75 Lao Tzu, *Te-Tao Ching*, trans. Robert G. Hendricks (London: Rider, 1991), 51.

76 H. Bergson, 'Introduction to Metaphysics', in William P. Alston and George Nakhnikian, *Readings in Twentieth-Century Philosophy*, (New York: The Free Press, 1963), 61.

77 Exod. 19:18.

78 Habakkuk 3:4.

79 Kierkegaard, *Concluding Unscientific Postsript,* 219.

80 John, I.1.

81 This is discussed in *Encyclopædia Biblica,* Tomus Sextus, Heironymous; Institute Bialik 74–75.

82 Diane Wolkstein and Samuel Noah Kramer, *Inanna, Queen of Heaven and Earth:Her Stories and Hymns from Sumer* (London: Rider and Co., 1983), 52.

83 I Kings 19:12.(in KJ version - "still small voice")

84 Martin Heidegger, *Being and Time.* (Oxford: Basil Blackwell, 1967)

85 Exod. 3:14.

86 Ernest Alfred Wallis-Budge, *Osiris and the Egyptian Resurrection* (New York: Dover Publications, 1973),

87 John D. Barrow and Frank J. Tipler, *The Anthropic Cosmological Principle* (Oxford: Oxford University Press, 1988), 16.

88 Steven Hawking, *A Brief History of Time* (Toronto: Bantam Books, 1988),164.

[89] Barrow and Tipler, *The Anthropic Cosmological Principle,* 5.

[90] Ibid., 21.

[91] Pierre Teilhard de Chardin, *The Phenomenon of Man*, cited in Ibid., 201.

[92] Moshe Idel, *Kabbalah: New Perspectives*. (New Haven: Yale University Press, 1988), 179–80.

[93] Ibid., chapter 8.

[94] Barrow and Tipler, *The Anthropic Cosmological Principle*, 22.

[95] Ibid., 23.

[96] Ibid., 23.

[97] Scholem, *Major Trends in Jewish Mysticism*, 214–215.

[98] Mircea Eliade, *A History of Religious Ideas* (Chicago: University of Chicago Press, 1978), 59–60.

[99] Svend Ranuif, *The Jealousy of the Gods and the Criminal Law of Athens: A Contribution to the Sociology of Moral Indignation* (London: William Norgate, 1933).

[100] Edmund Husserl, *Christian Meditations* (Jerusalem: Magnes Press, 1972), 54–57.

[101] Buber, *I and Thou*, 269–303. (New York: Scribner, 1958)

[102] Scholem, *Major Trends in Jewish Mysticism*, 275–276.

[103] Idel, *New Perspectives*, 103, 47.

[104] Maggid, *Deverav le Ja'acov*, chapters 4 (Jerusalem: Magness Press)

[105] A. Camus, *Le Myth de Sisyphus,* Bibliotheque de la Pléiade vol. 1 (Paris: Gallimard, 1965), 195–197

[106] 'The Gospel of Truth' in Foerster,*Gnosis* (Oxford: Clarendon Press, 1974), 54.

[107] 'The Hypostasis of the Arachons' in Gnosis, 47.

[108] Carl Gustav Jung, *The Trinity*.

Chapter Three

Epilogue and Overture

There is no pain you are receding
Like distant ship smoke on the horizon
You are only coming through in waves
Your lips move but I can't hear what you're saying
When I was a child I had a fever
My hands felt just like two balloons
Now I've got that feeling once again
I can't explain, you would not understand
This is not how I am
I have become comfortably numb
I have become comfortably numb
Pink Floyd: 'Comfortably Numb' in *The Wall*

One doorkeeper always deceives.
The other is always truthful.

You can resolve the conundrum
by framing the right question.

If I were to ask your companion
which door leads to the treasure

what would his answer be?
You then choose the opposite.

But always itself is fallacious.
The golden tongued doorkeeper,

growing sullen, calls iron down
to give strength to his fabling days,

his austerities tongue-in-cheek

when they are not deadpan, and so

always hard to interpret; his partner,
growing adventurous, ties a twist

in habitual fact as one might improvise
rabbits from handkerchiefs, or project

onto a wall familiar or fabled beasts
made out of finger-shadows, truth

which had once seemed self-evident
wrapped now in Cretan complexities

becoming at best comical or grotesque;
at worst, too obscure for admission.

How then shall we know anything other
than what is tautologous for certain?

or pass through a thousand doorways
expecting whatever lies on the far side

to acquiesce in ours is not the case?
Are doorkeepers not also husbands, wives?

Can we be creatures of fact, inventing lives?
Building fables, be other than fabulous?
John Gohorry: Fallacy of the Doorkeepers

Listen!
Let me tell
you my dream.
I saw
a child driving the wind and stones as if through water.
Under the water were bounties
locked as kernaes are locked
in a rush of becoming.
But why did I sorrow like hymns
from the kingdom of famine
and tears?

Listen!
I'm calling you to recognize
my voice
I am your
prodigal brother riding
the stallion of death to find
the door marked destiny.
Adonis

No species remains constant: that great
renovater of matter
Nature, endlessly fashions new forms from
old: there's nothing
in the whole universe that perishes, believe
me; rather
it renews and varies its substance. What we
describe as birth
is no more than incipient change from a prior
state, while dying
is merely to quit it. Though the parts may be
transported
hither and thither, the sum of all matter is
constant.
Ovid Metamorphoses

O Lady! We receive but what we give,
And in our life alone does nature live:
Ours is her wedding-garment, ours her shroud!
Gregory Bateson, 'Mind is the Pattern that Connects'
in *Anthropos*

The Gate, The Guard, and The Smuggler

It is time to sum up, and in the manner of a Camusian Sisyphus, stoop, lift the stone-burden, and survey the rocky mountain for new tasks. We have to consider, in this final chapter of our work, how the insightful claim of Claude Levi-Strauss, to the effect that a myth is a link between nature and culture, has been applied to bridge the basic dichotomies between subject and object, between individual and the group, history, and transcendence.

Our mythogene is supposed to create the mediational structures between these divergent dichotomies. In order to do this properly, we must examine carefully the nature of the barrier between the discordant elements of these dichotomies. Next, we must examine the composition, function, and dynamics of the mythogenic mediation between the dualities. Finally, we shall take stock of our accomplishments, if any, and look for new fields, adjacent to our present one, to plough.

We envisage four major barriers between the developmental phases of man: the ontological barrier between being and nothingness, the existential barrier between pantheistic participation and the crystallization of the individual self, and the ethical barrier between normative non-responsibility and ethical culpability. Finally, there is the transition from life to death.

Schematically these developmental phases, and the barriers dividing them, may be presented as shown in figure 3.1.

The first barrier divides non-being and being. In Judaism, non-being (ain), is the potential of being. This stems from an interpretation by the Maggid of a verse in Job, which asks: 'But where shall wisdom be found?'[1] in the affirmative rather than the interrogative form. The result is that 'from where?', (meayin) becomes 'from nothingness'. Hence, says the Maggid: 'This wisdom is within reach of the worthy yet in order to reach it, they have to think that they are dust...wisdom is nothingness.'[2] Therefore, 'the purpose of man is to abolish...reality and to return to the mystical ayin (nothingness) which preceded Creation.'[3] The ontological transition from non-being to being by birth is registered, as we have seen, by the neonate as a catastrophe, which has its mytho-empirical projection in the Kabbalist cosmic disaster of the breaking of the vessels. The existentialist counterpart of this catastrophe is the conception of birth by Heidegger as a Geworvenheit zum tod, a 'thrownness unto death'.

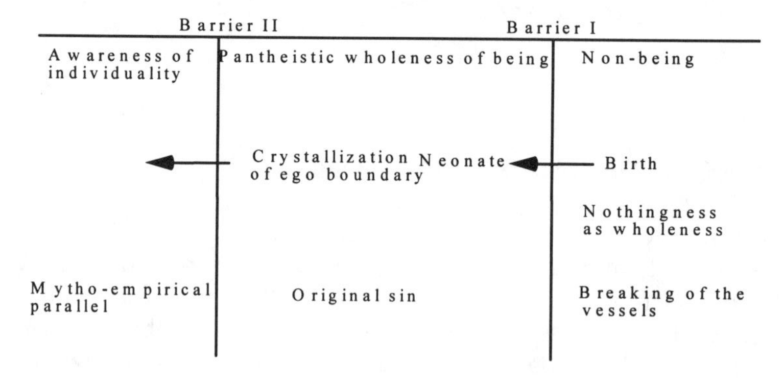

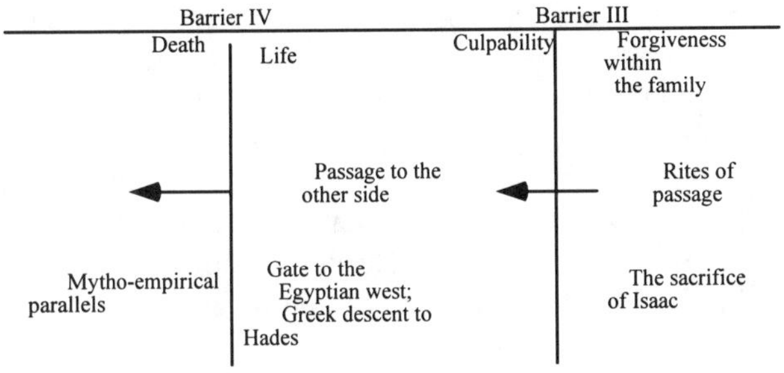

Figure 3.1

The second barrier bars the transition from the pantheistic togetherness of early orality to the individuality of later orality. Here the passage is registered by the infant as an expulsion, which is mythologically projected as an ejection from paradise. Indeed, the arrow of time points in a one-way direction of developmental growth; the way back is barred by the cherubim brandishing their flaming swords in every direction, preventing the return to the Edenic bliss of early orality. The enormity of original sin relates to the attempt of Adam to know God, or rather be reunited with Him, since *da'at*, knowledge, in Hebrew, is also union with the totality of pantheistic unity. This would have annihilated life, since creatures need their spatio-temporal boundaries in order to exist. Since the God of Genesis has created the world and its creatures as his magnum opus, therefore the annihilation of temporal existence and its reversal into the wholeness of pantheism is, indeed, a primal affront to the creator. We have dealt extensively in previous chapters with the normative barriers between the forgiveness of non-responsibility within the family fold and culpability outside it. The passage through of this normative barrier forced on us by our elders has been extensively dealt with by us while discussing the Isaac and Iphigenia syndromes.

The last transition, that from life to death, is massively documented mytho-empirically. Ancient Egyptian culture is almost totally based on a preparation for death, i.e., the passage from the domain of Horus in the here-and-now to that of Osiris in the west where the sun sets and the dead go to rest. The domain of life is separated from the domain of death by seven gates guarded by ugly monsters. They have names such as 'He whose face is inverted', 'He who eats the corruption of his hinder parts', 'He who lives on snakes', and 'He who cuts them down'.[4] The keeper of the door to the west, the domain of the dead, is Babai, alias 'He of sharp knife',[5] which brings to mind the cherubim guarding the gate to Eden with a turning sword of fire. In order to pass through the gates to the domain of Osiris in the west, one has to recite spells, manipulate the guards, and flatter and placate them with offerings.[6] Another way of convincing the gatekeepers to grant passage is to argue that one was sent as ambassador to Osiris by a god in the east, such as Re, Shu, or Tefnut;[7] better still, the supplicant claims to have a theurgical mission of mending the blemished god. This reminds us of the soul of the worthy in the Kabbala, which mends the less than perfect god, but in ancient Egypt, it was concrete, like the restoring of a gouged eye of Horus, which made complete the red crown of the deity and 'caused the plume to grow into the shoulder of Osiris'.[8]

In Mesopotamia, we find the transition from the world of mortality to the immortal realm of the gods guarded by the mountain Mashu. 'Its upper parts touch the skies' foundation, below, their breasts reach Arallu. They guard its gate, scorpion-men whose aura is frightfui, and whose glance is death. Their terrifying mantles of radiance drape the mountains. They guard the sun at dawn and dusk'. [9]

In Greece, Cerberus, the three-headed dog with a pelt of snakes, guards the gates of Hades, the underworld and the domain of the dead. Only Hermes, the professional border smuggler, was crafty enough to deal with the horrid Cerberus and safely conduct the souls of the dead to their abode in the underworld.

We shall now examine the barriers in the corresponding development, or rather formation, of energy-matter. Figure 3.2 shows the four phases of material existence that correspond to human development.

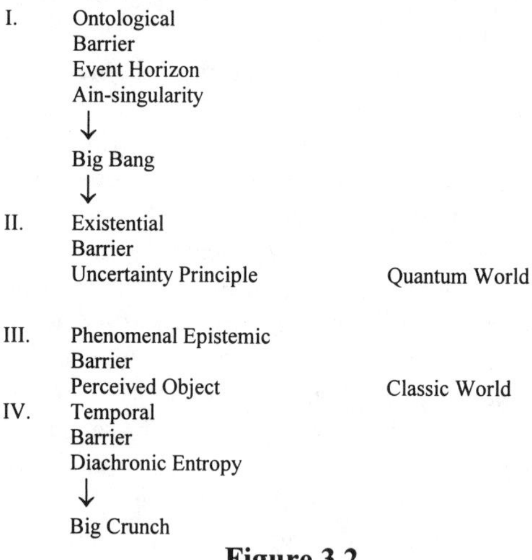

Figure 3.2

The ontological boundary of energy-matter is the event horizon, which is the boundary of a black hole. The singularity is situated within this region of super-gravity, from which even light cannot escape—hence, its blackness. The singularity is matter compressed into a region of zero volume, so that 'the density of matter and the curvature of space-time become infinite'. [10]

Mytho-empirically, the ain-nothingness, was conceived by the striking imagery of the Kabbala as the potential of the singularity with an event horizon around it, the initiation of the *tsimtsum* (contraction) by means of the creation of a round space and a concentrated point within it.[11] The potentiality of all the world's energy, as well as that of astral bodies, is envisaged by the contraction of infinity into a localized round space, *tehiru*, in which all the worlds have subsequently been created.[12] Describing conception of contraction by the sixteenth-century Safed School of Lurianic Kabbala, Scholem says:

> If, therefore, the Midrash says that, originally, the world was to have been based on the quality of strict judgment, *din,* but that God, seeing that this was insufficient to guarantee its existence, added the quality of mercy, the Kabbalist who follows Luria interprets this saying as follows: The first act, the act of tsimtsum, in which God determines, and therefore limits, himself, is an act of din which reveals the roots of this quality in all that exists; these roots of divine judgment subsist in chaotic mixture with the residue of divine light which remained after the original retreat or withdrawal within the primary space of God's creation. Then a second ray of light out of the essence of *en-sof* brings order into chaos and sets the cosmic process in motion, by separating the hidden elements and moulding them into a new form. Throughout this process the two tendencies of perpetual ebb and flow—the Kabbalists speak of *hithpashtuth,* egression, and *histalkuth,* regression—continue to act and react upon each other. Just as the human organism exists through the double process of inhaling and exhaling and the one cannot be conceived without the other, so also the whole of creation constitutes a gigantic process of divine inhalation and exhalation. In the final resort, therefore, the root of all evil is already latent in the act of tsimtsum.[13]

This is indeed a striking picture of the initial dialectics of separation (hithpashtuth) and participation (histalkuth) in forming both our initial symboloi structures as prime-movers, as well as the subsequent Promethean Holons.

After the 'contraction' of pregnancy, conceived by the Kabbala as vile *dinim* (stern judgment), in contrast to the hessed (grace) of non-differentiated infinity, a major catastrophe occurred, which to our mind, is the Kabbalist mytho-empirical projection of birth. Indeed, Vital expressly says that the death of kings, which in Kabbalist imagery is synonymous with the breaking of the cosmic vessels, is not real death but a descent from a higher to a lower echelon 'like a woman giving birth who also emits refuse'.[14] This conception of the breaking of the vessels as a mytho-empirical projection of birth is in line with some bio-psychological premises which envisage the experience of birth by the neonate as a catastrophe.

In the first chapter of *Salvation Through the Gutters,*[15] we showed that at birth the fetus is fully capable of registering the enormity of the shock of its expulsion from the womb, both bodily and mentally. In a publication on the psychology of childbirth, Leboyer describes the infernal experiences of the neonate during birth and just after it, thus:

> ...Hell exists and is white hot. It is not a fable. But we go through it at the beginning of our lives, not the end. Hell is what the child goes through to reach us. Its flames assail the child from every side; they burn its eyes, its skin, they sear its flesh; they devour. This fire is what the baby feels as the air rushes into the lungs. The air, which enters and sweeps through the trachea and expands the aveoli, is like the acid poured on a wound.[16]

The transition from the womb to the world is violent in all respects: the need to breathe instead of receiving oxygen directly from the bloodstream of the mother, the need to seek food and digest it, and the exposure to changing temperatures and hard objects instead of the constant warmth and cushioned, resilient walls in the womb. The expulsion from the womb is also accompanied by a period of varying intensity and length, of being squeezed and pushed into the rather narrow and inflexible birth canal which we mercifully do not remember, as a necessary defense against its intense bodily pains and psychic trauma, but is undoubtedly registered by our sub- or pre-conscious and projected, inter alia, as myths. The myth of the breaking of the vessels relates to the birth-giving mother and the ejection from the womb, whereas the myth of the scattering of the divine sparks, which in Lurianic Kabbala is a sequel to the breaking of the vessels, relates more directly to the neonate himself. The newborn feels himself as a precious particle of divinity, omnipresent and, hence, omnipotent, because at this stage of his life he cannot be aware of anything or anybody except himself. Yet, in his omnipresent egocentricity, he experiences a disastrous catapulting from blissful self-sufficiency into painful, troubled, and hostile surroundings which are not far removed from the mythical characteristics of hell.

It is also in line with the anthropocentric structure of the Kabbala that whatever happens in the divine realm has an immediate bearing on the temporal world and the fate of man. Conversely, the theurgic conception of the Kabbala considers every human act to have an immediate effect on divinity. This makes for a symbiosis between God and man. The less than perfect Kabbalist God, who is subject to catastrophes he neither foresees nor controls, needs man to mend (kabbalist tikkun) the catastrophe of the breaking of the vessels.

Furthermore, the nature of Lurianic Kabbala seems to be teleological; thus, it is less concerned with the catastrophic nature of the breaking of the vessels than with the fact that this cosmic catastrophe gives divinity a chance to cleanse itself of its polluted components and allows man to save himself while mending the blemished divinity.

It should be stressed, however, that Ibn Tabul, the second major disciple of Rabbi Isaac Luria, does not see the breaking of the vessels as a cosmic catastrophe unforeseen by divinity, but rather as an operation planned by God to cleanse Himself of dinim, the sinister elements within the infrastructure of divinity. After this planned breaking of the vessels, the theurgic mending (tikkun) by man will clean divinity of its vile residues. Again, a teleological theodicy of a catastrophe within divinity is concomitant with a mytho-empirical projection of the thrownness of man into temporality, because it gives divinity the opportunity to cleanse itself and man the opportunity to save himself.

We hold that the Kabbalist myth of the breaking of the vessels is also a projection of the birth of energy by the Big Bang—although its mytho-empirical projection is somewhat different and comes from another mythological layer than the breaking of the vessels, which relates to human birth. The Big Bang is described by Steven Weinberg as follows:

> In the beginning there was an explosion. Not an explosion like those familiar on earth, starting from a definite center and spreading out to engulf more and more of the circumambient air, but an explosion which occurred simultaneously everywhere, filling all space from the beginning, with every particle of matter rushing apart from every other particle. 'All space' in this context may mean either all of an infinite universe, or all of a finite universe which curves back on itself like the surface of a sphere. Neither possibility is easy to comprehend, but this will not get in our way; it matters hardly at all in the early universe whether space is finite or infinite.
>
> At about one-hundredth of a second, the earliest time about which we can speak with any confidence, the temperature of the universe was about a hundred thousand million (10^{11}) degrees centigrade. This is much hotter than in the center of even the hottest star, so hot, in fact, that none of the components

> of ordinary matter, molecules, or atoms, or even the nuclei of atoms, could have held together. Instead the matter rushing apart in this explosion consisted of various types of the so-called elementary particles, which are the subject of modern high-energy nuclear physics.[17]

We have seen that the Kabbalist myth of the breaking of the vessels is projected in a dual manner. One mythical layer, expounded by Vital, relates this cosmic catastrophe to a chance and, hence, to an uncontrolled, explosion more suitable for the projection of the Big Bang, whereas the other mythological layer expounded by Ibn Tabul, conceives the breaking of the vessels as an indeterministic self-cleansing act which is more suitable to the value-laden mytho-empiricism of human birth.

Moving further with the dynamics of human development and to the second existential barrier, which separates the quantum world from the classic one, we shall compare it to the coagulation of the separate human self out of the pantheistic mass of early orality and to the analogous creation of the Eigenstate of the separate particle out of the nondescript superposed energy. The mytho-empirical projection of these analogous processes is the expulsion from paradise and the fall from grace. After original sin, God condemned man to a cursed land in which he would live in sorrow all his temporal life. Psychologically, the pantheistic neonate learns through deprivational-interaction with his surroundings and, especially, with his mother or her surrogate who cannot fulfill all his wishes immediately and automatically as in the womb that he is not with everything, but against everything. The moment he becomes embodied in the scar-tissue of his delimiting individual ego boundary, his pantheistic participant togetherness gives way to the loneliness and the encapsulated existence of the human individualized separatum. This separation, the existential coagulation of the individual self, is also perceived by the organism as a catastrophe and projected onto mythology as the ejection from paradise following the original sin, which according to the Kabbala disrupted the equilibrium of all the worlds, both divine and temporal. The formation of the separate self, which according to our model occurs in the middle of the oral phase of development and marks the division between early and later orality, is not instantaneous but gradual. It is a transformation along a continuum, from a sense of partaking in a totality, to a feeling of separant individuation. Mytho-empirically, this coagulation of the separate self is envisioned by the Kabbala as a double process of Neoplatonic embodiment, from infinite divine light to the profanity of the body, coupled with a transition from grace (hessed) to the harshness of temporal stern judgment. This in our model is the mytho-empirical transition from the participant pantheism of early orality to the separant individuality of later orality.

Before the realization of creation and man within it, the light of infinity was boundless, eternal, imperceptible, and non-differentiated.[18] The motivation of emanating infinity in forming separate entities was to be able to confer grace onto them, because within the unity of infinity there can be no giving and no receiving.[19] Yet this divine emanation and formation of individual beings was also motivated by a desire to rule and dominate.[20] This might well be the mytho-empirical projection of the alternation at the oral stage between the graceful, nourishing good mother and the harsh bad mother withholding nourishment and care.

The embodied emanant matter are considered by the Kabbala as profane shells.[21] Moreover, according to Ibn Tabul, the differentiation of the emanent matter is effected by its swallowing of harsh dinim.[22] This alludes to the importance of the oral introjection of emanation in Lurianic Kabbala. It is stated expressly by Ibn Tabul[23] when he divides the suckling period of 24 months into three phases of 8 months each. Every life form and object in creation, as well as in divinity, is composed, according to the Kabbala, from endless combinations and permutations of ten rungs: *keter*, crown, which is part of divine infinity and has not emanated from it and is, thus, an emanating entity; *chochma*, wisdom, an archetype of divine masculinity; *bina*, intelligence or maternal divinity; hessed, grace or the goodness of God; *gevura*, signifying stern judgment or the sinister powers of divinity; *tiferet*, splendor; *netzah,* eternity; *hod,* awe; *yesod,* foundation, standing for the masculine components of the emanants, and *malchut,* kingdom or the feminine aspect of creation. Each rung may be likened to a holon, as conceptualized by the late Arthur Koestler to designate Janus-faced entities within a hierarchy.[24] Or better still, the holographic images of laser-based photography which are composed of endless combinations of the same images.

As for the formation of particles out of superposed energy, the mytho-empiricism of Lurianic Kabbala has the straight light stemming from the godhead as grace. Taking into account the participant bias of the Kabbala, this would stand for non-differentiated superposed energy. Then there is the refracting light, which has already interacted with emanant entities, and, thus, accordingly the Kabbala's participant bias, is less sacred and is already afflicted with stern judgment, which for the Kabbala represents vileness. The straight light of grace and the refracted light of stern judgment, which to us represent the participant and separant vectors within the connecting structure, then interact dialectically, in a process described by the Kabbala as 'blows' and 'thuds'. Out of their skirmishes the *reshimu* the coagulated particles of light are formed,[25] which due to the Neoplatonic participant bias of the Kabbala are considered as sinister and vile.

We have here the mytho-empirical projection of the coagulation of the separate human self out of pantheistic early orality, but also some layers of mythology projecting the encasement of particles into shells. This brings to the fore Penrose's quantum gravity theory which we have mentioned earlier and which envisages a general relativity dynamic which effects a space-time curvature around superposed energy to form an *Eigenstate* of a particle.[26] Also, the dual guardians, the 'cherubim and a flaming sword which turned every way, to keep the way of the tree of life' (Genesis 3:24), might well be the projection of Heisenberg's uncertainty barrier preventing both position and momentum of a particle or similar pairs of variables from being measured out of the quantum world boundaries. This brings us to one of the most important components of our model, namely, the barrier which exists between the quantum and the classical worlds.

At later orality a separate self has already emerged. A fixation on the early-oral pantheistic stage of development would result in a participant skewed personality longing to revert back to nothingness whereas a later oral fixation would effect a separantly skewed personality. The crucial point, however, is that a barrier separates a pantheistic totality from a separate individual. This barrier is necessary for the evolution of creatures. It is necessary for the formation of a feeling of solitude, of a lack and a longing for communication and dialogue. Finally, this barrier is indispensable for creativity and revelation. Consequently, the evolution of man as the anthropic mediator between consciousness and matter is dependent on the barrier forming around the individual. When the separate anthropos longs to reach the other life forms and objects, he becomes a revelatory Tantalus, a creative Sisyphus, and a meta-connecting Prometheus.

The analogous barrier in quantum mechanics cuts off the superposed energy from the classic level. Many problems in quantum mechanics stem from the inability of its exponents to decide where the superposition ends, and where to collapse the wave function. Where should we place the quantum barrier: in the observer's brain as not dismissed out of hand by Von Neuman or in the measurement instrument. We hold that the barrier lies with the measuring instrument. Once a particle has been detected on the classic level by the measuring instrument, the superposition ends, and the barrier between the superposed quantum world and the classic world has been established.

Passing over to the third barrier dividing the perceivable object from the non-perceivable particles, we shall compare it to that normative barrier dividing the individual from the social self. We have mentioned the processes of the formation of the social self, the rites of passage from adolescence to adulthood, and the painful expulsion from the cushioning family fold to the harsh and cruel interaction with the others as hell, to borrow Sartre's dramatic metaphor again. These dynamics of social separation imbue man with normativeness and, thus, make him capable of endowing meaning, values, and norms to the life forms and objects in his surroundings.

The strong nuclear force binds the quarks into protons and neutrons, and these into the nucleus of the atom. The strong nuclear force is short-ranged and strong enough to overcome the mutually repellent, positive charge of the protons. It is mediated by the spin 1 virtual gluons. The weak nuclear force has the opposite effect to that of the strong force. It disintegrates or dissolves fermion matter-building particles of spin 1/2 by radio-activity. The weak force is mediated by virtual vector bosons. The electro-magnetic force holds together the atom in a system-in-balance. The negatively charged electrons are attracted by positively charged protons. The electro-magnetic force is mediated by spin 1 virtual photons. A feature of this force which is most interesting to our present context is that the negative charge of the electron is mediated by a virtual cloud forming a field where vectors point inwards. In contrast, the vectors of the field surrounding the positively charged protons point outwards. The pointing outwards is a symbolic giving whereas the pointing inwards is a symbolic taking. If we compare this dynamic with the mytho-empirical Kabbalist imagery, then grace is participant giving whereas stern judgment is separant taking. To come back to our personality model, we should recall that the core personality is kept in a system-in-balance by the dynamics of the participant vector longing to revert back to the totality of unity of the pure ani-consciousness and the separant vector aiming to swallow the object and dominate it.

It should be pointed out that the four-fold division of the forces of nature (strong, weak, electro-magnetic, and gravity) is an artificial construct; except for the elusiveness of gravity, some successful attempts have been made to unify these forces. Abdus Salam and Steven Weinberg unified the weak and electro-magnetic forces. The grand-unified (gauge) theories (GUTS) integrated the strong nuclear force with electro-weak interactions, while Roger Penrose and Stephen Hawking have tried, not altogether successfully, to co-opt the gravitational force to this interaction. Still, if we accept Penrose's quantum gravity theory, the collapse of the *j* amplitudes function, which is a participant superposed state, and the creation of a particle Eigenstate, which is a separant concretization of matter, is effected by a space-time quantum gravity curvature.[27] On the macro level, the separant gravitational force mediated by the virtual graviton, which is responsible for the attraction of astral bodies, is countered by the participant centrifugal force. Still, even though the forces of nature have more separant and more participant aspects, all of them would be far removed on the separant pole of the participant-separant continuum in comparison to the rather chaotic participant force of entropy, which would be farther on the participant pole of the continuum.

The third epistemic barrier divides atoms, which are invisible to the human eye, from perceptible objects composed of masses of matter and is analogous to the barrier between individuals and human groups and aggregates. We have also described earlier the separant least interest principle, which prevents participation, since the reversal back to unity means the end of life. In energy-matter, Pauli's exclusion principle fulfills a similar function, since the participant cohabitation of spin 1/2 fermions would be the end of energy-matter. We have also mentioned that, mytho-empirically, this proscription against fulfilled participation is presented in the myth of original sin, where knowledge stands for the reversal to unity. The proscription of participant reversal in time is projected by the myth of Lot's wife, who was punished by being paralyzed into immobility, and the mytho-empirical proscription against the unification of language is presented by the myth of the Tower of Babel. The separant creator, the God of Genesis, protects his cosmos and the plurality of life forms and objects by the proscription of the contraction of space, the annihilation of temporal sequences, and the abrogation of the plurality of objects, representing a diversity of *symboloi* structures which secure the plurality and diversity of creation. We have also presented the need for a system-in-balance, the disruption of which destroys creatures and objects. And yet the innovative creators do commit the hübris of innovation and, hence, disrupt the system-in-balance and rock the boat of structural stability. They pay dearly for it: a Van Gogh, a Galileo, and a Giordano Bruno are martyred for their creative innovations, and Prometheus their mytho-empirical predecessor is chained to a rock. Their creativity is, thus, punished normatively by their sacrificial martyrdom, which is, thereby, infused with meanings, values, and norms.

The general theory of relativity tells us that gravity is responsible for the curvature of space, whereas entropy, as expressed by the second law of thermodynamics, decrees that in any closed system order tends to decrease and organization to disintegrate. Entropy, thus, indicates the arrow of time. The wrinkles in my face and the brown spots on my hands indicate to everybody, especially to myself, that I am over sixty and that I have a great future in my past. The system-in-balance between gravity and entropy indicates the integrated equilibrium between space and time. Space-time entails also a system-in-balance between the participant leveling of entropy and the separant encurving embodying and enclosing dynamism of gravity.

Penrose describes how the geodetic lines of the shortest routes, that of a positively curved surface would converge, whereas the geodetics on a negatively curved surface would diverge. Says he:

> Thus, our space-time, indeed, seems to possess a curvature analogous to that of our two surfaces, but more complicated because of the higher dimensionality, and mixtures of both positive and negative curvatures are involved for different displacements.
>
> With positive curvature the geodetic converge, whereas with negative curvature they diverge.
>
> This shows how the concept of curvature for space-time can be used to describe the action of gravitational fields.[28]

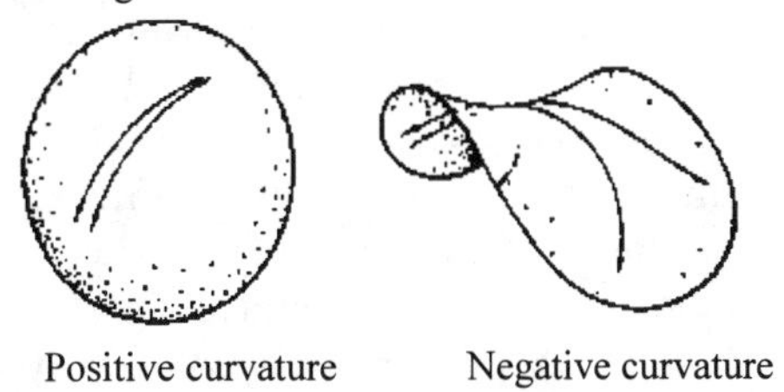

Figure 3.3 Geodetic lines on a curved surface[29]

This gives us a clue as to how gravity, effecting an elaborate process of space curvature, encases space around a symbolon structure in the process of creating a Promethean holon. The curvature of space through gravity as expounded by general relativity, thus, supplements the dynamics of special relativity which does not let matter escape from space by the limit of the velocity of light. Creatures and objects are thus encased within space-time as their viable context. Biologically, creatures can only exist within space-time. We have seen that Hawkings' two dimensional dog would not be able to retain anything in his two dimensional digestive tract, and that entropy and, hence, time, are of the essence in the developmental sequences of life. Space-time engulfs objects and life forms like the water in an aquarium, constitutes the essential life medium of goldfish, to utilize a crude metaphor. Entropy is a dynamic process, and so is time. Hence, the developmental transition from the Big Bang to the big crunch, from an ain singularity back to an ain singularity may be described, inter alia, by the thermodynamics of high and low entropy. The sense of time is also acquired through the developmental process of aging. The sense of the passage of time is acquired through our exterioceptors' and interioceptors' perception of our entropic bodily changes which could be reduced to energy-matter dynamics. The ani-consciousness is not subject to entropy and is, therefore, timeless. If we possess the right tools of introspection or mediation, we could sense that our ani-consciousness is as young or old now as it was when we were teenagers, adolescents, or infants. The ani-consciousness does not age because it is not subject to the developmental processes of thermodynamics generating the arrow of time.

Finally, we have to deal with the fourth temporal barrier dividing the decay, disintegration, and death of matter leading to another cycle, da capo, of life and death of matter, similar in a metaphoric sense to the growth, decline, death, and resurrection of life forms.

In chapter one, we have seen how the interaction between the participant and separant personality core vectors, which constitutes the Tantalus Ratio (TR) is the prime mover of human personality. By analogy, we have seen that the interaction between the canned ani-consciousness and superposed energy constitutes the prime mover and dynamic contents of the structure of the created particle. We hold that the human TR (and that of other life-forms) and the prime movers of artifacts and objects are structurally and dynamically similar and, hence, comparable to one another, except for the one major difference that the ani-consciousness of life-forms is indeterministic, whereas the 'canned' consciousness of artifacts and life forms is algorithmically deterministic. The analogic examination of the prime movers of objects and life forms is the subject of our present section. We shall deal, for didactic purposes, with these dualistic interactions out of their context because, in reality, they interact in endless holonic combinations and permutations both in life forms and objects. We have already mentioned the dualities of the basic forces of energy-matter and their comparability with the dual forces fueling human beings and life forms, but for clarity's sake we shall present the following two continua, the first relating to energy-matter, and the second relating to man as the anthropic connecting agent.

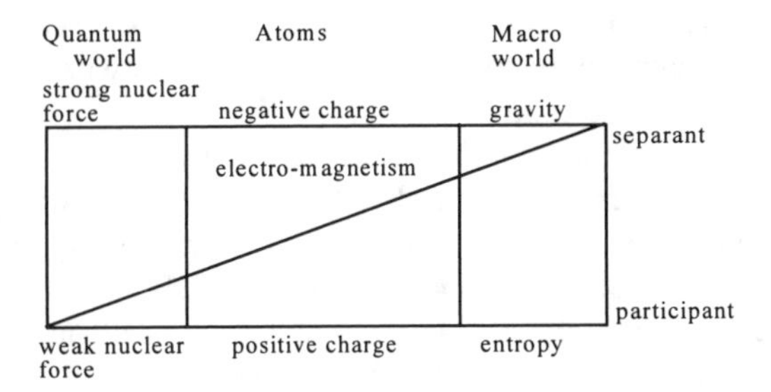

Figure 3.4 The Continuum of Energy-Matter

The quantum world contains the duality of the separant strong nuclear force binding and encasing the nucleus of the atom, whereas the weak nuclear force participantly decays particles by radioactivity. The analogous developmental stage on the anthropic continuum is the pantheistic early oral stage, at which the separant and participant core-vectors interact within an as yet amorphous and non-differentiated self.

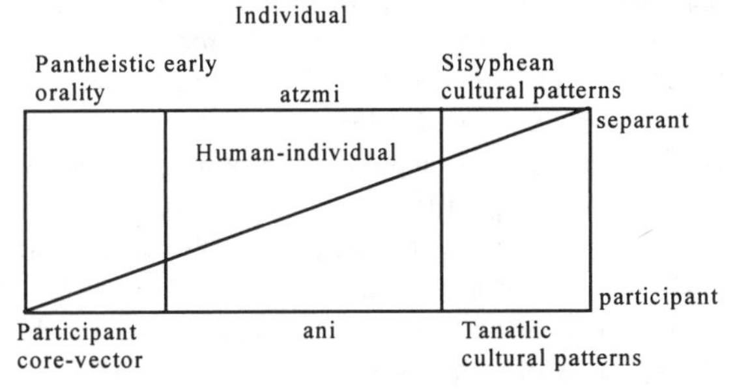

Figure 3.5 The Anthropic Continuum

The atom is the individualized unit of energy-matter held in an electro-magnetic system-in-balance through the separant negative charges of the electrons and the participant positive charges of the protons. The analogy here to the human individual is in the anthropic continuum, whose personality is held in balance by the interaction of the participant ani component of the self with its separant atzmi component. Both the atom and the human individual (or for that matter other life forms) constitute the connecting agents between the amorphic non-differentiated stage of their development and matter and human aggregates respectively. On the macro level, separant gravity delimits and encases matter, whereas entropy diffuses and disperses it. With human aggregates, the analogy is to the dialectics between Sisyphean and Tantalic cultural patterns to be at the basis of the developmental fluctuations of cultures.[30] We propose now to examine at greater length some of the analogies between the anthropic and the energy-matter continuums.

The most basic analogy lies in the fact that the creation of energy-matter was made possible through the disintegration of uniformities into imperfections and the breaking of symmetries into asymmetries. We have already mentioned Steven Weinberg's 'The First Three Minutes'[31], in which he describes the breaking of uniformities into diversities immediately after the Big Bang. Furthermore, a most lucid and concise description of this process is provided by Heinz Pagels:

> If we go back to the beginning of time, to the first moments of creation, the energy of the primordial fireball was so high that the four interactions were unified as one highly symmetrical interaction. As this fireball of swirling quarks, colored gluons, electrons, and photons expanded, the universe cooled and the perfect symmetry began to break. First, gravity was distinguished from the other interactions, and then the strong, weak, and electromagnetic interactions became apparent as they froze out of the cooling universe manifesting symmetry breaking. Exotic quanta like charmed particles decayed away, and soon mostly protons, neutrons, electrons, photons, and neutrinos were all that was left. After still further cooling, atoms could form and condense into stars, galaxies develop and planets emerge. As the surface temperatures of some planets dropped, complex molecules began to form the building blocks for life. Even in the evolution of life we see this process of symmetry breaking at work as organisms generally evolved from simple to more complex ones. Human societies, too, seem to become more complex as they develop. The universe from its very beginning to the present may be viewed as a hierarchy of successively broken symmetries—a transition from a simple perfect symmetry at the beginning of time to the complex patterns of broken symmetries we see today.
>
> At those immense energies at the beginning of time, life could not exist. Although interactions were unified and perfectly symmetrical, it was a sterile world. The universe had to cool and the perfect symmetries break before the complex interactions that gave rise to life could exist. Our world manifests a broken or imperfect symmetry. But out of that imperfection arose the possibility of life.[32]

Thus disruption, diffusion, and discrepancy mark the creation of energy-matter. Perfection and symmetry mark the potentiality of the singularity, which is the nothingness of the ain. The analogy to our anthropic continuum is the basic lack, the inability to achieve perfection which characterizes our core-vectors and which constitutes their prime movers. Both our Tantalic and Sisyphean vectors, as metaphorized by their mythological projections, are characterized by their inability to fulfill their aims. Hence, their unquenchable quests and unrequitable longings constitute their ontological fuel.

The basic asymmetry of the physical forces constitutes their prime mover because their teleological aim is to revert back to the unity of the singularity and to the potential equilibrium of the nothingness of the ain. Although the separant and participant forces function through diametrically opposed dynamics (telos), their aim (telos) is to revert to the potential of unity. This is the basic premise underlying the dynamics of our personality core-vectors. The separant vector aims to close the rift between the object and itself by swallowing it and achieving unity by incorporating the object or life form into itself. This goal, however, is not achievable. No power politics, manipulations, or creative molding can gain for the separant vector absolute dominion over the object life form. These attempts at dominion and creative efforts are projected as separant mythologies, and recharging the batteries of our separant core-vectors refueling them for further attempts at dominating the object and creating more art and artifacts. The unachievable goals of the separant core-vectors are projected as deities, perfections unallowable to mortals. These are, inter alia, the Greek gods and the separant components of a creator God, like the deity of the first chapters of Genesis. The participant core-vector, on the other hand, aims to achieve primeval unity by melting back into the object-life form. This goal is again unachievable, although revelatory and mystical experiences may give a momentary impression that it is possible. Hence, the non-fulfillment is projected as a myth of longing to fuel the participant core vector whereas the unachievable goals are projected onto religion as the abstract, unitary, and synchronizing God of Exodus ever immutable ehyeh asher ehyeh, I am that I am, in a continuous present. We have shown earlier that the TR, the contents of the symbolon structure which in its turn generates the Promethean holon, is indeed fueled and recharged by the mythologems projected by the experience of the separant vector and the unrequited longing of the participant core-vector.

Coming back to the quantum world, we have the strong nuclear force which binds together the particles that constitute the nucleus of the atom, e.g., protons and neutrons and are denoted as *hadrons*. However, a great proliferation of particles were discovered in the atom nucleus. The basic unit of matter within the hadron was named a quark, after a line from Joyce's *Finnegan's Wake* by the literate Murray Gellmann. These quarks were bound together by the separant strong force in a remarkable way which not only overcomes the mutual repulsion of the positively charged protons, but also confines the quarks in their prison bags with such strength that it is impossible to extract and isolate a single quark from the strong nuclear forces' grip. Moreover, the quarks within the hadron bag hardly feel the strong forces' push or pull. Only when the quarks try to escape from their demiurgical prison bag or, rather, straight jacket do they feel the confining potency of the strong force. A similarity may be noted here with the effects of fast velocities on space as decreed by special relativity. Low velocities have a negligible special-relativistic effect on space-time.

However, if an object approaches the speed of light, its time, for an observer, slows down, and its size flattens. As the speed of light would seem to be the archonic guardian of objects and life forms within spàce-time, so the strong force is apparently the demiurgical guard of the quarks within their hadronic prison. The quarks, which are also denoted by color (another measure of distinctness), are bound by gluons, which are also colored. These colored gluons interact not only with the quarks within the hadron bags, but also with themselves. This multiphasic hadronic interaction creates a strong force indeed. However, this very remarkable separant harnessing of energy-matter is far from the omnipotence which it seemingly aims to achieve. Beta-decay effected by the weak nuclear force causes the disintegration of a neutron into an electron which leaves the nucleus, while a stable proton remains within the hadronic core. On the quark level, the disintegration of a hadron like a neutron is mediated by the massive vector bosons ($W^+W^-Z^\circ$) which are the carriers of the weak nuclear force. The flavor of quarks—a differentiating measure coined seemingly in a moment of a poetic visitation or a culinary craving—may be 'up', 'down', and 'strange'. The weak force interacting with a quark may effect, for instance, a transformation from a down flavor to an up flavor causing an emission of a W vector boson which disintegrates into an electron which leaves the nucleus as an anti-neutrino. However, even the proton, the most common and most stable particle in the hadronic nucleus, is liable to disintegrate in a period of about 10^{28} times the age of our cosmos. Well time is an attribute of the anthropic agent interacting with the ani-consciousness and energy-matter. This is not the Kantean temporal filter in our minds, it is rather a quality of our conception of the anthropic principle as mediating between the ani-consciousness and energy-matter as a meta-symbolon structure. For the ahistorical ani-consciousness time does not exist, and, for the demiurgical energy-matter, time is meaningless. Both have eternity. What then is a mere ten billion billion billion years in which a proton may decay in the face of eternity?

The temporal proviso is important because on the scale of eternity all our universe will ultimately be sucked back by the big crunch into an ain singularity, which will explode again into a Big Bang to collapse again into a black hole, da capo ad infinitum.

These are the dynamics of existence observable both in the cosmological dimensions of energy-matter and in human societies. They are projected onto mythology as the cycles of creation and destruction of worlds and the death and resurrection of gods representing both energy-matter and life forms. If we come back to the weak interaction, it can affect the unstable baryons (the heavy ones stemming from the Greek βαρυs within the atomic nucleus), but does not influence the (historically) stable proton, whose life expectancy, we have seen to be about 10^{28} years. It also affects the leptons (Greek λεπτos = light) orbiting the nucleus, but not the electron itself, whose life expectancy is about 10^{21} years.

Since electrons and protons are the main building blocks of the atom, the decaying effects of the weak force are partial indeed. Hence, the teleological goals of the separant strong force and the participant weak force are partially achieved and partially frustrated, like the aims of the human participant and separant core vectors. The aims of these forces, viewed as absolutes, are not achievable, analogous to the goals of the human core-vectors as projected by the meta-myths of Sisyphus and Tantalus.

Turning to the atom, the basic structural unit of matter, we see its dynamic as a system-in-balance between forces: the positively charged electro-magnetic nucleus is balanced by the negatively charged leptons. Hence, the total charge of the atom is 0. However, what exactly is meant by a negative or positive charge? These are, of course, arbitrary notations, but represent an intrinsic variance. The positive charge lacks energy quanta, because it has given them out, whereas the negative charge has been taking in quanta. The negatively charged electron, thus, has an accompanying field with vectors pointing inwards, whereas the field accompanying the positively charged proton has vectors pointing outwards. The separant negative charge swallows or takes, whereas the participant positive charge is the givers. This is in line with our conceptualization of the dual structure of objects and life-forms and their interactional dynamics.

On the bio-psychological level, we have the female separantly absorbing and holding within her womb, whereas the male gives out participantly, injecting semen into the female. In chapter one, we have shown how the personality core-vectors are characterized by the separant vector aiming to incorporate, to swallow, whereas the participant vector aims to melt into, to give of itself, so to speak, to, the object life form. On the social level, we have recently completed a volume-length analysis of separant-Sisyphean carnivorous, aggressively martial cultures interacting with participant Tantalic self-effacing and normatively-sacrificial cultures.[33] We, thus, have an analogy between the separant-participant dynamics of the electro-magnetic force and the similar dual forces operating on the three bio-psycho-social levels of human and other life forms. On the mytho-empirical level, we have the Kabbalist hessed, which is a participant radiation, a giving out of grace, whereas din is an attribute of the separant depriver-taker. This analogy is replete with the attraction of non-likes and the repelling of likes, as phrased by Coulomb's law regarding electro-magnetic forces. This law states that, unlike electric charges, opposite magnetic poles will attract each other with a force inversely proportional to the square of the distance between them and proportional to the product of their force—producing electric charges or magnetic pole strengths. This is a special case of what we have denoted as the least interest principle. A separant personality type is repelled by another separant type, likewise a participant type[34] is repelled by another participant, whereas a separant type is attracted to a participant type, and vice-versa. However, the rule against the fulfillment of the vector goals puts a veto on a relationship that has become too close—love affairs peter out, friendships sour, and an I-thou dialogue deteriorates into an I-it petrification. We are not meant to reach a dialogical union for more than a limited, often a pitifully short, time. On the quantum level, Pauli's exclusion principle guards against too close a rapprochement between fermions. A too close human relationship gives rise to frictions which destroy the love, friendship, or dialogue, and, similarly, an overcrowding of fermions would play havoc with the structure of matter. On a higher level of abstraction, this injunction against a union or too close a proximity is a variation on the theme of original sin. We are not supposed to revert back to unity as craved and longed-for by our core-vectors. For life and matter to continue to exist, the distinctness of the atoms and the separate individuality of humans and life forms must be preserved—the alternative is disintegration, chaos, and death.

Finally, we propose to deal with gravity and entropy on the macro level. Due to its relative weakness, the impact of gravity on the quantum and nuclear levels is limited. Its most spectacular impact is in astrophysics and cosmology, as demonstrated by Einstein's general theory of relativity and more recently by Hawking's and Penrose's insights into the Big Bang and big crunch. We have already mentioned that, as early as 1928, Chadrasekhar hypothesized that a cold star of more than 1.5 times the mass of the sun would possess a gravity more powerful than the opposing Pauli's exclusion principle—hence, the star will collapse. Hawking demonstrated that this collapse would end up in a black hole in the center of which would be the singularity potential (our ain) surrounded by the event horizon which does not let most (not all) energy escape from the black hole.[35] The Sisyphean cycles of astral bodies, or for that matter of the universe itself as ordained by separant gravity, means that after a cooling of the gas explosively expanded by the Big Bang, some gravitational effects would produce irregularities in the expansion which would then effect a coagulation of astral bodies.[36] In time, as measured astronomically by thousands of millions of years, stars expand to red giants with a white dwarf in their center acquiring ever-larger density while sucking up the red stars' energy-matter. The white dwarf might cool and become a black dwarf—astral debris cruising insignificantly and invisibly in space. When the gravitational pressure is greater than the exclusion principle, a violent nuclear explosion could turn the white dwarf into a super nova. The explosion affects only the outer core, while the inner core still contracts and becomes a neutron star. The gravitational density of this mighty dwarf is immense. When it reaches the Landau-Oppenheimer-Volkov limit (2.5 Mo) and when the exclusion principle as applied to neutrons does not hold, the star collapses or, rather, is sucked into a black hole.[37] As the transition from the Big Bang to the big crunch is holonic, it applies both to individual astral bodies and to the meta-cosmogonical processes. The rather rugged representation of these cosmogonic transitions is presented by Penrose as shown in figure 3.6:

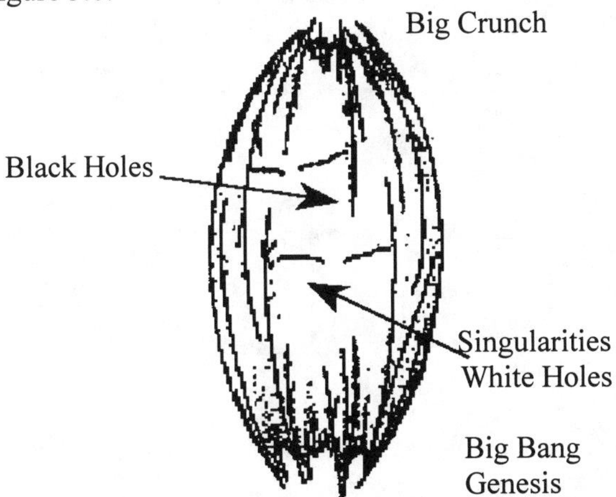

Figure 3.6[38]

The Sisyphean cyclic dimension of gravity is inherent in the fact that black holes re-explode into a Big Bang with the force of millions of H bombs. The separant spiral cycles of gravity may, therefore, be presented as a curved continuum as shown in figure 3.7.

This curved continuum shows us at the meeting point of the edges what we have described anecdotally in the previous pages, namely, that separant gravity not only does not achieve its goal of an absolute mastery over energy-matter, but is self-defeating. After it has overcome its most potent adversary, i.e., Pauli's exclusion principle, and presumably achieved mastery over its entrapped energy-matter, its trophy collapses into the nothingness (ain) of a point-singularity within a black hole. This is presented in the upper left point of the continuum where the separant cycle of gravity starts another spiral curve from the point-potential of a singularity. When we turn to entropy, on the participant extreme pole of our continuum, we may observe a similar self-defeating cycle. The high entropy radiation of the sun provides the means for photosynthesis, which sustains the flora that further sustains the fauna. The high entropic disintegration of life-forms and minerals provides the nourishment for flora which are consumed by fauna. The high entropy emanation of oxygen by plants allows fauna to breathe. The plant absorbs the carbon dioxide which is noxious to fauna, releases the oxygen, and ingests the carbon. Fauna then reverse this process into a recombination of carbon and oxygen da capo. This participant cycle of entropy is Tantalic because it is similarly self-defeating. A high-entropy participant process at the left-hand side of our continuum would be instrumental in producing a highly structured organism, whose entropic aging starts from the moment of its creation.

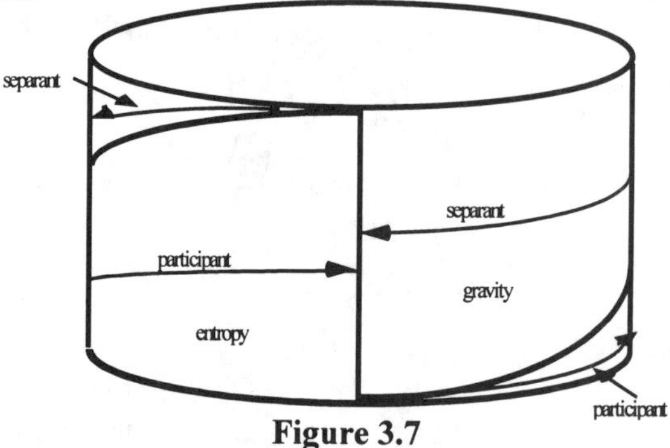

Figure 3.7

The analogy with human aggregates has been suggested by us in our recent study of the psycho-history of the Holocaust. In this study, we have shown that some participant experiences may push a Sisyphean social character to be even more aggressively Sisyphean. Likewise, extreme participant experiences of a Tantalic social character would effect a movement across the social character continuum towards a more separant reaction. Thus, the defeat of the Germans in the First World War—a participant experience—served as a dialectical lever for the ascent of the Nazis to power, whereas the Holocaust, a colossal participant experience, was instrumental in the creation of the State of Israel, which is quite power-oriented: as Golda Meir said, 'I shall never forgive the Arabs that out of the People of the Book (participants) they helped turn the Jews into arms merchants' (separants). This is not the place to go into these dialectics of the social characters, and interested readers are referred to our *Valhalla, Calvary, and Auschwitz*.[39]

Similar transformations on the social-aggregate level are taking place right now in Eastern Europe, but their examination likewise lies outside the scope of the present work.

To summarize our deliberations in this section, comparing the forces of nature and the forces that move man, the teleological aims of both the forces of nature and the core-vectors thereof are unattained and unachievable. This makes them not only the prime movers of man (and all life forms) and the fueling ding-an-sich of energy-matter, but also eternal. Energy-matter moves from the Big Bang to the big crunch, from singularity to singularity ad infinitum. Likewise, man is moved by Sisyphean cycles, never achieving his original ends, but undergoing creative experiences in the process which creates the separant myths that fuel his core-vectors da capo. Man's Tantalic aims are also not fulfillable by definition; but revelatory experiences recharge our participant core-vectors and feed our religions with Tantalic myths of longing. As our ani-consciousness is eternal, only our bodies rot away. We are endlessly reincarnated like Varuna, Mithra, Ahaswer, and the Flying Dutchman.

Another important analogy can be made between man's wish to revert back to earlier developmental phases, even ultimately to the non-being of unity, and the apparent striving of energy-matter, which is also ever-frustrated, to regain the perfect symmetry[40] at the beginning of time. With complete uniformity, there are no structures; with complete smoothness there is no differentiation. With no comparative information, there is a homogenous nothing. We have described in chapter one how the human being continuously wishes to revert back to earlier developmental phases: from the burdens of normative responsibility to the relative impunity of the family fold; from the loneliness of individuality to the pantheistic togetherness of early orality; from the deprivational interaction of being to the bliss of non-being in utero. The reversal to earlier developmental phases are, of course, impossible, hence, sublimatory processes might channel the participant longings and separant quests into creative and revelatory channels. For energy-matter, the initial perfect symmetry and the subsequent differentiation into forces and matter may be schematically presented as follows (figure 3.8):

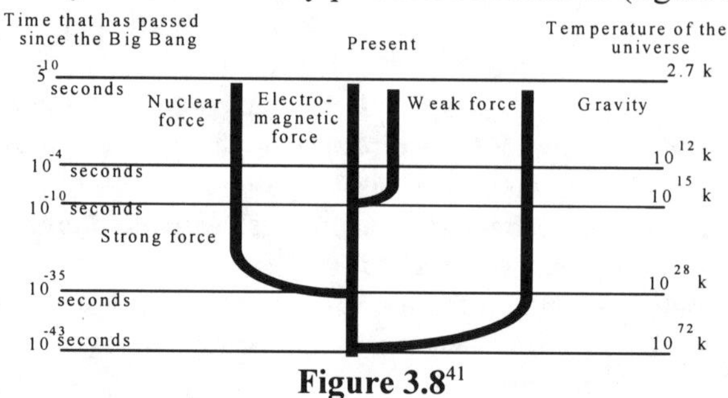

Figure 3.8[41]

By analogy with the human core-vector's quest to revert back to earlier developmental phases, we hypothesize a quest of energy-matter to revert back to the perfect symmetry at the beginning of time. Short of achieving this ultimate goal, energy-matter sublimates by ever striving to achieve symmetry after it has been spontaneously or purposely broken. It is, therefore, hardly surprising that some of the most revolutionary theories in modern physics are related to a mathematical restructuring of broken symmetries. These gauge symmetry transformations are responsible for the unification of electro-magnetism and the weak force noted by Weinberg and Abdus-Salam. They claimed that a spontaneous breaking of a symmetry invariance was at the base of the differentiation between the electro-magnetic and the weak forces. In the symmetrical invariance, all four bosons mediating the electro-magnetism and the weak interaction were massless. After the breaking of the symmetry, the photon-mediating electro-magnetism remained massless, but the three particles mediating the weak force (W+ W- Z°) acquired a large mass. The catalyst which triggered the spontaneous breaking of the symmetry was denoted the Higgs particle after its discoverer. It is important to point out that the Weinberg-Salam unification of the electro-magnetic and weak forces was made possible by Yang and Mills who developed the measurement criteria (gauges) by which to provide a complementary field to the broken symmetry in order to restore invariance.

The Yang-Mills gauge symmetry restoration principle has also been applied to the strong nuclear force. This gauge symmetrical theory, developed by Gellmann and Fritzch and denoted as quantum chromo-dynamics, relates to quarks and their color charges. These color charges were red, blue, and yellow: the three primary colors. If rotated these three primary colors achieved the invariant colorless symmetry of white. According to the gauge symmetry of quantum chromodynamics, all three quarks constituting the hadron have color charges. The quarks are glued together by boson power particles named gluons. This is effected by the eight color-carrying gluons that interact with the three quarks inside the hadrons as well as with themselves. The gauge symmetry invariance is restored here by the gluons. When a quark emits a colored gluon and thereby changes its color, it also breaks the symmetry of the (white) colorless invariance of the whole hadron, due to the complementary rotation of the three basic colors (red, blue, and yellow) of the three quarks. This broken symmetry is immediately restored by another quark within the hadron, absorbing the colored gluon and changing its own color in a complementary manner, which would restore a colorless symmetry to the hadron. An important point here is that whereas the breaking of symmetry in quantum electro-dynamics is spontaneous, the breaking and restoration of quantum-chromo-dynamics is hidden. There is no way to pry open a hadron and measure the charges of individual quarks.

Gauge symmetries have been applied in an attempt to transform bosons (power particles) into fermions (matter particles). This attempt has been denoted as the supersymmetry of grand unification theories (Susy Gut). The particle-antiparticle duality may also be related to a symmetry breaking restoration context. Dirac's original conceptualization of the particle-antiparticle relationship was anchored on the imagery of a sea of negative energy electrons in a vacuum. When a high energy photon hits one of the negative energy electrons it infuses it with energy so that it flies up excitedly filled with positive energy. What remains in the sea of negative energy electrons in the place of the electron which was excited out of its place and injected with positive energy is a hole. This hole is a lack, an absence of a negatively charged particle with negative energy. Two negatives make a positive and indeed this hole is a positron, the electron's antiparticle. Schematically, this may be presented as follows:

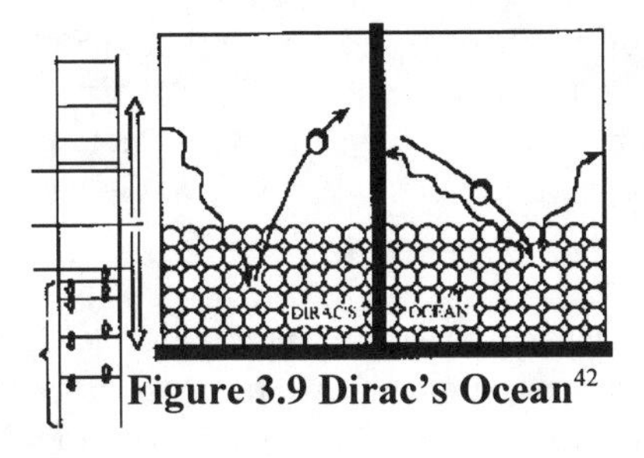

Figure 3.9 Dirac's Ocean[42]

This is clearly a breaking of the symmetry with the lack, the hole, wishing to be filled up again by a restoration of the symmetry; yet this longing of the electron and positron to reunite, to fill up the asymmetrical hole, is a self-defeating venture. When the electron and its anti-particle, the positron, meet, they annihilate each other, and the photon is emitted back into infinity. One moral of the story is that the fulfillment of a quest means annihilation and death. This could provide one clue to the fact that our participant longings and Sisyphean quests are never fulfilled, so that the processes of creation and revelation are endless. In a similar vein, the dialectical breaking and restoration of symmetries in the realm of energy-matter are also endless, in ever-recurring Sisyphean and Tantalic cycles. The Flying Dutchman is ever reincarnated, and the quest for a transformation from the karma of the samsara wheel to the Nirvana of a Mandala are unrealizable dreams. Mytho-empirically, this is projected by Lurianic Kabbala as the inability to achieve a complete tikkun, a complete mending of the rift between man and transcendence. The breaking of the vessels was the initial cosmic catastrophe catapulting man as a particle of divinity away from his sacred source. Thence, the efforts of man to mend a blemished God (and himself) by the manufacture of grace was again thwarted by original sin. Yet Sisyphus, Tantalus, and Prometheus stooped down, lifted their worn-out tools, and started to mend the injured God-man—only to be hurled back to the abyss by the sin of the golden calf. These alternations of grace-stern-judgment are endless and will continue ad infinitum. We shall never, states Haim Vital stoically in his *Etz-Haim*, achieve complete tikkun.[43] The dialectical spiral of the anthropic connecting agent effecting endless cycles of creativity and revelation by linking together the ani-consciousness and energy-matter will never cease. This is the thing-in-itself, the only reality; it is all there is.

As for the mytho-empirical evidence for the macro processes leading from the Big Bang to the big crunch and back to a resurrected genesis, there is an abundance of choices from almost every culture. We shall choose two representative myths—one from a participant, Tantalic culture and the other from a separant, Sisyphean one. The first is none other than the biblical myth of the Flood which has many counterparts in ancient Mid-eastern mythologies. Chapters 6, 7, and 8 of Genesis state, inter alia, as follows:

> 6:5.And God saw that the wickedness of man was great in the earth, and that every imagination of the thoughts of his heart was only evil continually.
> 6:6.And it repented the Lord that he had made man on the earth, and it grieved him at his heart.

6:7.And the Lord said, 'I will destroy man whom I have created from the face of the earth; both man, and beast, and the creeping thing, and the fowls of the air; for it repenteth me that I have made them.'
6:8.But Noah found grace in the eyes of the Lord.
6:13.And God said unto Noah, 'The end of all flesh is come before me; for the earth is filled with violence through them; and, behold, I will destroy them with the earth.
6:14. 'Make thee an ark of gopher wood; rooms shalt thou make in the ark, and shall pitch it within and without with pitch.
6:18. 'But with thee will I establish my covenant; and thou shalt come into the ark, thou, and thy sons, and thy wife, and thy sons' wives with thee.
6:19. 'And of every living thing of all flesh, two of every sort shalt thou bring into the ark, to keep them alive with thee; they shall be male and female.
7:4. 'For yet seven days, and I will cause it to rain upon the earth forty days and forty nights; and every living substance that I have made will I destroy from off the face of the earth.'
7:9.There went in two and two unto Noah into the ark, the male and the female, as God had commanded Noah.
7:21.And all flesh died that moved upon the earth, both of fowl, and of cattle, and of beast, and of every creeping thing that creepeth upon the earth, and every man:
8:1.And God remembered Noah, and every living thing, and all the cattle that was with him in the ark: and God made a wind to pass over the earth, and the waters assuaged;
8:17.Bring forth with thee every living thing that is with thee, of all flesh, both of fowl, and of cattle, and of every creeping thing that creepeth upon the earth; that they may breed abundantly in the earth, and be fruitful, and multiply upon the earth.
8:22.While the earth remaineth, seedtime and harvest, and cold and heat, and summer and winter, and day and night shall not cease.[44]

We have here the participant stress on the moral depravity of man as the basis for the world's destruction. However, in order to assure the eventual resurrection of the world the basic dualities of life were preserved by admitting couples of all fauna into Noah's Ark. Thence, after the revival of the earth's life forms, verse 22 of chapter 7 of Genesis promises the eternal recurrence of day and night the four seasons and the seeding-harvesting cycles.

A more violently separant destruction-resurrection myth involving, not only the fauna, but also the world's flora and its elements is the *Ragna Rok* or *Götterdämmerung*, the twilight of the gods of the Germanic *Eddas*.

> The sun becomes dark. Earth sinks in the sea. The shining stars slip out of the sky. Vapor and fire rage fiercely together till the leaping flame licks heaven itself.[45]

The wolf, Fenrir, swallows the sun, the separant life-giver and matri-normative symbol of dominion over fecundity and nature. The dissolution of culture and the family is marked by the emergence of the snake, the primeval phallus, escaping from its abyss and poisoning the sea with unchasteness, after which the land is flooded. Moreover, the proscription of incest, which sublimates forbidden sex into culture, breaks down, bringing about the disintegration of civilization.[46]

> Brothers shall fight and slay each other,
> Sisters' sons break kinship bonds,
> Hard it is on each with much unchasteness.[47]

Finally, the *Aesir* will be vanquished by their enemies; their swords and shields broken and cloven. The chaotic 'wind age, wolf-age' will reign supreme, and the world will sink under, as fire burns out the gods and creation. This is the end of a Sisyphean cycle. The Promethean fire which was instrumental in forging man's culture now destroys man, his artifacts, and his gods.

After the doom, a new Sisyphean cycle will be initiated, and the resurrection of the world initiated by a new sun. The god Balder will rise Christ-like from the dead, and Lif (life) and Lifthrasir (the one who holds fast to life), the new human couple, will repopulate the earth.

Here the resurrection not only involves the fauna, but the new Sisyphean cycle restructures a new cosmos, a new creation sired by resuscitated deities. Thus, the inability of our core-vectors as well as the basic forces of energy-matter to achieve their teleological aims raise the participant unrequited longings, the unfulfilled separant quest, and, especially, the dialectics between them to the stature of a universal prime mover. Mytho-empirically, this is beautifully portrayed by the myth of the heart and the spring recounted by Rabbi Nachman of Bratzlav: The heart and the spring are divided from each other by a mountain and cannot reach each other, yet the impossibility of their encounter makes their longing more intense. Hence, the unrequited longing in itself generates continuous energy. Rabbi Nachman was so convinced by the primacy of longing per se that he even risked the sacrilege of the affirmation of doubt, because the longing for a presumably unattainable perfection intensifies faith and raises it to a higher stature. In this, he shares the conviction of Kierkegaard that renunciation may enhance faith.

Renunciation of a goal turns the process into a goal in itself. Relinquishing the realization of the hopes for Godot's coming turned the waiting for him into a timeless vocation. Jesus' kiss on the forehead of Dostoevski's Grand Inquisitor might have symbolized his agreement to the latter's waiver of the Second Coming. The longing for the Second Coming may enhance the belief in God (and the interests of the church) more than the reappearance of the Messiah.

Renunciation of a goal and anchoring on the process creates ritualism which in sociology was tagged by Robert K. Merton as anomic deviance.[48] In our context, the ritualist is a success, since he anchors on the processes of life and on the continuous present, which if authentic could enhance revelation and creativity. The renunciation of achievements and ends enables one to realize that time-space and causality are cognitive filters, and that the underlying realities—the things-in-themselves—are yearnings, independent of their telos. The relinquishing of the telos frees us from beginnings and ends. The processes and the dialectics of yearning, as the transcendental things-in-themselves, render us into quanta without mass, into flows of energies which are common both to us and to God.

Renunciation is also extant in the mytho-empirical sale by Esau of his birthright to Jacob. This is a mythological projection of the normative directive of older children to relinquish their possessions and rights to their younger siblings. Renunciation is also apparent on a grand scale in the willing victims of the Isaac Syndrome. This sacrificial normativeness is inherent in the feeling of righteousness concomitant with sacrificing one's wealth, well-being, and, even, life for a norm or an ideal.

The Kabbalist account of Joseph Dela Reinha by Abraham Ben Eliezer Halevi[49] tells of the protagonist, a Spanish pre-expulsion practical Kabbalist, who tried to bring about redemption by prayer, rituals, and magic. Yet, in one of his rites, either purposely or inadvertently, he offered incense (*levonah*) to Satan. This, of course, further postponed salvation, and like Dostoevski's Grand Inquisitor vindicated the greater importance of waiting, longing, and yearning for salvation as against its realization. This is highlighted by George Steiner's Mount Nevo syndrome. Steiner claims that the spiritual excellence of the Jews was greater in the Diaspora, when their longing for Zion fueled their creative energies, than in Israel. In Hasidism, we find the statement by Rabbi Nachman of Bratslav, whose doctrine was influenced by Lurianic Kabbala, that 'when grace is postponed and (God) does not endow us with his peace, then we have to strive for his revelation'.[50] Hence, the striving for divine revelation is preferred by Rabbi Nachman to actual theophany. This can be seen as a mytho-empirical projection of the dynamics of the internal saboteur. A person who is successful in business, for instance, may make a grave error or a patently stupid move when he could or must have been aware of its disastrous effects. Such an error may be explained by our core dynamics. The suppressed participant core-vector of his personality surged up to sabotage the achievements of the separant core-vector, so that the renewed longing for success might resuscitate and recharge his presumably dwindling core energies.

For Kierkegaard, the renunciation of goals effects an extasis to a continuous present and to an authentic process of coming. He says:

> The principle that the existing subjective thinker is constantly occupied in striving, does not mean that he has, in the finite sense, a goal toward which he strives and that he would be finished when he reaches this goal. No, he strives infinitely, is constantly in a process of becoming. And this, his striving, is safeguarded by his constantly being just as negative as he is positive and by his having as much essential humor as essential pathos; which has its ground in the fact that he is an existing individual and reflects this in his thinking. This process of becoming is the thinker's own existence: from which it is, indeed, possible to make abstraction, but only thoughtlessly, in order to become objective. How far the subjective thinker has come along this road, whether a long distance or a short one, makes no essential difference. This is, indeed, only a finitely relative comparison; but, as long as he is an existing individual, he is in the process of becoming.[51]

And likewise: 'Earthly hope must be killed. Only then can one be saved by true hope'. The renunciation of the hope of realizing one's quests in the here-and-now prepares one for a leap of faith in transcendence. If Kierkegaard's waiver is sublime, the following renunciation is shmaltzy and kitschy:

> Nora stood up, 'Well, I'd better leave now…'
> 'I wish you happiness…'Sean said, putting his arms around her.
> For a moment they stood silently together. She was soft and sweet, an angel of love. He could feel her determination begin to melt into surrender. If he insisted now he could have her, he was sure, have a life with her in which the sweetness would never end. Images from their past love tumbled through his mind. Oakland Beach…Amalfi…Yet surely the sweetness would be short-lived. Not having her, he could love her forever. Not for Jimmy McGuire, not for all the priests of Chicago, not even for the Pope, but for Nora…yes, for Nora…he would do what his damn fool church and his damn fool God wanted him to do. He disengaged himself from the embrace. 'I've got to get ready for Mass.'[52]

Yet the effect is the same—a transition from ends to processes, from time to timelessness, from paradox to transcendence. By renouncing the theophany of Godot, Beckett's tramps may experience transcendence just by waiting for it. As one critic put it, they may sing a 'Kyrie without God'.[53] Finally, Camus's Dr. Rieux gives up all hope of vanquishing the plague, yet he can experience grace by treating its victims.

The linkage between the human developmental phases and passing over or smuggling the barriers between them and the developmental phases of energy-matter is effected by who else than man—the great anthropic mediator. The individual human being is endowed with a uniqueness which stems from his irreplicable link between the ani-consciousness and energy-matter in all their combinations and permutations and the various formations of human aggregates. The individual is the only human entity capable of authentic dialogue, revelation, and creativity. The phalanx, the army groups, are separant, carnivorous power structures. States, parties, and universities are demiurgical organizations, with no freedom of will, but rather algorithmically programmed to preserve themselves. The individual is the only entity empowered with real indeterminism, and, as such, God is mytho-empirically created in his own image. Finally, crowds and audiences are carnivorous organizations. Marilyn Monroe, Elvis Presley, and James Dean are the modern counterparts of Mithra, Horus, and Varuna. They may achieve dialogue with some members of their audience, but, as a crowd, any audience is a multi-headed Gorgon aiming to swallow ingest, and possess their idols. Often the fans drive them to suicide, drugs, and madness, performing a modern rite of human sacrifice, and, then, projecting it onto mythology as resurrected deities.

In thirteenth-century Spanish ecstatic Kabbala, man's participant longing to unite with God is expressed by one of Abraham Abulafia's disciples as follows:

> Man is the last of the compound entities and is, therefore, represented by the letter *yod,* that is, the number ten, which is considered the last primary number. He is the yod in this world, who has received the power from the all, and he comprises the all, like the yod in [the realm of] the sefirot. Understand, therefore, that there is no discernible difference between this yod and that yod, but a very fine one from the aspect of spirituality, and that it [the letter yod] is the *milluy* [contents] of the other yod...And this is the secret [of the verse] 'and cleave unto Him'—the cleaving of yod to yod, in order to complete the circle.[54]

In a similar vein, the Maggid Dov-Baer of Meseritz states in his *drash* (hermeneutic) on the meaning of the verse, 'Make thee two trumpets':

> Two halves of forms, as it is written 'on the throne, a likeness in the appearance of a man above upon it, as man [Adam] is but D and M, and the speech dwells upon him. And when he unites with God, who is the alpha of the world, he becomes 'Adam...and man must separate himself from any corporeal things, to such an extent that he will ascend through all the worlds and be in union with God, until [his] existence will be annihilated, and then he will be called 'Adam'.
> The Maggid bases his homily on the verse: 'Make thee two trumpets of silver, of a whole piece shall thou make them'. The Hebrew word for trumpets, *Hazozerot,* is interpreted as *Hazi-zurot,* that is, '[two] half-forms'.[55]

However, as actual union with God is impossible in the here-and-now, the longing for it in itself may effect a participant *experience* of a unio mystica.

The same holds true for Gnostic mytho-empiricism. The meaning of Gnosis is to revert back to the original perfection of non-being and to partake in the alien, ex-temporal God. The following Hermetic prayer is quite illuminating:

> Saved by thy light, we rejoice that thou hast shown thyself to us whole, we rejoice that thou hast made us gods while still in our bodies through the vision of thee. Man's only thanks-offering to thee is to know thy greatness. We came to know thee, O light of human life, we came to know thee, O light of all gnosis, we have come to know thee, O womb impregnated by the seed of thy father...In adoration of thy grace, we ask no other grace but that thou shouldst preserve us in thy gnosis and that we shall not stumble from the life so gained.[56]

We have here, first, the revelatory partaking in God, so that we become gods ourselves. Second, gnosis is contained in the womb, which is clear evidence of the projected quest to annul birth and revert to the non-being in the womb. Third, gnosis may be experienced by our soul in the evil here-and-now, while it is still entrapped in its profane body, through a revelatory vision of God. Gnosis is, therefore, a form of grace for the alien souls stranded in the squalor of creation.[57]

Hence, actual reversal to non-being is not necessary for a Gnostic revelatory *experience* of non-being—the longing for it may in itself provide the participant fuel to effect it.

We claim that our yearning, be it for Sisyphean possession of objects and life forms or Tantalic longing to fuse with them, is the essence of our being. The process of involvement kindles our energies and not the attainment of our goals, which are as unachievable as the aims of our participant and separant core-vectors. Nietzsche laments not so much his lost love for Lou as the destruction of his illusions of love and his ability to long for it.[58] Indeed, Plato describes this yearning for union as follows:

> For the intense yearning which each of them has towards the other does not appear to be the desire of lover's intercourse, but of something else which the soul either evidently desires and cannot tell, and of which she has only a dark and doubtful presentiment. Suppose Hephaestus, with his instruments, to come to the pair who are lying side by side and say to them, "What do you people want of one another?" They would be unable to explain. And suppose further, that when he saw their perplexity he said: "Do you desire to be wholly one; always day and night to be in one another's company? For if this is what you desire, I am ready to melt you into one and let you grow together, so that being two you shall become one, and while you live a common life as if you were a single man, and after your death in the world below still be one departed soul instead of two—I ask whether this is what you lovingly desire, and whether you are satisfied to attain this?" There is not a man of them who, when he heard the proposal, would deny or would not acknowledge that this meeting and melting into one another, this becoming one instead of two, was the very expression of his ancient need. And the reason is that human nature was originally one and we were a whole, and the desire and pursuit of the whole is called love.[59]

The essence of love is, thus, not the attainment of unity, but the longing for it. In a similar vein, our childhood memories have a life of their own detached from our adult present. The middle-aged men and women in class reunions seem de trop compared with our memories, and the encounter with our overweight, double-chinned, talkative first-love of a generation ago all but kills cherished memories. Moreover, our nostalgic participant yearning for the past and the separant longing for the future provide our activating energy. They are the real dynamics behind appearances; they are the thing-in-itself. In Gnosis, we find the gospel of truth claiming this:

> The Father, this perfect one who created the All, in whom the All is and whom the All lacks for he had withheld in himself his perfection, which he had not given to the All.[60] The lack is presented as a prime mover of the All which longs for the perfection withheld from it. This could provide a mytho-empirical anchor for the longing of the expelled particle of divinity (the human soul) to reunite with the godhead in primordial perfection. In the Hypostasis of the Archons, we find that when the powers of darkness saw the image of incorruption which was reflected in the water, 'they were inflamed with love towards it and wanted to seize it'.[61]

This would seem to be the mytho-empirical projection of the separant type's wish to reunite with the object/other by swallowing and incorporating it within himself. However, the Book of Thomas the Savior laments that the love of light symbolizing the godhead is unattainable.[62] This is the mytho-empirical vindication of our meta-myths of Sisyphus and Tantalus as metaphors for the unachievability of our yearnings as their energizing force.

In Theosophic Kabbala, we find that the participant quest of the strewn particles to reunite with their perfect nothingness is impossible, since it would lead to the annihilation of the temporal worlds.[63] As the godhead does not desire this ultimate union of man with infinity it cannot be realized. Indeed, just as the revolving sword of fire does not allow man to return to paradise so the particles of divinity strewn amidst the vile *kellipot* are not allowed to return to their divine source.[64] This is so, apparently in order to preserve their yearning to return to their source as a constant motivational force.

In Existentialism, we have Kierkegaard stating that the human mind yearns for the absolute, yet cannot reach it; hence, his quests become continuous. Man searches for the aesthetic idea which he can never dominate and, thus, becomes dominated by the quest. The aesthetic man anchors, according to Kierkegaard, on the outside, whereas the ethical man probes into his inner-self. His aim is to negate himself so that his historical self merges with the infinity of his inner-self. This aim cannot be achieved, and all that remains is the longing for it. The religious man, prompted by his unconditional faith, anchors on the insoluble paradox of the fusion of the historical with the non-historical. This faith, or if one wishes, this longing to solve the insoluble paradox fuels man's belief: credo quia absurdum.

Unrequited longing is a constant malaise, a constant lack. If these unfulfilled quests are our prime movers, then life indeed is characterized as Heidegger postulated, by *angst* (anxiety) and *sorge* (worry). We go even further than Heidegger by claiming that pain is the central phenomenon of life, both physical and mental, and only authentic revelation and creativity may provide a temporary relief from it.

Finally, the relationship between the man-God-object triad and the God-object-dyad is one of a self-other conflict and a godhead-demiurgos strife. If we abstract all these three relationships, we have lack, strife, and frustration, which are perceived by the individual as varying dosages and kinds of pain. Hence, the universal emotive principle is pain. This was expounded by Freud in his pleasure principle, according to which pleasure is the reduction of frustration, irritation, and pain. Freud confined the pleasure principle to intra-psychic dynamics, whereas we regard pain as governing both the temporal and transcendental relationships of man. Moreover, our programming, with its remarkable ability to utilize a very limited number of parameters—the four nucleotides of genetics, the four powers of physics, the two sexes required for procreation in most species, the two core personality vectors—to control and activate creation, utilizes pain not only to activate man but also to preserve him and regulate his relationships. Thus, pain guards the organism against injury, it serves as a communicative medium, it prods man to seek creativity and revelation. As we have seen, when internalized by Ego, suffering may form a basis for an existentialist system of ethics. In Existentialism, this is marked by the Heideggerean angst and sorge and by Kierkegaard's description of human existence as characterized by fear and trembling. Life is marked by varying degrees of deprivational interaction, yet its motivating efficiency is curvilinear. A moderate dosage of it prods us to act and create, but too much of it crushes us under the Sisyphean stone or the Tantalic rock, as in the earlier version of the myth. The Greek meden agan serves as a working maxim in this case too. One cannot create if afflicted by unbearable agony. For revelation, one should 'let pain flower' as Kierkegaard counseled, but a crushing blow damns the flow of grace and prevents it from reaching the victim.

Lack, pain, and frustration are ordained by the developmental phases of the human child and adolescent. The fetus is accustomed to a soft self-sufficient coziness in the womb only to be expelled into a world of changing temperatures, hard surfaces, and erratic feeding and care by the breast-mother. In early orality, we feel an Edenic pantheistic togetherness with our surroundings only to be confined into the scar tissues of the ego-boundary and the loneliness of later orality. Within the family fold, the adolescent usually enjoys an unconditional forgiveness for almost everything he says or does, until the sacrificial rites of passage of the Isaac Syndrome thrust him into the cruel rat race of socio-economic competition and full normative and legal responsibility. The openness of the infant and the adolescent expectations of an I-thou encounter with his surroundings are usually frustrated and meet with an I-it response. Hence, man's relationship with his surroundings is characterized by a deprivational interaction interspersed with occasional spells of grace. Mytho-empirically, this is represented by αχερων, the Greek river of woe surrounding hell. Man's communication with his infernal others, to extend Sartre's metaphor, takes place through a flow of agony. Moreover, man does not initially know that 'hell is other people'. On the contrary, he is conditioned by previous developmental phases to expect a welcoming and comforting other only to have his innocence bruised, scarred, and raped by the I-it other. According to Lurianic Kabbala, God also created the world in order to give and to share his flowing grace. However, the breaking of the vessels caused him to lose control over it and since then he has been confronted by the *Sitra Achara,* the sinister powers. Man in his struggle with his infernal other, thus, reflects an image of God in his conflict with the demiurgos. The message here is unequivocal: man in pain reflects a suffering God (Christ). Perfect theistic gods do not suffer. They make their creatures suffer, either to entertain themselves like Roman caesars watching the throes of man and beast in the arena or partake vicariously in the joys and sorrows of their creatures and, thus, extricate themselves from solitude in eternity. The God of Lurianic Kabbala is a suffering God and, hence, imperfect and blemished. The Gnostic God is pestered and attacked by the demiurgos and his archons. The Kabbalist rung of keter, which is an integral part of the godhead, is denoted by the *partzuf,* the countenance, of *arich anpin*—literally, the 'long suffering'—while Kierkegaard's existentialist God is effectively involved in his creation through his suffering son.

The suffering Christ on the cross broadcasts an appeal for communication and help on behalf of the blemished godhead and a maieutic message to man to seek revelation. Man has the choice whether to open or close himself to the God-man's cry of anguish. When this call of distress is felt within the inner-self, it represents the universal awareness of the godhead. In Gnosis, the soul was initially a part of the godhead, but afterwards,

> she fell into a body and came into this life, then she fell into the hands of the robbers. And the insolent tossed her to one another and [defiled] her. Some used her violently, others persuaded her by a deceitful gift. In brief, they dishonored her. She [lost] her virginity and played the harlot with her body and gave herself to everyone. And the one to whom she adheres, she thinks he is her husband. Whenever she gave herself to the insolent, faithless adulterers that they might misuse her, then she sighed heavily and repented. Again, when she turns her face away from these paramours she runs to others, and they compel her to be with them and to serve them like the lords on their couches. But from shame she no longer dares to forsake them. But they deceive her for a long time (by behaving) in the manner of true and genuine husbands, as if they honored her greatly, and at the end of all these things they abandon her and go. But she becomes a poor deserted widow who has no help—nor does she gain a hearing in her suffering; for she has no benefit at all from them, except the defilements which they gave her when they consorted with her. And those whom she bore by the adulterers are deaf and blind and sickly, their heart is bemused. But when the Father who is above in Heaven visits her and looks down upon her

> and sees her sighing with her passion and the unseemliness and repenting over her harlotry which she has committed, and she begins to call upon his [na]me that he may help her, [sighing] with all her heart and saying: 'Deliver me, my father. For behold, I will give account to [you], because I have forsaken my house and have fled from my maiden chamber. Once again I turn to you.' When he sees that she is of such a character, then will he resolve to make her worthy that he take pity on her, for much pain has come upon her because she abandoned her house.'[65]

The soul—the particle of divinity—was exploited, assaulted, raped, battered, manipulated, and manhandled after falling into its demiurgical body, yet the soul's cry of anguish pierced the boundaries of history and reached the godhead. In a similar manner, Isaac Yehuda Yehiel Safrin, the nineteenth-century Hasid and Kabbalist, recounts his revelatory experiences. Because of their importance, we shall quote them at length:

> In 1845, on the 21st day of the Omer, I was in the town of Dukla. I arrived there late at night, and it was dark, and there was no one to take me home, except for a tanner who came and took me into his house. I wanted to pray Ma'ariv and to count the Omer, but I was unable to do it there, so I went to the Beit Midrash alone, and there I prayed until midnight had passed. And I understood from this situation the plight of the Shekhina in exile and Her suffering when She is standing in the market of tanners. And I wept many times before the Lord of the world, out of the depth of my heart, for the suffering of the Shekhina in exile, and Her suffering when She is standing in the market of tanners. And I wept many times before the Lord of the world, out of the depth of my heart, for the suffering of the Shekhina. And through my suffering and weeping, I fainted and I fell asleep for a while, and I saw a vision of light, splendor, and great brightness, in the image of a virgin adorned with twenty-four ornaments...And she said: 'Be strong, my son' etc. and I was suffering that I could not see but the vision of her back and I was not worthy to receive her face. And I was told that [this was because] I am alive, and it is written, "for no man shall see me, and live.[66]

> It was his [R. Zevi Hirsch's] custom regarding the matter of holiness, to pray in order to bring upon himself a state of suffering, uneasiness, and affliction on every eve of Sabbath. This was done in order to efface himself completely before the Sabbath so as to be able to receive His light, be He blessed, during the prayer and the meal of the Sabbath [eve] with a pure, holy, and clear heart. This was his custom regarding the matter of holiness, due to his constant fear lest *arrogant* and *alien thoughts* would enter his heart. Once on the Feast of Shavuot, hundreds of people crowded around him. Before the [morning]

prayer, with the [first] light of dawn, I entered one of his rooms, but he did not see me, for he was pacing about the room to and fro, weeping and causing heaven and earth to weep with him before God. And it is impossible to write it down. And he humbled himself before God *with a mighty weeping*, supplicating that he not be rejected *from the light of His* face—then I was overcome by a great trembling, because of the awe of the Shekhina and I opened the door and ran away.[67]

His weeping and suffering mirror the crying and pain of the Divine Presence (the *Shekhina*) and this brings about the revelatory encounter between them. The pain Safrin radiated and the pain of the Shekhina received by him made him a flowing stream,[68] a communicative current of pain. In his revelatory experiences and his search for the roots of his soul, Safrin was convinced that he was the Messiah, the son of Joseph.[69] Indeed, his being a Messiah was necessary for synchronization between the ani (the inner-self) and the ayin (infinity), which contains the same letters in Hebrew but in a different order. The message here is that only a Messiah, a son of God, can serve as the mediator between the infinity (ayin) of the godhead and the historical self (ani). Only the man-God, who is at once both in history and outside it, can effect a union between the godhead and its particle (soul). Finally, Kierkegaard discusses the man-God's paradoxical offense of declaring himself to be God. Yet through the common suffering of man and God which meets in the man-God, the revelatory communion between man and God is made possible. Man suffering in history cries from his inner self, 'Out of the depths have I cried unto thee, O Lord'. This is reciprocated by the God-man's shriek of anguish, 'Eli Eli lama sabakhtani'. And both cries of pain are synchronized in Christ on the cross. In him the suffering is historical. The suffering of God and man integrates both history and eternity. This is the feat accomplished by the revelatory leap of faith through the communicative force of pain. A blemished suffering God and man, in fear and trembling in history, can communicate in an ever-suffering Christ. The savior's kiss continuously seared the forehead of Dostoevski's Grand Inquisitor as a painful communicative reminder of God's presence in the here-and-now. Camus's judge-penitent's refusal to heed the drowning girl's cry for help in *The Fall* was the existentialist original sin because it blocked the communication between man and transcendence. It prevented the judge-penitent from feeling the suffering of the girl within his inner-self and from communing with her by saving her. Her unanswered cry of anguish became a free-floating piece of scar tissue which encapsulated both protagonists in their solipsistic solitude.

An answered cry for help, on the other hand, extricates both man and God from their impending solipsism. Indeed, Kierkegaard demonstrates how the crucifixion in an eternal present crosses timelessness and history. The Gnostic messenger, the Kabbalist Shekhina, and Kierkegaard's Christ, who differs radically from the son of God of institutionalized Christianity, pierce the walls of the demiurgical tornado with their cries of anguish and reach the covert flow of grace within the eye of the storm. Brel's ne me quitte pas, which is a variation on the theme of separation anxieties, is absorbed into the innermost selves of the audience, thus, effecting a direct communication with the artist. Bosch's Christ transmits his suffering to St. Veronica, as symbolized by the image of his face which was imprinted on the handkerchief with which she wiped his face. Christ's suffering radiates from his agonized, yet graceful, face stoically calm amid the gaggle of vile, ugly, cruel, stupid, covetous, violent, and debauched faces surrounding him, until it seems to reach the innermost serenity of St. Veronica who contemplates Christ's image on the handkerchief. This image seems to be visible only to her since she is attuned to the pain emanating from the man-God. The poet Nelli Sacks sang of the pain she sensed was emanating from one of the stones of the Wailing Wall. Pierre Legendre, a world renowned legal anthropologist, confessed to the author, 'without misery I would feel lonely'. In Greek, *sympatheia,* sympathy, is literally the feeling of suffering with the other. Indeed, pain extricates both man and transcendence from ontological loneliness.

The communicative effect of pain was recognized by the sixteenth-century Safedean Kabbalists. Abraham Halevi Baruchim woke up every night at midnight and wandered the streets shrieking in a bitter voice: 'Wake up to honor God, the Shekhina is in exile, our temple is burnt down, and the people of Israel are in great trouble'. The circle of Lurianic kabbalists in Safed practiced the tikkun Rachel, behaving as follows: 'They took off their shoes, dressed their heads in mourning, and cried with all their might'. In this way they partook in the suffering of the Shekhina. The suffering of man and the pains of God coincide within the exiled Holy Presence. As for the effect of tears as a communicative medium between man and God, Haim Vital states the matter this way:

> When a person weeps and sheds tears for [the death of] a righteous man, he also causes tears to be shed on high, as it were, of God [Himself]. As it is said: 'The Lord God of Hosts will call to weeping and mourning' etc., [or] 'my soul shall weep in secret', etc., or as it is written: 'Oh that my head were waters [and my eyes a fountain of tears]'—namely, that I long for the act of the lower [entities], as by weeping below, they cause 'my head to be as waters and my

> eyes a fountain of tears.' May they do so, and, thereby, I may also weep for my dead.[70]

Pain, thus, almost automatically effects a dialogue between man and God.

According to Kierkegaard, the crucified Jesus effects an extasis, in the Greek sense, from the sequences of time, and, hence, his pain is continuously manifest in the perpetuity of the present.[71] The suffering of Christ is also introjected by man as pertaining to his own daily crucifixion. Thus, Christ pierces the imminent solipsism of man by partaking in his suffering self-image. The shriek of a normatively sacrificed Isaac meets the God's laments which are communicated to the innermost being of man through the tribulations of His son on the cross. The suffering of God as felt by man may break his heart; yet, as Rabbi Nachman of Brazlav taught, 'There is nothing so whole as a broken heart'. The calvary of Christ radiates Lacrimoe Rerum into man, but also fills him with the enthousiasmos (again in the Greek sense) which connotes the entry of divinity within man.

Physical pain is the demiurge's tool for guarding 'his property'—the body. Without the pain incidental to bodily injury, disease, and death, most human beings and many other creatures would probably take their own lives. The demiurgos controls a built-in safety mechanism to keep the inmates exiled particles of divinity—incarcerated in their temporal prison, i.e., the body. Without pain, the souls would easily destroy their prison-body and revert back to their origin in the Godhead. The demiurgical ananké, the coercive cosmic forces, as well as evolution, also avail themselves of pain in order to implement their aims. If one exceeds one's moira, the Furies strike with a vengeance in order to push the deviants back into line. Those who do not fit the designs of evolution are wiped painfully, yet unceremoniously, out of history. Suffering and history are true phenomena, yet pain is also instrumental in jolting man out of his complacency in his demiurgical body and his fear of eternity (death). Man's revolt against his demiurgical ananké and moira is, thus, prompted by pain, and some suffering (though not too much) is also necessary for revelation and creativity.

Dostoevski says that one should be worthy of one's suffering. In our model this would mean that one must first experience an impasse, a fall, a breaking of the vessels, an exile in order to embark subsequently on the rebellious road of creativity and revelation. This is expressed by Kierkegaard as 'letting the pain flower' and represented by Rabbi Nachman's seeking of hardship and suffering in order to reach a higher rung of grace.

In Existentialism, suffering, if it does not crush the protagonist, leads him to a deeper insight into himself and into his relationships with his surroundings and with transcendence. This is the professed reason for Rabbi Nachman's search for a *Machloikess,* disagreement or quarrel, with his surroundings in order to experience the cathartic pain and suffering leading to spiritual revelation. 'We begin to live', said Yeats in his autobiography, 'when we have conceived life as tragedy'.[72] As for creativity, we have Damocles, who never danced so well as when the sword was hanging over his head. A Celtic myth tells of a bird which impales itself on a thorn in order to sing its most beautiful song. Ezra Pound wrote his most powerful *Cantos* after the 'braves' of Pizza imprisoned him in a cage in the marketplace to be laughed and spat at by the passers-by.

Kierkegaard's and Rabbi Nachman's conception of the cleansing value of pain was shared by Kordovero who said, 'Those who suffer willingly will be cleansed and purified...until they become as clean and pure as silver (Psalms 130:1)'. Suffering is a precedent condition ordained by the Holy Presence prior to salvation.[73] In Mandean Gnosis, suffering and exposure to destructive lions and to the carnivorous dragon that surrounds the world preceded the healing and deliverance of the human soul from its demiurgical tribulations.[74]

The suffering of the other, as internalized by me, brings me first to recognize the other's existence as a separate entity, and enables me to sympathize and empathize with him. This non-verbal communication, which has to be reached through dialogue, generates within me a flow of grace which is shared—as inferred by me epistemologically—by the other. This is the essence of Dr. Rieux's feeling of grace when he treats the sick and tries to ease their pain, although he knows that he can never vanquish the plague. In order for the treatment of physical and mental ills to be authentic and, hence, effective, the healer must empathize with a concrete sufferer and not with an abstract or imaginary one. Often, people identify with the suffering of actors in films or characters in novels, thus, avoiding the need to identify with real sufferers or to help a concrete person in pain.

Opening up to the suffering of the other is a prime communication dynamic which extricates man from solipsism. It posits both healer and sufferer in the grace of an authentic encounter within a present which becomes continuous, in that it lends meaning outside sequential time both to the life of the helper and to that of the person helped. Thus, Mother Theresa, treating the lepers of Calcutta, sees in them the image of the suffering son of God. This might lend a new interpretation to St. John's dictum: 'For God so loved the world that he gave his only begotten Son, that whosoever believeth in him should not perish, but have everlasting life (John 3:16)'. God's need was for communication with man about his predicament and for man to effect a 'mending', a Kabbalist tikkun, through creativity and theurgic revelation. The causa causans for the sacrifice was, therefore, the crossing between time and eternity effected by the crucifixion, so that the Godhead's anguish outside of time would be heard and heeded by man within history. As each human being, or, for that matter, creature, is epistemologically transcendental to Ego, feeling of the suffering of the other and a readiness to respond to it facilitates a dialogue with both the transcendental and temporal son of God. The covenant between the man-God and the God-man represented by any authentic dialogue is wrought by common suffering.

We see, thus, that lack, deprivation, and pain constitute our prime movers. They are the fuel that activates us. They lead us to higher echelons of revelation and creativity. However, the relationship between revelation, creativity, and pain is curvilinear: too little is ineffective whereas too much pain risks our being crushed by the Sisyphean rock and by the Tantalic stone in the earlier version of the myth of Tantalus. Pain guards the structure and function of our bodies and serves as a prime communication agent. Pain is also the activating agent in the acquisition of morals. We have seen that normativeness needs the pain of sacrifice. Moreover, as the dialectics between participant longing and separant quests are the Ding an Sich (the thing in itself), the underlying reality of objects, artifacts, and life forms, and our prime mover—the refueling and recharging of the batteries of these core dialectics takes place through more deprivation and pain: this again occurs in a curvilinear manner and is structured properly by myths which are the prime form palatable to our core dialectics.

Thus, the myths of martyrs feed our Tantalic normativeness. The stunning efficacy of Christianity stems, inter alia, from the fact that Jesus Christ the arch martyr is ever crucified in a continuous present—thus continuously fueling the core-batteries of Christians with participant normativeness. Heroes and, especially, the myths about them, rejuvenate, refresh, and resuscitate the deflated separant core batteries of political ideologies. Finally, one is ever stunned by Vincent Van Gogh and by the force of the myths about the trials of this Promethean innovator as well as by the effects they have on artists and aspiring artists. This recharging of our core batteries is a continuous process. Each of our experiences can provide us with separant creative fuel or stifle us. The mass communication media as well as all literature and art expose us to an endless torrent of mythology, and it is our indeterministic decision whether or not to expose ourselves to the authenticity of a Jacques Brel or to the shmaltzy crooning of a Tino Rossi, to be inspired by the borderline crudeness of *Batman* or by the rebellious authenticity of a Keating in *The Dead Poets' Society*, to swallow the name-dropping and shallow profundities of a Simone de Beauvoir, only because her journals are reviewed by *Le Monde,* and *Le Figaro* and are discussed in *l'Apostrophe* or to read the all-but-forgotten, yet authentic and ever-relevant, journals of Karl Kraus. A burning instance of a fatally stifling experience is the encounter between Vincent Van Gogh and Paul Gauguin. Vincent wrote to his brother Theo that his drive to create was his life-line, or in our terms, the charging of his core batteries. 'My dear boy', he wrote, 'sometimes I know so well what I want. I can make do very well without God both in my life and in my painting, but I cannot, in spite of my sickness, exist without this thing which is bigger than myself, which is my life, and this is the power to create'.[75]

Vincent's drive to create which was his life and raison d'être was deflated by Paul Gauguin's brutal devaluation of Vincent's art. After this assault on Vincent's life-line against which he was seemingly defenceless, his life became meaningless, and he eventually committed suicide.

A prime mode of recharging our participant core-vectors in prayer is an idea given expressed by Van Gogh invoking Psalms:

> Hear my prayer, O Lord, and let my cry come unto thee.
>
> Hide not thy face from me in the day when I am in trouble; incline thine ear unto me: in the day when I call answer me speedily.
>
> For my days are consumed like smoke, and my bones are burned as an hearth.
>
> My heart is smitten and withered like grass; so that I forget to eat my bread. (Psalms 102:1–4)
>
> My days are like a shadow that declineth, and I am withered like grass. (Psalms 102:11)
>
> But thou, O Lord, shalt endure for ever; and thy remembrance unto all generations. (102:12)
>
> He will regard the prayer of the destitute, and not despise their prayer. (102:17)
>
> I love the Lord, because he hath heard my voice and my supplications.

> Because he hath inclined his ear unto me, therefore, will I call upon him as long as I live.
>
> The sorrows of death compassed me, and the pains of hell got hold upon me: I found trouble and sorrow.
>
> Then called I upon the name of the Lord; O Lord, I beseech thee, deliver my soul.
>
> Gracious is the Lord, and righteous; yea, our God is merciful.
>
> The Lord preserveth the simple: I was brought low, and he helped me.
>
> Return unto thy rest, O my soul; for the Lord hath dealt bountifully with thee.
>
> For thou has delivered my soul from death, mine eyes from tears, and my feet from falling.
> I will walk before the Lord in the land of the living. (116:1–9)
>
> Out of the depths have I cried unto thee, O Lord.
>
> Lord, hear my voice: let thine ears be attentive to the voice of my supplications.
>
> If thou, Lord, shouldest mark iniquities, O Lord who shall stand?
>
> But there is forgiveness with thee, that thou mayest be feared.
> I wait for the Lord, my soul doth wait, and in his word do I hope.
> My soul waiteth for the Lord more than they that watch for the morning: I say, more than they that watch for the morning. (130:1–6)
>
> Let Israel hope in the Lord: for with the Lord there is mercy, and with him is plenteous redemption.

Prayers like these may lift us up by our own bootstraps and inject some grace, hope, and joy even in the midst of misery, depravity, and squalor. The prayers do not change the objective conditions, and they may change the way we perceive them and help us to cloak these squalid conditions with different meanings and values. As intensive and sincere prayer recharges our participant batteries, it may act as a catalyst for revelation and give us certitude in our normative stance and support in our affective attitudes; hence, it may also enhance our creative capacities. Here again is another instance of the symbiotic link between Tantalic revelation and Sisyphean creativity.

The crucial point, however, is that each mythogene recharging our participant and separant core-vectors is unique because it follows a unique experience or a quest. Consequently, the dialectic between the core-vectors, the Tantalus Ratio, is unique and so is the symbolon structure. Finally, the Promethean connection which is the culmination of all these uniquenesses is certainly unique. Indeed the bio-psycho-social configuration of life forms makes each creature statistically unique, and Pauli's exclusion principle makes the fermion matter particles unique when all their measurable parameters are then taken into account. Why all these uniquenesses? We claim that the irreplicability of experiences and creatures is related to the necessity of our longings for our earlier developmental experiences—our childhood, our mother's grace, our past love—to be unrequited and for our dead beloved to be irreplaceable. There is no cloning or replication of our past experiences so that our quest for them will ever fuel our creative imagination. These are the meanings of myths which create unique gods, experiences, and creatures in their own unique image so that they will never be exactly recreated and our longing for them will be eternally unrequited. Evolution has perpetuated these uniquenesses as our prime movers so that Tantalus will never cease to chase his receding nourishment, Sisyphus will never stop pushing his stone up the hill, and Prometheus will be ever resurrected till the end of time, and all the three will thus effect unique revelations and acts of creativity ad infinitum. Hence, there will always be a gap, a disjuncture, an abyss between our longings and our quests and our ad hoc reality—a rift which ensures the continuity of our longings and quests and the revelation and creativity which they fuel.

As we have already mentioned, the Ding-An-Sich the prime mover lies not in the separate vectors but in the dialectics between them. Only the interaction between the two provides the ontological energy of being. As we have seen, the kabbalist zivug, mating, is the mytho-empirical projection of this core dialectic as prime mover. Indeed, the agapic mating between the supernal countenances of father (in Hebrew *Abba*) and mother (in Hebrew *Ima*) which also stand for the dialectics between grace and stern judgment is constant and provides the energy for the whole of creation.[76]

This is the TR, the raw energy. When structured into the symbolon structure and then invested into the creation of a Promethean Holon, the processes are ad hoc, depending on moods and needs. Hence the erotic mating of the lower countenances of the Kabbala: *ze'er anpin* (lower masculinity) and *nukbeh* (lower femininity) represent the processes of creativity whenever they take place.[77] The TR provides the basic energy which is value-neutral, but in the symbolon structures and the actual processes of revelation and creativity, evaluation and normativeness are imminent. Revelation and creativity may be authentic or inauthentic; when a dialogue flows between an I-and-a-thou both may experience grace, but when the dialogue degenerates into an I-it petrification the other becomes my hell à la Sartre and vice-versa. Indeed, the Kabbala envisages this theurgic tikkun, which we expound as a projection of creativity, as entirely within the value realm of man who may radiate grace or stern judgment. In our terminology, man has an indeterministic free choice to infuse himself with authentic revelation and, thence, to use it as a lever for authentic creativity, or to sink into the slumber and petrification of inauthenticity.

Revelation, creativity, theurgic tikkun, and the mending of a blemished God are, indeed, some of the modes of mythogenic mediation, linkage, and connection, which is the subject of the following section of our present chapter.

The Promethean Fire and the Burning Bush

The process of mediation is the smuggling over the ontological, existential, and aggregate developmental barriers of both humans and energy-matter. Then the synapses between the ani-consciousness and energy-matter are linked by man as the anthropic connecting structure within which the elements of consciousness and energy-matter interact in a maieutic-Socratic manner. It should be stressed that man as the anthropic connecting structure obeys the laws of evolution. We hold that man had evolved to be what he is—as a function of his fitness to link between consciousness and energy-matter. Once a more efficient mediator evolves between the two, man would become extinct, or run around in zoos, like his predecessors in the tree of genetic transition. This could be linked to the fact that any barrier building behavior is shunned, proscribed, and punished. On the ontological level, the quest for non-being may take the form of a spiritual unio mysticia, and the longing for the perfect non-differentiation in perfect unity could effect a revelation by prayer, yet the wrong behavior would build up the barriers between history and transcendence. An apt illustration is in the Lurianic Kabbala, which describes sin as feeding the kelipot, or shells, which are literally the partitions between history and transcendence. However, one ought not to go to the other extreme of reverting back to non-being. This was one of the meanings of original sin, since the exposure involved (*da'at*) in the knowing of transcendence might lead to the nihilation of the boundaried individual and his ability to mediate the primal dualities of universal consciousness and to the nullification of energy-matter. The existential barrier may be passed by an I-thou dialogue between two individuals, but the alternative I-it mutual petrification actually thickens the boundaries between human beings. Also, various substances, like alcohol and drugs, resorted to in order to achieve a smoother and easier rapport with one's environment, may eventually become a hindrance to dialogue since they give an illusion of concord and harmony, but actually twist the perception of objects and others and, hence, exacerbate the rift between the self and its human and objective surroundings. Finally, the social barrier may be overcome by authentic creativity which may give one a sense of freedom and fulfillment even in the confines of a normative mesh. Per contra, the ambitious social-climber, dominated by the expectations of the generalized other would find his isolation augmented the harder he tried to climb the achievement pyramid. Also, once he amasses power and wealth he is bound to feel more lonely amongst the hordes of lackeys, camp followers, and spongers who follow him only so long as he hands out positions and money.

Since the aim of creativity is better to bridge between consciousness and matter, whatever is not authentically creative may boomerang back at a person or group and stifle, injure, or degenerate it. Authenticity in this context is creativity which is preceded by an inner revelation as to the most appropriate manner of creativity, which would lead to a sense of pure fulfillment free of the dictates of the generalized other. This, of course, is paradoxical. Yet precisely this paradox may lead to a more effective link between consciousness and matter since of the endless modes of individual creativities some would be more viable mediators than others among man, objects, and life forms. This is evolution on a primary interactive scale. Creativity and revelation are individual attributes, yet man the creator works in a group, in a society, which demands conformity to its rules lest it be injured or, in extreme cases, disintegrate. Here again we witness a paradox: The creative innovator who enhanced the well-being, development, and aesthetic pleasures of a society is usually suppressed, oppressed, and off-times ostracized by the very same society which benefits from his creativity. This may be related to a need of a group or a social or cultural system to guard itself against too great innovation, for which a society may not be ready, and which may hence rock the boat, shake its system-in-balance, and even disrupt it. This may be the reason for the Greeks' injunction against hübris, which may disrupt the contextual balance of society. Revelation may also be too extreme and, hence, be proscribed by the directional ethics like that of the Jews. We have already mentioned the celebrated apocryphal mishna of four who entered the mystical orchard. Of the four, one died, one lost his mind, and a third turned away from God. The password of a successful linkage between consciousness and matter is a balanced complementarity between revelation and creativity. The aim is to create self-sustaining connecting structures, the nature of which we shall examine in extenso in the following pages, to link the divergent dualities of consciousness and energy-matter.

There is still no comprehensive theory on the link between consciousness and energy-matter on the quantum level, although there is a fair amount of consensus as to the existence of such a link. This may be contrasted with the plethora of attempts to bridge over the basic dualities of the macro world, e.g., Descartes's bridging over consciousness and the objects by the mediation of the good and truthful God, five hundred years of German philosophy trying to link between epistemology and ontology, and more recently the Existentialist striving to achieve dialogue with the other through one's inner-self.

We hold this division between macro and micro worlds to be necessary and justified by their apparent nature and differences. Otherwise, some unwarranted hypotheses might be proffered. A recent exposition, for instance, trying to link mind and quantum mechanics advocates an isomorphism between quantum and macroscopic states, especially as far as superposition is concerned.[78] Well, as Lockwood does not posit any limit to the macro-superposition state, it could encompass the whole universe and the observer.[79] The world with all its galaxies and nebulae is, thus, dragged back from limbo into reality by a conscious act of observation. This, to us, is untenable. Superposition is an attribute of waves. Even if we take particles to be pockets of waves à la de Broglie and Schrodinger, then after they are structured in atoms, molecules, objects, and organisms Pauli's exclusion principle would not allow more than one fermion-matter particle (spin 1/2) in one state. Hence, these original wave packets (particles) are not likely to allow an instantaneous crowding in on them of masses by other wave packets competing for the same exclusive positions. For living organisms, this going in and out of superposition would entail death and resurrection. We hold, therefore, that superposition is an attribute of unbound waves of and the fuzzy quantum world. Thus, structured matter and organisms in the macro world cannot be subject to superposition. This view, incidentally is shared by Penrose,[80] Lockwood's endorser. Moreover, we hold consciousness to be non-spatio-temporal; hence, it cannot be superposed. Finally, the isomorphization of the quantum and macro worlds ignores the uncertainty barrier which does not allow any direct observation of the superposed unstructured micro world behind it. Thus, we hypothesize a multiplicity of energy-matter states, ranging from the potential ain singularity, through the fuzzy unstructured, superposed quantum world and the atom, which is the structure unit of matter, to the molecule, objects, and life forms.

Consciousness, on the other hand, is unique and unitary. Quantum theoreticians with their usual materialist, physical biases are trying to link consciousness to some measurable, observable, or quantum processes in the brain. Thus, Roger Penrose tries to explain such unity of consciousness by the quantum correlation phenomenon such as the particles flying in opposite directions in the EPR and Bell's inequality violation experiments. Penrose states:

> Quantum mechanics involves many highly intriguing and mysterious kinds of behavior. Not the least of these are the quantum correlations...which can occur over widely separated distances. It seems to me to be a definite possibility that such things could be playing an operative role over large regions of the brain. Might there be any relation between a state of awareness and a highly coherent quantum state in the brain? Is the 'oneness' or 'globality' that seems to be a feature of consciousness connected with this? It is somewhat tempting to believe so.[81]

Lockwood goes even further and cites the cases of patients whose corpus callosum had been severed and who consequently displayed two different streams of consciousness.[82] This, as Lockwood himself noted, is not entirely accurate, because the Gestalt nature of the brain induces one hemisphere to develop or sublimate the functions of the other, with relative unity being regained through the unsevered brain stem. However, this to us is unnecessary. Penrose's query as to the source of the cognitive unity of consciousness is readily answered by us. We see it as stemming from the unity of the ani-consciousness, which is reflected indeterministically in the consciousnesses of all life forms and deterministically in the contained consciousnesses of all artifacts and objects.

The differences between the cognitive perceptions of each life form are related to their specific bio-psycho-social configuration, which indeed renders their consciousness sui generis. In artifacts and art the contained consciousness varies according to the purpose, use, or message meant to be conveyed. As for Sperry's commissurotomic patients, even if their split mind does not rectify itself through the Gestalt functions of the hemispheres and brain stem, both minds reflect a single ani-consciousness. No one tries to belittle the functions of the brain since every mental and physical function is either generated or mediated by it, but the ani-consciousness which is a non-historical structure is integrated within the human personality in the manner described by us in chapter 1.

We have accepted Wheeler's dictum that observer and observed collaborate in the act of creation; he does not, however, elaborate on the dynamics of this partnership. We hold that Existentialism of the Kierkegaard-Buber dialogica variety does expound how the ani, the archetypal observer, interacts and initiates the processes of becoming. Buber postulates primary words which are spoken from the innermost being. Primary words signify a relationship. 'Primary words do not describe something that might exist independently of them, but being spoken, they bring about existence'.[83]

We hold that the primary word concept articulated by the ani-consciousness is a revelatory happening which structures the symbolon. The primary word spoken, not in isolation but, in intentional dialogue already entails a relationship, an I-thou, or an I-it. This fits our model, insofar as the TR structured within the symbolon contains within it an integration of ani-consciousness and energy-matter. Our atzmi, or interactive component of the self, is a conceptualization of one such integration. Hence, the speaking of a primary word integrates the I-thou of the ani and the I-it of the atzmi into a self-contained unit which stems from the self, but which is directed towards the object. It, thus, initiates the process of creation or, rather, provides a vectorial seed or tool of creation which is the essence of our connecting symbolon structure. 'And God said, Let there be light, and there was light'[84] is, indeed, the speaking of a primary word-concept which forms a symbolon structure directed at creation and serving as a primary tool for it.

The Mediation

Most philosophers dealing with quantum mechanics refrain from postulating that the observer—by himself, or through the measuring instrument—actually creates the particle, presumably lest they be accused of metaphysical inclinations. Thus, Lockwood says, 'As a first approximation, one could think of awareness as a kind of searchlight sweeping around an inner landscape—literally inner: inside the mind. The searchlight may be thought of, in part, as revealing qualities that were already part of the landscape rather than as bringing these qualities into being'.[85]

In a similar vein, Dummet says, 'Our investigations bring into existence what was not there before, but what they bring into existence is not of our own making'.[86]

We claim that the symbolon structure is of our making and so—through the measuring instrument—is the Eigenstate, the particle.

We hold that the connecting symbolon structure is generated by a process of inner revelation. The vectorial intention of the symbolon is conscious, but the actual integration of the TR within it and its structuring is unconscious. The symbolon seed is utilized as a connecting or, rather, integrating agent between the ani-consciousness and energy-matter to catalyze the creation of a Promethean holon, be it the Eigenstate of a particle, a chanson, or a sculpture. In this matter, we agree with Churchland's claim:

> ...the world of inner sense, the world of sensations, and of thoughts, and of emotions, is...a constructed world. As with its access to the external world, the mind's access to itself is equally mediated by its own structural and conceptual contributions. It has access to itself only through its own self-representations.[87]

This, in a sense, would be what Foster calls 'mentalistic realism' according to which phenomenal qualities are self-revealing.[88] However, our conception of the revelation which gives rise to the symbolon structure and the process of creation of the Promethean holon is sui generis and we propose to describe it *in extenso.* Historically, revelation was related to religious experiences, to the exposure of the individual to transcendence. For us, however, all these accounts of revelatory religious experiences have a mytho-empirical value because they constitute a mythological projection of core personality experiences. These are transmitted by the ani to the level of consciousness and to mythology, although the core personality processes are largely subconscious. Thus, although our empirical anchors in the present context are taken from belief systems, our aim will be to understand the revelations triggering creativity. Creative activity presumably displays dynamics similar to the revelatory processes underlying the exposure of the individual to his ani in the process of structuring the symbolon connecting agent. Indeed, we claim that mytho-empiricism is probably the sole method for gleaning information about the otherwise unfathomable dynamics of structuring the symbolon.

The psychological basis for the quest of revelation is the participant vector's directive to the personality core to revert back to the Edenic pantheism of early orality and to the blissful omnipresence and self-sufficiency in utero. As these goals are unattainable, the revelatory processes allow their sublimation. But we believe in the conservation of psychic energy. Hence, the energy of the participant core-vector unexpended in the sublimatory process of revelation is projected mytho-empirically onto transcendence.

The way to a participant revelation is a one-way journey into the inner self. This is also the irreversible direction of salvation because the pure ani without attributes is the manifestation of divinity. To seek revelation and redemption outside the self is, thus, not only ineffectual, but also sacrilegious according to some participatory belief systems. Indeed, for Kierkegaard the subjective inwardness constitutes the self-evident truth whereas the subject-object relationships are dependent on the mediation of inferences to uphold their shaky hypotheses. Kierkegaard proclaims, therefore, with the categorical finality of a preacher that 'God is a subject'. Authentic existence is, therefore, lonely, and Kierkegaard declares with his irrepressible irony, 'Let no one invite me, for I will not dance'.[89] It takes two to tango, but, according to Kierkegaard, authentic being-in-the-world is a game of solitaire.

The solitude of the individual is a unique loneliness because his inner core is linked by an umbilical cord to unity. Of this the individual can be aware of only if he turns inwardly to his pure ani.

By prodding into his inner-self, man is revealed to truth and to God, which are synonymous. To this end, the outside, the objects, and the others are unnecessary and confounding and should be relegated by Occam's razor to the realms of superfluity.

Tautologies are sometimes not only useful but necessary.

'I am, therefore, I am' is one such tautology. It points to the primacy of the existing self, whose awareness is not inferred from anything extraneous to itself. It rejects the Cartesian cognito, because in order to think one has to exist first, and therefore, existence does not have to be inferred. It manifests itself through the inner attributeless self which is the primary channel of awareness both of oneself and of one's surroundings. This pure self was theorized by Husserl and conceptualized by Heidegger as Dasein, which is the state of being in the world and knowing it.[90] The Dasein man's being-in-the-word is uncovered (*aufgedeckt*) by, and from, its very being and does not, or cannot be, inferred from anything else.[91] Marcel also points out that the inner-self exists without the pure-self [92]: the Dasein is the veritas transcendentalis, the transcendental and phenomenological truth.[93] The unveiling, the disclosedness, the uncovering of being stems from the being-in-the-world itself and from a direct awareness of it without the mediation of logic or inference from human thought processes. Indeed, man's revelatory potential stems from this basic unveiling of the self by himself and to himself.

The participant stance that all sense perception is illusive and that all truth stems from the inner sense of being which is the manifestation of the infinite and indivisible unity is projected, mutatis mutandis, in most monotheistic creeds and proclaimed, inter alia, in the first commandment of the *Decalogue*. The primacy of the self as a chip of divinity was expounded by the Neo-Platonists, adopted by mystics of most denominations, and developed as the anchor of a whole philosophical weltanschauung by Kierkegaard. Heidegger reasserted the dasein as the expression of the 'I' about itself which is not itself a predicate, but the absolute subject.[94] Niels Bohr, a lifelong Kierkegaardian, was motivated in his studies of physics to unearth his truthful inner-self. Heidegger's philosophy is central to contemporary Existentialist thinking; hence, it is useful to compare his conceptualization to ours. Heidegger's conception of dasein as the unveiling and disclosure of being, as the basic ontological truth which needs no further proof,[95] is quite similar to the extreme participant pole of our personality continuum with its objectless pure-self (ani). This is the pole towards which the individual would move or yearn when his revelatory experiences are likely to manifest themselves.

The separant pole, however, where the interactive self (atzmi) is posited, anchors on logic and causality and would be quite amenable to the Cartesean cognito as proof of its existence. We do not, however, envisage an either/or alternative of either the dasein pure-self (ani) or the Cartesian cognito and the interactive self. In our model, both the inner-self and the interactive-self are part of the same continuum of being, though at opposing poles. This is where we differ from Heidegger and Descartes. Heidegger sees his dasein as being within space[96] whereas our ani is the primary awareness of being without the attributes of space and time.

Many of our mytho-empirical anchors are Gnostic and Kabbalist. These two disciplines are dualist and, hence, fit our basic conception of all creation as a perpetual interaction of the ani-consciousness and energy-matter through the mediation of symbolon structures.

Our first mytho-empirical anchor is taken from *Sha'arei Zedek*, a thirteenth-century Spanish Kabbalist tract, which states that lower man and the 'higher man sitting on the divine throne'[97] are both signified by the letter *yod*—this is the first of the Tetragrammaton and has the graphic shape of half a circle in Hebrew. These two yods, the two semi-circles, long to be united into a whole circle when lower and upper man are elevated to the Throne of Divinity. This could serve as a mytho-empirical anchor for the revelatory process of structuring the symbolon. The lower man representing the mortal human being is exposed to the upper man, who could signify the exposure to the inner ani-consciousness. This results in the integration of the two half circles into one. Translated into the conceptual context of our model, the interactive atzmi separant vector is integrated with the ani participant vector into the TR which forms the contents of the subsequently structured symbolon. This symbolon then triggers the creation of the Promethean holon, be it a Christmas dinner or an Eigenstate of a particle.

In a similar vein, the Gnostic Gospel of Philip speaks about truth and its image. 'Truth', it says, 'did not come into the world naked, but it came in types and images. It (the world) will not receive it in any other way. There is a rebirth and an image of rebirth. It is truly fitting to be reborn through the image. What is the resurrection and the image? It is fitting that it rise through the image'.[98]

We claim that the truth here, for the fiercely participant Gnostics, stands for the attributeless, pure ani-consciousness. The created world of spatio-temporality cannot accept it in its nakedness. It needs a go-between, an image which we interpret mytho-empirically as being our mediating symbolon structure.

In Gnosis, light, which with its participant bias would stand mytho-empirically for the ani and darkness, which represents the profane energy-matter, intermingle to create the world.

In the theosophic Kabbala, the ten sefirot contain an image of God clothing himself, yet these sefirot are an integral part of the divinity, 'like the garment of the grasshopper whose clothing is part of itself'.[99] These are the mytho-empirical manifestations of named archetypes, which are both an inner ani-consciousness dynamic and coined denotations facing creation. These holonic manifestations also represent the initial formations of the symbolon structures. The sefirot are then structured into five countenances which are the mytho-empirical projection of full-fledged symbolon connecting structures. As we shall see later, the coupling interaction or intercourse of these countenances constitutes acts of creation. In our conceptualization, the countenances are symboloi connecting structures which produce the Promethean holon, the entire holonic product, creation, or artifact.

According to the Kabbala, each life form and object has a transcendental root. This we could take to be a mytho-empirical projection of the symbolon structure as constituting the transcendental model or blueprint for creation. These roots constitute an integration of grace and stern judgment. Here again the participant bias of the Kabbala would conceive grace to be the projection of the ani-consciousness and stern judgment the projected profanity of energy-matter as represented by the interactive atzmi. The intermingling of sacred and profane elements in these Kabbalist roots is universal even at the risk of sacrilege. Thus, Moses had his root not only in Abel (grace), but also in Cain (stern judgment).

The initial stages of the symbolon formation are within the ani-consciousness. It is an intra-psychic revelatory dynamic—a dialectic between the ahistorical, pure ani and the historical Tantalic participant vector within the historical self. Mytho-empirically, this could be found in the Kabbalist notion of the divinities, self-entertainment. This dynamic could be a projection of the individual's prodding into his inner-self for the structuring of the symbolon through the revelatory intercourse (zivug) with the ani, pure transcendental consciousness.

The Kabbala conceived this revelatory process as a divine game of solitaire with the unitary God playing faute de mieux with himself.[100] This divine game of solitaire resulted in the formation of the symbolon connecting structure.

Mytho-empirically, this intra-psychic revelatory dialectic resulting in the formation of the symbolon is envisaged by the Kabbala as the process of creation, which started with God clothing himself in garments woven from the Torah and the letters of the Tetragrammaton. It is of crucial importance here to note that words and letters as intermediaries, i.e., as symboloi connecting structures between God and Creation were known in Jewish mysticism as early as *Sefer-Yetzira* (3rd to 6th century).[101]

The symbolon, which structures the TR within it, contains both participant ani-consciousness components and separant energy-matter components. The main asset of the symbolon is that it integrates within it the ahistorical ani-consciousness and spatio-temporal energy-matter. Thence, it can serve as a synthetic seed for further creation. Since revelation is not communicable, the revelatory components of the Tantalic ani must interact with temporal energy-matter in order to be communicable and to serve as a trigger for further cycles of creativity.

To sum up our present deliberations, we may envisage the revelatory intra-psychic dialectic as culminating in the structuring of the symbolon. The symbolon not only reveals what to do, i.e., lends meaning, but also how to do it and in which direction, i.e., lends value to the subsequent act. This when implemented in the act of creation will lend meaning and value to the created Promethean holon. The act of creation is, therefore, a dual process: an intra-psychic ontological dialectic leading to the formation of the symbolon and a subsequent epistemic process of creativity linking the ani-consciousness and energy-matter by the symbolon structure, thus creating the Promethean Holon. Schematically, this may be presented as follows (figure 3.10):

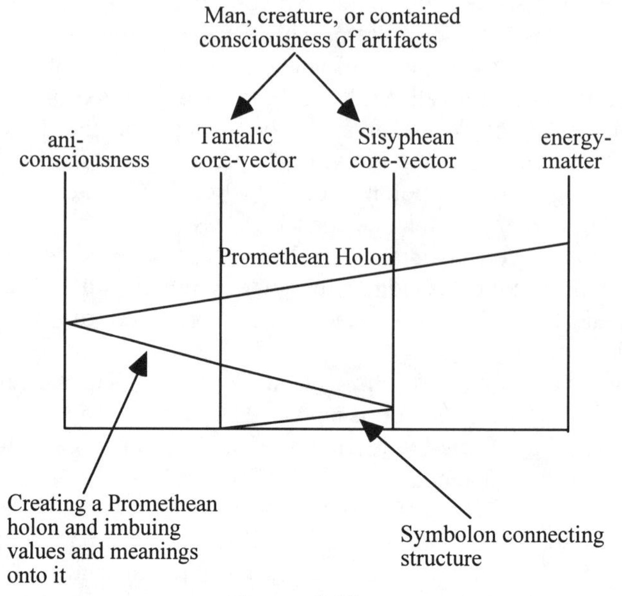

Figure 3.10

In its center, the scheme presents the dual Tantalic and Sisyphean core-vectors of man as the most elaborate synthesis of the basic dualities of creation. Alternatively, it could also represent any other creature or artifact with contained consciousness, like our quantum measurement instrument. The intra-psychic revelatory dialectic structures the symbolon and with it creates meanings and values to be subsequently transmitted to the created Promethean holon. The actual act of creation is represented by the creative process linking the outer columns of the scheme. We may note that the two consecutive processes form a spiral which represents our basic dual processes of the symbolon structure formation and the Promethean holon creation.

Before embarking on the actual process of creativity and, in our present context, the creation of the particle Eigenstate, let us examine the tool of the coupling creativity, i.e., the symbolon structure itself.

The symbolon, being the contents of the relational process, constitutes the raw mixture of elements of the ani and the cognitive elements of the object-other embodied in the atzmi within the self. The essence of the symbolon is the first ontological manifestation of the togetherness of the interacting elements different from its initial components. In so doing, the various symboloi overcome the ontological, existential, and social barriers. This happens because the cognitive relationships between the elements of ani-consciousness and atzmi elements which contain cognitions of energy-matter may create cognitively meaningful links between transcendence and history; self, objects, and others and relate oneself as an individual to the demands of society. Apart from this relationship within the symbolon there cannot be any meaning and, indeed, there is not. The symbolon is, therefore, our prime mover as far as our being-in-the-world is concerned since the measurement relationship between the ani-consciousness and energy-matter actually creates the Eigenstate of a particle. The symbolon linking the 'I' and thou actually create the meaningful relationship between the self and its surroundings and the authentic revelation within oneself projected outwardly are the mythogenic symboloi linking the 'pure ani with transcendence'. Still, the symbolon is not operative as a linking agent without its existential structuring. Hence, the tool of passing barriers and the linking between the ani-consciousness and its physical and metaphysical surroundings is the symbolon structure.

The Structure

The content of the symbolon structure is the TR, i.e., the ani-consciousness as reflected in our participant core-vector interacting with the atzmi components of the separant core-vectors of the self. These, when structured within the symbolon, would contain superimposed waves and/or virtual particles. However, at this stage we cannot offer a hypothesis as to how the ani and atzmi components of the TR actually interact within the symbolon structure. There was a time when brain researchers knew that there was a biochemical and electromagnetic interaction within the synapses between axons and dendrites of neurons, but did not know how the interrelationship and transfer of information actually took place. We are, by analogy, at a similar stage of knowledge—or rather ignorance—as to how the ani and atzmi actually interact and communicate within the symbolon structure. It may be that some spectacular advances in quantum mechanics and neuro-science will shed light on the basic interactions between consciousness and energy-matter within the symbolon structure. It is more likely that we shall never discover these basic dynamics because they are linked to the basic paradox of our being.

This paradox relates to Ego's feeling and his realization that he was chosen to be the channel of awareness through his ani-consciousness, not only of his own being but also of the whole of creation. This makes for a solipsistic sense of being a unique and exclusive center of the cosmos. Schopenhauer admitted that one cannot argue with a solipsist but only send him to a madhouse. Surely, if the solipsist is willing to extricate himself from his quandary he may do so through our conception of an imperfect, ever-striving transcendence in the following manner. He should realize that the awareness of the ani is not his alone. The unique awareness perceived in his pure ani-consciousness—without interactional attributes—is a unity and, hence, common to all fauna and flora. Each lifeform, as well as Ego, feels this basic awareness through this unique bio-psycho-social configuration and, therefore, perceives this ani awareness in a kaleidoscopic manner specific to itself. This space-time kaleidoscope cuts off Ego from the other life forms and from the realization that the basic awareness in his pure ani-consciousness and transcendence are one.

The immutable ani-consciousness peers through ever-changing configurations of life forms, artifacts and objects, and this combination of immutability and kaleidoscopically changing plurality makes for the uniqueness and irreplicability of each creature. Hence, the reflected historical ani in a specific self and the transcendental, pure ani-consciousness cannot be creative in unity: as Sisyphus has to have his stone in order to be creative, so Ego has to feel apart and separate from the transcendental ani for the interactive experience of creativity or, for that matter, for all experience, except for revelation, to take place. Hence, Ego is a partner of the transcendental ani in creativity.

Mytho-empirically, we have the description of the Maggid of Meseritz following certain Kabbalist traditions according to which God contracted himself so that he could experience man's adventures vicariously through human cognition. 'The sages', says the Maggid, 'affect God through their mind; so that He thinks what they think. If they think in love, they bring God into the realm of love as stated in the Zohar. A King (God) is imprisoned in the tresses of the (human) mind'.[102] The kaleidoscopic presence of divine unity in every object and life form is also apparent in the following passage from Plotinus:

> It is a common conception of human thought that a principle single in number and identical is everywhere present in its entirety, for it is an instinctive and universal truism that the divinity which dwells within each of us is single and identical in all.[103]

In Lurianic Kabbala, the doctrine that God is present in every life form and object is basic. 'There is nothing in the world,' says Vital, 'and in all the worlds and in all parts of creation; the inanimate plants, living and talking, that does not have in it sparks of divinity which are embedded in their profane shells.'[104]

All creation, not only man, was thrown into spatio-temporality, and all flora, fauna, and inanimate objects are, in this respect, equal to man, with exiled cores of divinity encased in every created separatum and every vestige of spatio-temporality. Ibn Tabul describes this sequel to the breaking of the vessels as follows: 'And the *reshimu* of (Divine) light...was scattered within and amongst the (sinister) powers of judgment, and these were crystallized like containers which served as a body for a soul and, thus, a light particle is clothed by a (profane) container',[105] Hence, each object and life form of creation is composed of divine particles embedded within containers of less sacred, and, in the lower spheres, downright profane, matter.

The barrier between Ego and transcendence must be hermetically sealed; otherwise, the creative interaction between experientially different entities cannot be effected. Ego is, thus, interacting with a less than perfect transcendence which needs him for its feeling of creativity, yet cannot allow him to know that he is part of it. Ego is moved and motivated as we have seen by the dialectical quests of the TR, which are the things-in-themselves and, hence, part of transcendence. The longing for a perfect transcendence cannot and should not be realized, otherwise the seemingly all-important relationship between Ego and transcendence cannot be creative or even sustained. Hence, we have a double paradox: an imperfect transcendence makes for existence, creativity, and revelation whereas a perfect absolute transcendence, if achieved, is tantamount to nihilation and extinction of both transcendence and Ego.

The possible solution of this paradox is that imperfection is perfect in the sense that it lends life and creativity to the dyad of Ego and transcendence, whereas the perfection of transcendence spells inertia, sterility, and the perfection of absolute death.

However, we still have another paradox and this is the question of why the universal ani-consciousness chose a specific, atzmi historical, interactive self, such as a particular lump of energy matter or, in the author's case, a unique 95 kg. heap of flesh, bone, marrow, blood, and sinew, to be the seat of the awareness of the whole cosmos. This paradox seems to have no answer, and it may be that this is our metaphysical prime mover which keeps us ever looking, probing, and searching for the transcendental meanings of our existence, our origins before birth, and our destination after death. If the TR is our prime mover within our personality, the second paradox relating to the unexplained choice of our body as the channel of universal awareness and consciousness may be our transcendental prime mover. There could be no better illustration of our present premise than Roger Penrose's self-searching question as to why he wrote the book which we rely on in our present work. Penrose says:

> ...there is a simple bottom line reason for believing that consciousness must have *some* active effect even if this effect is *not* one of selective advantage. For why is it that beings like ourselves should sometimes be troubled—especially when probed on the matter-by questions about self? (I could almost say; 'Why are *you* reading this chapter?' or 'Why did *I* feel a strong desire to write a book on this topic in the first place?') It is hard to imagine that an entirely unconscious automaton should waste its time with such matters. Since conscious beings, on the other hand, *do* seem to act in this funny way from time to time, they are, thereby, behaving in a way that is *different* from the way that they would if *not* conscious—so consciousness has *some* active effect! Of course, there would be no problem about deliberately programming a computer to seem to behave in this ridiculous way (e.g., it could be programmed to go around muttering, 'Oh dear, what is the meaning of life? Why am I here? What on earth is this self that I feel?') But why should natural selection bother to favor such a race of individuals, when surely the relentless free market of the jungle should have rooted out such useless nonsense long ago![106]

The answer to Penrose's query might well be the paradox which we have presented here; a paradox of a universal consciousness having chosen a specific body, mine (or Penrose's) through which to be aware of the whole of creation. This paradox may well provide Penrose's (and my own) motivation to probe into the relationships between consciousness and energy-matter.

This paradox is exacerbated, or rather complemented, by the basic paradox of quantum mechanics: the duality of particles and waves which has fueled the efforts and imaginative questions of quantum physicists from Bohr to Wheeler, from Feynman to Everett, and from Bohm to Penrose. They and many others have tried to solve this paradox with apparent success only to realize that the vicissitudes of the paradox re-emerge again from unexpected angles and quarters. Our own work is no exception. We have tried to integrate this paradox using new tools and a hitherto untried frame of reference, yet here again, when all is said and done, a doubt sets in, and either we or somebody else, prodded by the ontological and metaphysical paradoxes which we have presented above as well as by the quantum mechanical paradox, will again try to solve these contrarieties by new methods and from new angles. This is the Sisyphean essence of all creative ventures.

To sum up our deliberations on the symbolon structure, we might as well return to our spiral model linking the symbolon structure to the Promethean holon.

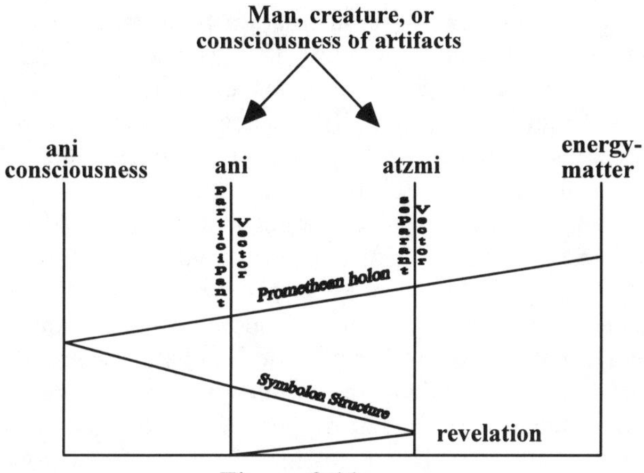

Figure 3.11

The act of revelation created the symbolon and imbued it with contained consciousness. The symbolon is, thus, provided with a deterministic goal. The creation of a Promethean holon (PH) in the form of the quantum measuring instrument is an indeterministic decision by the human observer. However, once the instrument has been constructed, the deterministic task of the contained consciousness of the instrument is to create a PH in the form of a particle. It cannot innovate, improvise, or decide to measure. Its contained consciousness is strictly commissioned and deterministically programmed to perform preordained tasks.

In this respect, there is no difference between a measuring instrument and the most sophisticated computers. Both are programmed by their contained consciousnesses to perform deterministically pre-ordained tasks. The human observer may conceive of another symbolon structure and then decide indeterministically to construct with it another PH, but as far as the previous PH is concerned, he is out of the game. He cannot have direct recourse to the micro quantum world; only the PH, the measuring instrument, can do thus. The human observer can decide to cut off the power to the measuring instrument or otherwise neutralize it, but this is another ball game, another symbolon structure. Man is ever-conceiving new symbolon structures. This characterizes more than anything else his mental functioning. Subsequently he will decide to implement only a few of these symboloi into Promethean holons.

The creation of the symbolon structure is a participant dynamic and mostly unconscious; whereas the creation of the PH is a separant process and mostly conscious. Thus, the creation of everything from a micro quantum mechanical Eigenstate of a particle to the twin towers of the New York Trade Center is an alternation between participant symboloi and separant Promethean holons. This is the universal rhythms of revelation and creation. This is also our conception of complementarity, in contrast to the non-realistic disconnected probability and, at the same time, mechanistic complementarity of the Copenhagen interpretation.

Mytho-empirically, this is projected by the Kabbala as the constant agapic mating of the two supernal countenances of Abba (father) and Ima (mother). The erotic mating of the lower countenances, *ze'er anpin* (the lower masculine countenance) and *nukbah* (the lower feminine countenance), are not continuous but sporadic for ad hoc needs.[107] This mytho-empirical mating represents the Kabbalist world of *tikkun,* the world of mending or of making whole. In our conceptualization, this would represent the processes of transition from the mental (agapic) structuring of the symbolon to the actual construction or (erotic) procreation of the PH by the seed of the symbolon structure. Indeed, the supernal mating between the Kabbalist upper countenances of Abba and Ima produces the da'at, the knowledge of revelatory grace. We hold that da'at represents the revelatory symbolon structure mytho-empirically. It is the shout of *Eureka!* when the parts of the model fall into place and when the design of the quantum measurement seems to us to be complete.

The erotic mating between the lower countenances which we hold to be the actual creation of the PH is facilitated by the theurgic, mending efforts of man.[108] This is the complete mytho-empirical dynamic of the revelatory formation of the symbolon structure and the creation of the PH through the mediating services of man. One important result of the complementarity between the supernal revelatory agapic mating and the lower erotic creative mating is that every life form and object must have a particle of divinity in it.

Mandean Gnosis posits that the will of the Father (the Godhead) flows into every object and life form. The Kabbala postulates a panpsychism with particles of light present in all objects and life forms.[109] Kordovero, the sixteenth-century Safedean Kabbalist, held that God is embedded in all creatures and all objects,[110] and Rabbi Nachman of Bratzlav declared that everything, animal and plant, contained a spark of divinity in its core. Buber's Existentialism envisaged a hidden thou in each life form and object, capable of being discovered by dialogue.

This is the mytho-empirical projection of the presence of the reflection of the universal, pure ani-consciousness, integrated with energy-matter, in all life forms, artifacts, and objects.

We may sum up our deliberations on the symboloi structures by pointing out that they can be conscious or subconscious and, thus, be in the realm of potential non-being. They constitute the ego-boundary formed around the self at the end of early orality to form an individual self, which is distinct from his objective and human surroundings and the ego-identity, which is the individual's normative structure vis-à-vis the social and normative structures. Once a link between consciousness and energy-matter between the inner-self and the outside objects and others, between the historical-self and transcendence, have been formed, it is subject to evolution, and the nascent symbolon structure is viable according to its ability to better link between the ani-consciousness and its human objective and metaphysical surroundings. Therefore, our conception of functionalism as related to structuralism is the aptitude of the symbolon structure to help the ani-consciousness better pass over its ontological, existentialist, and social barriers and link it to energy-matter. Man is the crown of creation so long as he is the best available creator of symboloi structures. Once a better (i.e., more functional) mediator evolves, man is sure to be dethroned.

At this stage, however, man is the mediating agent between his psyche and the created work of art and the artifact as well as between the measurement instrument and the Eigenstate of a particle.

Once the symbolon structure has been formed, it is fueled by the separant quests and participant longings within its TR, but the transition from the potential of the symbolon structure to the act of creation takes place through an indeterministic act of intention. This intentionality, as we have mentioned earlier, lends meaning to our acts. This has been noted by Husserl and fits the vectorial teleology of our model. The transition from the thought to the word, from the Logos to the Act, has been admirably described by Goethe's Faust, as follows:

> It is written: 'In the beginning was the word'. Here am I baulked: who now can help afford? The Word?—impossible so high to rate it; And otherwise must I translate it, if by the Spirit I am truly taught. Then thus 'In the Beginning was the Thought' This first line let me weigh completely, lest my impatient pen proceed too fleetly. Is it the thought which works, creates. 'In the Beginning was the Power', I read. Indeed? Yet, as I write, a warning is suggested, that I the sense may not have fairly tested. The Spirit aids me: Now I see the light. 'In the Beginning was the Act', I write.[111]

The evolution of a Faust progresses from the word, the core of a holistic idea, to the thought: the derivation of being from the Cartesian cognito. The power is the dialectical energy which is generated within the TR and which finally finds its outlet in the act, in the object manipulation of the atzmi. Indeed, there could be no better description of the flow of energy from the self to the object than this outward bound progression of the Faustian atzmi.

In our conceptualization, the transition from the potential of the symbolon structure to the creative act is by an indeterministic intention which lends meaning, not only to the act but also, to the Promethean holon produced by the act of creation. This intentionality also reflects the unity of the ani-consciousness, which we hold to be at the basis of the experimentally observed unity of consciousness, as well as the unifying nature of perception.[112] We also claim that our perception is then selectively directed by our indeterministic intention to choose from our surrounding energy-matter, objects, and life forms those items and patterns which fit the design of the symbolon structure for the construction of the Promethean holon. We have already pointed out that perception is biased by the bio-psycho-social configuration of each individual, but we now add a more basic bias of perception according to the vectorial contents of each symbolon structure. The selectivity of perception is an ad hoc dynamic determined by the intention to look for raw material for the construction of the Promethean holon as decreed by the symbolon structure.

It might be useful to refer again to our spiral model as a visual aid for our explanation as to the relationship between the symbolon structure and the Promethean holon in the act of creation.

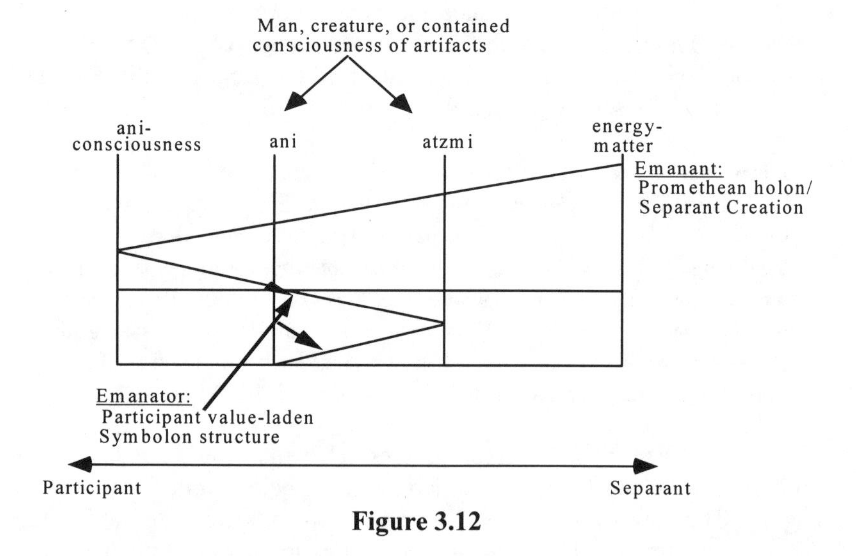

Figure 3.12

The symbolon structure when embarking on its creative task following an indeterministic decision by the creator connects the ani-consciousness with energy-matter to form, according to its seed blueprint, the Promethean holon, the historical creature object. The link of the ani component of the symbolon structure with the pure ani is direct and instantaneous. The ani-component of the symbolon is just the reflection of the pure ani-consciousness. Both are ahistorical. Hence, there is no need for non-local pilot waves or tachion particles which fly faster than light to convey information from one particle to another in the EPR thought experiment and the Bell-Aspect inequality violation experiment. Distance, diachronicity, and locality are spatio-temporal dynamics, whereas the link between the ani component of the symbolon and the pure ani-consciousness (Buber's universal Thou) is synchronic, direct, and non-local, because both are manifestations of the same ahistorical entity.

Moreover, our solution would not encounter special-relativity difficulties as other models do,[113] because the communication through the ani-consciousness is instantaneous. The particles in the EPR thought experiment and the Bell and Aspect experiment were correlated before flying off to different directions and, thus, had the same ani component which further facilitated the instantaneous non-local communication between them. Yet, as Penrose rightly says,[114] most if not all particles in creation are entangled and correlated. Hence, the possibility of instantaneous non-local communication through the ani-consciousness contained within these particles is universal. However, we should stress once more that this instantaneous communication is possible only on the quantum level and not on the classical level. There 'monads have no windows', to borrow Liebnitz's enigmatic phrase again. We also exclude any ESP phenomena on the classical level as bases for the arguments in our present work.

Per contra, the link between the atzmi component of the symbolon and energy-matter is elaborate and rather indirect. This might be related mytho-empirically to the link effected by the kabbalist or *yashar* (direct light) streaming from the Godhead, whereas *or hozer* (returning or refracted light) characterizes the dynamics of the lower sefirot (holonic rungs) and the world of creation, which is the mytho-empirical projection of energy-matter. The atzmi and energy-matter, both being spatio-temporal, obey the rule of the attraction of non-likes and the repelling of likes which prevails both in physics and in socio-personal relationships. This rule, which we have denoted as the least interest principle, operates in the manner we shall now outline.

Most of our experience in deprivational interaction with our surroundings is negative, because of our basic separant competitive orientation towards other human beings and our achievement-motivated efforts to control our environment. Such efforts usually fail because others also aim to control their environment, including the ego itself, and because the more one succeeds in one Sisyphean task the more one increases one's Sisyphean goals which, thus, become progressively unattainable. This is one of the main separant mechanisms guarding against a too close rapprochement between the ego and its surrounding objects and life forms. However, the most effective separant safeguard against participation is the least interest principle, which ordains that the more the ego strives to gain control over its surroundings or to gain possession of goods, power, and money, the less it is likely to succeed in its aims. The least interest principle operates on all levels of human behavior and may, therefore, be denoted as a meta-dynamic. It functions in a curvilinear relationship with separant goals. Some achievement motivation is needed for the ego to muster all its energies to achieve its Sisyphean aims, but, at a certain intensity of motivation and effort, it becomes counterproductive. Beyond a certain level of exertion to achieve a separant aim, the marginal returns decrease. The least interest principle operates, thus, as a negative feed-back cycle effecting a rupture between the ego and its goal whenever the efforts to attain it become too strenuous or frantic. Consequently, when the ego's attitude towards the achievement of separant goals is almost neutral or nonchalant, it has the best chance of gaining them. The least interest principle operates in full force in the emotional relationship between the sexes[115] and in power-based interaction in politics and business.[116]

Dialectics, as the unifying mechanism of existence, ordain that man can never achieve his Sisyphean quests and Tantalic longings but only a synthesis between them, which then serves as a thesis for another dialectical zig-zag ad infinitum. Consequently, man's fate is ever to seek something and always attain something else. This is masterfully portrayed by Beckett, whose Watt always longs to go north while his legs lead him southwards.

The synthetic result of dialectics is the compromising middle range principle of the golden rule—or, the Greek, 'nothing in excess'—which was projected onto transcendence as the main principle governing both life and the heavenly bodies. Even the planets will be scourged by the Furies if they leave their ordained course. If one exceeds the middle course and one's moira, one commits the capital sin of hübris, punishable most strenuously by the Olympians. If one does not maneuver oneself skillfully between the extremes of Scylla and Charybdis, one is sure to perish.

In physics the least interest principle is apparent in the attraction of nonlikes and the repelling of like ones in electromagnetic charges. It also operates in the short range of the strong nuclear force, which is just strong enough to offset the repelling force of the positively charged nucleus and in Pauli's exclusion principle, which does not allow Fermions of spin 1/2 to occupy more than one physical state. The dialectics between the repelling and attracting forces within the atom are responsible for its system-in-balance; otherwise, all matter would be squeezed back into singularities.

To return to the interaction between the atzmi and energy-matter, in view of the least interest principle, which guards against successful participation in unity, marking the end of life and creation, the interaction must be indirect and maieutic in the following manner: The ani component of the symbolon structure ingrained in the measurement instrument of the double-slit experiment transmits to the ani component (the contained consciousness) of the photon emitting instrument that it intends to measure a particle. When the superimposed energy flowing into the physical system (double slits) comes into contact with the atzmi component of the symbolon structure contained within the measurement instrument (the particle counter) it serves only as a maieutic trigger which catalyzes the actual particle formation. This is so because the information (order, decision) to form the particle was already transmitted synchronically by the ani component contained in the measuring instrument to consciousness contained within the energy source (the photon gun the ani). The contact with the energy-matter component (the atzmi) of the symbolon structure triggers the emergence of a packet of energy from the superposition in the physical system into an Eigenstate of a particle. We have here a complementarity between the formation of a particle transmitted outside spatio-temporality through the synchronicity of the ani-consciousness, and the actual atzmi component of the symbolon structure embedded within the measurement instrument.

The trigger could be effected by a local junction between a virtual particle or a resonant tangential junction stemming from the atzmi component of the symbolon structure embedded in the measurement instrument and the superposed energy within the physical system. Such a trigger is unobservable and also unhampered by the uncertainty barrier.

This is our conception of the complementarity between consciousness and energy-matter in the formation of a particle in the double-slit experiment. Similar complementarities may explain the Bell inequality violation, as well as the transmission of the stunning force of a fifteenth-century Bosch painting to the author, who recently visited the Prado Museum in Madrid.

The Neoplatonic Plotinus envisaged that the creative transition from transcendental unity to the world soul, which contains the temporal created world, is mediated by the *Nous,* the cosmic intelligence.[117] The Gnostic Gospel of Truth envisages the Father (Godhead) mingling with matter through the mediating services of the savior-messenger (Logos).[118]

We, however, hypothesize an intermingling of the transcendental ani-consciousness and energy-matter which already takes place in the mediating symbolon structure. Hence, it can trigger the Promethean holon which is the product created in its own image. The crucial point, however, is that the measurement act raises the quantum event to the classical level.

Apparently this transition is effected by a quantum jump through the barrier dividing the classical and quantum worlds. This is the basic enigma of quantum mechanics. Roger Penrose's elegant mathematical formula linking the amplitudes of the time-evolving wave function (u) with the indeterministic act of measurement (R) is an immensely useful computation. It does not, alas, explain the processes represented by the mathematical formalism. We, however, try to explain this quantum jump over the boundary separating the quantum and classical worlds by a convergence of two processes: the instantaneous transmission of information by the ani-consciousness component of the symbolon structure contained within the measuring instrument, followed by a maieutic triggering of virtual particles and processes stemming from the separant energy component of the symbolon structure which catalyzes the formation of the PH particle. The quantum jump is, thus, effected, not by a direct, local link, but by a maieutic trigger which algorithmizes—this is a preposterous expression, but it does describe the process—a particle out of the superimposed energy waves. This is an act of creation, ex nihilo. We do not accept the implication of Penrose's description of an orthogonal combination of states from which the measurement act chooses one which jumps into reality.[119]

Thus, the act of measurement creates—although maieutically and by means of an indirect trigger—the spin of a particle and the particle itself.

The System-In-Balance

Once the particle has been created, it requires a system, in, balance for its subsistence in its Eigenstate. If Roger Penrose is right, this system-in-balance is between quantum gravity and entropy.[120]

Even if Penrose is not right, then some other forces will prove to sustain the system-in-balance of the particle. This system-in-balance is universal and stems from the holonic duality of life forms and objects. We postulate that nuclei of atoms are held together by a system in balance between the strong nuclear force and the repelling force of the positive charges of the protons in the nucleus, that the electromagnetic force and Pauli's exclusion principle hold the atom in a system-in-balance while gravity and the centrifugal force hold the solar system in-balance. Life forms, from the cell to the organism, are held in a system-in-balance by forces which we do not have the ability or the knowledge to examine. In chapter one, we showed how the human personality is held in a system-in-balance by its participant and separant core-vectors. We hold that such a system-in-balance of objects and life forms is necessary for their space-time existence and evolutionary survival. It is reflected in our model of the system-in-balance of the symbolon structure between the ani-consciousness and energy as well as in the holonic balance between the Tantalic and Sisyphean forces within the PH. If we return to the particle, so long as the system-in-balance holds, so does the particle. Once the balance is disrupted, the particle may decay into other particles or revert back to a superposed wave-like form.

Following our method, we shall trace some of the mytho-empirical anchors for the necessity of a system-in-balance of both life forms and objects on all levels of existence.

Any conspicuous difference between individuals and groups may lead to an increase in their mutual suspicions. Such differences reduce one's tendency to identify with others and make it easier to project guilt upon them in the form of social stigma. Thus, one of the most ancient sources of ethnocentrism lay in the perception of members of the outgroup not only as different, but actually as dangerous. Sumner tells us that 'each group nourishes its own pride and vanity, boasts itself superior...and looks with contempt on the outsider...The Tupis called the Portuguese by a derisive epithet descriptive of birds which have feathers around their feet on account of their trousers'.[121]

The significant point, however, is not success, but rather conspicuousness. The Azande will proclaim persons who are deformed, ill-tempered, glum, or who behave in a bizarre manner to be witches. All these signs show their potential danger, and they are, therefore, stigmatized and ostracized.[122] When Azande say that an action or feeling is bad, they mean that it is socially deplorable and condemned by public opinion. It is bad because it may lead to witchcraft and because it brings the offending person into greater or lesser disrepute. It is in the idiom of witchcraft that the Azande express moral rules which mostly lie outside criminal and civil law. The stigmatized person is outside the realm of the normative system of the tribe; he is a dog-like being whose huts may be burned and whose women and children destroyed with impunity.[123] We mentioned earlier that the criteria for proclaiming a person a heretic in the

Middle Ages were peculiarities of conversation, strange language, dress, manners, or unusual restraint in conduct. If a Jew is strangely attired, a black man has a strange family life and different sexual mores, if a foreigner acts queerly, or if an intellectual has strange and dangerous ideas, he is different and incomprehensible and, therefore, arouses anxiety. The stigmatizer cannot identify with them. They are 'not like us' and are, thus, suitable objects of the stigmatizer's projection and displacement mechanisms.

For example, in the ancient tribal society of the Middle East, fratricide was among the worst crimes, since it undermined the basis of social organization—family relations. The bearer of the original Mark of Cain was not only damned by man; the land that he cultivated was cursed: 'When thou tillest the ground, it shall not henceforth yield unto thee her strength; a fugitive and vagabond shalt thou be in the earth'. The pollution presumably stems from the identity of social norms and religious ones in ancient times. The offender acted against the divine order and was, therefore, considered a representation of evil. He, thus, became a source of moral pollution.

Ranulf cites a seventeenth-century English Puritan sermon: 'Sinne leaves a kind of blemish and stain upon the soul after the commission of it...The Scripture calls it the excrement of naughtiness, though the act of sin is gone yet there is a blemish on the soul....So a man after sin shall find himself dull to any good, and prone to any evil'.[124] This is a perfect illustration of the symbolic value of the derogatory tag. This pollution was deemed to be contagious; the stigmatized offender was very often segregated and ostracized. Frazer cites instances of this stigmatized pollution.[125] In ancient Attica, murderers were ostracized and outlawed, and anyone could injure or kill them with impunity. If another trial was pending against a murderer, he could return to defend himself, but he had to do so on board a boat, while the judges conducted the trial on the seashore. The murderer was not allowed to touch the shore lest he pollute the land and the people by contagion.

Thucydides tells the story of Alcmeon, who wandered the earth after the murder of his mother; he had been told by the Oracle of Apollo that he would never find peace until he discovered some place which had not yet been in existence nor been seen by the sun at the time he slew his mother; only there could he settle; the rest of the earth was accursed to him.[126]

Thus, stigma and its social consequences historically preceded the normalization of sanction. Sanction was originally an expiatory act that was supposed to cleanse and purge the pollution and stigma incurred by the violation. Philological support for this premise is to be found in the origin of the word punishment (*peine* in French, *poena* in Latin, and *poine* in Greek), which derive from the Sanskrit root PU, which means to cleanse, to purify. The crime offends the gods and pollutes the community; formal punishment cleanses the community of its pollution and, thus, appeases the gods.

The phenomenon of stigma for violation of norms is almost universal. There are numerous examples in mythology, drama, and history. In Aeschylus' House of Atreus, the Oracle of Apollo instructs Orestes to avenge the blood of his father Agamemnon because the murderer has been cursed by the wrath of the gods. If the sin is not expiated by punishment, the whole community might suffer diseases and disasters.[127] The Manteans of ancient Greece purified themselves after they met the murderers of Arcadia. The Kikuyu tribesmen in Kenya used to purify themselves after a chance meeting with a murderer; every chattel or object which came in contact with the murderer also had to be destroyed. The Chama Indians forbade the murderer to wave his hands, comb his hair, or dine with his fellow tribesmen, and in the hunting period he had to camp far away from the tents of the rest of the tribe.[128]

Another instance of stigmatization has been described in a study of the Amazon Indians. This is of special importance because until recently these tribes possessed a whole system of purification rites, the sole purpose of which was to cleanse the tribesmen from the polluting presence of a murderer or other offender against tribal taboos.[129]

In a primitive society, stigma in the form of taboo is the most prevalent sanction for non-normative behavior. Stigmas are applied to enforce dietary, familial, and sexual norms and to sanction rules pertaining to property, war, ghosts, religion, and group solidarity.[130] Frazer cites many instances in which usurpers of the chief's authority, unauthorized users of his property and clothes, and uninvited participants in his meals became taboo. Being declared taboo in a primitive society is the strongest sanction imaginable, sometimes tantamount to a death sentence. Frazer's examples include a New Zealand native who died of painful convulsions after becoming taboo for eating his chief's food and a Maori chief's tinder-box that actually killed several persons who lit their pipes from it because they died of fright on learning to whom it belonged. Death from taboo, although induced by shock from imaginary fear, is a potent reinforcement to the norm. For the savage, taboo is not a spiritual or intangible entity; for him it is, to quote Frazer, 'as real as gravity and may kill him as certainly as a dose of prussic acid'.

It is not only the anthropomorphic Greek gods or primitive tribes who punish man's disruption of the system-in-balance severely. Lurianic Kabbala sees original sin as inherent in Adam's hübris, as expressed by his over-eagerness to copulate with Eve. He disrupted the cosmic system-in-balance by carrying out his mating zivug before the Sabbath—an optimal time for a zivug of mending, tikkun. In addition, he performed a disrupting and polluting mating with Lilith-Satan's consort, thereby, bringing about the profane zivug of Eve with the snake.[131] In a like manner, Moses also committed hübris by striking the rock, instead of talking to it as ordained by God, in order to free the water within. Moses, thus, also caused a disrupting zivug instead of a harmonious one.[132] The fiercest excesses and their ruthless punishment are found in Amos chapter 6:1–14:

1.Woe to them that are at ease in Zion, and trust in the mountain of Samaria, which are named chief of the nations, to whom the house of Israel came!

2.Pass ye unto Calneh, and see; and from thence go ye to He'math the great: then go down to Gath of the Philistines: be they better than these kingdoms? or their border greater than your border?

3.Ye that put far away the evil day, and cause the seat of violence to come near;

4.That lie upon beds of ivory, and stretch themselves upon their couches, and eat the lambs out of the flock, and the calves out of the midst of the stall;

5.That chant to the sound of the viol, and invent to themselves instruments of musick, like David;

6.That drink wine in bowls, and anoint themselves with the chief ointments: but they are not grieved for the affliction of Joseph.

7 Therefore now shall they go captive with the first that go captive, and the banquet of them that stretched themselves shall be removed.

8.The Lord God hath sworn by himself, saith the Lord the God of hosts, I abhor the excellency of Jacob, and hate his palaces: therefore will I deliver up the city with all that is therein.

9.And it shall come to pass, if there remain ten men in one house, that they shall die.

10.And a man's uncle shall take him up, and he that burneth him, to bring out the bones out of the house, and shall say unto him that is by the sides of the house, Is there yet any with thee? and he shall say, No. Then shall he say, Hold thy tongue for we may not make mention of the name of the Lord

> 11.For, behold, the Lord commandeth, and he will smite the great house with breaches, and the little house with clefts.
>
> 12.Shall horses run upon the rock? will one plow there with oxen? for ye have turned judgement into gall, and the fruit of righteousness into hemlock:
>
> 13.Ye which rejoice in a thing of nought, which say, Have we not taken to us horns by our own strength?
>
> 14. But, behold, I will raise up against you a nation, O house of Israel, saith the Lord the God of hosts; and they shall afflict you from the entering in of He'math unto the river of the wilderness.[133]

We have here the luxurious excesses of hedonism, the hübris of assuming to be like King David, God's abhorrence of the hübristic excesses of Israel, and his smiting of those who falsely claimed to have vigor (horns). The hübris of pride, indeed, disrupts man-transcendence relationships. Hence, 'everyone that is proud in heart is an abomination to the Lord[...]he shall not be unpunished.'[134]

We have already pointed out that the breaking of the vessels was a violent disruption of the system-in-balance of the Godhead, whereas original sin and the golden calf represented dramatic disruptions in the process of his mending.

Indeed, man's system-in-balance on all three levels of his being—biological, personal and social—is very precarious. In *The Myth of Tantalus*, we discussed the vulnerability of the Sisyphean and Tantalic types to outside stimuli. On the cortical level, the activist Sisyphean needs the initial arousal more than the Tantalic type in order to initiate his functioning. On the personality level, the Tantalic type is averse to stimuli, whereas the Sisyphean is hungry for them. On the social level, the Sisyphean is a group performer, whereas the Tantalic type is a loner.[135] These traits, as measured along continua, can be used to indicate the vulnerability of the various types to the disruption of the system-in-balance on these three levels which are, of course, interrelated within the individual as a holistic unit. When one of these levels, or the whole person, is exposed to a traumatic experience, they try to mend themselves on another level of being. However, when these tikkunim are not successful, the individual may die, become insane, or become alienated. There is no intrinsic difference between the vulnerability of the system-in-balance of man or of God. Both have to be mended if their inner equilibrium has been disrupted. This makes for constant change, both in man and God. Both mortal and divine are in a constant process of becoming. They undergo processes, but, in line with their Tantalic and Sisyphean meta-myths, they never reach their goals.

A system-in-balance also constitutes a prerequisite for revelation and creativity. Revelation can flow through a balanced infrastructure and then be transmitted to others and to God as a universal thou. Man, through his creativity, is also the connecting link between the mindless, valueless demiurgos and the powerless and silent Godhead. Man creates the viable equilibrium between psyche and soma, between God and his creation. There can be no abdication for a creative Sisyphus; without him everything reverts to chaos.

The Spiral

The act of creation brings us back to our original spiral. The symbolon structure is the structured operational containment of the Tantalus Ratio (TR), which in turn is the prime moving dialectic between the ani-consciousness and energy-matter. As we have seen, this symbolon structure triggers the creation of the particle as a Promethean holon (PH). We have seen that although the PH could be any artifact or life form, in all cases the holonic dynamics of creation are similar. Yet the spiral does not stop there. We have seen that the participant longing and separant quests inherent in our prime moving TR can never be achieved, so where, then, does this non-expended vectorial energy move to. We hold that after the act of creation the vectorial non-expended energy inherent in the TR is projected onto transcendence as separant myths of experience and participant myths of longing. These in turn refuel the batteries of the TR, which has been deflated, which then invests its energies into more symboloi structures which trigger the creation of PHs, da capo. Graphically, our spiral would then look as follows:

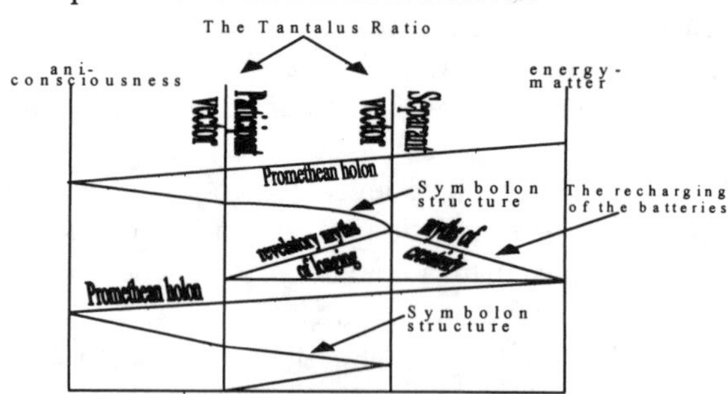

Figure 3.13

Our scheme, thus, presents the whole dynamic progression from the TR as prime mover, its structuring within a symbolon to its maieutic triggering of a PH.

Since the continuum of these Tantalic and Sisyphean myths—the projection of which is generated by the unachievable goals of our core-vectors—corresponds to the participant and separant dualities of the TR, the symbolon structure. Then, mytho-empirically and even etymologically, this duality is apparent from the Greek and Hebrew words for the world. In Greek, it is cosmos, i.e. order, the separant arrangement of objects and life forms in a pre-determined scheme. In contrast, the Hebrew word for world is *olam,* which is related to *healem,* the clandestine nothingness, representing participant wholeness. This is related to our core continuum, ranging from separant being to participant nothingness.

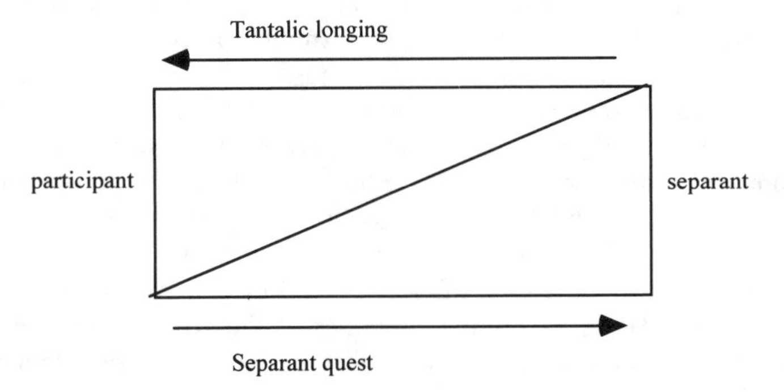

Figure 3.14

The recharging of our participant core vectors by Tantalic myths of revelation would correspond mytho-empirically to the Kabbalist *hessed*, the Gnostic *ogdoad* and the Buberian universal Thou. In Eastern creeds, this would have its equivalent in the mandala and other revelatory mythologenes. The separant recharging of batteries would be by Sisyphean mytholegenes ranging from the Greek archetypal anthropomorphic gods through the Germanic war gods to the contemporary American myths of the superman, the cowboy, Horatio Alger and his rise from rags-to-riches. The participant mythological recharging of our ani core vectors make for a mytho-empirical projection of our ani-consciousness as a particle of divinity. In fact, the mytho-empirical projection of our ani core-vector as part of divinity makes our TR an initial link between transcendence and history. The dialectical quests of the TR are both in history and outside it. The fact that my body has been chosen to be the channel for transcendence is the initial metaphysical factor which motivates our transcendental quests. This is the insoluble riddle which leads us to turn to God for answers. 'Behold the fire and the wood, but where is the lamb for a burnt offering?', asks Isaac, and Abraham answers, 'God will himself provide for a burnt offering'.[136] But he does not. Isaac is offered as a burnt whole, and the sacrificial Isaac syndrome actually provides the basis for morals and normativeness, both for man and transcendence. The link between the transcendental thing-in-itself and the prime mover in history is provided by revelation. Transcendence is revealed to history through exposure and the flow of grace. The participant giving of transcendence is supplemented and complemented by separant receiving.

The myths of participation are myths of yearning, of our ani-consciousness's core-vector, and, hence, are also expressed in theological mythologies of the Godhead. The myths of experience are projections of the prime movers of the demiurgical quests of possession and power. The Tantalic mythologies, thus, fuel our primal dialectical yearning, while the separant mythologies project myths of man's development as well as of cosmogony. Hence, both man and God are in a constant process of becoming linked to the dialectics between Tantalic myths of yearning and Sisyphean myths of experience generating the signs of language and the symbols of religion.

The demiurgos is the God of creation and of history, of space and of atomic energy. He is the divine container of the Kabbala receiving the flow of the light of grace from the Godhead. The demiurgos interact with the Godhead through creativity to produce creation. Sisyphus, thus, imbues his stone with grace, and the inert Godhead is able to vicariously experience the authentic triumphs and disasters of a Mozart, a Van Gogh, or a Brel. Existentially inauthentic creativity, which is unpalatable to him, is left to the demiurge as Gnostic error or Kabbalist din and kellipot. Creativity, if authentic, may generate the energy for an I-thou dialogue, linking the Godhead (the universal thou) and creation. If inauthentic, flawed creativity would degenerate into the petrification of an I-it relationship.

The Gnostic messenger, the Kabbalist initiate performing the tikkun, the mending, the go-between of revelation, links the thing-in-itself of transcendence with the prime mover emanated into history. This is why Tantalus the protagonist of our meta-myth is a Titan: part god who is still in transcendence and part man; he is God's image and emanant theophany within history. The dialogic prayer between the self in history and the transcendental universal thou actually generates the energy of revelation. It is the process of revelation in itself without any further goal beyond it.

Revelatory prayer is God. Sisyphus, likewise, is the creative link between the Godhead and the demiurgos. He symbolizes the integration between man's desperate creative spirit and the demiurgical stone which is both his burden and his destiny.

The Descent into History

The most formidable barrier is the ontological one between being and nothingness, since whatever is on the side of non-being stems from and longs to revert to metaphysics. The mediation between transcendence and history preceded Christianity. In India, the *avatara* signifies a descent of a God into history. Vishnu, for example, as an avatara, assumed many forms, both human and non-human. There would, indeed, be mediating agents between temporality and transcendence. When in history the avatara serves as such an independent connecting structure it has been self-regulating and equal in significance. Since the linking function involves the structured mixture within itself of both connected elements, the connecting structure has a dual nature, temporal and divine. Developmentally, early oral non-differentiation would make for the linkage in a single consciousness as the arena, a nascent-self, and a residual outside transcendence. Hence, a universal pure-self would be anchored onto pantheistic early orality. The plurality of objects crystallized at later orality would, therefore, be conceived as subsequent to, and stemming from, the unity of early orality. The mytho-empirical primary mediator between unity and plurality would be the Son of God, the Kabbalist adam kadmon, or the son of man which in Christianity is embodied in Jesus Christ. There are many instances of a man-God mediating between history and transcendence, but the figure of Christ predominates. The mediation of the man-God creates a trinity, the most common mode of linkage between two divergent entities.

Jung examines the psychological sources of the trinity and starts with the Pythagorean assertion as to the perfection of the number three. 'One is the first from which all other numbers arise, and in which the opposite qualities of numbers, the odd and the even, must therefore be united; two is the first even number; three is the first that is uneven and perfect, because in it we find beginning, middle, and end'.[137] Indeed, if dialectics is as potent and all-inclusive as it seems to be, the third is the synthesis resulting from the interaction between the first and the second.

In our context, a trinity stands for the basic procreative triad of the father, mother, and child. The Christian Trinity has the Holy Ghost instead of the mother, because of Christianity's overt aversion to sex, which we have explored elsewhere. Feuerbach, for instance, states:

> It is true that the Virgin was not so placed between the Father and Son as to imply that the Father had begotten the Son through her, because the sexual relation was regarded by the Christians as something unholy and sinful. But it is enough that the maternal principle, the Holy Ghost, was associated with the Father and Son.[138]

Not so in other creeds and mythologies, which sanctify the trinity of the archetypal nuclear family. Some representative examples are the Egyptian trinity of Osiris, Isis, and Horus and the Greek triad of Zeus, Semele, and Dionysus. Our concern, however, is the triadic nuclear family, as projected on transcendence, with the divine siblings having a religio-normative status of their own vis-à-vis the created world and human society. This relates, naturally, to our third phase of separation where the adolescent offspring are pushed out of the protective family fold by means of some rite of passage to bear the burdens of social responsibility. Such placement within the mesh of the normative system of society has been dealt with by us through the Isaac Syndrome,[139] with the positing of the offering of Isaac as a mytho-empirical anchor for the normative separation of adolescents from the forgiving protection of the family. Both Isaac and Jesus had been willing normative victims of the authoritarian separant mandates of the archetypal father. In a similar vein, Iphigenia was a willing victim to the normative, patriotic mandates of Greece as imposed by her authoritarian father Agamemnon. All had been mytho-empirical normative sacrifices, symbolizing the harnessing of the young into their separant social burdens. Here we near the separant extreme of our continuum of gods: The son/daughter are normative success stories because they willingly sacrifice themselves to the normative standards of their society through the authoritarian services of the father and are projected on transcendence as separant sun-gods and martyred redeemers.

This trinitarian system is a clear separant development introducing plurality into Christian theism. The Council of Nicaea rejected the Arian doctrine of the Son being created by the Father and, hence, subordinate to him, instead adopting the Athanasian doctrine of consubstantiality of three separate divine persons. This separation is the metaphysical projection of the surrogate sacrifice parent pushing out the pubescent young into the trials of societal strife, whereas the triunite formula is the transcendental expression of the young adult's participant quest to return to the cushioned forgiveness of the family fold.

Our interpretation of this basic Christian dogma as a transcendental projection of the socio-normative separation of young adult male children and their ejection into the normative loneliness of responsibility for their own deeds and life explains its otherwise absurd logical inner contradictions. The Athanasian formula, sanctified by the Council of Nicaea, stresses the distinctness and separateness of the three divine persons. They are distinct selves: 'The Father is God, the Son is God, and the Holy Spirit is God'.[140] This separate distinctiveness is then merged into unity: 'And yet', continues the Athanasian doctrine, 'there cannot be three Gods but one God'.[141] No amount of scholastic hair-splitting could evade this logical contradiction, despite attempts to explain its viability over the centuries. It may, indeed, be explained by its intra-psychic reinforcement of the normatively ejected adult, trying to regain the togetherness within the fold of the archetypal triad of the nuclear family. It is a longing for unity in a trinity, which comes only as a metaphysical projection of the lonely adult's yearning for his lost cushioned forgiveness in his pre-adolescent family.

The self-sacrifices of Isaac and Jesus had been to assert the authority of the father, as representing the normative structure of society. The purpose of divine legitimation of this paternal authority has been its imputation to God the Father. Christ himself asserts that 'the Father is greater than I'. The father commands and the son obeys.

We have mentioned in an earlier chapter that the interpreters of the myth of the offering of Isaac claim that he bound himself to the altar.[142] This to us symbolizes the self-enclosing of the obedient son to the separating social norms promulgated by the archetypal father. Both Isaac and Christ were active partners to their normative sacrifice. Jesus carried his own cross and Isaac carried the wood for his sacrifice on his shoulders, forming a cross, with his own body. This is a mytho-empirical account of successful separant socialization.

Isaac was believed to have been sacrificed and then resurrected so that the myth of his offering also parallels the crucifixion and resurrection of Christ. The implication is that when the Son of Man sacrifices himself willingly to the paternal normative mandates of society he is projected on transcendence as a Son of God.

Everyone in human society has undergone some rites of passage or other from childhood to adulthood. The surrogate sacrificial processes make for a strong identification with the archetypal suffering Son of Man, especially when he is projected ultimately as a Son of God. A paternal victim who becomes God is the strongest possible model for identification for a struggling adult, who has been pushed to paternal authority from the family fold to 'become a man', a responsible citizen/subject/party member in a depriving, competitive, cut-throat society. This is reinforced by the victimized son of man becoming a separantly omnipotent son of God, who can at will manipulate his objective human environment.

The importance of this premise, which is beyond the scope of the present work, is that the surrogate sacrificial rites of passage from childhood to adulthood serve as a major dynamic for the reinforcement of social norms in adolescents and young adults. We have already pointed out elsewhere that the Freudian Oedipal aggressiveness of children towards their parents and its resolution is a necessary, but not sufficient, dynamic for the acquisition of morality. Such an Isaac syndrome is the supplementary dynamic of implanting social norms in the young and their enmeshing into the normative system of society.[143]

Indeed, by his suffering, Christ became normatively pure.[144] His victimization was instrumental in his promulgation of a higher code of social norms and the announcement of ideals for human behavior. He also decreed through his sacrifice (and in like manner through the archetypal offering of Isaac) the need to obey social norms as invested by paternal authority and his own mandate to judge others through the authority of God the Father and his church.[145] This most separant power, to pass judgment on the world, has been relegated by the Father to the Son so that he may proclaim the Kingdom of God on earth. This kingdom is the separant active control of God of all human affairs. The direct manipulation of all life forms, man and objects is relegated to Jesus through the reign of God the Father.[146] These are the wildest dreams of the separant type come true. The obedient Son has gained not only the vicarious, but the direct, authority of the father to impose his commands and mandates over his objective surroundings and life forms. The normative system which has been implanted in the Son by rites of passage and surrogate sacrifices is imposed by the conformist Son with divine paternal authority. With the proclamation of the Kingdom of God through the Son, the object-manipulative goals of the separant core personality vector have achieved their projective fulfillment. However, the price for this separant omnipotence is complete conformity—*perinde ac cadaver*, i.e., 'obey like a corpse', as the Jesuits put it. One has to surrender completely to the authority of the Messiah-King 'for his sake' and to be worthy of him.[147]

The separant authoritarian cycle now becomes clear: become a willing victim to paternal authority as manifest by the normative structure of society, and its institutions permit one to demand obedience from others. Hence, all absolutist rulers reigned not with grace, but through the projected separant tyranny of God. Indeed, Kabbalistic authority stems from vile stern-judgments and not from divine grace.

One step further from the deification of a son who complies with paternal authority is the beautification of the normative system as a whole, which is the expansion of the authority of the archetypal father and its relegation to the whole body of societal laws and mandates. This makes for the enshrined status of legal systems among lawyers and law-makers. When God is dead or absent, the law becomes God.

The original Indian avatara was a god who descended (*ava* means 'down') into history; his parallels in other religions were mortals who became gods. Surely, these opposite directions of linking history and transcendence have theological significance, but for our present purposes this is secondary, since we are mainly concerned with the function of linkage itself and not whether it was initiated in history or transcendence. St. Mark co-opts Elias and Moses to Jesus as divine mediators, but singles out the latter as the beloved son of God.[148] Also, Jesus saw himself as a door or a linking structure through which one may enter and be saved in the ever-after.[149] Jesus is the image, the refraction into history of the abstract invisible God. He is the archetypal model, the avataric blueprint for every creature.[150] He is the potential, as the primary symbolon structure for the creation of everything.[151] Still, Jesus saw himself as the Son of man.[152] This could mean the elevation of a human, like Enoch and Elijah, to the throne of God or the sanctification of martyrs like Isaac and Jesus, who achieved divine status by taking upon themselves the sins of others—Isaac of Israel and Jesus of humanity as a whole. Another possibility is that Jesus, or rather his followers, saw in him the ideal man in the Platonic sense, which endowed him with the perfection of the Platonic idea from which all humanity has been fashioned. The importance of this view of Jesus for our context is its effort to pierce the veil between history and transcendence by devising anthropocentric means to reach out to the perfection of holiness. Also, the second coming of Christ is a truly avataric event, since Christ, who has become God, appears on earth, and would, thus, be recrossing the border from transcendence to history, so that the barrier between being and non-being is traversed back and forth. However, the Eucharist, a partaking of the body and the blood of Christ, is a ritual crossing over to transcendence by means of ingesting the divine substance of a man who became God, and re-enacting thereby the transition of Christ from here to eternity. The essence of Christ as the prime mediator between history and transcendence is extended to whoever believes in him.[153] Christ, then, is a kind of universal exchange. Whoever plugs into him will experience a revelatory crossing of the barrier in the way that Jesus himself did. Hence, according to St. John, to believe in Christ is to shed off the temporal fetters and partake in eternity, while still in the here-and-now.

In Jewish tradition, we have the interpretation of Goldzieher and Popper that Abraham was a Titan (an interpretation stemming from the etymology of his Hebrew name *Av Ram*) and, thus, linked by mythogenic structures between history and transcendence.[154] God appoints a servant—an elect who will be imbued with his spirit and bring forth judgment to the nations.[155] This again is a linkage, an avataric theophany of God within history. Moses was the mediator between the children of Israel and God, since he spoke to them through Moses. The adam kadmon (Lekhol kedumim), the primeval anthropos was the mediating agent according to Lurianic Kabbala between God and his creation. Job says, 'In my flesh shall I see God'.[156] This is a mediating struggle which is initiated in a diametrically opposite direction to the avataric descent into history and to the dictum of St. John, 'that the word (the Logos) was made flesh, and dwelt among us'.[157] It is more in line with the Lurianic Kabbala's doctrine, that sparks of divinity are imbedded in every creature. However, the end result is really a link between history and transcendence, irrespective of whether the connection was initialed in the former or the latter. Likewise, the Neoplatonic doctrine of Plotinus postulates an intermediate entity which he called *vous*, the intellect, which was the ahistoric structure containing the Platonic forms—ideas, which connected between the transcendental abstract one and the individual soul. The Hasidic tzaddik was also a go-between for the Holy Presence and the community. In the various Gnostic sects, we have the intermediary messenger which links the profane creation and pure 'righteous alien God'. Thus, in Mandean Gnosis, the go-between is 'manda Hayé' the messenger of *Kushta*—truth. In the second-century texts of Poi-mandres of Hermes Trismegistus, the vous is the father from which emanates the word 'Logos', and then the mind-artificer (nous-demiurgos). These two intermediaries lead to primal man (anthropos).[158] In Valentinian Gnosis, christos is the icon which may pass through the *horos*: the barrier between the Pleroma and the Cosmos and harmonize them.[159] Krishna, being the avatara, the temporal incarnation of the Hindu God Vishnu, is the divine messenger sent down to earth to reveal to humans the way to abandon the profane pleasures and turn to divine enlightenment. In Egypt ma'at, the concept of truth is an avataric descent of cosmic transcendental origin to endow harmony and justice to the created world and its creatures.[160] Also, the Pharaoh was worshipped as the God Horus and, thus, was the link to transcendence and the ever-after since when the Pharaoh Horus died he became the God Osiris, Lord of the West, the realm of the dead. The function of primal man in connecting history and transcendence was of the nature of a complementarity since, on the one hand, he was created in the image of God,[161] and, on the other hand this imago dei is reflected in all human individuals, although every human being is different from every other.[162] Hence, within man as the prime symbolon structure there is a complementary interaction which complements and unites the here-and-now and the ever after. Indeed, the Midrash specifies that man was both created from supernatural and earthly elements so that the barrier between being and transcendence was traversed by the creation of man.[163] We have already mentioned that God used the Torah as a prime tool for the creation of the world. Hence, whatever mediating function between time and eternity is effected by the avataras, sons of God and Jesus Christ is carried out in Judaism by the Torah. It befits the abstract nature of the Judaic God, since the abstract Logos is an apt mediator between God and history.

The Torah also lends its traversing powers to its temporal abode, the Ark of the Covenant, the Tabernacle, and to the Temple itself. Indeed, God instructs Moses that the communication between them shall take place from the Ark of the Covenant: ‘And there will I meet with thee’, says God, ‘and I will commune with thee from above the mercy seat, from between the two cherubim which are upon the ark of the testimony of all things which I will give thee in commandment unto the children of Israel’.[164] Man expects reciprocity from God. He assumes that his efforts to cross the barrier towards transcendence will be met by a corresponding approach from God. Hence, God’s sacrifice of his son to save humanity is an apt response, especially if we are to accept the hermeneutic of Kierkegaard to the effect that the sacrifice of Christ is continuous and takes place in a continuous present. Also, the Indian avatara is expected to remain in the here-and-now until his task is completed. Man may also strive to cross the border of transcendence in order to ‘mend’ (the kabbalistic/Hasidic tikkun) a blemished God. Christ is by definition a blemished God, yet his suffering is mostly regarded as a means for identification with Him, so that whoever empathizes with him will believe in Him and be saved.

Not so Lurianic Kabbala. We have mentioned previously and elsewhere[165] that the cosmic catastrophe of the breaking of the vessels was due to the inability of God to prevent it. Hence, God is less than perfect. Thence, the task of the Kabbalist and the Hasid is to effect a *tikkun*, a mending of God by collecting the particles of divinity, which have been strewn in the mires of profanity and lift them back to their sacred source. This lends meaning to the life of man. He is not just a subject of a perfect God to whom he has to pay daily homage and flatter him from time to time, but he is a partner, albeit a junior one, to divinity by helping to cure its blemishes and ineptitudes. Likewise, Horus and Orisis are mutilated, losing their eyes, so that the mending and restoring of their eyes is of prime importance in the eschatological Egyptian religion: the righteousness of those who wish to pass safely to the barrier of the ever-after in the west is measured by the ability of their good deeds to restore the blemished limbs of the gods. This is aptly phrased in the following spell from the Egyptian *Book of the Dead*:

> The plume is stuck into the shoulder of Osiris, the Red Crown shines in the bowl, the Eye is eaten and he who sought it is fetched. I know it, for I have been initiated into it by the Sem-priest, and I have never spoken nor made repetition to the gods. I have come on an errand for Re in order to cause the plume to grow into the shoulder of Osiris, to make complete the Red Crown in the bowl and to pacify the Eye for him who numbered it. I have entered as a Power because of what I know, I have not spoken to men, I have not repeated what was said.
> Hail to you, souls of Hermopolis! Know that Re desires the plume which grows and the Red Crown which is complete at this temple, and rejoice at the allotting of what is to be allotted.[166]

Indeed, the task of the dead passing over to the realm of Osiris on a theurgic mission for Re, the sun god and chief deity, is to repair the crown of Osiris and cure his blemished eye as well as to cause the plume to re-grow on his shoulder.

The essence of the mending of a blemished god is that man, by his righteous deeds, theurgically transmits the restoring energies and grace with which the divinity may make himself whole again. The feeling of pain of a suffering god like Christ on the cross induces man to empathize with him and generate grace with which to restore him. This grace, which is formed in man and flows towards a needy transcendence, creates a symbiotic relationship between man and God and effects a reciprocal flow of grace through the barrier of non-being. This is the meaning of the dictum of the Zohar that man's deeds should be for the theurgic unification, or rather the coupling, of God and his Holy presence. In Hasidism, this mending is effected within the consciousness of man. God the king says that the Maggid of Meseritz following the tikkun ei hazohar 'is imprisoned within the tresses of man's mind'.[167] Meaning that God, as a spark of divinity or as a reflection of his unity as a potential wholeness, is contained within the consciousness of man. Hence, whatever has to be mended in, or of, divinity may be effected in the intropsychic dialectics of the individual human being. Indeed, the phrase 'and thou shalt know your God' said when tying the phylacteries in the morning prayer is taken by the Bratzlav Hasidim to mean an agapic copulation, because *yada* means both knowledge and sexual intercourse in Hebrew. Hence, intentional concentrated prayer is meant to effect a dialogue between man and God through the barrier of transcendence. The meditative prayer which links the soul of man and God effects also an extasis of the psyche of a man at worship, although momentary from diachronic time to the synchronicity of timelessness. The goal of prayer is to pass over the threshold of temporality and reach God in timeless eternity. However, the ultimate union with God is effected through sanctification of the name of the Lord, by sacrificing oneself for one's faith in Him. Then the martyred soul ascends, according to Lurianic Kabbala, directly to heaven and unites with God.[168]

The Indirect Passage

We have seen that ontological, existential, and social barriers are necessary; otherwise man would no longer be able to develop his proficiency as mediator between his subject and the material world. He would not be prodded to strive towards temporal and metaphysical goals, since a free passage to the unknown would make it graspable, familiar, and easy, like the tip of a mountain that has been climbed and explored. This might be another layer of the proscription of knowledge in the myth of original sin. The direct assault on metaphysical barriers is proscribed by most religions. The Jewish God cannot and should not be seen and no man can know his place.[169] Likewise, Greek mortals should not avail themselves of the rights and privileges of the gods lest they be smitten for their hübris. Hence, the crossing of barriers must be roundabout, indirect, and clandestine. One may pass over the threshold of a partition only in a maieutic manner; meaning that the sender of intentions and desire to communicate such generates a symbolon structure which may transmit energies, words, and mythogenes which may not even pierce the relevant ontological, epistemic, and social barriers, but which may engender in the other partner of the dyad, on the other side of the barrier, a feeling, a message, or a belief that he himself created the idea, the design for an artifact or tenet. Such roundabout communication is intended to franchise the barrier between history and transcendence through interpersonal dialogue and between consciousness and quantum processes. Let us return to the maieutic relationship between history and transcendence. We may envisage the call of man: 'Out of the depths have I cried unto thee, O Lord; Lord hear my voice; let thine ears be attentive to the voice of my supplications'.[170] This is the call of prayer to be reciprocated by a maieutic response from transcendence. If revelation comes following authentic directional prayer, this is indeed a dialogue between man and God, since all mediation between subject and object, consciousness and energy-matter, history and transcendence, must take place within the cognitive processes of man, the meta-connecting agent. This is all that can be postulated, and, in all probability, this is all there is. In the Gnostic text, describing the revelation experienced by Zostrianos, through his rapport with Ephesek, we read thus:

> ...these same powers exist in the world. Within the Hidden Ones corresponding to each of the aeons stand glories, in order that he who is in [the world] might be safe beside them. The glories are perfect thoughts living with the powers; they do not perish because they are models of salvation by which each one is saved when he receives them. He receives a model and strength through the same (power), and with the glory as a helper he can, thus, pass out from the world.[171]

Indeed, there is an extatic revelatory link with hidden powers through the receiving of a cognitive model of salvation. This is, in our conceptualization, a maieutic enthousiasmos in the Greek sense, which is an experience of the divine through a cognitive trigger of a connecting symbolon structure believed to have been expedited by transcendental powers. Whether this is so is irrelevant since the experience of revelation in itself is sufficient to effect a religious belief in a link with God. This is even more apparent with Marcionite Gnostics who believed that 'the adopted souls that listen to, and accept, the message of the stranger of God are saved by their own experience of faith, not because they receive some sort of Gnosis'.[172] Gnostic salvation is triggered by an inner process of maieutic revelation, irrespective of whether a message has or has not been sent by the 'stranger alien God', as reffered to by the Gnostics, who might have been even perennially silent, as postulated by Camus in his exposition of the metaphysical predicament of man.[173] The effective teacher is like a midwife; he helps his pupils give birth to ideas which they cherish as their own much more than if they had been coerced by authoritarian teachers, who force their ideas on their charges ex cathedra. Aside from Socrates, the archetypal maieutic teacher, Mahavira, the founder of Jainism and Gautama the Buddha, who were almost contemporaries of Socrates, also preached their doctrine by personal example and roundabout metaphors. In all probability, Christ was also a maieutic teacher who had the charismatic quality of sparking in his disciples a revelation which they felt to have been generated within their inner-selves. Such maieutic transmission is the essence of Buberian dialogue. Buber regarded the I-thou dialogue as the prime ontological existence. The hyphenated I-thou *dialogos*, entering through the word in the Greek sense, creates maieutically an essence of being with which the

'I' or the thou by themselves cannot effect. Such miraculous passing through the barrier of the subject-other is a moment of grace since the natural inter-personal relationship is an alienated I-it.[174]

Moreover, the flow of grace in an I-thou relationship creates God, who is the universal thou. Hence, in the Buberian context, an authentic I-thou dialogue also pierces the barrier between temporality and transcendence, since I-it is an historical relationship fettered in the prison of time, whereas an I-thou relationship is metaphysical. Buber distills some basic notions of Lurianic Kabbala and Hasidism into his dialogic philosophy. Thus, the creation of the universal thou through an authentic I-thou dialogue may be linked to the kabbalist premise that Akatriel, one of God's countenances, asked Ishmael, the high priest, to bless him[175] and to the Ba'al Shem Tov's statement that God is the shadow of man.

Dialogue is also the great equalizer, since an I-thou relationship can happen only between free equals. Subjugation invariably leads to an I-it petrifaction. Can love, both erotic and spiritual, cross the interpersonal barrier? We have dealt elsewhere with love as a variation on the theme of dialogue.[176] The conception of the dyad of love as an unattainable dialogue has been expressed thus by Georg Simmel:

> The fact that male and female strive after their mutual union is the foremost example or primordial image of a dualism which stamps our life-contents generally. It always presses toward reconciliation, and both success and failure of the reconciliation reveal this basic dualism only the more clearly. The union of man and woman is possible, precisely because they are opposites. As something essentially unattainable, it stands in the way of the most passionate craving for convergence and fusion. The fact that, in any real and absolute sense, the 'I' can *not* [sic] seize mutual supplementation and fusion seem to be the very reason for the opposites to exist at all. Passion seeks to tear down the borders of the ego and to absorb 'I' and thou in one another. But it is not they which become a unit: rather a *new* unit emerges, the child.[177]

Simmel's ingenious observation, which is not very far removed from our own conception of the unachievable aims of the core-vectors, is that the impossibility of union between man and woman leads to the dialectical synthesis of the child. This seems to us as too mechanistic a concretization of dialectics. We envisage that man and woman are induced by a mirage of participation that emanate from sex and love to mate analogously to the way racing dogs are lured to win by an ever-receding plastic rabbit running in front of their noses. Male and female do not directly intend to perpetuate the species by their sex and love. They are tricked into it by their programming. They are driven to mate by the quest of orgasm, which is meant to be a quick glimpse of participation, and by the Tantalic visions of eternal love, which is a surrogate image of the unattainable aims of our participant core-vectors.

The agonies of love described by the myriads of lovers, from pulp magazines to the *Song of Songs*, stem from Ego's feeling that 'he opened up' towards his beloved Alter and that he/she did not respond to him as expected. This is the inevitable gap between Ego's amorous expectations and Alter's response. Ego many times experiences the chagrin of the disenchanted lover for having invested so much emotion in such an unworthy person. Ego would rarely have the inclination, or the ability, to realize that he projected on Alter his inner craving for participation and expected him to fulfill this core longing by their love. As intersubjective communication is an ontological impossibility. Alter cannot perceive Ego's expectations and is even less able to fulfill them. 'That love is suffering', says Capellanus, 'is easy to see, for before love becomes equally balanced on both sides there is no torment greater, since the lover is always in fear that his love may not gain its desire and that he is wasting his efforts'.[178] Love, however, cannot be equally balanced on both sides because Ego's amorous expectations from Alter, and vice-versa, are determined by their differences in gender, in neuro-endocrinology, in personality core-vectors, and in cultural imprints. Furthermore, Ego's expectations are bound to change with time and place so that Alter's ability to meet these expectations are diminished further.

What characterizes love at its peak is that the lover, spurred by an intense longing for participation, claims the exclusive attention and time of his beloved. Ego desires (sometimes accompanied by overt demands) to share all the thoughts and all experiences of Alter. At that very place and time, Alter may not be able or be willing to totally attune to Ego and match his staccato display of emotions. Alter may have reached his own emotional crescendo at another time or place, and he cannot or will not match his emotional crescendo at another time or place, and he cannot or will not match his emotional peaks with those of Ego. The pangs of love and the romantic agonies stem from the disparity of expectations between lover and beloved. Love is either Sisyphean or Tantalic because we tend to project on our beloved expectations of which we ourselves are not aware, so that the beloved cannot be expected to be aware of them. If we aspire for our love to be what it cannot be, we make it impossible. Consequently, the impossibility of love is related to Ego's projection of his personality core longing for participation. As Alter cannot fulfill this longing in the form, content, and duration expected by Ego, love is bound to be a temporary and often lonely trip of Ego brushing occasionally and tangentially with the emotional orbits of Alter.

We shall deal extensively with the continuum ranging from the Sisyphean separant lover who aims to include, subjugate, and swallow his beloved to the participant Tantalic who longs to be immersed, excluded, and, so to speak, consumed by his love. The latter has been depicted in literature and art as l'amour sacré, the spiritual and sacred love for a person who stands for and symbolizes an archetype such as the Great Mother, the Virgin Mary, an absolute value, the divine presence or God himself. This love of an ethereal purity is tailor-made as a surrogate participation dynamic: by immersing oneself in the spiritual love of an unattainable woman one enacts the longing of the core participant vector to partake in the absolute. The Tantalic nature of these sacred loves calls for their partial, at least, impossibility. The less attainable they are, the more pure, spiritual, and sacred they become. Temporary blindness and selective perception is of great help in such cases. Without them a Don Quixote can hardly be expected to sing odes of love and worship to a Dulcinea the way she really is. The main function of the beloved in a Tantalic participant dyad is to trigger and reflect the lovers' own longing to partake in an omnipresent absolute and melt into an all-engulfing wholeness.

Both the form and contents of the participant expectation of the lover are determined by his biological parameters including gender, his participant or separant personality structure, and his socialization in a Sisyphean or Tantalic culture.[179]

For Ego's amorous expectations as determined by his bio-psycho-cultural configuration to be met by Alter, the latter's expectations, as determined by his configuration must be exactly complementary, which is a statistical improbability. Second, as we have stated in the *Violence of Silence*, meaningful communication is more feasible on shallow and routine levels of encounter, whereas on deeper levels of encounter communication is hardly possible.[180] The expectations of love are for the deepest level of encounter and for the most complete fusion of bodies and souls, yet communication between the lovers as to the intricate nuances of their mutual expectations is almost impossible. Consequently, the more a couple are in love, the less able the partners are to convey to each other the depths, range, and intensity of their emotions and mutual expectations of each other.

Third, we know that an extreme need dulls all the other functions of the body and personality. It generates biased perceptions, even hallucinations. For example, hungry subjects perceive food-related stimuli, ignoring a wide range of others.[181] Likewise, a sex-hungry subject or one who is emotionally infatuated by love cannot evaluate the stimuli and expectations of his beloved except in the context of his turbulent emotions. Ego, the lover, is bound, therefore, to twist his perception and expectations of his beloved Alter according to his emotionally biased perceptions, which are twisted in turn by his own intense motivated expectations. The more intense the love is, the more the impossibility of a meaningful communication between the lovers to enable them to realize their participant aim. Love seems to be dominated by a self-defeating negative feedback cycle.

Finally, the investigators of the least interest principle have shown that when Ego is very high in his emotional involvement, Alter seems to cool off, and vice-versa.[182] Although this phenomenon is well documented, as far as we know no one has yet offered an etiological explanation it. We, however, are able to do so: a separant Ego who aims to conquer Alter will losė interest once he achieves his aim. This is especially so when Ego's desire to overpower Alter is dominated by his separant core personality vector, which is not satisfied by an intermediate conquest, but which is ever craving to subjugate and swallow more bodies. A participant Ego, with his ever-ready submission, will be taken and had by the separant Alter only to be rejected immediately afterwards, as just another item in the conqueror's log book. If both Ego and Alter are separants (or participants), an amorous encounter between them would be quite unlikely from the outset. As their expectations are diametrically opposed, they are more likely to be repelled by each other than attracted to each other.

If sex is bait, and the exclusive communion through love cannot be attained, what reinforces the torrents of emotion invested by couples throughout the world trembling with desire for each other? What sustains the furtive longing glances of girls and boys in societies which forbid public manifestations of love? What makes a Tristan and Isolde so turbulently immortal, or the death for love of a Romeo and Juliet so intensely and continuously relevant? What makes Solomon's love song ever fresh and the clichés of Segal's *Love Story* sell millions of copies? The answer is that the longing in itself for the communion of love, and not its attainment, is the necessary and sufficient reinforcer. Moreover, in many cases, some amorous longings should not be quenched, so as to ensure their viability. Solomon of the *Song of Songs*, after trying to fulfill his amorous longing with a thousand spouses, reached the abysmal despair of Ecclesiastes. Ephraim Kishon, the Israeli satirist, had the ingenuity of continuing the story of Romeo and Juliet who have been saved, been married, and have sunk into the nagging life of a bourgeois boredom. Kierkegaard, on the other hand, renounced the realization of his love, thereby freeing it from the bonds of its fulfilment. By making his love independent of its fulfilment, Kierkegaard assured its continuity.

Participant union by sex and the grace of communion by love, as spurred by our core-vectors, are unattainable. Yet the common longing for them by people in love creates a bond and a frame into which their different participant cravings might be expressed. Love encloses the lovers within a common boundary in which their separate and disparate visions of union seem to each one of them as if flowing in unison. We have stated earlier that without the pleasure of orgasm species would probably not engage in sex. Yet the need for reproduction and for the ever-evolving more effective links between spirit and matter produces in the orgasm, if mutual, the most intensive sense of union between human beings in the here-and-now.

It seems as if our programming has a desperate need to bring about reproduction for reasons known only to itself, with the process of reproduction being the aim of the exercise, while the reproducing life forms seem to be tools or secondary instruments to the process of reproduction itself. Moreover, we have seen that sex is a very consuming activity, both physical and mentally. It involves some violent conflicts with other males and some cramped, painful, and sometimes dangerous positions during mating itself. No life form is likely to engage in reproduction, which seems to be the target of our programming, unless we have been baited, as indeed we are, by short-lived experiences of participant bliss in orgasm and non-realizable visions of the communion of love. Our programming seems to be indifferent to the fact that the Tantalic fata morgana of love cannot be fulfilled as long as it helps to blunt the violence and stress incidental to courting and mating and brings the life forms to reproduce successfully. We are anaesthetized by sex and love to carry on reproducing in circumstances which are at best repetitive and at worst violent and painful. The name of the game is reproduction. Yet our programmer did not divulge why it is all so important to him or to us. Moreover, it seems to offend our sense of fair play that the baits of sex and love, although effective, have not been construed with more sophistication, so that they would seem, at least, more credible and viable.

Reproduction seems to be the raison d'être of life. Animals stop their fighting and courting after mating, flowers wane after fertilization, and pregnant women lose their eagerness to flirt. In most cultures, especially separant ones, youth is worshipped as a corollary to fertility, whereas sterile old age is dreaded and considered non-aesthetic. Only in some of the more participant cultures in the Far and Middle East, which anchor on transcendence and other worldliness, is old age revered. In a similar vein, the infatuation of love seems to wane with marriage and childbirth, as if the bait of love takes one up to reproduction and becomes superfluous after it. Also, with sexual arousal, and during intercourse, the body of the mate and its odors feel and smell attractive, but right after orgasm, some parts of the mate's body might seem repulsive and disgusting.

After reproduction, the bait of sex and love has fulfilled its purpose. The rose petals fall off the swelling of the fertilized hips; pregnant women lose their expectant freshness, and the queen ants, after their mating flight, are shorn of their wings and the drones chased away. Life has fulfilled its purpose. The time for play is over, and the nest should be prepared for the young. The centrality of reproduction to life may be apparent in the frantic efforts of injured or sick plants to muster their last vestiges of energy to flower prematurely and produce seed. Lastly, the worst blow to a human being is the death of his offspring because it deprives him of his programmed raison d'être of reproduction. Yet the ecstasy of orgasm is short. It is, however, adequate for the function of reproduction, and it conditions us to seek more and more orgasm in order to experience again the fleeting sense of union.

'After intercourse all animals are sad', says the Latin proverb. Is it because the pitifully short bait of ecstatic orgasm has vanished and the participants are re-confronted with their separant state of existential drudgery and misery? With the human male there is an abrupt post-orgasmic loss of sexual tension and a momentary loss of erotic interest in his partner. Although women are slower in their post-orgasmic loss of stimulation susceptibility and many are capable of multiple orgasms, Masters and Johnson have established that there is a marked similarity between man's and woman's post-orgasmic resolution phases.[183] As for lower animals, males do experience varying kinds of orgasmic ecstasies during ejaculation, but it is an open question as to what extent female fauna experience orgasm.[184] Nevertheless, most female fauna do disregard sexual approaches after a copulation by which they have presumably been fertilized, while most female insects even stop the secretion of sexually attractive pheromones after mating.[185] Following are some observations by Briffault, which although outdated, have been supported by subsequent research:

> With a large proportion of mammalian species, the association between the male and the female does not extend beyond the primary purpose for which the sexes come together—the fecundation of the female. After that function is fulfilled there appears to be, as a general rule, an actual repulsion between the sexes. 'As soon as pairing is over,' says Brehm, speaking of mammals generally, 'great indifference is shown towards one another by the sexes.' Among most carnivora, cohabitation of the male with the female takes place for a short time only during the rutting season, and in many species there is no cohabitation at all. Weasels continue together during the mating season for a

> week or more, then separate completely. Bears do not cohabit after sexual congress; 'no one yet has found two adult black bears in one den; mother and half-grown cubs have been taken together in the same winter quarters, but never two old ones.' 'I have never seen the two (male and female) together at any time of the year,' says an experienced observer of the species; 'they meet by chance and again separate.' The same is reported of the Indian, and of the polar bear. The jaguar cohabits with the female during one month of the year only; and the cougar during a few weeks. The leopard male and female live entirely separate.[186]

The conclusion is that after copulation and mating, the abating of orgasm and its instantaneous glimmering of participant bliss have fulfilled their purpose and are, henceforth, unnecessary. The males have impregnated the females, and the species is hooked on its task of reproduction. From this point on our programmer seems to lose interest in the moods, ecstasies, and sexual attraction of the parents. Its interest is already fully concentrated on the fetus. Orgasm is a short-lived exposure to a subjective peak experience of participant bliss cleverly manipulated to serve the purposes of our programming, which are unknown and unknowable by the sexual partners.

The Spanish call orgasm *la poca muerta*, hinting at its participant and annihilating nature of longing to fuse with the sexual partner. Karen Horney realized the greater participatory significance of the nature of orgasm for the male than for the female. Man, she says, secretly longs for extinction through sex as a surrogate wish for reunion with woman-mother, whereas for a woman, sex is only the initiation of a new cycle of procreation.[187] The more separant role of woman in sex has thus been recognized by one of the pioneers of psychoanalysis. The participant component of orgasm is apparent in its temporary blunting of separate awareness and in the feeling of union with one's environment, bringing about a transitory sense of non-being. The Tantalic nature of the participant longing for orgasm is apparent in the physical and emotional build-up towards it. When the climax has been reached and a flicker of a sensation of union has been experienced, the orgasm is terminated, and the ecstatic participant revelation ends almost before it has begun. The longing for participation is the prime mover of orgasm because actual union with the object is, of course, not achieved. There is a marked similarity between the rhythmic movements of the devout in a participant mood of prayer and the pelvic thrusts striving towards orgasm. This might lend a serious hue to the 'wise guys about Jerusalem' who observe that the Wailing Wall is a very sexy place because men move to and fro in front of it, and the women behind their partition groan in ecstasy.

Ferenczi envisaged the participant craving of man in orgasm as brought about by his identification with his penis, which itself identifies with the sexual partner in penetration; in ejaculation that identification is transferred to the semen.[188] Individuals with a weak ego boundary may experience in orgasm a participant loss of body contour, a crumbling and melting down of the partition between themselves and their surroundings, including their sexual partners. This may account for the reluctance of individuals who have anxieties about their ego boundaries and body image to reach orgasm. For them to experience a participant melting down of their ego boundaries is tantamount to madness, for in their daily existence they relate a dissolution of their shaky ego boundary to just this. The enormity of orgasm and its overpowering effects on the senses have made people impute divinity to it. Indeed, the Greeks denoted genitalia as *aidoion* (inspirers of holy awe).[189] Many religions frown on the pleasures of sex, and most condemn sexual activity which is geared only towards pleasure. Such condemnation seems to stem from the religious sanctioning of our programming to reproduce. Our programmer and his religious guardians feel cheated if we enjoy our sexual experiences without reproducing.

The separant component of sex is the epitome of Sisypheanism. Ego's craving to overpower and swallow Alter through intercourse may be phantasized during the short span of orgasm, only to be confronted immediately with the post-orgasmic reality. Yet the separant ego is sure to resume his pursuit of more sex and more orgasms, culminating in identical Sisyphean failure, followed by the inevitable renewed effort to overpower the sexual partner through the peak imagery of orgasm. We should remind ourselves at this point that the separant-participant components of orgasm constitute a continuum, with women biologically predisposed to be nearer its separant pole and men to its participant pole. These biological predispositions are the results of many factors and may be shifted to smaller or greater extents by oral fixations and later cultural imprints.

The separant nature of the human female orgasm is not so much related to the vaginal or clitoral excitation as to the orgasmic platform which develops at the outer third of the vagina, contracting rhythmically at the onset of orgasm, embracing and containing the penis, and absorbing its flow of semen.[190] The more participant nature of the human male's orgasm is inherent in the penetration and ejaculation of the penis spurting out spermatozoa to be absorbed by the ova (although some male orgasm may occur without ejaculation).

Subjective phantasies in orgasm involving both body image and object perception are initiated by a participant blurring of the contours of both the self and partner by both men and women. The voluntary control of body movements is felt to be impaired, along with a feeling of emptiness, an internal void,[191] as well as a diffuse floating and flying sensation.[192] Both Kinsey et al and Masters and Johnson have reported a temporary lapse of contact with reality during orgasm. Kinsey and his associates have stated:

> All of our evidence indicates that there is a considerable and developing loss of sensory capacity which begins immediately upon the onset of sexual stimulation and which becomes more or less complete, sometimes with complete unconsciousness, during the maximum of sexual arousal and orgasm. At orgasm, some individuals may remain unconscious for a matter of seconds or even for some minutes. There are French terms, 'la petite mort' (the little death) and 'la mort douce' (the sweet death), which indicate that some persons do understand that unconsciousness may enter at this point.[193]

The above is precisely our conception of a temporary participant diffusion of the ego boundary and body image. After such initial participant baiting inherent in the orgasm of both males and females, we may note the following marked differences: women see in intercourse and orgasm just the first phase of reproduction. Consequently, even their phantasies at sexual arousal, intercourse, and orgasm are related to the link between sex and reproduction, whereas men focus more during intercourse on their immediate sexual gratification.[194] This indicates that even in the throws of orgasm the woman does not lose awareness of her separant programming to reproduce. Kinsey et al have reported that women find more satisfaction during intercourse in their separant sensation of receiving, whereas men find their psychological rewards and satisfaction mostly in their participant feeling of penetrating.[195] Of special importance is Kinsey's report that:

> The slower responses of the female in coitus appear to depend in part upon the fact that she frequently does not begin to respond as promptly as the male, because psychologic stimuli usually play a more important role in the arousal of the average male and a less important role in the sexual arousal of the average female. The average male is aroused in anticipation of a sexual relationship, and he usually comes to erection and is ready to proceed directly to orgasm as soon as or even before he makes any actual contact. The average female, on the contrary, is less often aroused by such anticipation, and sometimes she does not begin to respond until there has been a considerable amount of physical stimulation.[196]

The more object-oriented woman needs substantive tactile stimulation to be sexually aroused, whereas the more participant abstract male may be easily aroused sexually by erotic phantasies and imagery. The more down-to-earth functions of woman seem to permeate right through her need to be more directly and physically manipulated in order to be sexually aroused and satisfied. As a woman is more firmly aware of her bodily contours and boundaries, she is also bound to have more anxieties of being, that is of losing her body image, during orgasm.[197] The more separant woman needs a firm anchor on her objective surroundings, and if these fade in orgasm she is liable to be frightened.

Masters and Johnson report that their female subjects had a feeling of receptive opening during orgasm, whereas the male feels at the onset of orgasm the inevitability of his penetrating ejaculatory thrust.[198] This again vindicates our portrayal of the more separant Sisyphean role of woman and the more participant Tantalic role of man in sex and orgasm. Man and woman are predisposed to seek different aims. These aims can never be achieved, and even their baited imagery are diametrically opposed. Sometimes the latter are complementary, but mostly they are not.

The fruits of orgasm are, indeed, a successful union between those involved in the act of sex and in love. The child synthesizes within himself the genes of his parents, their personalities, as transmitted to it during early socialization and the socio-normative imprints, as ingrained in it both by the parents and other socialization agencies. The child is the convergence of the desires, hopes, and longings of his parents. No wonder that it was projected mytho-empirically as the archetypal mediator: the Son of God. Indeed, the Trinity of Christian dogma, as well as the trinity of the Demetrian Tesmophoria, is the mytho-empirical incarnation of the synchronicity of the parents and offspring in the biological personal and cultural senses. This is also the resolution of the paradox of a plurality within unity as stated in the New Testament:

> For as the woman is of the man, even so is the man also by the woman; but all things of God.[199]

The Kabbala postulates a complimentarity between the erotic and agapic love as follows:

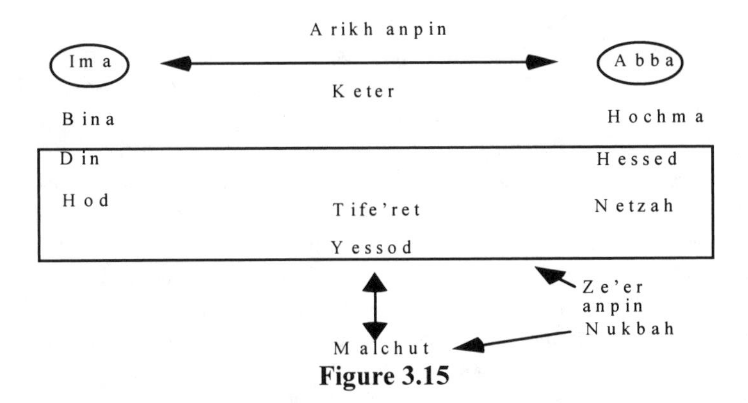

Figure 3.15

The ten rungs are divided into five countenances. The upper countenance is the *arikh anpin,* the long suffering imperfect God whose imperfections induces him to create and long for a mending tikkun with the demiurgical history. Abba and Ima the supernal father and mother, have to mate continuously in an agapic constant mating otherwise the work of divinity will perish. The lower two countenances of *ze'er anpin,* the male and *nukbah,* the female, mate for the purpose of reproduction and the complementarity between the supernal and lower countenance. Thus, they link transcendence and history. In Christianity, we also have the agapic mating which gave birth to Jesus through an immaculate conception and, likewise, the agapic spiritual love between Saint John of the Cross and Saint Theresa d'Avilla. We may ask, therefore, if love is agonizing, painful, frustrating, unattainable, illusory, subjugating, petrifying, and well nigh impossible, what then kindles its fires? What induces us to indulge, da capo, in the amorous cycles of involvement, infatuation, and disenchantment? We claim that our yearning for love, be it the Sisyphean covetousness of possessing our beloved or the Tantalic longing to fuse with him or her, is the essence of love. The process of involvement kindles our amorous fires and not the attainment of our love goals, which are as unachievable as the aims of our participant and separant core vectors. Nietzsche laments not so much his lost love for Frau Lou Andreas Salomé as the destruction of his illusions of love, indeed, of his ability to long for it.[200] Plato describes such yearning for union in love as follows:

> For the intense yearning which each of them has towards the other does not appear to be the desire of lover's intercourse, but of something else which the soul of either evidently desires and cannot tell, and of which she has only a

> dark and doubtful presentiment. Suppose Hephaestus, with his instruments, comes to the pair who are lying side by side and says to them, 'What do you people want of one another?' They would be unable to explain. And suppose, further, that when he saw their perplexity he said: 'Do you desire to be wholly one; always day and night to be in one another's company? for if this is what you desire, I am ready to melt you into one and let you grow together, so that being two you shall become one, and while you live share a common life as if you were a single man, and after your death in the world below still be one departed soul instead of two—I ask whether this is what you lovingly desire, and whether you are satisfied to attain this?' There is not a man of them who when he heard the proposal would deny or would not acknowledge that this meeting and melting into one another, this becoming one instead of two, was the very expression of his ancient need. And the reason is that human nature was originally one and we were a whole, and the desire and pursuit of the whole is called love.[201]

The essence of love is, not the attainment of unity but, the longing for it. Which of us did not experience the thrill, the elation, the quickening of the pulse when revisiting the place of our first kiss and embrace. The yearning for an amorous encounter is enough to fill our hearts, even though its realization is remote or even impossible. The craving for love takes us out of our daily routines and drudgeries and lends a dimension of elation to our Sisyphean quests and infuses revelation into our Tantalic longing. Such independent potency of the yearning for love, which has an essence and a dynamic of its own irrespective of the object of love, might well be the reason for our being baited by it to mate and reproduce. Love songs, tales, myths, and drama are anchored on the yearning for amorous union and not on the processes of mating, reproduction, and growth. Camus succeeded in capturing the essence of this yearning by describing 'the Adulterous Woman', who exudes a free-floating longing for love towards no specific object, but radiates this longing in all directions to the earth, sky, sea, and stars to be borne along by the evening breeze.[202]

Man is in love with love. The objects of our amorous involvement, however, are transitory. What is permanent throughout our life is our yearning for love and to be loved. The Tantalic longing for love has been projected onto religion as the pure Mother of God, the graceful Sophia, and Shekhina. The timelessness of love is a function of the longing for it. A sacred love is a love for an inaccessible object. The rebellion of the participant lover is to immerse himself into his longing for his beloved, however unattainable he or she may be and however impossible the love might be. The rebellious lovers' motto is to love at all costs and to hell with the consequences. Adele H., of the movie portraying some of the actual trials of Victor Hugo's daughter, carries on her Tantalic love irrespective of the indifference of her beloved, oblivious to his rejection of her. The professor in *The Blue Angel* carries on his debasing love affair with the cabaret dancer even though he is fully aware that he is being destroyed by it. In a similar ideational context, but a different setting, Beatrix in Claude Grote's film *The Lace Embroidery* can only achieve a pure and perfect love in the total isolation of an insane asylum.

Kierkegaard performed his metaphysical rebellion concurrently with his renunciation of the consummation of his love for Regina Olsen. By so doing, he elevated his love to a stature of permanence. He extruded it from the precariousness of spatio-temporality and made it timeless. He also prevented it from souring through the leveling down and petrifying routines of matrimony. He renounced a love object and gained a permanent love-longing. To yearn for a love irrespective of the possibilities of its realization, and even being certain that it is unattainable, is to render it absolute. By the same logic, but for diametrically opposite ends, Sade aimed to destroy the longing for love and, thereby, annihilate love itself. He realized that the prime mover of love is the yearning for it. Hence, the destruction of such longing will bring with it as a necessary corollary the extinction of love. This fits Sade's radical nihilistic design of killing sex through boredom by repetitive perversion. He wished to be society's ultimate executioner, because, without a yearning for an amorous encounter and a longing for an emotional dialogue, man enters a state of indifference and loneliness and, hence, a lack of empathy and desire for involvement with his human surroundings. Without the longing for union, the act of sex becomes a mere banality which eventually destroys the erotic passions. Without the Tantalic longing for grace and the Sisyphean dreams anchored on sex, the contours of flesh, the texture of skin, and the glow of eyes lose their bait value, and love peters out. By killing erotic desire and the yearning for love, which sustain the human core-vectors, Sade meant to halt reproduction, dissolve the human family, and disrupt the normative system which he hated. He knew that by depriving man of the longing for love, human life, which he despised and aimed to annihilate, would become not only unbearable, but totally meaningless, and, hence, not worth living. Sade's negation highlights the basic assertion of life inherent in the longing for love.

The mutual longing of lovers for an emotional dialogue provides a framework, a context, a scaffolding for their love. Two lovers holding hands on a moonlit shore might have different expectations and be on the opposite poles of the participant-separant continuum. Yet, their mutual longing for love provides them with a channel through which their divergent Tantalic revelations and Sisyphean aspirations may flow out and provide them and their offspring with some sort of a viable future. Only the longing for love can provide the human being's thrownness unto death with a silver lining of grace.

To Storm the Wall Between One and the Many

The barriers between the individual and society are both structural and normative. Since this is not a social or anthropological tract, we shall not engage in the present context in the interrelationship, either conformative or deviant, between the individual and society. We have elaborated extensively on these vast focal concerns elsewhere. Here we may deal with the various methods by which an individual may cross the structural and normative barriers of society. We should distinguish here between two barrier dichotomies: authentic versus inauthentic revelation and authentic versus inauthentic creativity. The crossing of these continua forms the model seen in figure 3.16:

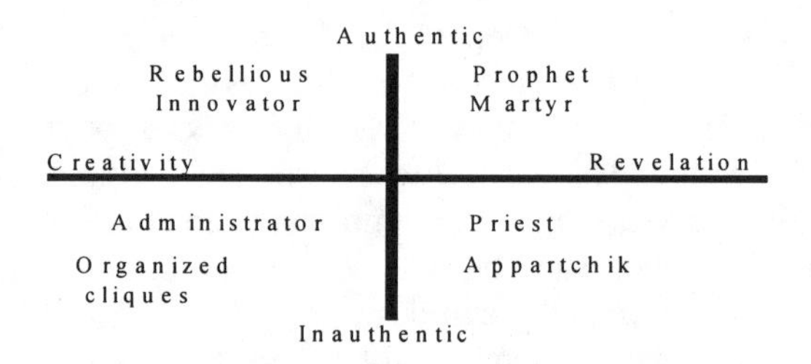

Figure 3.16

The prophet is the man who reveals ultimate meanings to his community of believers because he had a divine revelation concerning truth or the proper behavior. He either has the tablets of the Law like Moses or the Logos, the word of God, like later prophets. These ultimate meanings, when communicated to members of the community, irrespective of his social position, becomes, as Rabbi Joseph Sloveitchik has stated a community of the Covenant.[203] This is based on the summing up of Moses in Deuteronomy:

> 'Ye stand this day all of you before the Lord your God: your captains of your tribes, your elders, and your officers, with all the men of Israel; your little ones, your wives and the stranger that is in thy camp, from the hewer of thy wood unto the drawer of thy water. That thou shouldest enter into covenant with the Lord thy God with you only do I make this covenant and this oath; but with

> him that standeth here with us this day before the Lord our God, and also with him that is not here with us this day.'[204]

This community of the Covenant enables each individual to cross the veil between himself and the group and feel at one with it. The same holds for ideologies. The charismatic leader-prophet reveals the social and political truths to be followed by each individual comprising the group, which may then serve as the economic glue which ties the group together and serves as the basis for every individual to identify with it. However, to make such solidarity possible, group martyrs are necessary. These martyrs, in the Greek sense, are witnesses—in Arabic even today every person who dies for a cause is a *shaheed,* a witness. The martyrdom effects the belief or ideology to emerge extatically in the Greek sense of extasis from the sequences of time and exist in an eternal present like the Christian belief that the crucifixion of Christ takes place everyday. Also, martyrs as mythogenes charge the batteries of all those who would follow in their religious and ideological steps and pay the price. Jesus Christ, el-Hlage, and Rabbi Akiba fired the beliefs and readiness for self-victimization of would-be martyrs; Socrates, Galileo, and Giordano Bruno strengthened those who were ready to renounce their truths. Jan Patocka, who signed the charter 77 together with Havel and Hayek in Communist Czechoslovakia and paid with his life,[205] is just an instance of the myriad of political martyrs who fuel the altruistic solidarity of millions of ideological rebels and would-be rebels and, thus, help them to cross the barrier between themselves and the group and feel solidarity with it and act accordingly. Per contra, the priests of institutionalized religions, as well as the political apparatchiks who succeed the martyrs and self-sacrificing revolutionaries, reap the temporal rewards and build ramparts of power, suppression, and oppression, which strengthen and thicken boundaries between the individual and his membership groups. The institutionalized power brokers of the church have no use for martyrs and prophets. Dostoevski's Grand Inquisitor tells Christ, who made good on his promise for a Second Coming, to go away. The power structure of the church has no use for troublemakers who rock the boat. Likewise, Koestler portrays masterfully in his *Darkness at Noon* the way the apparatchik Gletkin crushes the old Bolshevik Rubashov and convinces him that the last service he can offer the party is to confess that he was an imperialist spy who sabotaged the latest five year plan and, thus, serve as an expiating scapegoat for the failures of the Stalinist regime.

The creative innovators fare no better. The process of branding the creative innovator deviant starts with the essence of innovation, which is the ability to see the commonplace and the familiar from new angles. This seeing things differently than most people makes the innovator point out different aspects and voice different opinions to the reasonable man about town. Hence, innovation is by definition non-normative, which raises the probability of non-conforming behavior. Indeed, many times genius is not more (yet not less) than the ability to perceive contrary to normative conditioning and socialization in a given family and culture. The ability to innovate is linked to one's aptitude to extricate oneself from the harness of stereotypes and clichés imposed by the reigning mandates of the generalized other and to project a novel and, therefore, rebellious vision onto one's creativity. Here again the revelatory component of creativity is a crucial ingredient of innovation. The innovator is also a perpetual child ever astounded by his curiosity, perceptions, and experiences and not stultified by drudgeries or normative routines.

Creativity also necessitates a certain detachment. True, without objective involvement there can be no creativity, but the relationship is curvilinear. A too intense involvement may paralyze the creator. Hence, a measure of distance, apartness, and dissociation is necessary for the artist to gain the right perspective for creation. The artist could very easily be tagged by the normative branding agencies as alienated or deviant. This tag might be reinforced by the fact that the authentic creator is immersed in the process of creativity and is relatively oblivious to money and fame. This is apparent *in extremo* with a Kafka, who was not even willing to have his work published, or with an Erich Neumann, who was determined to go on writing even if no one read his work, or with a Van Gogh, who continued painting with a staccato urgency while knowing he had no chance of being recognized in his lifetime by the art establishment. There might be no better way of illustrating our premise than the advertisement of the Time/Life Library of Art of its Van Gogh volume which says: 'It took the eyes of a madman to see the world in a new light and to paint it that way'. Indeed, to see the world in a new light may predispose one to be stigmatized as a madman. We may, therefore, propose a hypothesis for empirical investigation that most great innovations and creations have been carried out by creators who have been considered as outsiders, outcasts, deviants, and madmen in their own lifetime. This is a variation on Kropotkin's hypothesis that *all* great discoveries and epoch-making researches were carried out outside academic institutions or, we may add, by deviants and outsiders within academia.[206] The persecution of Galileo, the pestering of Bach, and the early loneliness of Einstein are just celebrated instances representing a host of others.

The extreme forms of creator-audience relationships present Scylla and Charybdis choices. The extremely isolated and non-communicative artist is embedded in the solipsism of being both creator and audience.

This might be illustrated by Dostoevski's *Man in The Underground*. On the other extreme, we have the poet laureate and the court jester who are not so far apart in their total dependence on some relevant others and in their need to cater to the tastes and whims of their audience. However, these are extreme poles of a continuum; most artists can be positioned between them. The more the artist anchors on his participant revelatory inner core, the less is his creation marketable, although its participant uniqueness enhances its durability or even timelessness. The participant creator tries to ensure the authentic sincerity of his art, but he cannot evaluate its reception by the consumers of his creation. He may also decide that the process of creativity is more important to him than the peddling of his art, so that he would be discovered after his death or even not at all. We can only guess how many Bachs are totally forgotten, because they did not have a Mendelshohn-Bertoldy to rediscover them; how many Van Goghs have been consigned to oblivion because they did not have a brother Theo to love, cherish, and preserve their work for posterity; even how many Johnsons are untraceable because they did not have a Boswell to pester them and record their utterances for generations to come. Often the participant revelatory artist immersed in visions of his inner-self is not willing to compromise with his audience and insist à la Artaud to be accepted on his own esoteric terms, not realizing that he is asking for the impossible. Mostly, however, the artist receives feedback of his worth from a specific audience or from people whose opinion he values most. This is even more apparent in the case of the performing artist, whose art is focused on his ability to pass over to his audience. A prominent Israeli actress once said that the stage for her is a sacrificial altar on which she prays to achieve revelatory elation; yet even for her, the audience was essential because the actor-audience relationship is the creative unit of the dramatic performance. Many times an actor sacrifices his personal well being, his health, and his livelihood for the actor-audience dialectical interstrains and interplay which are the essence of his art and its main reward.

As we have tried to show earlier, creativity aims at communication with objects and people—this is its authentic raison d'être. However, when the end product is complete, its promotion and exposition may be pursued for recognition, fame, and money. These two processes have hardly anything in common. The quest for communication in creativity anchors on the process of creation and fuels the self-expression inherent in this process, whereas the sale of the end product depends solely on promotion, image-building and public relations not very different from the technique of selling detergents and cereals. Writing a book with a wish that someone pick it up today or a hundred years from now and feel an affinity with the author's ideas is a dynamic of communication inherent in the process of authentic creativity. Per contra, the part of one's motivation to write for pecuniary gain or recognition by the generalized other is extraneous to authentic creativity.

The initial sale of creations and works of art is inversely related to their authenticity and revelatory depth, which stems from the uniqueness of the creator's inner-self. This is based on promotion techniques, which cater to the lowest common denominator of public tastes, in order to ensure a widest possible exposure and largest sale. When an author tries to communicate the intricate feelings, conflicts, thoughts, and interpersonal relationships as experienced by his unique psycho-cultural configuration, he is bound to experience difficulties in expressing himself with the rather inadequate means of language. Words at best are only approximate echoes of one's thoughts and feelings and at worst twist the level of the uniqueness of the author's experience. Also, an authentic creator anchored on the process and not on the end product of his art is not likely to make compromises with his audience to facilitate the easy understanding and absorption of his creation. Hence, his audience is bound to be rather limited. On the other hand, an author writing for the generalized other with a view to selling as many books as possible will utilize the shallow clichés and streamlined stereotypes which are palatable to the modal tastes of the masses. In extremo, this trend is manifest in the currently commercially very successful, no-frills books. The motto of the publishers of these books is 'avoid originality'. The Westerns in this genre of literature usually end with an immortal line like 'Joe (the cowboy hero) rides and fades into the sunset' and the romance novels with 'wordlessly, he swept her into his arms, and their spiral of ecstasy began'. The marketing of a creation, like the selling of any other product, is a function of power, money, and skill. Publishers, for instance, look for bestsellers, and if they have enough of them, allow themselves to publish occasional, quality, prestige pieces, which are good PR, even if they don't bring in enough money. Yet, one shouldn't exaggerate! When Herman Melville insisted on writing more of his think pieces, his publishers retorted that they had enough of these, and the public would prefer some racy adventure stories. Melville declared like Luther before the Inquisition that he could not do otherwise. He was then rejected into oblivion until he was rediscovered in the twenties after the centennial of his birth. Mostly, however, a certain creation will be recognized, accepted, and rewarded with money and fame because of vested economic and political interests, fads, or snob appeal. This is irrespective of the timeless value of a creation or its authenticity, which might be similar to other works of art which have not been discovered and publicly recognized. Some books, for instance, are carried onto the bestseller list by a new diet, a wave of feminism, or the marriage of the Prince of Wales. Others, like Arthur Koestler, Jacob Bronowsky, and Kenneth Clark are master popularizes for the masses of intricate scientific doctrines, philosophical theories, and art movements. Also, some great artists like Picasso, Dali, Graham Greene, and Ernest Hemmingway, who became financially successful in their lifetimes, were astute businessmen. Finally, chance, luck, and coincidence may play a major role in the rediscovery of creative giants like Bach and Melville. A great number of profound writings are probably still buried in oblivion because a convergence of factors did not generate a renaissance of interest in them, the likes of which happened to the works of Melville and Herman Hesse.

Fame and money, however, have quite often asphyxiated creativity by a kiss of fat, inducing the artist to rest on his laurels. The greedy bourgeois so much despised by the authentic artist may, thus, have the last word. Especially painful is the case of Jacques Brel, whose last record, which he considered to be his rebellious testament, was callously commercialized by the carnivorous bourgeois peddlers who he so masterfully ridiculed in his songs.

Creativity, being Sisyphean, is marked by fierce competitiveness, which tends to push it into an inauthentic quest of marketable products. The participant component of creativity makes for blunting this competitiveness and anchors the processes of creation. There is, however, enough venom and malice within ambition-crazed cliques to push many unheedful creators of the success pyramid into the abyss of oblivion. In the lore of the combative artistic cliques, this is expressed by the observation that the moment one starts climbing the ladder of public recognition and success there are those who already engineer his downfall. This, together with what is known in Hollywood as 'the curse of the Oscar' and in scientific circles as 'the noose of the Nobel Prize', constitutes the self-defeating component of public recognition. A best-selling author, an Oscar winner, or a Nobel laureate may be swept by success from his state of mind, which may be optimal for authentic creativity, and hurled into the momentarily loving but carnivorous bosom of the admiring public. Their roots may subsequently be severed from their sources, drained their juices of creativity, with a resultant blackout of production, which may last until a readjustment is effected. This temporary creative recession related, at least partly, to public recognition and glory was suffered by Rod Steiger and Albert Camus and is dreaded by John Le Carré with every new bestseller. This is the reason for his constant refusal to accept very lucrative invitations from Hollywood.

We may denote mytho-empirically such fear, or flight from public acclaim, as the Jonah syndrome. Apart from the realization that material success is liable to deflate the dialectical energy underlying creation, the Jonah syndrome may also be motivated by the creator's agoraphobic dread of an excess of stimuli to which he may be exposed.

It is quite understandable, according to our model, that a separant carnivorous public, which cannot distinguish between the artist and his art, would devour both physically and mentally some muddle-headed performers like Rita Hayworth, Marilyn Monroe, and Elvis Presley. The institutionalized art establishment may also muffle the rebelliousness of creative artists by burying them in the coziness of its soft and overflowing contours. This happened to Jean Genet. After Sartre wrote a blockbuster of a book that turned Genet into the first existentialist saint, Genet, it is reported, could not write for five years. All he did was drive around in a Rolls Royce, changing his young male companions every few days. De Sade was completely institutionalized by the academic establishment which showered him with torrents of pompous verbosity—no doubt making the divine marquis turn in his grave. More disturbing, and yet proof of the universality of our model, is the fact that Camus himself, expounder of the myth of Sisyphus, succumbed to the vicissitudes of success. Public acclaim deprived him of the dialectical strain so vital for creativity.

However, most creators search for recognition and the wealth that goes with it as a reinforcement of their sense of separant worth. If public acceptance fails to materialize, they may be resentful, basking in the halo of the genius unrecognized by the Philistines. This is sure to place our acclaim-thirsty artist under the dominion of the generalized other whose recognition he is trying to gain. This, in turn, further decreases the chances of authentic creation. The course which may finally prove to be both more authentic and more politic is to immerse oneself in the process of creativity and, thereby, gain one's sense of inner dialectical fulfillment. If public acclaim does come, one may accept it as a fringe benefit to authentic self-realization. Another fringe benefit might be, for those who are bent on it, vengeance against one's real or imaginary enemies. However, when one invests one's limited energies, in time and effort—consuming schemes to get even with one's opponents, one loses even if one gains, since the expended energies came to naught and the benefits are momentary, emotional satisfactions which are soon filed and forgotten. On the other hand, authentic creativity is rewarding to the creator as well as the best means of having one's enemies eat their hearts' out. Hence, even if the creator's motivation is strongly fueled by a desire to show them up (meaning his colleagues and competitors and the generalized other), his course of action should still be authentic creativity.

Talent is not democratic. It has not been equally distributed among human beings. But nor does it favor the power elites of artistic cliques. The powerful and talentless within competitive groups, therefore, begrudge the talents of others in the group, especially if they are powerless and, hence, appropriate objects for stigmatization and scapegoating.[207] The powerless talented are, therefore, predisposed to be tagged as deviants among the powerful pacesetters of professional, academic, and artistic groups. Moreover, in many forms of art and creativity, the cliques are also the arbiteri elegantiari. They use their power to brand as mediocre and worthless the work of the authentic creators who reject their authority or do not conform to the rules of the clique. The innovative outsider is usually ill-equipped to fight this judgment because he is mostly powerless, roaming somewhere on the fringes of institutionalized art or outside it. Therefore, the test of the artistic worth of an artist is outside time and place. Only in retrospect can we appreciate the excellence of a Mozart, a Van Gogh, or a Melville. The sad fact is that most innovative creators are recognized only after their death. During their lifetime, they are evaluated by cliquish interests and power structures averse to those who rock the boat. When the creator's critics and rivals are dead, as well as he, his creation can be given its rightful due in a disinterested context. Creators and their creations must effect an extasis in the ancient Greek sense in order to be evaluated in their proper perspective. Mere operators who enjoy wealth and acclaim because of their position of power will not even be remembered in footnotes, whereas the creative outsiders will be recognized for their contributions without the marring, blocking, and twisting effects of vested interests and power politics.

The vested-interest and clique-based evaluation of the creator not only dates him, but also binds him in a derogatory manner to a given place. This could be denoted as the Muhammed syndrome, exemplified by the saying, 'there is no prophet in his own country'. The people of Mecca, Muhammad's hometown, did not accept him as their prophet, so he moved to Medina, where he was acclaimed as the emissary of God. Muhammad's trip from Mecca to Medina, the hejira, was considered so crucial that it came to serve as the baseline for the Moslem calendar. Indeed, we could hear the gentry of Mecca muttering, 'This runny-nosed epileptic a prophet? Never!' The British say that 'familiarity breeds contempt', while Proust remarked that we cannot impute genius to the tablemate who picks his teeth after dinner. The deeper basis for the Muhammed syndrome is that the vested interests and power élite are wary of the creative innovator and try to suppress him. The authentic creator is more likely to fulfill himself creatively without the stifling normative prejudices of the indigenous others when he leaves, in a rebellious mood, for another place. Hence, authentic creativity is boundless.

Artistic cliques are composed of a few artists, with many camp followers, lackeys, groupies, critics, managers, and spongers—all centered around a hard-core leadership that draws its power not from creative excellence but, from the control of budgets, journals, theaters, and radio and TV stations. They are separantly dependent on the clique for favors, employment, and for a sense of relative achievement which comes from stigmatizing their colleagues. The cliques, through their public-relations organs, create celebrities and destroy them. When someone has been declared brilliant by the public communications channels, the declaration becomes a self-fulfilling prophecy. Even if everybody knows, including the artist who received the praise, that the critic responsible for the praise is a shallow mediocrity, the laudatory image receives the sanction of public opinion and vox populi, becomes vox Dei. This image of a given artist and his art created by the reigning pace setters and their PR organs, of course, have very little to do with authentic creativity, but are almost exclusively related to sales, power politics, and the egomania of some artists, reinforced by their camp followers and groupies.

There are, however, many instances in which authentic creators need the good services of cliques, institutions, and establishments in order to expose their works to groups and individuals with whom they wish to communicate. These are, inter alia, professional organizations, congresses, publishing houses, theaters, and galleries. Camp followers, as well as sincere friends and constructive critics, give the artist the feedback he so ardently needs as a reinforcement of his sense of worth and an evaluation of the communicative worth of his creation. The creator may thereby become easy prey to flatterers who exploit him materially and emotionally. Because of his separant need for reinforcement, he is in a poor position to distinguish between flatterer and sincere critic. The institutionalized outlets for his creations may shower him with prizes, honors, and positions that might stifle his creativity with a thick mesh of complacency and quench his authentic rebellion with pomposity and self-satisfaction.

Creative people are usually too absorbed in their work to be willingly involved in administration and institutional power politics. Deans, directors of granting agencies, museum curators, and administrative directors of orchestras are usually people who have stopped being creative or have never been so. Yet they have power over creative people because they control the budgets and other essentials for the creator's work. Creative people soon find themselves at the mercy of such administrators, who are liable to abuse their power. The creator may rebel, but soon finds himself powerless. When he persists in standing on what he considers his legitimate rights, he is likely to be branded as a troublemaker or poor team member, be denied tenure, or even find himself without a job. His non-involvement in power politics—since his creative efforts absorb most of his time and energy—also predisposes him to loneliness, whereas the power-anchored controllers operate in cliques. Lilliputians always have to band together to fell a creative giant.

The pseudo-bohemians, the synthetic bums and the salon rebels seek, and sometimes get, the best of two worlds: they are very good at adjusting to both fads and power shifts. They pose as artists and have the mannerisms, the expressions, and the bearing of poets, actors, and novelists. Apart from wearing the uniform, they also sit in the coffeehouses or bars which are reputed to be the watering holes of celebrities. What the pseudo-bohemians do not possess is the raison d'être of the artist—the process of authentic creativity itself which no material remuneration or social acclaim can rival in its sense of fulfillment. T.S. Eliot was usually clad in a conservative suit and tie. Modigliani frequented coffeehouses only to sell his paintings for a few francs to buy the cheap wine that eventually corroded his liver. Bach had the appearance and household of a harried shopkeeper. Yet all three felt what the synthetic bum could never feel—the majestic undulating of their inner eagles' wings lifting them from their places and times onto the boundless eternity of authentic creativity.

As authentic creativity is a continuous process, one should continually seek new ways of expression and novel techniques of artistic communication. Any resting on laurels is tantamount to stagnation. However, in extremo, this constant pursuit of innovation may turn into a cult of newness which accepts anything, pseudo-art included, provided it is novel. 'We have learned so well how to absorb novelty', says Richard Hofstader, 'that receptivity itself has turned into a kind of tradition—the tradition of the new. Yesterday's avant garde experiment is today's chic and tomorrow's cliché.'[208] Many phony artifacts or performances which intend to shock, overwhelm, or simply fool audiences may thus pose as art. However, most of the authentic innovators are stigmatized and ostracized by the processes we have described earlier in this section. This process may be described mytho-empirically as the transformation of the creative Sisyphus into the tortured Prometheus. Mythological transformations are very common, and we have elsewhere studied the transformation of Korê, Demeter's 'good' daughter, into 'horrible'

Persephone.[209] The process of transformation in the present context is the creative hübris of the Sisyphus, which evokes the jealousy of the Olympian gods, who are the mythical projections of separant men. The gods then punish Prometheus, just as the jealous and competitive power élite stigmatize and ostracize the unruly and rebellious creative innovators. The rock-burden of Sisyphus is, thus, symbolically transformed into the rock to which Prometheus is chained. It is also symbolic that the regeneration of Prometheus' liver and his subsequent torture by the vulture are cyclic, paralleling the cyclic trials of Sisyphus and his stone. (It is interesting in this context that the makers of Persian carpets deliberately introduce a flaw in it in order not to commit the hübris of perfection and thereby incur the wrath of the jealous gods.)

The plight of the creative Prometheans may be pathetic when they do not understand the dynamics of relationships between innovators and the power structures of society. They may complain that their innovation benefited the group and humanity at large—so why have they been punished? Haven't the Promethean innovators brought light to humanity? Of course they have! But in the process they have rocked the boat. They have threatened the vested interests of, for instance, gas companies, which are bound to be threatened by Edison's electric light bulb. Above all, however, the creative innovators have raised the jealousy of the Olympians, the mythical separant projections of the competitive power élite in society. They are much more concerned with maintaining their power than with artistic excellence, scientific progress, or the welfare of humanity. Creative, Promethean outsiders demand, with typical naiveté, that they be accepted by a public which is led and controlled by the power élite and vested interests against whom they have rebelled and whom they have injured. Their misfortune is, thus, exacerbated because they are asking for the impossible. They do not realize that by being excellent they make the power élite appear even more mediocre and sterile than they are. Their difference and otherness fill the vulgur with apprehension and anxiety. Finally, their creativity makes them seem powerful, though socially and materially they are the opposite. Promethean outsiders are powerless power symbols and, as we have shown in *The Mark of Cain*, this combination makes them perfect scapegoats.[210]

On the macro level of metaphysical programming, the power élite, artistic cliques, and academia might offer an apology smacking of science fiction—that stigmatization of creative innovators serves as a guard against too much innovation, for which society is not prepared. The Inquisition, which in Galileo's time stood for stability, good order, propriety, and probity, and which, of course, was the staunch defender of the universal church, had to torture him to make him recant his atrocious contentions—which might have led to cosmic, social, and religious chaos. Yet Galileo could not help it. Being a rebellious creative innovator, he could not but declare against all convention *'and yet it* (the earth) moves'.

As we have shown throughout the present work, myths are projections onto mythology of human experiences. We, therefore, conclude our explorations of creativity and revelation with a mytho-empirical anchor of our theoretical model.

Both our protagonists, Kierkegaard and Rabbi Nachman, have made public their revelatory Messianic experiences, and they have had to pay for their hübris by social ostracism, debilitating social stigmata, and life-long misery.

Both the self-sacrificing creators like Van Gogh and self-victimizing prophets like Jan Hus break the barricades and melt the veils between the individual and the group whereas the false prophets, church rulers, and artistic power brokers break the ramparts between the individual and society. The authentic willing victimization of a Jesus Christ effects an *extasis* out of time and place and fuels the belief of millions in a continuing present. Likewise, the authentic sacrificial creativity of a Van Gogh made his art timeless and passes over group and institutional boundaries to fire the creative imagination of viewers and would-be artists in a timeless synchronicity from here to eternity.

Seeing Is Believing: Hearing the Logos and Seeing with the Eye of Horus

The epistemic barriers between man and his surroundings are legion. This is mainly related to the fallibility of human perception. Philosophically, the failings of the human senses has been expounded on by David Hume. We have shown elsewhere in a volume-length exposition the epistemic and cognitive obstacles to perceive whatever there is out there.[211] Indeed, we are not concerned here with optical or visual illusions, such as the fact that the Muller-Lyer illusion shows the line with arrowheads pointing outwards to be shorter than the line with its arrowheads pointing inwards, although the two lines are of exactly the same length.[212] We are concerned with the twisting of perception by motivation, needs, values, and personality differences. We are, however, interested by the fact that the sticks in the Muller-Lyer illusion appear to be of different lengths to different people and to the same person at different times and places. In this issue we side with the motivational approach to perception according to which we are very likely to misperceive because of a projection of needs and wishes on the stimuli. Consequently, we cannot adhere to the psycho-physical approach of

Gibson and his disciples, which stresses the 'correspondence between certain mathematical properties of the retinal image and certain phenomenal variables of the visual world'.[213] The psycho-physicist anchors on the stimulus with a scientific zeal for measurements, whereas we join the motivationists in trying to relate the individual's perceptual response to his needs and motives. Moreover, we hold that because Ego's motives and wishes, as determined by the dialectics of his personality core-vectors, largely determine his precepts and perceptual responses, they also play a crucial role in his interaction with his surroundings. To be more precise: our interest in Ego's value involvement with things, nature, and people makes us more concerned with the relationship between his motives and his perceptual responses than with the epistemic nature of the stimuli which impinge on his senses.

There are, of course, some links between stimuli and their precepts which are not based on motivational pressures and their projections. These have been studied and supposedly measured by an impressive number of experimental psychologists, from G. Fechner to modern psychophysicians.[214] We do not believe, however, that the non-motivational components of the perception can be effectively isolated from the motivated and projective ones, and then related separately to the stimuli. The science of man has not yet reached the level of sophistication to conduct the controlled experiments which are necessary for these kinds of measurements. Yet, we may carry on our reasoning and theorizing by assuming a given constancy of relationship between the stimuli and their non-motivated perception (which serve as a raw material for the final product of perception). This, in turn, is influenced and molded by the vast array of motivational and wish-based personality traits and cultural pressures. This assumption may be questioned by some scientific psychologists. Our defense is by reference to one of their own cherished assumptions: the behaviorist black box analogy of intrapsychic dynamisms which is very much like our present assumption about the consistencies of relationships between stimuli and their sensory perceptions.

Even if there are some psycho-physical constancies in the relationship between stimulus and precept, they are bound to be twisted and remolded by the dynamics of the organism and the psyche. The form and quality of perception may be influenced by the intensity of the needs of the body, by some endocrine secretions, diseases, and drugs on the biological level, by developmental fixations and core personality characteristics on the psychological level, and by cultural imprints and social character traits on the social level. The complexity and variability of the configurations of these variables are so vast that the chances of one person having even a closely similar perception to the one perceived by another person of the same stimulus are very remote. Yet perceptual theory links meaning and reason to similarity.[215] Consequently, the inevitable dissimilarity of perceptions makes the possibility of meaningful communication of precepts from one person to another sadly remote. Meaningfulness in the present context relates to the intersubjective domain and not to the mere mechanical transmission of symbols and signs.

Worse still, even the meaningfulness of Ego's own perception is related, according to perception theory, to the resemblance of a given perception to a previous one. There is evidence that time differences may be related to different motivations, body chemistry, moods, and sex are also bound to influence the form and contents of the perception.[216] Thus, the meaningfulness of a perception varies not only with the motivations, fixations, and cultural imprints on Ego's personality, but also on the time of perception by Ego himself. We may conclude, therefore, that the meaningfulness of Ego's perception is, not only non-communicable from the ontological point of view but in all probability also, statistically unique. This premise that perception is essentially a private language will have wide implications for our subsequent examination of Ego's ability to reach a meaningful dialogue with his surroundings.

Our central thesis is that effective interpersonal communication is so unlikely that it borders on the impossible. This is so because Ego's cognition is related first of all to his biological potential, to his core personality fixations, to his peripheral personality parameters, and to the cultural imprints on his personality effected by socialization. The permutation of all these factors makes the cognition of Ego unique to himself and not shared by any other human being almost like his fingerprints. Consequently, there is no cognitive common denominator between Ego and Alter, and, even if there was, there are no adequate means of transmitting Ego's cognition to others. We assume that there are no effective direct means for intersubjective communication. Telepathy, even if it exists, is not developed and widespread enough to serve as an effective and universal means of interpersonal communication. Language operates on a very shallow level of encounter and is subject to the same twists and biases as other modes of cognition.

To begin our argument we present the following model of dyadic interpersonal perception (figure 3.17):

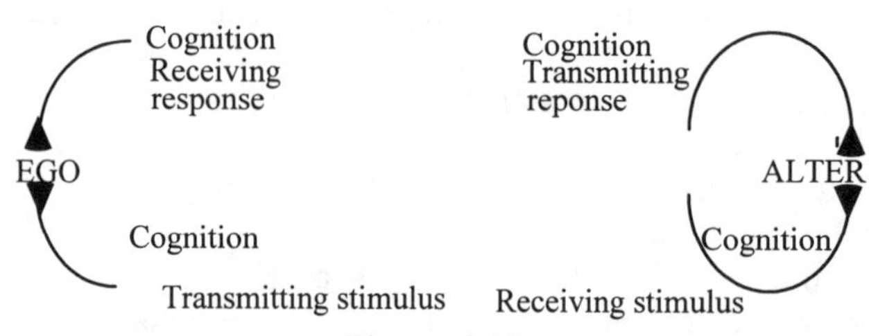

Figure 3.17

Each stage of perception and response is subject to the biases and twists of both Ego's and Alter's cognition. The specific and virtually unique combination of Ego and Alter's cognitive processes intervene and stand between the reception and transmission of both stimuli and responses. As the cumulating and permutation of bio-psychogenic and socio-genetic factors make the twists and biases within the cognitive process unique for each person, the effective transmission of stimuli and responses on a common denominator of meanings between Ego and Alter is practically impossible. As for the value-laden attitudes and affects inherent in the cognitive processes of an individual, they are even less transmittable. The personality-and culture-bound attitudes and affects color each precept and cognition of Ego in hues and nuances peculiar to himself. They cannot be shared with Alter or communicated to him.

The gist of our argument is first of all statistical, namely that the vast permutations of cognitive twists and biases, along with the combinations of effects and value judgments, make the cognition of Ego peculiar to himself and the possibility that they are shared by Alter is so remote that it is virtually non-existent. Second, all kinds of symbolic and non-verbal means of human communication are blunt, coarse, and inadequate tools for effecting an intersubjective rapport of meanings. Finally, Ego's psychological defenses and his congruity based longing for dialogue may create an illusion of communication. This illusion may constitute a further barrier against interpersonal communication because the illusion itself and its projection on Alter is peculiar to Ego and cannot be transmitted to Alter. Moreover, when this illusion of communication is projected onto the group, the collective, or society at large, it creates expectations by the individual from the group which are again peculiar to a given individual and are not shared by others. This makes for the vast heterogeneity of views as to the social and political functions of society and the inevitable rift between Ego's expectations from his membership and reference groups and the latter's ability to fulfill them.

The guideline for our analysis of the disjunctures in the process of dyadic communication is presented schematically as shown in figure 3.18:

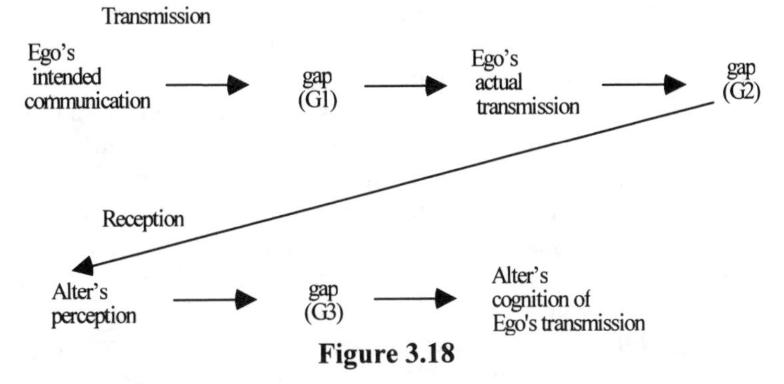

Figure 3.18

The first gap, denoted G1, is between the communication which Ego meant to transmit and his actual communication. This gap may be related to a wide range of reasons. Some instances are that Ego lacks the necessary proficiency, verbal or non-verbal, in order to convey his meaning. Many times language or other means of communication available to Ego cannot depict or, hence, convey the depth of his emotions, the range of his ideas, or the subtlety and nuances of his meanings. In art, especially the performing arts, the artist may feel that he did not come through or that the music in his heart was not translated by his fingers into the music that actually emitted from the piano. Due to twisted perception and defense mechanisms of projection, displacement, pretense, illusion and elusion (double illusions boomeranging back at Ego),[217] one may present a communication in a form and content quite different from the manner in which Ego intended to transmit it.

The second gap, G2, relates to Ego's communication as stimulus and Alter's twisted perception of it, due to biological, personality, and cultural factors. The third gap, G3, is the transformation of Alter's precept by his cognitive processes and the biasing effects of his defence mechanism, personality peculiarities, and cultural imprints. The cumulative disrupting effects of these gaps on Ego's endeavors to communicate with Alter are brought home to Ego by Alter's dissonant reaction to his communication. Ego is then likely to experience a frustration because of this initial breakdown of communication. Man is motivated by his early developmental phases to be a congruity driven animal. Consequently, Ego is bound to try to overcome these gaps of communication (depending on his personality type) by either a separant inclusionary effort to reach Alter by conveying his communication to him in an overpowering manner or by a participant exclusionary effort to achieve congruity by accepting Alter's version of the communication as processed by him and fed back to Ego. When these congruity-based efforts to close the gaps in the process of dyadic communication fail, the breakdowns in the communication process are final and are recorded as such by Ego's psyche.

The failure of dyadic communication is, of course, relative and varies in degree for every communication. Totally detached autistic psychotics are a very small minority in any human society. On the other hand, a mutually meaningful and successful dialogue borders on the miraculous. The middle range consists of near-failures, semi-failures, and partial dissonances. The main impediment to any measure of dialogue is that Ego is ever-motivated by his core personality vectors to achieve a deeper level of encounter with Alter and his contextual object than the level he deems himself to have achieved. This is the fate of man's Sisyphean ressentiment and Tantalic illusions that he ever chases a stone he cannot control or a communication he cannot achieve. However, the efforts of man to overcome the epistemic barrier between himself and his surroundings have been attempted by mythogenic means throughout the ages. These efforts are strongly related to the social character of the individuals attempting it. We shall, therefore, illustrate for our purposes the mythogenic efforts to overcome the epistemic barrier by means of the senses in the ancient Egyptian and the biblical Judaic social character. It would be useful to guide our analysis by a continuum as shown in figure 3.19:

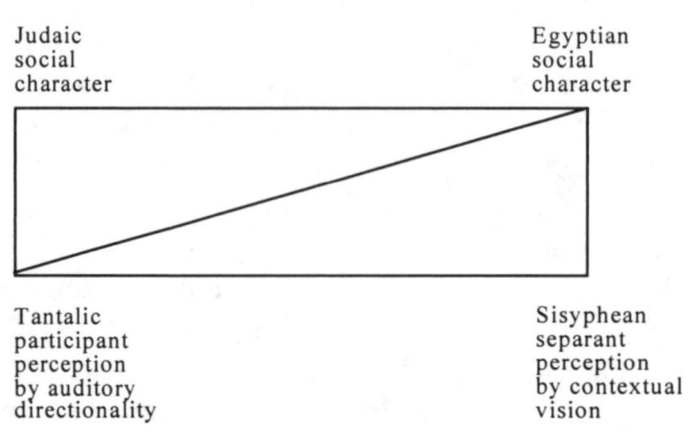

Figure 3.19

Thus, in Egyptian scripture, when Horus comes to look for his father Osiris, he sees Ra (the Egyptian chief deity) and he *knows* Ra.[218] This direct epistemic visual exposure to God is seemingly anathema to the Mosaic conception of the abstract, unique God which was the antithesis to the polytheism of concrete Egyptian deities. Hence, original sin is direct exposure to knowledge of God and, therefore, is considered to be the most heinous transgresson in both Judaism and Christianity. The visual organ occupies a central role in ancient Egyptian cosmology, mythology, and ritual. Egyptian cosmology identifies the sun and the moon as the two eyes of the falcon-god Horus.

> Thou art the God who came into being when no (other) God had yet come into existence, when no name of anything has yet been proclaimed. When thou openest thy eyes so as to see, it becomes light for everyone. The falcon radiating light from his eyes. The sun and moon are his eyes.[219]

This identification is somewhat peculiar. It confers upon the eye a function which is dissonant, if not opposite, to our present-day knowledge and way of thinking. We are accustomed to think of vision as the perception of light. However, from the cosmological statements above, it is clear that the Egyptian eye is no less a symbolical instrument of illumination than it is an organ of receiving light. The visual faculty of the god Horus is, at the very same time, a source of light radiation. His vision gives us our light. This conception of the eye as a light source, as an organ which actively participates in the creation of its own datum, is highly significant and deserves further attention.

The sun and moon themselves occupy an immensely important role in Egyptian cosmology and mythology. The solar and lunar cycles of light and darkness are one of the essential bases, if not the fundamental one, to understanding the Egyptian preoccupation with the transformations between life, death, and resurrection. The rising of the sun, birth, ascension to the throne, victory, and the coming into being of light are intertwined to form a complex of partially related meanings in the Egyptian discourse. On the other hand, the dimming of light, the setting of the sun, death, and defeat are strongly associated together. The great, unfathomable abyss between life and death, and between reality and transcendence challenges each individual and every society with their respective cultures and religions to supply a satisfactory conception of what the bridge over this abyss might be. It is highly significant to our thesis that the specific conception supplied by the Egyptian religion to give meaning to the metamorphosis of life unto death relies so heavily on symbolism of light or its absence. The sun is life, and its rising means birth. Sunset means death, but as the sun returns to rise, life returns to rise in the ever-after. Life comes forth by day following a successful passage through darkness.

Life is the presence of light. Death is the absence of it. Resurrection is the re-emergence of light. The two celestial luminaries, the sun and the moon, appear respectively in the day and the night. The fact that they are both symbolized as the two eyes of Horus transcends and resolves the seemingly unbridgeable gap between light and darkness and between life and death. The phenomenally shocking metamorphosis of human life into a human corpse, is, thus, made coherent within the transcendental face of the falcon-god, in which the sun and moon are equal partners. Indeed, it seems as if the universal medium, or ether, or space, in Egyptian cosmology is made of light. Where there is darkness, one cannot walk. The dead must be armed with the eye of Horus.

The eyes of Horus, the fact of their co-presence within the same godhead, is far from taken for granted in Egyptian mythology. The universal continuity between life and resurrection has been symbolically secured and guaranteed not only through the resurrection of Osiris, but through the victory of Horus over Set, in the course of which Horus took possession of his eye or eyes unrightfully stolen from him by Set. It is customary to view the Osirian process as the essence of the Egyptian theory of eternal life, but, in truth, the Osirian process would be incomplete without the complementary significance of Horus and his eyes. Osiris is a one-way ticket to away and beyond. Osiris is the vehicle from reality to transcendence. But Horus, the son of Osiris, is the vehicle from transcendence to reality, and much of the complete, round trip, depends on his eyes. The story comes in numerous variations, but in all of them it is clear, that before or after Osiris is safely reconstituted, resurrected, and mounted on his rightful throne as king of the dead, there develops a cosmic battle, or conflict of some sort, between Horus, the son of Osiris, and Set, his sinister brother-shadow, in the course of which one of Horus's eyes, or both of them, get stolen or damaged. The result is darkness. Absolute death, the sort of death which is not permissible in the Egyptian frame of mind, threatens to take hold of the universe. The exact manner of resolution of this threat varies from story to story, but in all of them the end result is the same: Horus regains possession of his eyes, and light returns to the world. A horrible threat on universal order is thus removed. In the next step Horus gives his eye to Osiris and, thus, complements the process of reconstitution. Horus's eye grants Osiris the gift of eternal life and the ability to rule the kingdom of the dead. The mythological picture here is somewhat incomplete. Common sense has it that Horus's gift to his father would leave the son blind again. But, as Budge convincingly demonstrates, the transfer of Horus's eye to Osiris does not damage Horus's own visual/enlightening faculty.

How should we understand the meaning of the eye of Horus, in the context of this mythological array?

We have two gods, father and son. The son loses his eye while avenging the death of the former, the loss constituting a universal catastrophe. The son wins his eye back, the catastrophe is averted. Then son transfers an eye to the dead father, who is thereby given powers of eternal life and authority. This time the transfer of the eye does not threaten the universal order. Indeed, it only strengthens it, since the eternal life and government of Osiris ensures the proper functioning of the crop cycle, to mention only one essential Osirian responsibility towards the human race. The eye, the visual sense, its image, symbolism and mythogenes are, therefore, the prime means by which the ancient Egyptians tried to bridge the epistemic rift between themselves and their surroundings.

The eye has to bathe in humidity; the life-giving wetness of the Nile in order to survive. Hence, Seth, the evil Weidergeist symbolizing nihilation and death, is ever dry. Seth pushes his finger of dryness into the eye of Horus, and it dries and destroys it. But then Horus cries, and from his tears all human beings are created.[220] Hence, humanity was conceived in pain and agony. This might well be linked to the notion of a blemished God in both Christianity and Luranic Kabbala whom man's duty is to help mend (tikkun). However, there is a daily resurrection of the sun and the day since Osiris, the god of death, gives Horus the eye and resuscitates, thereby, both him and the new day. Indeed, the Egyptians had eye-shaped saffron cakes, and their ingestion was like partaking of the host in Christianity. In all probability, there was a certain link between these two rituals: The eating of the symbolic eye of Horus sanctifies the eater, very much like the eucharist swallowed by the Christians. Also, Osiris eats the eye and is resurrected.[221] In Egypt, the facts of life and resurrection are related to seeing and perceiving the concrete image. Per contra, in Judaism and sometimes in Christianity seeing is shunned as related to the visual concretizing image. Eidolon, an idol which stems from the Greek eidon (to see), is of course related to the heinous sin of idolatry both in Judaism and in Christianity. The medieval church proclaimed derisively: "Quod Legendibus Scriptura, Hoc Idiotibus Pictura". As the written word is to the literate, so is the picture to the illiterate—decreeing the supremacy of the Logos to the visual image. Indeed, Moses assures the children of Israel: 'Take ye, therefore, good heed into yourselves; for ye saw no manner of similitude on the day that the Lord spoke unto you in Horeb out of the midst of the fire.'[222] The Mosaic God has no image he cannot be seen only heard. This, of course, is mytho-empiricized by the exhortation: 'Hear O Israel: the Lord our God is one Lord'.[223] The most important assertion of monotheism is related to abstract hearing and not to concrete seeing. Characteristically, the priests are sanctified by tipping their right ears with the blood of a sacrificial ram[224] since it is with their ears that they have to receive the word of God. This is why the golden calf, the concrete visual image of an eidolon, was so starkly contrary to the essence of an abstract unseen and unseeable God. 'Thou canst not see my face: for there shall no man see me and live'.[225] The God of Israel can only be heard. *Mashma'ut* (meaning in Hebrew) stems from the root שמע, to hear, which implies that meanings may be gleaned by hearing. Mishma'at—"obedience" in Hebrew—also stems from *shma* or hearing. Indeed, God commands Israel: 'Obey my voice, and I will be your God, and ye shall be my people'.[226] Here the hearing of the voice of God seems to be a condition precedent to the theophany of God of Israel, His agreement to be their God and to accept them as his people. In prayer, man calls, and God mercifully hears his prayer.[227] The gist of our argument here is that, in directional Judaism, the inner revelatory conviction is effected maieutically through an inner voice which is taken to be divine. One cannot see himself interacting with one's surroundings and with other human beings; yet one can hear oneself in discourse with others. Hence, man who wishes to convey a directional meaning or norm projects onto others a sincere authentic exhortation with the intention that this other hears maieutically in his inner-self a resonant echo of Ego's exhortation. This is the attempt of Ego to cross the epistemic barrier between himself and Alter.

To Dance with Particles

Our final deliberation on a possible way to bridge over epistemic barriers will be a description of the possibility of crossing the rift between consciousness and matter which entails the crossing over from the classic into the quantum world. A volcano erupts and the earth revolves around its axis without knowing whether what they do or what happens to them is good or bad. Knowledge entails a complementarity relationship between man and physical systems both quantic and classic. This is apparent from the mytho-empirical interpretation of the myth of original sin which we have explained previously. The mytho-empirical method regards myths as, inter alia, a projection of developmental phases of the individual human being. Hence, the knowledge of original sin proscribed by the absolute directional abstract and unique God since he regards knowledge as his own prerogative, gained by interaction with a physical object, the apple. After the complimentarity interaction with the objects around him which gains his cognition ethical knowledge, the developing infant is able to distinguish between good and bad. Even before this when man was still in the Edenic non-differentiated phase of his development, he had the ability to label with a word the objects and life forms around him. This is epistemic knowledge, a purely cognitive intra-psychic dynamic which is followed by the interactional ethical knowledge of the original sin. Indeed, the word Logos is a prime directional tool.

Moses, the inventor of directional ethics, lost his chance to enter the Promised Land because he smote the rock at the waters of Meribah instead of speaking to it to make it give forth water as ordained by God.[228] This, indeed, is central to the directional creed. The Jews are the people of the word, the Logos, of the book whereas the gentiles and, especially, the Greeks act and use force to effect order, kosmos, in their contextual surroundings. Hence, Moses and Aaron committed sacrilege, and not just a trivial offense, by hitting the rock instead of talking to it.

This mytho-empirical digression highlights the complementarity of ethics in the same way the observation effects a well-defined physical Eigenstate out of the probabilistic superposition of the wave function. This measurement interaction confers a physical definition and is, hence, meaningful to the stochastic diffusion of the Schrödinger wave function. This complementarity between observer and observed confers meaning on the measuring artifact and the physical system complex, not only according to the Copenhagen Interpretation of quantum mechanics but also, according to the other major interpretations of the quantum measurement problem.[229] If we take Von Neumann's mathematical formula, which described the collapse of Schrödinger wave functions into defined physical Eigenstate, we may point out the following problems. First, the Schrödinger wave function on which the probability of finding a particle is smeared, according to Born on the wave function and measured by the square of its amplitude, is linear and deterministic. The collapse of the wave function by the measurement of the quantum system as formulated by Von Neumann is stochastic and non-linear. Hence, there is a dynamic disconnectedness between the movement of the wave function and its collapse into a physical Eigenstate. A second point of criticism is that, according to Von Neumann, the collapse may be effected anywhere between the physical system and the brain of the observer, yet the dynamics are bound to be different if the collapsing measurement is effected by the measuring instrument or the observing brain. According to our reassessment of the Copenhagen Interpretation, a complimentarity relationship takes place between a meaning and a value endowing human psyche and quantum systems. The formation of a clearly defined physical phenomenon is as follows. The act of measurement plunges the measured quantum system, the measurement instrument as well as the observers' brain, into a superposition of states. This is the murky quantum soup of non-defined entangled probability waves and their squared amplitudes.

The subsequent collapse of the wave function is carried out by a virtual particle originating in the human brain and engulfed by a hermetic force field. We denoted this force field hermetic after Hermes, the messenger of the Greek gods, since its function is to link the cognition of the observer as contained in the measurement instrument (including the human brain) and the measured quantum system. The virtual particle has only a shadowy physical existence since it can violate the uncertainty barrier. The uncertainty relationship postulates $\hbar/2\pi < \Delta E \cdot \Delta T$, where E is energy, T is time, and $\hbar$ is Plancks' constant. If ΔE is near to O, ΔT is moving towards ∞. Hence, a virtual particle which has borrowed a minute amount of energy may exist for a relatively long time. As we do not grasp quarks, bossons, and gluons, but perceptible phenomena, the collapse of the wave function into a defined physical state is essentially a cognitive one. This is brought about by a hermetic force field cloning a virtual wave function, which engulfs the physical wave function like a cognitive halo. The cognitive collapse into a well-defined phenomenon does not affect either the physical system or the measurement apparatus which still remains in a superposition of states. The link between the cognitive system and the physical one is carried out by the hermetic force field through a maieutic resonance. The Socratic maieutic dialogical relationship was not foreign to Bohr, since it was expounded by Kierkegaard who influenced Hefding, Bohrs' friend. This maieutic relationship entails a mediating birth-giving trigger by the cognitive virtual particle and the hermetic force field. These clone a virtual wave function, which fits like a cognitive halo around the wave function. Then the cloned virtual wave function interacts with the wave function through a resonance. These nucleon resonances have proved to be excited, short-lived states that are momentary flirtations of a pion Π -Mesons, the strong force-carrying particles binding the protons and neutrons together) with a nucleon (proton or neutron). In pion nucleon scattering, a pion can be caught in the momentary embrace of a nucleon; the two orbit each other briefly before separating once again. Think of two dancers coming together in a square dance, embracing warmly and swinging fondly before parting again and going on their way.[230] This resonance minuet is the maieutic interaction by means of which the virtual cognitive collapse is effected and a minute quality of energy is transmitted to dent it in its superposed state so that whoever observes the physical state will perceive the same object. The resonance triggering a maieutic interaction between the cognition of the observer and the quantum system must result in a well defined observable stable for all observers.

David Bohm's 'Hidden Variables' interpretation of quantum mechanics utilizes the point particle concept, which is very much like our virtual particle and is more of a cognitive entity than a physical one. Bohm envisages a Hamiltonian which evolves deterministically from initially known conditions. The pilot wave then chooses one branch of the probability density wave function and the other branches become, thence, ineffectual. Bohm's interpretation is realistic in the sense that, unlike the Copenhagen interpretation which postulates probabilistic relationships between the observer and the physical system, Bohm envisages real quantic processes among the measuring instrument, Hamiltonian wave, and physical system. Hence, Bohm's interpretation encounters Lorenz's invariance and relativity problems. As we envisage a virtual collapse of the wave function which is largely cognitive, we do not encounter any relativity problems.

The many worlds interpretation of Evertt and DeWitt has a science fiction aura. All the probabilities of the wave function materialize since each relationship between observer and observed does result in a well-defined Eigenstate, although in a world to themselves. Hence, there is no need for the wave function to collapse because all squared amplitudes of its probability wave are realized in a different space-time universe. Consequently, each measurement creates a separate world for the measurer, the measurement instrument, and the quantum system. The acute problem here is that if each observer disappears with the measurement instrument and the Eigenstate of the observed into a world of their own, what happens if the same observer and the same instrument measure another quantum system? Will they occupy another world completely cut off from the first? How then will persons keep a continuous stable identity if every single observation catapults them to a separate world? Also, the Schrödinger wave function does not contain any provisions for world splitting. Our interpretation would help the many worlds interpretation to evade some pitfalls since it envisages a dualism of consciousness and energy-matter. A hermetic force field sent by a particle originating in our consciousness clones the time-evolving Hamiltonian and leads the virtual particle to one wave packet whereas all the others became ineffective. Since this dynamic is cognitive and virtual and does not happen in the physical system each observer generates a different hermetic force field corresponding to his cognition.

A variation on the theme of the many worlds' interpretation is the many minds interpretation of Albert and Lower. It postulates that each probability in the wave function has a corresponding state of mind and each probability materializes. Apart from the lack of the observer identity problem which is common to the many worlds and many minds interpretations, the many minds exposition is also vulnerable to the danger of solipsism since one observer functions as if his mind is the sole one in existence and unaware of other minds. If Albert and Lower had adopted our stance and synchronized it with theirs, they would not have succumbed to the dangers of solipsism. We postulate only one consciousness which is reflected kaleidoscopically in every life form. The resulting classical phenomenon, which is indeed a unique relationship between one mind and a physical system, is a cognitive reflection of the mind in the physical system, and does not preclude a similar cognitive reflection of another mind. Hence, the dangers of solipsism are avoided by means of our interpretation, and we also assure the continuous identity of the observer. The interpretation of Ghirardi, Rimini, and Weber postulates that there is a spontaneous collapse of the wave function of the measurement instrument into a particle which collapses by a domino effect the whole measurement instrument and, thence, the quantum systems. This happens because the measurement instrument is a macroscopic classic object big enough to have one of its particles collapse randomly and start the whole chain reaction, collapsing both the measurement instrument and the quantum system into a well-defined Eigenstate. The stochastic collapse is effected by the Gaussian (the normal) curve of the measuring instrument, which clones the wave function of the instrument which then collapses both the instrument and the quantum system. The problem here starts with the collapse, which poses relativistic inconsistencies. Also, the tails of the Gaussian curve never reach a zero, and, hence, the collapse cannot lead to a complete Eigenstate of a quantum system. Finally, Ghirardi, Rimini, and Weber do not explain the domino effect by which the first collapsed particle collapsed all the others, both in the measuring instrument and in the quantum system. We try to solve these problems by envisaging a separate hermetic force field for each probability amplitude of each particle in the measurement instrument. The hermetic force field clones the Gaussian curve which takes the shape of the wave function of the instrument. Then the spontaneous collapse of a particle in the pointer occurs, the virtual particles which emanate from one consciousness transmit this information to all other hermetic force fields of the particles in the measuring instrument and quantum system. However, both the measuring instrument and the quantum system remain in superposition since the collapse of both the instrument and the quantum system are virtual and cognitive. In this manner we hopefully provide a more viable interpretation of quantum mechanics by utilizing a complementarity dynamic between consciousness and energy-matter.

This basic duality of physics stems from Bohr's conviction that the basic duality between the observer and observed is the essential dyad of being. Indeed, if a relationship between an observer and a physical system is all there is—the minimum condition of ontology is a dyad between duality. This holds true, not only for physics but also for ethics as shown by the Dialogica philosophers, like Kierkegaard and Buber. In history, Croce and Colingwood assure us that history is generated by a relationship between the historian and his objects of study. Some major trends in religion and mysticism are patently dualistic like the various branches of Gnosticism and the Kabbala. Finally, evolution is effected by a relationship of the creature with his environment.

Differentiation of forces and coagulation of matter came later. Indeed, Einstein's lifelong dream was to find a unified theory of physics. Although not entirely successful, Steven Weinber, Abdus Salam, Sheldon Glashnow, and Stephen Hawking have made giant strides towards a unification of physical theory.[231]

Even if the grand unifying theories (GUTS) in physics have not succeeded up to now in incorporating gravity within their domain, the common, homogenous origin of all energy-matter is enough to contrast it with the historical and non-physical universal ani-consciousness.

The next logical problem lies in trying to explain how, according to our model, energy-matter and consciousness are coupled together so as to form matter-particles, objects, and, eventually, life forms. In order to do this, we propose to return to the double-slit experiment and show how our interpretation differs from the Copenhagen interpretation. There are three actors in the double-slit experiment: the human-observer-experimenter, the classic measuring instrument which records the quantum event, and the observed quantum physical system. Man, the observer, and homo faber, the instrument maker, is, not only the most elaborate and sophisticated seat of the ani conscious but also, the most advanced connecting agent between consciousness and energy, the two basic dualities of creation. This he performs by means of the symbolon, the connecting structure. The original Greek symbolon signified an animal bone broken in the middle, with one half given to each of the two parties to the contract. The bone fibers were broken in a specific non-replicable manner and served as conclusive proof of partnership to the contract. In a similar manner, our symbolon as a connecting structure is also unique, insofar as it synthesizes the initial model of a phenomenon subsequently to be realized by an act of creation.

We would like to point out the specific nature of our symbolon connecting structure. Our symbolon is all this except that its transformations do lead to outside components of the structure because it is a creative structure. Our symbolon triggers the creation of a phenomenon by synthesizing the ani-consciousness and the energy-matter as a means for the subsequent creation. More than anything else, man is a manufacturer of symboloi. Man's atzmi, his interactive self, synthesizes symboloi by connecting his ani-consciousness with well-defined or diffuse parts of his environment. Hence, each symbolon is dynamic, unique, and irreplaceable in another space-time configuration.

As we have mentioned above, algorithms characterize computers as well as the contained consciousness of our measuring instrument. An algorithm is a programmed input which determines the function of a device. In this sense, an algorithm is the internal state of a device because it constitutes the inner specifications according to which a certain device should function.[232]

On the other hand, the indeterministic consciousnesses of creatures are not algorithmic because they are not computable. Penrose rightly says that creatures, especially man, have self-awareness, but that computers measuring instruments programmed by an algorithm to perform defined tasks do not and cannot have self-awareness.[233]

Searle has also shown that any machine, including the most sophisticated computer, does not have the faculty of understanding which man has. Hence, man is not just 'a computer made of meat', as Marvin Minsky quipped. 'The human mind', as Penrose says, 'is more than a collection of tiny wires and switches'.

The communicative proficiency of the contained consciousness within an artifact operates through the symbolon structures ingrained in it by its creator. This communicative ability is necessary to substantiate our claim of an interdependence among the observer, the measuring instrument, and the quantum of the physical system. A contained vectorial consciousness is ingrained, for instance, into a work of art and, through it, is communicated to an observer.

The Quanta Events

The universe started from a singularity with the Big Bang and will end by reverting back to a singularity with the Big Crunch. This Sisyphean cycle is replicated in the birth and death of stars. It is not surprising that this dynamic was hypothesized by the Indian Chandrasekhar, whose tradition postulates Samsara cycles of creation, which are equivalent to our Sisyphean cycles relating only to matter and energy, because participant ani-consciousness is immutable and ahistorical. This notion of shrinking back into a singularity of infinite gravity and zero size was attacked by such giants of Occidental science as Einstein and Eddington, but Chandrasekhar was right. The dynamics of energy-matter are outbursts from singularities and sink back to them da capo ad infinitum. Singularities, however, cannot be observed. Not only are they outside space-time, but they are protected by black holes from which light cannot escape because of extreme gravity. These black holes are bordered by event horizons which form further barriers against the observation of singularities. This inability to detect, observe, and verify the existence of singularities led Penrose to expound the cosmic censorship hypothesis, according to which our programmer did not intend his creatures to be exposed to a singularity; hence, it is unobservable by man.[234] We hold, following Koestler's holonic principle, that there is no reason to suppose that the Sisyphean cycles of energy-matter from singularity to singularity are confined to macro-events only. Singularities might well be the unobservable source of quantic energy and its final telos, from which another Sisyphean cycle will eventually sprout forth, in infinite Samsara incarnations. This sprouting of quanta energy from a potential was hypothesized by Heisenberg quite early on in quantum theory.[235] Out of this potential, quanta energy spouts out in wavers and waves superpose. This is due to the additive nature of the wave amplitudes when interfering with each other.

For de Broglie and Schrödinger, who conceived of particles as packets of waves, the superposition was of real waves, whereas for Born the waves were probabilities. They give the probability function of finding a particle at a given position by acquiring the amplitude of the probability wave at that position. These probability waves also superpose as described by Dirac as follows:

> When a state is formed by the superposition of two other states, it will have priorities that are in some vague way intermediate between those of the two original states and that approach more or less closely to those of either of them according to the greater or lesser weight attached to this state in the superposition process. The new state is completely defined by the original states when their relative weights in the superposition process are known, together with a certain phase difference, the exact meaning of weights and phases being provided in the general case by the mathematical theory. In the case of the polarization of a photon their meaning is provided by classical optics, so that, for example, when two perpendicularly plane-polarized states are superposed with equal weight the new state may be circularly polarized in either direction, or linearly polarized at an angle 1/4π, or else elliptically polarized, according to the phase difference.[236]

The non-classical nature of the superposition process is brought out clearly if we consider the superposition of two states, A and B, such that there exists an observation which, when made on the system in state A, is certain to lead to one particular result, say *a*, and when made on the system in state B, is certain to lead to some different result, say *b*. What will be the result of the observation when made on the system in the superposed state? The answer is that the result will be sometimes *a* and sometimes *b*, according to a probability law dependent on the relative weights of A and B in the superposition process. It will never be different from A or B. The intermediate character of the state formed by superposition thus expresses itself through the probability of a particular result for an observation being intermediate between the corresponding probabilities for the original states; the result itself is not intermediate between the corresponding results for the original states.[237]

Born's probability waves and Dirac's formulation of their superposition are both a staple of the Copenhagen interpretation. But how can probability waves imprint an interference pattern on the photographic plate in the double slit experiment?! Only *real* waves can do this. The Copenhagen interpretation gives a viable mathematical exposition of the superposition of the probability amplitudes of finding particles in given positions, but it refrains from stating anything about the reality represented by this mathematical formalism. Penrose introduces some sophisticated mathematical formalism to denote the spreading out of a particle over large regions of space,[238] to describe the evolution of the wave function over time. He claims that the wave function's reality is represented by its amplitude, while, at the act of measurement, this amplitude turns into a classical probability, which, incidentally, is one of Bohr's claims in his exposition of the Copenhagen interpretation. It is hard to see why Dirac's denotation of energy waves superposed as vector states in quantum linear superposition is probabilistic, whereas Penrose's amplitudes of a particle smeared out over a large region of space are real. To us, they seem as probabilistic as an amplitude of a spread momentum. Until an act of measurement has dragged out the superposed energy into quantum reality, we are dealing with probabilities, whatever the elegance of their mathematical formalism.

The decision to detect a particle collapses the probability waves. This is not specific to quantum mechanics, but stems from probability theory, according to which a certain result, such as the measurement of a particle which renders its probability one, reduces all their other probabilities to zero. The collapse of the probability function relates only to the Copenhagen interpretation. If we adopt the realistic de Broglie-Schrödinger interpretation, together with our conception of a vectorial consciousness contained within the measuring instrument, the measurement act drags out the energy necessary to form a particle from the superposition of waves. This is not unlike the measuring or dragging out of one color from white, which is the superposition of all colors. The problem of the Copenhagen interpretation is where to cut the measurement chain, or, more specifically, is where the superposition of probability waves collapses: whether before the measurement instrument, after it, or in the observer's brain, does not arise in our interpretation. We hold that the ani-consciousness, being ahistorical and attributeless, cannot be and is not in a superposition with waves. Hence, the superposition stops at the measuring instrument, which has a contained consciousness and certainly cannot engulf the human observer. Hence, the so-called Wignes's friend paradox cannot be applicable to us. The paradox is as follows:

> [the observer] was in a state of suspended animation before he answered [the] question. It follows that the being with a consciousness must have a different role in quantum mechanics than the inanimate measuring device. In particular, the quantum mechanical equation cannot be linear if the preceding argument is accepted. This argument implies that 'my friend' has the same types of impressions and sensations and, in particular, that, after interacting with the object, he is not in that state of suspended animation which corresponds to the wave function. It is not necessary to see a contradiction here from the point of view of orthodox quantum mechanics, and there is none, if we believe that the alternative whereby my friend's consciousness contains either the impression of having seen [a live cat] or of having seen a [dead cat] is meaningless. However, to deny the existence of the consciousness of my friend to this extent is surely an unnatural attitude approaching solipsism, and few people, in their hearts, will go along with it.[239]

We also postulate a limit, a Greek *horos* or barrier, between the classic and quantum worlds. This barrier, represented by Heisenberg's uncertainty relations, does not allow more than a single glimpse of related phenomena behind the barrier. Hence, the superposition of quantum waves themselves cannot be measured. We can record either their interference pattern or the particle created from them by the interaction of the symbolon structure embedded in the measuring instrument and the super-imposed quanta energy. It should be stressed that the interference pattern is recorded when there was no intention to record a particle. Thus, the interference pattern is the more basic state of the superposition of waves. Only when the vectorial symbolon needed to create a particle comes into contact with the superimposed waves is the particle created and recorded. The superposition of waves might not necessarily have disappeared from the observed quantum physical system; it just cannot be observed because of the uncertainty barrier. Hence, the singularity is a potential for energy waves, and the superposition of waves is a potential for particles. Thus, the hierarchy of the quantic phenomena vis-à-vis the uncertainty barrier might be presented as shown in figure 3.20:

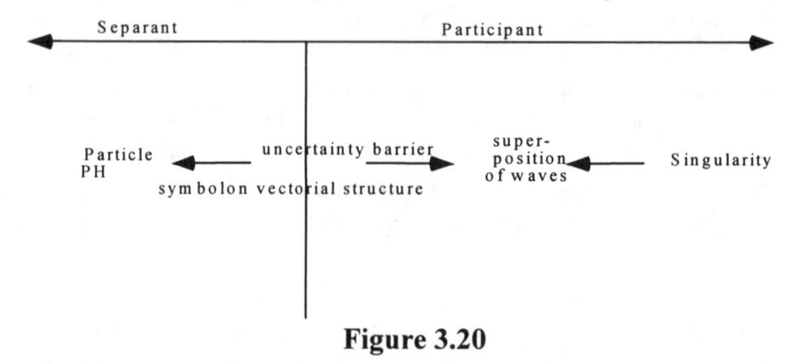

Figure 3.20

The singularity, unobservable within the quantum world, is the potential of superposed waves. These are behind the uncertainty barrier superposition, which manifests itself by a separant, measurable, and measured physical Eigenstate. This is why Dirac's denotation of quantum linear superposition, which stands for a complex vector space, combines real and imaginary non-observable number entities. Indeed, complex numbers are particularly suitable for our purposes because our dualistic model combines the non-measurable participant ani-consciousness with largely measurable separant energy-matter. These two divergent entities are integrated both in the connecting symbolon structure and the ultimate Promethean holon, be it a life form or an artifact. To represent the symbolon structure, the Promethean holon and the processes leading to them, one must use complex numbers, as presented by an Argand plane as shown in figure 3.21:

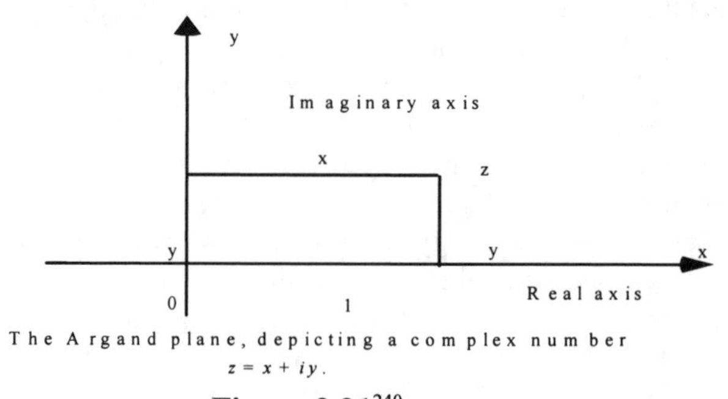

The Argand plane, depicting a complex number $z = x + iy$.

Figure 3.21[240]

Thus, a particle passing through both slits at once cannot be represented, except by complex numbers combining both real and imaginary ones. In a similar vein, the converging encounter between the evolving determinist-time linear Schrödinger equation of superposed waves and the indeterministic measurement act resulting in a particle eigenstate can be represented only by complex numbers combining real, separant processes and imaginary, non-measurable participant dynamics.

An Act of Creation

The Copenhagen interpretation does not really relate to the underlying dynamics of the wave-particle duality of energy-matter. 'The paradoxes of the dualism between the wave picture and particle were not solved', said Werner Heisenberg. 'They were hidden somehow in the mathematical scheme'.[241] However, we do wish to relate to the processes by which particles are created from the superposed waves behind the uncertainty barrier of quantum events. The Copenhagenists' contention that the act of observation not only infuses energy onto the observed quantum event, thus, biasing its momentum and position measurements, but possibly also in itself, creating a particle, is only partially true. The detector which counts particles in the double-slit experiment does not infuse any energy into the observed quantum event; yet we claim that the contained vectorial consciousness inherent in the symbolon structure embedded in the particle detector, which is intended to count particles, does actually create them. This it does by a dialectical encounter with the superposed energy waves behind the uncertainty barrier in the quantum world. We have already hinted that the uncertainty barrier is not partial to waves or particles. If one passes the barrier, the other cannot, and vice-versa. However, an undisturbed state of motion, which, in quantum mechanics (QM) terminology, stands for the undetected superposed flow of waves within, for example, the double-slit experiment, will emit an interference pattern of superposed waves, which will accordingly be recorded, on the photographic plate. This will change the moment the symbolon structure in the counting detectors interacts with the superposed waves in the undisturbed state of motion to create particles. Once the contained consciousness of the particle detector is removed, the undisturbed state of motion is again enabled by the uncertainty relations to record an interference pattern. Not that the superposed waves disappear from the quantum world. They are just not allowed to pass the uncertainty barrier once the particle detector is operating. The particle and wave are quantically complementary; hence, only one can pass the uncertainty barrier, but this complementarity has a much deeper significance for us than for the Copenhagen interpretation, as we shall presently see. One can regard the superposed waves in the quantum world as raw material or raw energy for the creation of a particle, such as a Promethean holon (PH).

We have seen that the particle, as a PH, results from the interaction of the raw energy with the consciousness of the symbolon structure contained within the particle detector. Hence, as we have already pointed out, the measuring instrument is the one to collapse the wave probability function. However, in our model, it does more than that. With its contained vectorial consciousness, it forms the symbolon structure with which it reaches out to the superposed waves of energy in the physical system and creates a particle by a vectorial act of observation. Man the observer cannot do this anymore. Once he has relegated the act of observation to the instrument and imparted to it his contained consciousness, he is functus officio and cannot intervene any more, as a deus ex machina in the act of particle observation and particle creation by measurement. Man can fly to the moon only through the mediation of a space probe, and he can reach the quantum world only through the particle counter. The ani-consciousness is not within space-time and cannot be found in a wave superposition. Hence, it can interact with energy matter only through the mediation of the Tantalus Ratio as ingrained in the symbolon structure.

The famous, or rather notorious, Schrödinger cat paradox stated in the words of the master himself runs as follows:

> A cat is penned up in a steel chamber, along with the following diabolical device (which must be secured against direct interference by the cat): in a Geiger counter there is a tiny bit of radioactive substance, so small that perhaps in the course of one hour one of the atoms decays, but also, with equal probability, perhaps none; if it happens, the counter tube discharges and through a relay releases a hammer which shatters a small flask of hydrocyanic acid. If one has left this entire system to itself for an hour, one would say that the cat still lives *if* meanwhile no atom has decayed. The first atomic decay would have poisoned it. The function of the entire system would express this by having in it the living and the dead cat (pardon the expression) mixed or smeared out in equal parts.[242]

For us, this paradox resolves itself by imparting a contained vectorial consciousness to the measuring instrument—in this case, the Geiger counter—which collapses the probability function of $\varphi = 1/\sqrt{2}$ (φ dead + φ alive) into the certainty of a dead or live cat.

The act of creating a particle is executed by the symbolon structure of the measuring instrument dragging out energy from behind the quantum barrier to interact with the contained consciousness within it. But what is the nature of this barrier which divides the classic and quantum worlds? We might as well begin by considering the speed of light, which is a constant (299 792.5 kilometers per second) and forms the basis of the special theory of relativity engulfing spatio-temporality. Objects approaching the speed of light would become shorter for an outside observer until they disappear riding on a ray of light. Time slows down for the observer watching objects approaching the speed of light until it stops when riding a light beam.

Thus, the speed of light as a barrier of history would seem to imply that in order to exist in spatio-temporality as a four-dimensional object, one must stay within the limits of the speed of light. The barrier dividing the classic four-dimensional world contained by the speed of light which cannot be exceeded and the QM world is Planck's constant, which lies at the basis of Heisenberg's uncertainty principle. This constant relates energy to frequency, so that ħ is a constant of action, which specifies that allowed frequencies of light packet or quanta, emitted in Planck's case by a heated blackbody radiation in which a very small number is negligible in macro-classical physics, while in micro-physical events it specifies the frequencies allowed to pass through the uncertainty barrier. Indeed, Heisenberg's uncertainty principle is expressed in terms of Planck's constant as $(\Delta E)\cdot(\Delta T)= \hbar$, where E is energy and T is time. Hence, if we measure E accurately, we cannot measure time and vice-versa. However, as ħ is a constant of action, it is expressed in terms of energy and time. Yet it seems to engulf the micro-world of quantum events, jealously guarding its secrets like the cherubim with their flaming swords guard the entrance to heaven. The constant of action lets out only one item of information at a time and suppresses the information on its complementary item. Thus, our ability to know and observe quanta events is precarious and uncertain. The ability to predict events in the macro-world deterministically does not apply to the quantum world. We cannot predict the future state of a quantum event from its present state. Schrödinger and Born provided us with a probability wave, the intensity of which at a given region gives us the probability spread, smear, or smudge of the occurrence of a quantum event. Quantum phenomena are sometimes waves and sometimes particles, and we have no way of knowing how the energy waves are superposed behind the uncertainty barrier. The spin, the angular momentum of particles, is also a sui generis phenomenon peculiar to the quantum world. The particles do not really revolve around their axis. The particles which constitute matter are those which have a spin of 1/2, i.e., they must revolve twice in order to have the same face to us. Force particles are those with spin 0, which look the same in all directions, those with spin 1, which must revolve 360° to present the same face, and those with spin 2, which must turn 180° to present to us the same face.

Finally, virtual particles, like force-carrying particles, e.g., gravity, mediated by virtual gravitons, electro-magnetic force, mediated by the virtual photons, the weak force, mediated by virtual vector bosons, and the strong force, carried by virtual gluons, cannot be detected by particle detectors because they cheat the uncertainty barrier and perform their task in a time too short to be detected. Thus the micro-world is less real, less tangible, and less deterministic than the macro-world. The quantum world is aptly enclosed within an uncertainty barrier. It is the no-man's land, the twilight zone, between the being of the macro-world and the nothingness as wholeness, of the potential of ain, of the singularity. The latter cannot be observed. It is bounded by an event horizon which protects the phenomenality of the singularity. The quantum world is only partially latent. If we carry our holonic metaphor to the extreme, we might say that the quantum world is the meta-symbolon structure connecting the potential of the ani-singularity to the macro-world of classical physics.

A Quantum Houdini

The quantum barrier, as we have seen, is only partially, or rather selectively, closed. Particles can perform an Houdini act and jump over a barrier, or rather disappear and materialize on the other side of the barrier. This phenomenon is termed tunneling and is at the basis of both the electronic microscope and the decay of a nucleus due to the tunneling out of it of an alpha particle. Tunneling is based on the ability to perform a confidence trick on the uncertainty barrier. Time and energy are related to Planck's constant as follows: $h/2\pi \leq \Delta E \cdot \Delta T$, where E is energy and T is time. Hence $\Delta T \geq h/2\pi \bullet \Delta E$. Thus, a particle can borrow energy to get over a quantum barrier so long as it repays it within the time of $h/2\pi \bullet \Delta E$. This is short indeed, but sufficient, if the materialization on the other side of the barrier is quick enough. However, the most widespread border cheating in the quantum world, and the one which we intuitively perceive as most relevant to our present context, is that one which we intuitively perceive as most relevant to our present context, is that done by the virtual particles we mentioned earlier. These virtual particles are force-carrying bosons with angular momentum of 0, 1, 2. The Fermion particles with spin 1/2 are subject to Pauli's exclusion principle, according to which no two-matter particles can occupy the same physical state. Force-carrying bosons, on the other hand, can be crammed together. More important, a light, massless, virtual photon carrying the electromagnetic force can cheat the uncertainty relationship for a longer distance and for more time. This, in contrast to a heavy virtual particle like the gluon mediating the strong nuclear force, which can cheat the uncertainty principle for only a short distance and a very short time. Virtual particles, as specialized border-smugglers, are, thus, admirably suited to carry our symbolon structures, and we shall describe presently our hypothesis as to how they do so. The virtual graviton photons, vector bosons, and gluons mediate all the forces of nature by being emitted and absorbed by matter particles. This transmission for the electro-magnetic force is shown in figure 3.22:

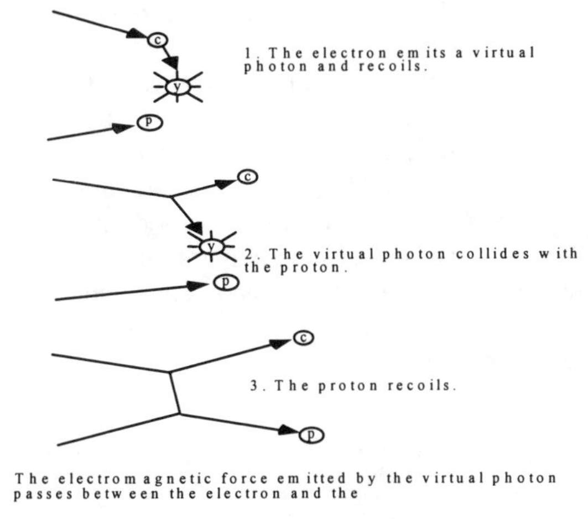

Figure 3.22

Their ephemerality, as far as the macro-world is concerned, makes virtual particles more amenable to interact with the contained *symbolon* consciousness within the measuring instrument. Our hypothesis is that the separant non-detectable and, hence, virtual energy component within the TR of the symbolon structure embedded in the measuring instrument is the communication agent for reaching a virtual particle in the observed physical system. Both particles interact and, thereby, transmit information or particle formation instructions. The crucial point, however, is that this information is in itself already a synthesis between the energy inherent in the atzmi, the interactive self or the Buberian I-it, and the ani-consciousness within the symbolon structure of the measuring instrument. This symbolon structure, which integrates the seeds of both epistemology and ontology, transmits these integrated messages and triggering instructions over to the observed physical system. There are two important dynamics at work here, which lie at the heart of our existentialist interpretation of QM:

(A.) A dyadic dialogical integrative interaction takes place within the symbolon structure contained within the measuring instrument between a separant component of virtual energy-matter and the ani-consciousness.

(B.) The ani-consciousness, which, because it is ahistorical, permits instantaneous communication.

Our first postulate is based both on our exposition of the TR and on the nature of virtual particles. We have pointed out that within its synaptic junctions, the TR integrates the participant longing of the Tantalic vector to regain the totality of the ani-consciousness and the separant quest of the Sisyphean vector to revert to the omnipotence of the ani energy potential (singularity). Neither the Tantalic nor the Sisyphean vectors can fulfill their teleological aims, and, hence, they constitute the prime mover. The nature of both Tantalic and Sisyphean vectors as continua are of crucial importance. To express this in Buberian terms, both the I-thou and I-it contain components of both consciousness and energy-matter. In our terms, the Tantalic vector has mostly participant ani-oriented components, but also has some interactive components epistemologically oriented towards objects and energy-matter. The TR may, thus, be presented graphically as shown in figure 3.23:

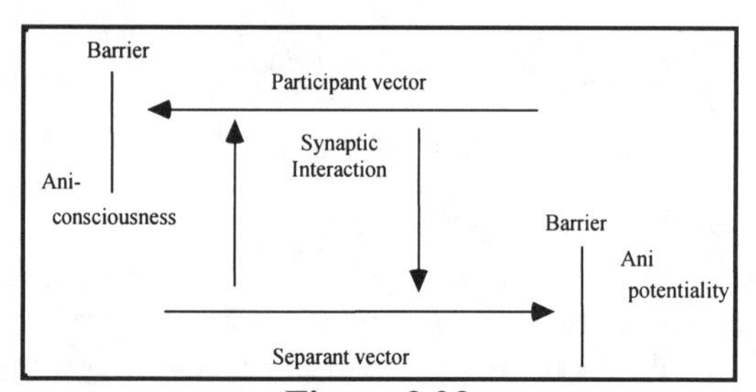

Figure 3.23

The barriers signify the inability of the vectors to regain their teleological aims, which lends continuity to their actions. When this TR is structured within the symbolon, it constitutes the connecting medium between the ani-consciousness and energy-matter. The full dynamics of our model may be seen in figure 3.24:

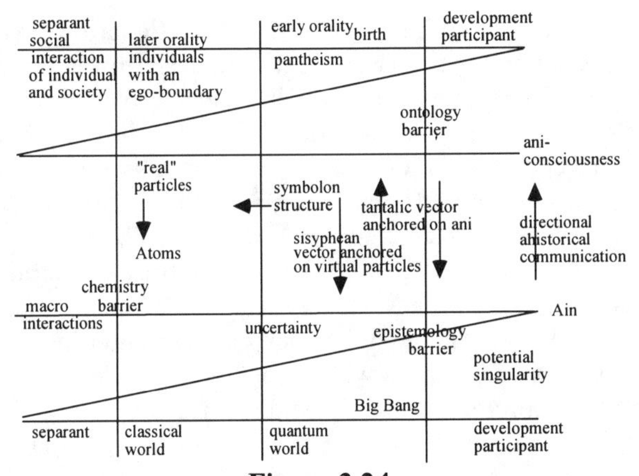

Figure 3.24

The upper part of our model represents the development of individuals, stemming from the ani singularity. For the sake of convenience, we shall begin the analysis of our model from the second column. The symbolon structure is situated within a quantum world swarming with superposed waves and virtual particles. The ephemerality of this world is parallel to the early orality-anchored ephemerality on the Tantalic vectors of the human personality. The Tantalic vectors operating on the early oral subconscious layers of the ani-consciousness become structured within the TR and the symbolon, where they interact and become integrated with the virtual particles, which are potentialities as far as the classical world is concerned. The latter are kept within the quantum world by the barrier of the uncertainty principle. However, as we have seen, these virtual particles are professional go-betweens, mediators, and messengers. To mediate between forces, they can cheat the uncertainty barrier and interact with the ani-consciousness within the symbolon structure. They are, therefore, the most suitable communicative agents, together with the ani-contained consciousness, for triggering the potentialities of superposed waves and other virtual particles into a Promethean holon, a real, measurable, and recorded particle which may then become the building block of the real classical world. Of crucial importance is column 1 in our model, which presents the potentialities of both the ani and the ain singularities, on which our core Tantalic and Sisyphean vectors are anchored.

Behind the ontological and epistemic barrier, the pure ani-consciousness and the ain potentialities may exchange information directly and instantaneously because they are outside space, time, and locality (physics terminology for causality). Hence, the Tantalic vector, anchoring on the *ani*, and the Sisyphean vector, stemming from the ain, can interact through their ahistorical sources, instantaneously and non-locally, provided they are still in their seed form within the pantheistic and ephemeral symbolon structure. This is because the possibility of communication between the ani-consciousness and energy-matter decrease with each column. In ahistorical column 1, communication is direct, instantaneous, and non-local. In column 2, it can only be effected within the TR as structured within the symbolon. In the real world of column 3, we have individuals, both human (and other life forms imbued with freedom of choice) and energy-matter individuals such as real particles imbued with contained consciousness. The communication in column 3 can only be dialogical.

For humans this is possible, but Buber tells us that dialogical communication borders on the miraculous. In particles, dialogical interaction takes place as resonances which Riordan describes poetically. 'These nucleon resonances have proved to be excited, short-lived states that are momentary flirtations of a pion which can be caught in the momentary embrace of a nucleon; the two orbit each other briefly before separating once again. Think of two dancers coming together in a square dance, embracing warmly, and swinging fondly, before parting again and going their way'.[243]

Another dialogical interaction between particles takes place when they interact initially and then fly apart. Relevant examples include the EPR thought experiment, in which pairs of photons are correlated within their positron atom source and are then fired in opposite directions. Also, in Bell's inequality experiment, as well as in the double-slit experiment, particles are fired from the same source and interact before flying out. In these cases—and here is the punchline—the initial interaction makes for a mutual ani and ain, so that they have a common symbolon structure. Thus, the questions are: How does the flying particle in the double-slit experiment know that the other slit is open or closed, and how does one particle in the EPR of Bell experiment know about the spin or polarization of its twin particle. These are readily answered. The communication between initially correlated particles, which have a common symbolon structure, is carried out through the underlying ani and ain sources of the separant and participant vectors in the TR of the symbolon structure. The communication is, thus, instantaneous and non-local. This instantaneous communication can be much more widespread than one might initially expect because a great many acts of creation in nature start, as we have already mentioned, from a correlated interaction.

Roger Penrose argues that this non-local communication between particles, both in the EPR thought experiment and in the Bell and Aspect type of experiment, makes the correlated particles dependent and non-separated entities.[244] He does not, however, offer an explanation as to how this faster-than-light communication takes place from the superposed wave amplitudes (Penrose U) to the collapse of the wave function into an Eigenstate of position, momentum polarization, or spin (Penrose R), depending on the type of experiment. Indeed, such an explanation is impossible unless one assumes, as we do, a non-spatial, non-temporal, and acausal—i.e., non-local—synchronic, holistic entity like the ani-consciousness, which serves as the immediate link between physical states of energy-matter.

The time differences also do not constitute a problem since the time arrow with its relativistic effects starts to move only in columns 3 and 4 of our model. In column 2, behind the uncertainty barrier, time is either partially fuzzy or nonexistent, whereas column 1 is ahistorical. Column 4 is the demiurgical I-it relationship of the individual and the group, in which an authentic I-thou dialogue is impossible and discourse is either on a routine or power-based level. The diagonal lines dividing the upper and lower parts of our model signify the continuum nature of the separant-participant structure of both consciousness organisms and energy-matter structures.

The Creative Intercourse

The virtual particles within the symbolon do find an epistemic outlet from the classic world by cheating the uncertainty barrier for a short period of time, which is inversely related to their energy. They also have an epistemic way of communicating with other particles by absorption and emission. A virtual particle may combine with another virtual photon in the cloud surrounding an electron to create a pair of real particles. A photon may jump over the uncertainty barrier and borrow energy on the other side, creating an electron-positron pair—all this for a very short while within the limits allowed by the uncertainty relations—and then combine back into a photon. A virtual photon may be exchanged by one of the quarks in the proton or electron. This is the basic exchange between a virtual force-carrying boson, undetectable in the real world, and a quark, the most basic Fermion energy-matter particle, also undetectable in the real world. These virtual processes, although brilliantly described by Richard Feynman diagrams replete with conceptual (but not realistic) jumps back and forth in time (although undetectable in the real world), are represented in column 3 of our model. Yet, precisely because of the virtuality and ephemerality of these processes, they are admirably suited to be the communicative agent within the symbolon structure. We must stress again that our model does not ascribe any magical occult faculties to energy-matter à la Fritjoff Capra. We do accept that energy-matter particles, although virtual, must fully obey the ananké, the coercion of the rules of nature, as formulated by theoretical and experimental quantum physics. Our present endeavors just exploit to the hilt the Copenhagenists' idea of co-opting consciousness with energy-matter, as the co-creators of physical reality. The Copenhagenists did not wish to think out the psychological, phenomenological, and existentialist implications of this co-option, nor could they have, whereas we at least try to do so. The gist of our argument is that the virtual processes, as structured within the symbolon, are transmitted together with the participant ani-consciousness, which interacts with the virtual energy within the connecting structure. The ani-consciousness, which is outside history, is given a free ride in and out of spatio-temporality by the virtual-particles, and, thus, together they create matter and artifacts.

The ani-consciousness appears to give the order to create a particle, but it is the virtual particle within the Tantalus Ratio of the symbolon structure which actually passes over the message to other particles (virtual, real, or anti) and to waves in quantic superposition and triggers the act of creation. The symbolon structure is both the blueprint (seed), the messenger, and catalyst of the act of creation, while the end product is a synthesis of energy and consciousness, as a PH which is the basic building unit of the whole of creation. Hence, we do not need the superrealist image of solitons as particles structured out of crests of localized, yet mobile, solitary waves,[245] in order to solve the double-slit paradox. Our particle is a novel synthetic creation, a PH intended and ordained by consciousness and executed by energy as a common endeavor through the mediation of the symbolon structure.

If we compare our interpretation with other endeavors to solve the quantum world paradoxes, we might find support for them in Bell's hidden variable hypothesis as vicariously formulated by Heinz Pagels:

> We have described the experiment and Bell's inequality in some detail because it is rather elementary and illustrates the crux of quantum weirdness. Bell was motivated to find a way of testing if there are hidden variables that exist out there in the world of rocks, tables, and chairs. He showed that the violation of the inequality by quantum theory did not necessarily rule out an objective world described by hidden variables, but the reality then represented had to be non-local. Behind quantum reality, there could be another reality described by these hidden variables, and in this reality there would be influences that move

> instantaneously an arbitrary distance without evident mediation. It is possible to believe that the quantum world is objective—as Einstein wanted—but then you are forced into accepting non-local influences—something Einstein, and most physicists, would never accept.[246]

We relate to Bell's hidden variable hypothesis for illustrative purposes only, since a more elaborate hidden variable hypothesis has been developed by David Bohm.[247]

Our ani-consciousness is, indeed, the kind of hidden variable needed to account for the non-locality of Bell's inequality infringement. This is rather significant because of Bell's centrality in recent developments in quantum mechanics, theoretical and experimental.

We have mentioned Everett's[248] and De Witt's[249] *many worlds* hypothesis, according to which all the probabilities in Schrödinger's wave function, the particle and wave alternatives, and the spin up and spin down alternations of the EPR thought experiment materialize, but in different worlds. These many worlds are not linked, as in the 'monads have no windows' of Leibnitz. We do not accept this absolute separation, since the quantum world as represented by column 2 of our model and the ahistorical potentialities of column 1 are interlinked and interconnected. Only the real, classic, and macro-pluralities are disconnected, but, even in them, a miraculous Buberian dialogue may occur and a flow of grace sometimes radiate to a crowd from an authentic performer like Jacques Brel. Particles, objects, and life forms as presented in columns 3 and 4 of our model are indeed secluded by the boundaries around them, but windows may be found perchance through which virtual energy, dialogue, and grace may interchange. This dialogue might lend meaning to the ani-consciousness as well as to the energy-matter, objects, and life forms interacting with it.

Our interim conclusion is that authentic revelation and creativity might link us to other people, objects, and energy-matter as well as to transcendence and may perchance extricate us from the meaninglessness of an absurd existence.

The Overture

Summing up our rather long deliberations is not easy, but necessary. We call our stock-taking an overture since all summations serve as a stepping stone to further enigmas to explore.

We initiated our exploratory study of myths by utilizing the ingenious insight of Claude Levi-Strauss that myths are structures connecting nature to culture. We claimed for our mythogenes much more, since mythology sanctifies history, by introducing God into it. Also mythogenes link subject and object, individuals to their membership groups, and consciousness to energy-matter. A mythogene, as a generating structure, follows first of all Bergson's notion of élan vitale, life as a self-generating dynamic. Piaget was so impressed with Bergson's insight that he conceptualized a self-generating, self-sustaining dynamic which suits our notion of a mythogene: a generating myth. A mythogene is ahistorical. Indeed, there is no historical record of Moses, an Egyptian prince, who led a massive slave revolt in Egypt. Yet this myth was structured into a religion and still fuels the Judaic ethos to this day. A mythogene is also a symbolon, a connecting structure in the Greek sense. The Torah, for instance, was God's tool, according the Midrash, for the creation of the world. As the act of creation is continuous, so the Torah as a creative mythogene is also timeless. We propose to summarize our deliberation on mythogenes by surveying its ontological, existential, and relational aspects, relying mostly on Judaic mythogenes. We might as well start our ontological survey by examining the nature of the Mosaic deity, denoted as '*Eheyeh Asher Eheyeh*' or 'I am that I am'. This is, indeed, an abstract, non-spatial mythogene, in contrast with the concrete Egyptian deities against which Moses presumably rebelled. It is also diametrically opposite to the Greek conception of tangible deities. The Judaic conception of an abstract deity influences Judaism's whole ethos. World in Hebrew, *olam,* is related to *Healem,* non-being, whereas the corresponding Greek concepts are kosmos, ordered universe, related to cosmeticos, or contextual aesthetics. This might account for the largely non-aesthetic Judaic ethos and its negation of concreteness and proscription of graven images. Still, in Judaism god is spaceless: he is nowhere and everywhere. Hence, the spaceless Mosaic God is a mythogenic nothingness who is a potential for everything. Existentially Eheyeh Asher Eheyeh is synchronic, timeless, in contradistinction with Cronos or, as some denote the son of Uranus, time who eats his children, implying a temporal diachronic passage which passes from the future to the past and, thus, negates itself. By being synchronic, it negates the temporal cycles and pagan fertility rites. The Greek Tesmophoria and the Demetrian and Dionisian procreation rituals depict the impregnation, growth, death, and resurrection by actually emulating the cycles of nature. In the process, the mystriarchs and bacchants, participants in the fertility rites, commit incest, idolatry, kill the sacred king, and eat his flesh. Hence, incest, idolatry, and murder have become, by exclusion, the capital sins of Judaism. It is characteristic that the ultimate salvation in Judaism is related to a synchronic extasis from the diachronic sequences of time: 'And it shall come to pass in that day', says Zechariah, 'known to the

Lord which is not day not night'.[250] In that synchronic extasis, man and all creation shall be liberated from the diachronic fetters of time.

The authentic relational dialogue is between the Logos, the word of God, and the maieutic acceptance of God's word in man's inner-self. This dialogue is essential in Judaism. The Mosaic God speaks whereas the pagan god acts. Hence, the gross transgression of Moses at the waters of Meriba: instead of talking to the rock, he struck it in a pagan manner. That transgression of Moses was heinous enough to punish him by not permitting him to enter the Promised Land. The mythogenic primacy of the word in Judaism is related to the importance of the audible sense, in contrast with the visual, which is of paramount importance in Egyptian and Greek mythology. The synchronic essence of God is imbued in the burning bush mythogene in Judaism which links the divine fire of transcendence with the temporality of the bush. Not so in Greek mythology, where Prometheus must bring the fire down from the mountain of Olympus to another dimension of space and time where mortals dwell. Since man prays to God in words which are pregnant with grace, the accosting of God in authentic prayer creates the presence of the wholly other, the universal thou. Hence, an authentic dialogue between man and transcendence actually generates divinity; therefore, as the Ba'al Shem Tov put it, God is the shadow of man.

NOTES

1 Job 28:12.

2 Dov Baer of Mezhirech: Maggid Devarav Leya'akov (Jerusalem, 1962), 15.

3 Ibid., 16.

4 R. O. Faulkner, *The Ancient Egyptitan Book of the Dead,* trans. Carol Andrews (London: The Trustees of the British War Museum, 1989), 144.

5 Spell 17, in Ibid., 49.

6 Spell 144, in Ibid., 133.

7 Spell 114–15, in Ibid., 112–13.

8 Ibid.

9 N.K. Sandars, ed.,*The Epic of Gilgamesh*, (Harmondsworth, Middlesex: Penguin Books, 1964), 95.

[10] Steven W. Hawking, *A Brief History of Time* (Toronto: Bantam Books, 1988), 49.

[11] Haim Vital, *Etz Haim* (Jerusalem: Research Centre of Kabbalah, 1978), 19.

[12] Gershom Gerhard Scholem, *Shabbatai Zvi:* vol. 1 (Tel Aviv: Am Oved Publishers, 1967), 24 (Hebrew).

[13] Gershom Gerhard. Scholem, *Major Trends in Jewish Mysticism*, 263.

[14] Isiah Tishby, *The Doctrine of Evil and the Kelippah in Luranic Kabbalism* (Jerusalem: Schocken Publishing, 1942), 37.

[15] Shoham, *Salvation Through the Gutters* (Washington, D.C.: Hemisphere Publishing, 1979), Chapter 1.

[16] F. Laboyer, *Birth without Violence* (London: Wildwood House, 1975).

[17] Steven Weinberg, *The First Three Minutes: A Modern View of the Origin of the Universe* (New York: Basic Books, 1977), 5.

[18] Haim Vital, *Sha'ar Hahakdamot* (Jerusalem: Research Centre of Kabbalah, 1984).

[19] Vital, *Etz Haim*, 27.

[20] S.A. Horodezki, *Lurianic Kabbalah* (Tel Aviv: The Hebrew Writers' Association, 1947), 35–41.

[21] Vital, *Etz Haim.*

[22] Ibn Tabul, *Drosh Heftziba,* 3.

[23] Ibid., *Drosh,* 8.

[24] Arthur Koestler, *Janus* (London: Hutchinson, 1978), 33.

[25] Vital, *Etz Haim*, 50.

[26] Roger Penrose, *The Emperor's New Mind* (New York: Penguin, 1991), 367–68.

[27] Ibid., 207.

[28] Ibid., 207.

[29] Ibid., 207.

[30] Shoham, *The Myth of Tantalus,* Chapter 2, and *Valhallah, Calvary, and Auschwitz*, Introduction.

[31] Weinberg, *The First Three Minutes*, 5.

[32] H. R. Pagels, *The Cosmic Code* (New York: Bantam Books, 1983), 233–34.

[33] Shoham, *Valhallah, Calvary, and Auschwitz* (Cincinnati: Bowman & Cody Academic Publishing, 1995), Chapter 1, 2.

[34] Shoham, *Sex as Bait* (St. Lucia: University of Queensland Press, 1983), 4.

[35] Hawking, *A Brief History of Time*, 87.

[36] Penrose, *The Emperor's New Mind*, 328.

[37] Ibid., 332.

[38] Ibid., 341.

39 S.G. Shoham, *Valhalla, Calvary, and Auschwitz*, (Cincinati: BCAP Inc. and Ramot: Tel-Aviv University, 1955)

40 Heinz Pagel's book dealing with the basic processes of cosmosgony is entitled *Perfect Symmetry: The Search for the Beginning of Time* (New York: Bantam Books, 1986).

41 John Gribbin, *In Search of the Big Bang* (Toronto: Bantam Books, 1986), 337.

42 Tony Hey and Patrick Walters, *The Quantum Universe*, (Cambridge: The Cambridge University Press, 1987), 125.

43 Vital, *Etz Haim*.

44 Gen. chapters 6, 7, and 8.

45 Larousse, *Encyclopedia of Mythology,* trans. Richard Aidington and Delano Amos (London: Batchworth Press, Ltd., 1959), 258.

46 Ibid., 266.

47 "Eddic Mythology," *Social Theory and Social Structure* (New York: Free Press, 1957), 339.

48 R. K. Merton, *Social Structure and Anomie*,

49 A. B. Eliezer Halevi, *Iggeret Sod haGe'ulah*, Jerusalem, 1519 (Hebrew)

50 Green, *Tormented Master*, 237.

51 Kierkegaard, *Concluding Unscientific Postscript,* trans. David Swenson and Walter Laurie (Princeton: Princeton University Press, 1968), 84.

52 A. M. Greely, *Thy Brother's Wife* (New York: Warner, 1982) cited in *Time* July 8, 1966.

53 *Time* Magazine, July 8, 1966.

54 Moshe Idel, *Kabbalah: New Perspectives* (New Haven: Yale University Press, 1988), 63.

55 Ibid., 65.

56 Jonas, *The Gnostic Religion*, 63.

57 Ibid.

58 R. Binion, *Frau Lou,* (Princeton: Princeton University Press), 75.

59 Symposium, *The Dialogues of Plato*, (New York: Random House, 1937), 318–19 (Symposium 191–93).

60 *The Gospel of Truth* in Foerster, *Gnosis,* 57.

61 *The Hyposthasis of the Archons* in Ibid., 41.

62 *The Book of Thomas* in Ibid., 113.

63 Idel, *New Perspectives,* 83.

64 Tishby, "Doctrine of Evil and the Kelippah," *Lurianic Kabbalism* (Jerusalem: Shocken, 1924).

65 "The Exegesis on the Soul": in Foerster, *Gnosis,* 103–104.

66 Idel, *Kabbalah: New Perspectives*, 83.

67 Ibid., 85.

68 Ibid., 86.

69 J. I. Safrin, *Megillat Setarim*, (1944).

70 Vital, *Etz Haim*.

71 Kierkegaard, *Training in Christianity*, 28–29, 94–99.

72 W.B. Yeats, *Autobiography* (London: MacMillan, 1961), 189.

73 Gershom Scholem, *Shabbatai Zvi,* vol. 1 (Tel Aviv: Am Oved Publishers, 1987), 45.

74 Ibid.

75 V. Van Gogh; from a letter to his brother Theo from Arles, Sept. 1988 in *The Complete Letters of V. Van Gogh* (Greenwich, W.S. Graphic Society, 1959)

76 Moshe Idel, '*Metaphores et Praitques Sexuelles dan la Cabale*' in Charles Mopsik, *Lettre sur la Saintete* (Paris: Verdier, 1986), 330.

77 Idel, *Kabbalah: New Perspectives*, 144–153.

78 Michael Lockwood, *Mind, Brain, and the Quantum* (Oxford: Basil Blackwell, 1989), 224.

79 Ibid., 216.

80 Penrose, 'Quantum Gravity and State Vector Reduction,' in R.Penrose and C.J.Esham, eds., *Quantum Concepts in Space time* (Oxford: Oxford University Press, 1985), 129–46.

81 Penrose, 'Minds, Machines and Mathematics,' in C.Blackmore and S.Greenfield, eds., *Mindwaves* (Oxford: Basil Blackwell, 1987), 274.

82 R.W.Sperry, 'Hemisphere Deconnection and Unity in Conscious Awareness,' *American Psychologist,* (1968), 723–33.

83 Martin Buber, *I and Thou* (Cleveland: Meridian Books, 1956), 269.

84 Gen. 1:3

85 Lockwood, *Mind, Brain and The Quantum*, 163.

86 M. Dummet, *Truth and Other Enigmas* (London: Duckworth, 1978), 1–24.

87 Paul M. Churchland, *Matter and Consciousness (*Cambridge:MA: MIT Press, 1988), 84–85.

88 J. Foster, *The Case for Idealism* (London; Routledge, Kegan Paul, 1982), 1103–107.

89 Kierkegaard

90 Martin Heidegger, *Being and Time* (Oxford: Basil Blackwell,1967), chapter 1.

91 Ibid., 69.

92 G.Marcel, *Metaphysical Journals* (Paris: Gallimard, 1927) p. 329 330.

93 M. Heidegger, *Existence and Being* (Chicago: Regency, 1949), 82.

94 M. Heidegger, *Being and Time* (Oxford: Basil Blackwell, 1967), 369.

95 Ibid., 271.

96 Ibid., 148.

97 Scholem, *Major Trends in Jewish Mysticism* (New York: Schoken Books, 1944), 1st Lecture.

98 "The Gospel of Philip," in Foerster: *Gnosis*, 89.

99 S.G. Shoham, *The Bridge to Nothingness*, 313.

100 I. Saruk, *Sefer Limudi Atzilut* (S. Khan Verlag Munkacs, 1937), 3 (Hebrew).

101 Scholem, *Major Trends in Jewish Mysticism*, 76.

102 *Maggid Devarav Leya'akov* (Jerusalem: Magness Press, 1962), 16 (Hebrew).

103 *Complete Works of Plotinus* (London: George Bell & Sons, 1918), 314.

104 Haim Vital, *Mevo-Shearim, Part 2, Chapter A*; Cited in Tishby: *The Doctrine of Evil*, 36.

105 Ibn Tabul, *Drosh Hefziba* as cited in Ibid., 24.

106 R. Penrose, *The Emperor's New Mind,* 408–9.

107 Gershom Scholem, *Kabbalah* (Jerusalem: Keter Publishing House, 1988), 141.

108 Tishby, *The Doctrine of Evil*, 94.

109 Jonas, *The Gnostic Religion*, 58.

110 Tishby, *The Doctrine of Evil,* 125.

111 J.W. Von Goethe, *Faust*, (New York: The Modern Library, 1950), 43.

112 M. Lockwood, *Mind, Brain, and the Quantum,* 62.

113 R. Penrose, *The Emperor's New Mind,* 281.

114 Ibid., 297.

115 S.G. Shoham, *Sex as Bait*, 182–185.

116 S.G. Shoham, *The Violence of Silence,*

117 *Complete Works of Plotinus,* 119, 153, 314.

118 "The Gospel of Truth", in Foerster, *Gnosis*, 65.

119 Penrose, *The Emperor's New Mind,* 274–75.

120 *Entropy* is a term related to the Second Law of Thermodynamics. It refers to the disinegration, disorder or degeneration of a closed system. According to the Second Law, the entropy of a system will remain constant or increase with the passage of time.

121 William Graham Sumner, *Folkways: A Study of the Sociological Importance of Usages, Manners, Customs, Mores, and Morals* (New York: Mentor Books, 1960), 28.

122 Edward E. Evans-Pritchard, *Witchcraft Oracles and Magic Among the Azande* (Oxford: Clarendon Press, 1937), chapter 3.

123 Ibid., chapter 3.

124 Svend Ranulf, *Moral Indignation and Middle-Class Psychology* (Copenhagen: Levin and Munksgaard, 1938).

125 James George Frazer, *Folk Lore in the Old Testament: Studies in Comparative Religion, Legend, and Law* (London: Macmillan, 1923).

126 Thucydides, *The Greek Historians*, vol.1 (New York: Random House, 1942).

127 Æschylus, *The House of Atreus,* 83–84.

128 James George Frazer, *Psyche's Task: A Discourse Concerning the Influence of Superstition on the Growth of Institutions* (London: Macmillan Co., Ltd., 1920).

129 Sumner, *Folkways,* 43.

130 Frazer, *Psyche's Task.*

131 Tishby, *Doctrine of Evil,* 94.

132 Ibid.

133 Amos, chap. 6.

134 Proverbs, 16:5.

135 Shoham, *The Myth of Tantalus*, ch. 2.

136 Gen. 21:7–8.

137 Zeller, *A History of Greek Philosophy,* vol 1, 429, as cited in C.G. Jung, *Psychology and Religion,*
West and East, trans. R.F.C. Hull (London: Routledge & Kegan Paul, 1969), 118

138 Ludwig Feuerbach, *The Essence of Christianity,* trans. George Eliot (New York: Harper Torchbooks, 1957), 70.

139 Shoham, *The Myth of Tantalus*, ch. 8.

140 Henry, R. Percival, ed., *The Seven Ecumenical Councils of the Undivided Church,* Vol. XIV of *Nicene and Nicene Fathers*, 2nd series, ed. Philip Schaff and Henry Wace (R. Edinburgh: T&T Clark, 1988)

141 Ibid.

142 Shoham, *The Myth of Tantalus,* 314.

143 Ibid., ch. 8.

144 Appolinarius, as cited in in J. Hastings, *Encyclopedia of Ethics and Religions* (New York: Charles Scribners' and Sons, 1957), 536.

145 In the Gospel according to John we find the following proclamation of obedience to paternal authority: 'What things soever he (the Father) doeth these also doeth the Son likewise'. John 5:19.

146 Matthew 10:7, 12:28, 6:10; Mark 9:1, 13:24; Luke 17:24.

147 Matthew 10:34.

148 Mark 9:2–7.

149 John 10:7, 9.

150 Colossians, 1:15.

151 Colossians, 1:19.

152 Matthew 19:18.

153 John, 17:17–26.

154 *Encycopedia Biblica*, 64.

155 Isaiah 42:1.

156 Job 19:26.

157 St. John 1:14.

158 Jonas, *The Gnostic Religion*, 154.

159 Ibid., 184.

160 Jan Assmann, *State and Religion in the New Kingdom*, in *Religion and Philosophy in Ancient Egypt* (New Haven: Yale University Press), 66–67.

161 Gen. 1:26.

162 Talmud Bavli, Sanhedrin 37:1.

163 Genesis *Raba*, vol. 1., 56–57.

164 Exod. 25:22.

165 Shoham, *The Bridge to Nothingness*.

166 Faulkner, *The Book of the Dead*, 112, 113.

167 Maggid Devarav Leyaakov, chapter 4.

168 Haim Vital, *Sha'ar Hakavanot* (Jerusalem: Ashlag Edition), 137.

169 Midrash on Pslams, chapter 103.

170 Psalms 130:1,2.

171 Giovanni Filoramo, *A History of Gnosticism,* trans. Anthony Alcock (Oxford: Basil Blackwell 1992), 104.

172 Ibid., 165.

173 A. Camus, *The Rebel* (Hammondsworth: Penguin Press, 1962)

174 Buber, *Or Haganuz* (Jerusalem: Schocken Books, 1987), Hebrew.

175 Scholem, *Major Trends in Jewish Mysticism* (New York: Schocken Books, 1941), 356.

176 Shoham, *Sex as Bait: Eve, Casonova, and Don Juan* (St. Lucia: Queensland Press, 1983), 13–17.

177 Kurt Wolff, ed., *The Sociology of Georg Simmel* (London: The Free Press of Glencoe, 1964), 128.

178 Andre Le Chapelain, *Art of Courtly Love*, trans. John Jay Parry (New York: F. Ungar Pub. Co., 1959), 28.

179 Shoham, *The Myth of Tantalus*, chapter 2.

180 Shoham, *The Violence of Silence*, chapters 1–3.

181 H.S. Gvetzkow and P.H. Bowman, *Men and Hunger: A Psychological Manual for Relief Workers* (Elgin, Ill.: Brethren Press, 1956).

182 F. Heider, *The Psychology of Interpersonal Relations* (New York: Wiley, 1968), 198.

183 W. H. Masters and V.E. Johnson, *Human Sexual Response* (Boston: Little Brown & Co. 1966), 286.

184 A.C. Kinsey et al, *Sexual Behavior in the Human Female* (Philadelphia: W.B. Saunders & Co., 1966), 286 et seq.

185 C. Butler, "Insect Pheromones", *Biological Review* 42 (1967), 42–87.

186 R. Briffault, "The Origins of Love", *Biological Review* 42 (1967), 42–87.

187 K. Horney, 'The Dread of Woman", *International Journal of Psychoanalysis* 13 (1932), 348–360.

188 S. Ferenczi, 'Thalassa: A Theory of Genitality", *Psychoanalytic Quarterly vol__* (1938), 18.

189 G.R. Tayler, 'Historical and mythological Aspects of Homosexuality', in *Sexual Inversion*, Judd Marmor ed. (New York: Basic Books, 1963), 146.

190 Some male orgasms may occur without ejaculation.

191 T. Agoston, 'The Fear of Post Orgasmic Emptiness', *Psychoanalytic Review* 33 (1938), 197,214.

192 Erich Fried, *The Ego in Love and Sexuality* (New York: Grune & Stratton, 1960), 3.

193 A.C. Kinsey et al, *Sexual Behavior*, 613–14.

194 T. Benedek, 'Discussion of Sherfey's paper on Femal Sexuality' *Journal of the American Psychoanalytic Association* 16 (1968), 424–48.

195 Kinsey et al, *Sexual Behavior*, 592.

196 Ibid., 626–27.

197 Fisher, *The Female Orgasm* (New York: Basic Books, 1973), 53–4.

198 Ibid., 52.

199 Corinthians I, 11:12.

200 Binion, *Frau Lou*, 75.

201 Plato, "The Symposium" in *The Dialogues of Plato,* trans. B. Jowett (New York: Random House, 1937), 318–19.

202 Albert Camus, 'The Adulterous Woman' in *Exile and the Kingdom* (Harmondsworht: Penguin Books, 1961).

203 J.B. Soloveitchick: *The Man of Faith* (Jerusalem: Massad Harav Kook).

204 Deut. 29:10–12.

205 A.Tucker, 'Sacrifice from Isaac to Patock'; *Telos* (91 Spring 1992), 117–124.

206 Petr Aleksecvich Kniaz Kropotkin, *The Conquest of Bread* (New York: 1926), 103.

207 Shoham and Rahav, *The Mark of Cain*, 299, 302.

208 Cited in *Times Literary Supplement* (May 30, 1980).

209 Shoham, *Sex as Bait.*

210 Shoham and Rahav, *The Mark of Cain* (Santa Lucia: Queensland UP, 1982)

211 Shoham, *The Violence of Silence* (New Brunswick: Transaction Books Rutgers University Press, 1983).

212 G. Vesey, *Perception* (London: Macmillan, 1972), 3.

213 G.S. Klein, *Perception, Motives, and Personality* (New York: Alfred Knoph 1970), 49.

[214] Ibid., 49 et seq. Z.Giora, *Psychopathology* (New York: The Gardener Press, 1975), 53–54.

[215] Vesey, *Perception*, 5.

[216] Ibid., 43–44.

[217] R.D. Laing, *Self and Others* (Harmondsworth: Penguin Books, 1972), 44 et seq.

[218] Ernest Alfred Wallis-Budge, *Osiris,* vol. 1 (New York: Dover Publications 1973), 126.

[219] Henri Frankfort, *Kingship and the Gods: A Study of Ancient Near Eastern Religion as the Integration of Society and Nature* (Chicago: University of Chicago Press, 1978), 37.

[220] Robert Thomas Rundle Clark, *Myth and Symbol in Ancient Egypt* (London: Thames and Hudson, 1959).

[221] Wallis Budge, *Osiris*, vol.1, 89.

[222] Deut. 4:15.

[223] Deut. 6:4.

[224] Exod. 29.

[225] Exod. 33:20.

[226] Jeremiah 7:23.

[227] Psalms 4:1.

[228] Numbers 20:8.

[229] Based on Shoham and Meir Hemmo, "The Hermetic Interpretation of Quantum Mechanics" in *Filosofia Oggi,* Anno XVII (67) F. III July-September, 1994, 315–334 .

[230] Riordan, *The Hunting of the Quark* (New York: Simon and Shuster, 1987), 78.

[231] Glashow, "Towards a Unified Theory: Threads in a Tapestry"(Nobel Prize in Physics Award Address 1979) and Hawking, *A Brief History of Time,* Chapter 10.

[232] Penrose, *The Emperor's New Mind*, 38.

[233] Ibid., 379, 407.

[234] Roger Penrose, "Black Holes in Cosmology Now" in L. Johns, ed. (London: BBC Publications 1974).

[235] Werner Heisenberg, *Physics and Philosophy* (New York: Harper & Row, 1962), 148, 160.

[236] Paul Adrien Maurice Dirac, *The Principle of Superpositon in The Principle of Quantum Mechanics* (Oxford: Oxford University Press, 1956).

[237] Ibid.

[238] Penrose, *The Emperor's New Mind*, 252.

[239] Cited in John D. Barrow and Frank J. Tipler, *The Anthropic Cosmological Principle*, 468.

[240] Penrose, *The Emperor's New Mind*, 90.

[241] Werner Heisenberg, *The Physicist's Conception of Nature.*

[242] M. Riordan, *The Hunting of the Quark* (New York: Simon and Schuster, 1987), 46.

[243] Ibid., 78.

[244] Penrose, *The Emperor's New Mind*, 297.

[245] F. David Peat, *Synchronicity* (New York: Bantam Books, 1988), 74.

[246] Heinz Pagels, *Bell's Inequality*, 481.

[247] David Bohm, "A Suggested Interpretation Theory and Measurement," *The Cosmic Code,* ed. J.A. Wheeler and W.H. Zurek (Princeton: Princeton University Press, 1983).

[248] H. Everet, "The Many Worlds Interpretation of Qauntum Mechanics", Rev. Mond Phys. 29(1957),454.

[249] B.S. de Witt & N. Graham, *The Many Worlds Interpretation of Quatum Mechanics* (Princeton: Princeton Univeristy Press, 1973).

[250] Zechaira 14:7.

Glossary

Agapé: Spiritual and religious attraction, stemming historically from the 'love feast' held by the early Christians.

Ain: Singularity. A point at which the space-time curvature becomes infinite. Hence it is a potential of energy-matter manifesting itself as nothingness. Hence this nothingness (Ain in Hebrew) is wholeness.

Algorithm: A programming of an artifact to perform tasks.

Alpha Particle: A helium nucleus compromising two protons and two neutrons.

Ani: The participant component of the self that aims to transcend spatio-temporality. It longs to waive the object and to reach inward toward pre-differentiated unity.

Ani-consciousness: The Universal unitary consciousness present in all life forms and objects.

Anthropic Principle: The Weak Anthropic Principle (W.A.P) states that certain properties of the universe are necessary if it is to contain human beings. The Strong Anthropic Principle (S.A.P) states that the universe must have those properties which allow life to develop within it as some stage in its history. Final Anthropic Principle (F.A.P) states that intelligent information-processing must come into existence in the universe, and once it comes into existence, it will never die out. These definitions were taken from: J.D Barrow and F.J Tipler: The Anthropic Cosmological Principles; Oxford, 1988, Oxford University Press.

Antiparticle: A particle with identical mass but with an opposite charge of its corresponding particle.

The Atzmi: The interactive relational component of the self reaching outward towards the manipulation of the object.

Baryons: The heavy particles within the atom nucleus.

Big Bang: The explosion of the universe at the beginning of time, which started its expansion.

Big Crunch: Energy-matter collapsing into the super-gravity of a black hole.

Black Hole: A region of super-gravity from which even light cannot escape—hence its blackness.

Bosons: Force carrying particles and Fermions (matter particles—see glossary) which do not obey the Pauli Exclusion Principle (see glossary).

Breaking of the Vessels: A Kabbalist myth according to which a disaster, not intended by Divinity, damaged both Divinity and Creation and Sparks of God were scattered into spatio-temporality and embedded into each object and life-form.

Complex Numbers/Vector States: Numbers (or vector states) composed of real numbers and of imaginary numbers such as $\sqrt{-1}$.

Copenhagen Interpretation: Interpretation of quantum mechanics by Niels Bohrs and his associates.

Contained Ani-consciousness: Algorithmic deterministic consciousness encased (canned) in all artifacts, from the paleolithic spear to the most sophisticated computer.

Continuum: A continuous series of elements, usually a duality, with one changing in proportion to the other(s).

Corpus Callosum: The connecting 'cable' of neurons linking the two brain hemispheres.

Cosmogony: The creation of the cosmos.

Dasein: According to Heidegger, the state of being-in-the-world and knowing it.

Determinism: Linked by a continuous causal chain.

Demiurgos: The Gnostic evil entity, which by the Gnostic participant bias is responsible for the creation of the world, is judged vile by the Gnostics.

Diachronic: The movement of sequences from one space-time point to another.

Dialectics: The integration of opposites into a third synthetic state.

Din: According to theosophic Kabbala, the 'Stern Judgement' rung of Divinity.

Early Orality: The developmental phase of the infant at which no separate ego-boundary has as yet been coagulated around the nascent self.

Ego Boundary: The coagulated separate identity of the infant—after leaving the pantheistic unity of early orality and crystallizing an individual 'I'.

Electromagnetism: The interaction between electrically charged forces, it attracts dislikes and repels likes, it thus holds together the atom by the interaction between the negatively charged electrons and the positively charged protons. Electromagnetism is one of the four fundamental forces of nature.

Electron: The negatively charged particle that circles the nucleus of the atom.

Eigenvalue/Eigenstate: Observable quantum mechanical phenomena.

Entropy: A term related to the 2nd Law of Thermodynamics, which states, inter alia, that the entropy, the disorder of an isolated system is always increased by any transfer of heat within or out of it.

Epoche: Phenomenological reduction which lifts layer after layer of a life-form or object's attributes until it's 'pure core essence' is reached.

Ephiphenomenalist: A view which holds that conscious states are concomitant with brain functions.

Event Horizon: The boundary of a black hole.

Fermion: Matter particles of spin 1/2 (see glossary) which obey the Pauli Exclusion Priciple (see glossary).

Fixation: A developmental trauma contributes the crystallization of personality patterns.

Gluons: Particles carrying the strong nuclear force.

Gnosis: The dualistic creeds developed in the Middle-East before and concomitant with Christianity, according to which Good and Evil have independent existence.

Godel's Incompleteness Theorem: States that mathematical systems (by which physical systems are represented) must contain statements the truth-value of which cannot be proven.

Grand Unifying Theories (GUT): Theoretically integrating the electromagnetic, strong and weak forces.

Gravitational: The weakest of the four forces of nature, yet for large astral bodies is the force of attraction between them. It acts over large distances.

Graviton: The particle carrying the force of gravitation.

Hadrons: The particles which constitute the nucleus of the atom and interact through the strong nuclear force.

Hessed: According to Theosophic Kabbala, the Grace rung of Divinity.

Hilbert Space: An infinite dimensional complex vector space; used as the state space for quantum-mechanical systems. From: M. Lockwood: Mind, Brain and the Quantum, Oxford, Basil Blackwell 1989. p. 330).

Holon: A stable, integrated structure, equipped with self-regulatory devices and enjoying a considerable degree of autonomy.

Holonic: A hierarchy of sub-wholes.

Indeterminism: A dynamic containing a free-will decision.

Iphigenia Syndrome: Surrogate sacrificial rites of passage and the imposition of the duties of the normative system of society by the father on his daughter.

Isaac Syndrome: Surrogate sacrificial rites of passage and the imposition of the duties of the normative system of society by the father on his son.

The Ity: The structured Tantalus Ratio within the self. Its synthesizing integration makes it the coordinator of human action.

Kabbala: The main body of the Jewish mysticism, developed mostly in 13th century Spain and 16th century Safed in Palestine.

Kavanah: In the Kabbala prayer, with a concentrated intention.

Later Orality: the developmental phase of the infant after a separate ego-boundary has been formed around the individual's self.

Least Interest Principle: In dyadic relationships, like business contracting partners, mates or lovers, the partner who is more interested in the relationship is weaker than the other partner.

Leptons: The light particles orbiting the nucleus of the atom.

Local Causality: The rule in physics which states that events must be related in a space-time continuity.

Lurianic Kabbala: The 16th century Jewish mystical school developed by Isaac Luria and his disciples in Safed, Palestine.

Maieutically: Teaching by a Socratic midwifery so that the student feels as if he 'gave birth' to his knowledge himself. In physics an indirect trigger.

Matrinormative: The inculcation of norms through maternal authority.

Mythoempiricism: The utilization of myths as empirical anchors for physical, metaphysical and bio-psycho-social processes.

Mythologem: According to C.G Jung, a unit in the structure of a myth.

Neutron: The uncharged particle in the nucleus of the atom. Is of approximately the same mass as the proton.

Normative Anthropic Principle: States that man, as the meta- integrator between the *ani*-consciousness and energy-matter, lends significance and norms to this interaction, which would be meaningless without him.

Nucleon: The particles within the nucleus of the atom, protons or neutrons.

Participation: The identification of Ego with a person, object or symbolic construct outside himself, and his wish to lose his separate identity by fusion with this other object or symbol.

Patrinormative: The inculcation of norms through paternal authority.

Pauli Exclusion Principle: The uniqueness of an individual Fermion-matter-particle (see glossary) as measured by its quantic attributes (quantum numbers). The effect is that no two-matter particles can occupy the same physical state.

Photon: A particle/quantum of light, which carries an electromagnetic force.

Pion: A π meson particle with a mass that is between that of an electron and a proton.

Positron: The anti-particle (see glossary) of the electron with a positive charge.

Promethean Holon (PH): The integrated product of the *ani*-consciousness and energy-matter, the creation of which was triggered by the Symbolon Structure (see glossary).

Proton: The positively charged particle in the nucleus of the atom.

Quantum numbers: Numbers which stand for quantum attributes of a quantum system.

Quark: The most basic constituent of elementary particles.

Resonance: Energy transmitting encounters of particles.

Sefirot: According to the Kabbala, the ten rungs which constitute the building holonic entities of both Divinity and Creation.

Separation: The wish to sever, disjoin and differentiate Ego from his surrounding life-forms and objects.

Sisyphean Personality Type: The separant type fixated by developmental traumas after the coagulation of the separate self.

Solipsism: The self's sense of being a unique and exclusive possessor of real consciousness and knowledge of the cosmos.

Spin: The angular momentum of the particles around themselves.

Strong Nuclear Force: Holds the nucleus of the atom together and binds the quarks in the protons and neutrons. Although very short ranged, is the strongest of the four forces of nature.

Structure: A holistic system characterized by transformation and self-regulation.

Superposition: The products of physical states added together.

Symbolon Structure: The agent which connects the *ani*-consciousness and energy-matter, structured into a model of a phenomenon, to be realized subsequently by an act of creation.

Synchronic: Coincidence in point of time.

Tantalic Personality Type: The participant type fixated by developmental traumas before the separation of the separate self.

Tantalus Ratio: The gap between our quest of participation and our subjectively defined distance from our participatory aims and the dialectical strain between these two factors.

Tantalus-Ratio (T.R): The dialectic between the *ani* participant-vector aiming to merge into the totality of Unity and the *atzmi* object-bound separant vector.

Teleological: From the Greek *telos*. Directed toward specific aims, goals or purposes.

Theogony: The creation and formation of gods.

Theurgy: Human interaction with Divinity.

Tikkun: In Kabbala the theurgic 'mending' of God by man, by means of prayer and righteous behaviour.

Tunneling: The 'jumping' of quanta through regions, against the laws of classical physics.

Turing Halting Theorem: Postulates that a computer, or any other artifact activated by an algorithm, cannot fully understand itself.

Uncertainty Principle: Associated with Werner Heisenberg. One cannot measure with certainty both the position and momentum of a particle.

Universal Thou: Buber's conceptualization of transcendence in dialogue, which has elements of our 'pure' *ani*-consciousness.

Vector: A directional power.

Vector Bosons: Particles which carry the weak nuclear force.

Vectorial intention: The directional energy of the Symbolon, which creates a Promethean Holon.

Virtual Particles: particles which cannot be detected and measured. Their existence is so short that their passing from the quantum world to the classical world and back does not violate the uncertainty principle.

Weak Nuclear Force: One of the four fundamental forces of nature. It is responsible for radio activity (Beta decay) and acts on Fermions (see glossary).

Zivug: In the Kabbala, the coupling of the *Midat HaRahamim*, the rung of Hessed representing participant masculinity and the feminine *Midat HaDin*, the Stern Judgment.